Human Information Processing

Human Information Processing

Vision, Memory, and Attention

Edited by Charles Chubb, Barbara A. Dosher,
Zhong-Lin Lu, and Richard M. Shiffrin

DECADE
of BEHAVIOR
2000-2010

American Psychological Association • Washington, DC

Published by
American Psychological Association
750 First Street, NE
Washington, DC 20002
www.apa.org

To order
APA Order Department
P.O. Box 92984
Washington, DC 20090-2984
Tel: (800) 374-2721;
Direct: (202) 336-5510
Fax: (202) 336-5502;
TDD/TTY: (202) 336-6123
Online: www.apa.org/pubs/books
E-mail: order@apa.org

In the U.K., Europe, Africa, and the Middle East, copies may be ordered from
American Psychological Association
3 Henrietta Street
Covent Garden, London
WC2E 8LU England

Typeset in New Century Schoolbook by Circle Graphics, Inc., Columbia, MD

Printer: United Book Press, Baltimore, MD
Cover Designer: Mercury Publishing Services, Inc., Rockville, MD
Cover Art: Mossy Bikoni, b. 1970. Whirlwind Question, 2010. 24" × 36". Mixed media on canvas.

The opinions and statements published are the responsibility of the authors, and such opinions and statements do not necessarily represent the policies of the American Psychological Association.

Library of Congress Cataloging-in-Publication Data

Human information processing : vision, memory, and attention / Charles Chubb . . . [et al.].
    p. cm. — (Decade of behavior)
 Includes bibliographical references and index.
 ISBN 978-1-4338-1273-6 (alk. paper) — ISBN 1-4338-1273-8 (alk. paper) 1. Human information processing. I. Chubb, Charles, PhD.
 BF444.H86 2013
 153—dc23

2012035660

British Library Cataloguing-in-Publication Data
A CIP record is available from the British Library.

Printed in the United States of America
First Edition

DOI: 10.1037/14135-000

APA Science Volumes

Attribution and Social Interaction: The Legacy of Edward E. Jones

Best Methods for the Analysis of Change: Recent Advances, Unanswered Questions, Future Directions

Cardiovascular Reactivity to Psychological Stress and Disease

The Challenge in Mathematics and Science Education: Psychology's Response

Changing Employment Relations: Behavioral and Social Perspectives

Children Exposed to Marital Violence: Theory, Research, and Applied Issues

Cognition: Conceptual and Methodological Issues

Cognitive Bases of Musical Communication

Cognitive Dissonance: Progress on a Pivotal Theory in Social Psychology

Conceptualization and Measurement of Organism–Environment Interaction

Converging Operations in the Study of Visual Selective Attention

Creative Thought: An Investigation of Conceptual Structures and Processes

Developmental Psychoacoustics

Diversity in Work Teams: Research Paradigms for a Changing Workplace

Emotion and Culture: Empirical Studies of Mutual Influence

Emotion, Disclosure, and Health

Evolving Explanations of Development: Ecological Approaches to Organism–Environment Systems

Examining Lives in Context: Perspectives on the Ecology of Human Development

Global Prospects for Education: Development, Culture, and Schooling

Hostility, Coping, and Health

Measuring Patient Changes in Mood, Anxiety, and Personality Disorders: Toward a Core Battery

Occasion Setting: Associative Learning and Cognition in Animals

Organ Donation and Transplantation: Psychological and Behavioral Factors

Origins and Development of Schizophrenia: Advances in Experimental Psychopathology

The Perception of Structure

Perspectives on Socially Shared Cognition

APA Decade of Behavior Volumes

Child Development and Social Policy: Knowledge for Action

Children's Peer Relations: From Development to Intervention

Cognitive Fatigue: Multidisciplinary Perspectives on Current Research and Future Applications

Commemorating Brown: The Social Psychology of Racism and Discrimination

Computational Modeling of Behavior in Organizations: The Third Scientific Discipline

Couples Coping With Stress: Emerging Perspectives on Dyadic Coping

Developing Individuality in the Human Brain: A Tribute to Michael I. Posner

Emerging Adults in America: Coming of Age in the 21st Century

Experimental Cognitive Psychology and Its Applications

Family Psychology: Science-Based Interventions

Gender Differences in Prenatal Substance Exposure

Human Information Processing: Vision, Memory, and Attention

Individual Pathways of Change: Statistical Models for Analyzing Learning and Development

Inhibition in Cognition

The Journey From Child to Scientist: Integrating Cognitive Development and the Education Sciences

Measuring Psychological Constructs: Advances in Model-Based Approaches

Medical Illness and Positive Life Change: Can Crisis Lead to Personal Transformation?

Memory Consolidation: Essays in Honor of James L. McGaugh

Models of Intelligence: International Perspectives

The Nature of Remembering: Essays in Honor of Robert G. Crowder

New Methods for the Analysis of Change

On the Consequences of Meaning Selection: Perspectives on Resolving Lexical Ambiguity

Participatory Community Research: Theories and Methods in Action

Personality Psychology in the Workplace

Perspectivism in Social Psychology: The Yin and Yang of Scientific Progress

Police Interrogations and False Confessions: Current Research, Practice, and Policy Recommendations

Primate Perspectives on Behavior and Cognition

This book is dedicated to George Sperling, whose 50 odd years of research have provided example after example of the best way to apply the theoretical methods of the hard sciences to the analysis of perception, attention, and cognition. In his hands, extensive data collected in exquisitely crafted conditions have produced detailed quantitative models that provide deep insights into mind and brain. His work has inspired us all and will continue to inspire generations to come.

Contents

Contributors

Charles Chubb, PhD, Department of Cognitive Sciences, University of California at Irvine

Stephen E. Denton, PhD, Department of Psychological and Brain Sciences, Indiana University, Bloomington

Barbara A. Dosher, PhD, Department of Cognitive Sciences, University of California at Irvine

Jean-Claude Falmagne, PhD, Department of Cognitive Sciences, University of California at Irvine

Karl R. Gegenfurtner, PhD, Department of Psychology, Justus-Liebig University, Giessen, Germany

Norma Graham, PhD, Department of Psychology, Columbia University, New York, NY

Stephen Grossberg, PhD, Departments of Mathematics, Psychology, and Biomedical Engineering, Boston University, Boston, MA

Chang-Bing Huang, PhD, Institute of Psychology, Chinese Academy of Science, Beijing, China

Geoffrey Iverson, PhD, Department of Cognitive Sciences, University of California at Irvine

Eileen Kowler, PhD, Department of Psychology, Rutgers University, New Brunswick, NJ

Martin Lages, PhD, Department of Psychology, University of Glasgow, Glasgow, Scotland

Zhong-Lin Lu, PhD, Department of Psychology, The Ohio State University, Columbus

Isabelle Mareschal, PhD, Division of Optometry and Visual Science, City University, London, England

Misha Pavel, PhD, Departments of Biomedical Engineering, Computer Science and Electrical Engineering, Oregon Health & Science University, Portland

Adam Reeves, PhD, Department of Psychology, Northeastern University, Boston, MA

Richard M. Shiffrin, PhD, Department of Psychological and Brain Sciences, Indiana University, Bloomington

Joshua A. Solomon, PhD, Division of Optometry and Visual Science, City University, London, England

Miriam Spering, PhD, Department of Ophthalmology and Visual Sciences, University of British Columbia, Vancouver, Canada

Hal S. Stern, PhD, Department of Statistics, University of California at Irvine

Michel Treisman, MB, BCh, DPhil, Department of Experimental Psychology, University of Oxford, Oxford, England

Jan van Erp, PhD, Toegepast Natuurwetenschappelijk Onderzoek (TNO), Soesterberg, the Netherlands

Peter Werkhoven, PhD, Toegepast Natuurwetenschappelijk Onderzoek (TNO), Delft, the Netherlands

Alissa Winkler, PhD, Structural Brain Mapping Group, University of Jena, Jena, Germany

S. Sabina Wolfson, PhD, Department of Psychology, Columbia University, New York, NY

Charles E. Wright, PhD, Department of Cognitive Sciences, University of California at Irvine

Yifeng Zhou, PhD, School of Life Science, University of Science and Technology of China, Hefei, Anhui, China

Foreword

In early 1988, the American Psychological Association (APA) Science Directorate began its sponsorship of what would become an exceptionally successful activity in support of psychological science—the APA Scientific Conferences program. This program has showcased some of the most important topics in psychological science and has provided a forum for collaboration among many leading figures in the field.

The program has inspired a series of books that have presented cutting-edge work in all areas of psychology. At the turn of the millennium, the series was renamed the Decade of Behavior Series to help advance the goals of this important initiative. The Decade of Behavior is a major interdisciplinary campaign designed to promote the contributions of the behavioral and social sciences to our most important societal challenges. Although a key goal has been to inform the public about these scientific contributions, other activities have been designed to encourage and further collaboration among scientists. Hence, the series that was the "APA Science Series" has continued as the "Decade of Behavior Series." This represents one element in APA's efforts to promote the Decade of Behavior initiative as one of its endorsing organizations. For additional information about the Decade of Behavior, please visit http://www.decadeofbehavior.org.

Over the course of the past years, the Science Conference and Decade of Behavior Series has allowed psychological scientists to share and explore cutting-edge findings in psychology. The APA Science Directorate looks forward to continuing this successful program and to sponsoring other conferences and books in the years ahead. This series has been so successful that we have chosen to extend it to include books that, although they do not arise from conferences, report with the same high quality of scholarship on the latest research.

We are pleased that this important contribution to the literature was supported in part by the Decade of Behavior program. Congratulations to the editors and contributors of this volume on their sterling effort.

Steven J. Breckler, PhD
Executive Director for Science

Virginia E. Holt
*Assistant Executive Director
for Science*

Preface

George Sperling was educated in the public schools of New York City and then went to the University of Michigan to study science. At Michigan he majored simultaneously in biology, chemistry, physics, and mathematics, receiving a BS in 1955. After earning an MA in psychology from Columbia University in 1956, he went on to Harvard. During the summer of 1957, George Miller arranged for Sperling to borrow a tachistoscope to carry out an experiment Sperling had proposed in a student report. With the help of S. S. Stevens, Sperling turned these summer experiments into his doctoral dissertation in 1959. In this now-famous experiment, Sperling used what has become known as the "method of partial report" to measure the time course of visual persistence (sensory memory), subsequently renamed "iconic store" by Ulrich Neisser.

This was the start of a remarkable career that has yielded fundamental discoveries in three research domains: vision, memory, and attention. Although these three areas are often considered in isolation, Sperling's work reveals the important interconnections among them and shows how much is to be gained by refracting our understanding of each area through an understanding of the others. This is the inspiration for the current volume, which brings together research on the frontiers of vision, memory, and attention by scientists, all of whom have been strongly influenced by Sperling in their thinking and methodological approaches. Many of the contributors participated in a conference celebrating Sperling's accomplishments at the University of California at Irvine in July 2007.

This book is aimed at readers interested in using cutting-edge computational models to understand cognition, an approach common to all of the chapters included here and a cornerstone of Sperling's research throughout his career. In fact, several of the chapters (e.g., Chapter 9 by Dosher and Lu; Chapter 5 by Wright, Chubb, Winkler, and Stern) are explicitly concerned with introducing model-based empirical methods for probing cognitive processes in new ways. As this might suggest, to get the most out of this book the reader should be comfortable with equations and familiar with the standard mathematical tools of cognitive science, including psychometric functions and signal detection theory. At least one chapter requires facility with calculus (i.e., Chapter 4 by Iverson and Chubb), and Chapter 14 by Falmagne requires an understanding of the basic concepts of graph theory.

It has been a great pleasure putting this book together. We hope readers will find the chapters as useful and inspiring as we have.

Acknowledgments

Support for the chapter by Barbara A. Dosher and Zhong-Lin Lu was provided by the National Institutes of Mental Health (Grant R01MH81018) and the National Eye Institute (NEI; Grant EY-17491); in addition, over the years, the Air Force Office of Scientific Research (AFOSR), the National Science Foundation (NSF), the National Institutes of Mental Health, and the NEI supported the experimental and theoretical work described.

Support for the chapter by Michel Treisman and Martin Lages was provided by an Engineering and Physical Sciences Research Council studentship to Lages and a Biotechnology and Biological Sciences Research Council grant to Treisman.

The work reported by Norma Graham and S. Sabina Wolfson was supported in part by the NEI (Grant EY-08459); the authors also thank Boris Grinshpun, Ian Kwok, Stephanie Pan, Alisa Surkis, and Jiatao Wang, all of whom did modeling that is not discussed explicitly but that has been important for the development of the ideas. Graham and Wolfson also thank their observers for their hours of effort, and finally, they express years of gratitude to George Sperling for many contributions and, particularly, for his consistent use of rigorous mathematical models that are complicated enough to capture interesting behavior but simple enough to give understanding and insight into the processes producing the behavior.

The chapter by Stephen E. Denton and Richard M. Shiffrin was supported by NSF Grant 6804643 awarded to Shiffrin. The authors thank David E. Huber for helpful comments on earlier versions of their chapter.

Joshua A. Solomon and Isabelle Mareschal thank Michael J. Morgan for collaborating on almost every phase of the research reported in their chapter. They also belatedly acknowledge Steven C. Dakin, who directed them toward investigating the relationship between cortical separation and the size of the tilt illusion. Financial support came from the Cognitive Systems Foresight Project (Grant BB/E000444/1).

Charles E. Wright, Alissa Winkler, Hal S. Stern, and Charles Chubb thank their colleagues Scott Brown and Geoff Iverson for helpful discussions during the preparation of their chapter; financial support came from NSF Award BCS-0843897.

The work reported by Eileen Kowler and Misha Pavel was supported by National Institutes of Health/NEI Grant 15522 and AFOSR Grant 49620-96-1-0081; in addition, the authors thank Brian Schnitzer for his many useful contributions to the visual search experiments and for valuable comments on this chapter.

The chapter by Zhong-Lin Lu, Chang-Bing Huang, and Yifeng Zhou was supported by the Natural Science Foundation of China (Grants 30128006 and 30630027), National Basic Research Program (Grant 2006CB500804), and the NEI (Grant EY017491-05).

The research reported in the chapter by Adam Reeves was supported by AFOSR grant FA9550-04-1-0244 to A. Reeves and B. Scharf; Theo Voinier and Zhenlan Jin programmed the experiments, and John Suciu and David Richters ran subjects. The approach taken by Reeves in the experiments he reports was inspired by George Sperling's lectures in basic processes, and the problem was introduced to him by Bertram Scharf.

Human
Information
Processing

Introduction

Charles Chubb, Barbara A. Dosher,
Zhong-Lin Lu, and Richard M. Shiffrin

The chapters of this book are all energized by the same central question: What are the processes that operate within us to enable our action in the world and to produce the stream of our experience? Different chapters take different points of entry into this realm. Some focus on vision, others on memory, and others on attention.

These three fields have traditionally formed separate branches of cognitive science, each with its own central questions. Vision science focuses on the processes that operate automatically to construct the visible world that we effortlessly apprehend as soon as we open our eyes, memory research focuses on those processes through which information is retained across time for the purposes of influencing future behavior, and attention research focuses on the flexibility exhibited by human participants to adjust their behavior in complex task situations in response to changing demands.

Despite their deep differences in focus, the fields of vision, memory, and attention are strongly linked. Researchers in the fields of vision and memory are well aware that performance in the tasks they use typically depends strongly on the state of attention of the participant. For this reason, vision and memory researchers routinely design their experimental procedures carefully to control the participant's state of attention. In addition, attention plays a central role in various theories of memory; for example, the levels-of-processing model (e.g., Craik & Lockhart, 1972) implies that memories formed as by-products of various sorts of information processing are likely to be more durable if the processing that produced the memories involves greater levels of attention. The field of attention is linked to vision in that many of the central questions concerning attention deal specifically with its visual deployment. For example, Posner's (1980) classic experiments analyzed how orienting covert attention to different spatial locations influences the probability of detecting a briefly flashed visual target. Similarly, the field of memory is linked to vision in that many important memory processes have evolved specifically to retain visual information. For

DOI: 10.1037/14135-001
Human Information Processing: Vision, Memory, and Attention, C. Chubb, B. A. Dosher, Z.-L. Lu, and R. M. Shiffrin (Editors)

example, visual sensory memory (Sperling, 1960) is a rapidly decaying memory store that briefly retains the visual input in image form. Finally, the field of vision is linked to memory in that many aspects of visual perception depend crucially on the past experience of the participant. In the McCollough effect (McCollough, 1965), for example, the participant views a red horizontal grating alternating for a few minutes with a green vertical grating. Following this brief exposure period, the participant typically sees a black-and-white horizontal grating as being greenish and a black-and-white vertical grating as being pinkish; remarkably, this effect can last for months (Jones & Holding, 1975). As the strong links among the fields of vision, memory, and attention suggest, to achieve a deep understanding of any of them is likely to require understanding them all.

When we try to imagine what life would be like without memory, we fall into a void. To see this, begin by applying your imagination to erase your own past. Your childhood, your parents, the people you love—let them all go, along with all the places you've ever been, where you live, where you work. Let there be nothing before what you see right now in front of you. You will see that along with the past, the future has also been lost; the plans and dreams that formerly arced ahead of you, built as they were on all of your hard work in the past, have evaporated. You are now adrift, literally without hope. We can dig deeper, however: Next, erase everything you've ever learned, all numbers, all letters, all words, all shapes and patterns, and the meanings they carry. Suddenly, the panorama before you collapses into chaos—not even chaos, for chaos implies the possibility of order. Whatever grip you had on your situation has been dissolved. You are an infant—not even an infant, for an infant is a memory sponge, but you absorb nothing. The play of physical energy across your sensorium changes nothing. You are a block, a stone, a void.

We see, then, that memory is an essential prerequisite for action and experience. But how does memory work? In particular, how does experience alter the structure of our brain to change how we see, think, understand, and respond to future events? In other words, how do we *learn?* It is now well documented that many sorts of learning processes operate to alter information encoded in various memory structures throughout the brain. Some of these processes operate automatically, outside the scope of awareness, and others depend strongly on efforts of attention. How many such mechanisms are there? How do they operate? An instant of insight can change us forever. How does this happen? Such questions ignite much of the work described in this volume.

For example, Chapter 6, contributed by Michel Treisman and Martin Lages, calls into question some of our basic assumptions about memory. A standard model hidden at the core of nearly all models of memory proposes that when an observer views an object, a representation embodying information about the object is stored somewhere in the brain; under this model, memory for the object is made available, if we need it later, by retrieving and consulting this representation. This conception may have some plausibility when it is applied to our final perceptions and cognitions. However, as Treisman and Lages show in their chapter, memory works entirely differently when used to compare properties of incoming stimuli with previously experienced stimuli. Their nonrepresentational model of how past information controls sensory decision making provides important insights not only into how memory operates at the level of perception but also into the development of sensory skills, as well as how context influences perception.

Stephen Grossberg (Chapter 10) is also focused on fundamental questions about learning and memory. Specifically, Grossberg asks, how do we learn about objects—their boundaries, shapes, identities—without any external supervision? How does the brain learn to recognize a complex object from multiple viewpoints? We make scanning eye movements to a variety of points of interest, or views, on the object. How does the brain know that the views that are captured on successive fixations of the eye belong to the same object? How does the brain avoid the problem of erroneously learning to classify parts of different objects together? Grossberg's ARTSCAN neural model is a theory of how the brain processes that control three-dimensional vision, figure–ground separation, spatial attention, object attention, object category learning, and predictive eye movements all work together to learn what an object is.

As we see, then, the concept of attention plays an important role in Stephen Grossberg's chapter, but what *is* attention? As William James (1890) observed, the answer seems obvious from the perspective of one's own experience:

> Everyone knows what attention is. It is the taking possession by the mind, in clear and vivid form, of one out of what seem several simultaneously possible objects or trains of thought. Focalization, concentration, of consciousness are of its essence. It implies withdrawal from some things in order to deal effectively with others. (pp. 43–44)

Although we may know what it feels like to focus our attention, it is far from clear what effects this operation has on our ability to process information. As has been documented many times, we are better at detecting or discriminating visual stimuli presented in attended regions of the visual field than in unattended regions. The question that has had no resolution since it was first raised more than a century ago is: What exactly is attention doing to improve our performance in this task?

This is the topic explored by Barbara A. Dosher and Zhong-Lin Lu in Chapter 9. Many have argued that what attention does is strengthen the visual signal within the attended region. Others have argued that attention instead alters the selectivity of the detection process, decreasing its sensitivity to irrelevant, potentially distracting aspects of the visual input relative to its sensitivity to the target. A third way in which attention might work to improve performance is suggested by analogy to piano playing: One can play a piece carelessly or carefully. Careful playing yields fewer errors. Similarly, one can imagine that the processing in a given task may be more stringently regulated in an attended region than in an unattended region. Dosher and Lu have pioneered the development of psychophysical methods for measuring the relative contributions of these different potential effects of attention. Their chapter describes these methods and the basic patterns of results that they have found when attention is used to control performance in a range of tasks drawn from the domain of visual perception. Indeed, much of the research in this volume is focused on vision. A single, basic question energizes most of this work.

How does the brain construct the visible world as we experience it? The retina receives an image, a postage stamp of changing light, but what we experience is the panorama of the world and all it contains, arrayed for us in space: mountains, coffee cups, waterfalls, lizards, and faces, each thing pregnant with the past and alive with future possibility. Our vision embodies inference, the intelligence of which outstrips our own capabilities of thought, immediately sorting out the people and things in a scene, their identities, distances, spatial relations, and potential patterns of interaction. It is as though a genie is at work crafting the solid world before us out of light, but there is no genie: This is all accomplished by some miraculous machinery in the brain. The question is, how?

Thus, the qualities of the visual world as we experience it differ dramatically from the properties of the input received by the retina. The chapter contributed by Stephen E. Denton and Richard M. Shiffrin focuses on one such difference (Chapter 7). When we move our eyes across a scene, unless we are tracking a smoothly moving object, our eyes take sudden jumps, called *saccades,* from one location to another. When we make a saccade, the image that gets produced on the retina is smeared, and any part of the scene that was formerly imaged in one region of the retina is now abruptly shifted to a different region. Despite this massive disturbance in retinal input, we experience clear perception of an unshifted visual world. The question explored by Denton and Shiffrin is: How does our visual system accomplish this magical adjustment?

Chapter 8, by Eileen Kowler and Misha Pavel, focuses on the relation between saccadic eye movements and attention. When we are searching a scene for some target (e.g., looking for a can opener in a cluttered kitchen drawer), we make saccades to various locations in the scene. Often the saccades we make land at useless locations, requiring correction by subsequent eye movements. The question addressed by Kowler and Pavel is: Why are our eye movements so crudely selected? They make the case that these eye-movement selection strategies, which on the face of it seem suboptimal, may actually represent an efficient use of resources because they minimize the attention devoted to saccadic planning. The net cost of these "useless" saccades is low because the saccadic system is able to program corrections quickly. Errant saccades to useless locations may cost more time, but they do not undermine scene analysis because the true filter of what we apprehend from a scene occurs at the level of what we choose to attend and remember, not at the level of saccadic decisions.

Our eyes can move only in saccadic jumps when we take in a stationary scene. However, they operate very differently when we view a smoothly moving target. If you move your finger back and forth in front of you, you will find that you can easily track it smoothly with your eyes. (However, you will also find that it is impossible to make those same smooth eye movements without the aid of your smoothly moving finger.) The slow rotations of the eyes that we produce in such instances are called *smooth-pursuit eye movements,* and it is this class of eye movements that is the central topic of Chapter 3, by Miriam Spering and Karl R. Gegenfurtner. These sorts of eye movements are closely related to how we perceive visual motion. Among the questions addressed by Spering and Gegenfurtner are the following: How are we able to "lock on" to a moving object and use our eyes to track it? How does the analysis of motion by human vision inform this process? And how does tracking an object with a smooth-pursuit eye movement change our perception of that object?

Other chapters centered on vision are concerned with the ways in which various sorts of patterns are encoded by human vision. For example, Chapter 1, by Norma Graham and S. Sabina Wolfson, explores a remarkable effect with important implications for our understanding of human pattern vision. In their basic experiment, participants adapt to a square array of identical tokens (Gabor patterns) on a gray background. Each of the tokens in this array has medium contrast (ranging in luminance from medium dark to medium bright). The participant adapts to this display by fixing her gaze on a central cue spot for some period of time. Following adaptation, a 100-ms test display is presented in which either the rows or the columns of tokens are made to alternate in contrast; the screen then changes back to the adapting display. The observer's task is to judge the orientation (vertical vs. horizontal) of the contrast-defined pattern. Graham and Wolfson's chapter begins with the following mysterious finding: If the contrasts of the tokens in the test pattern are either all lower or all higher than the adapting contrast of the tokens, then this task is easy; however, if the high and low contrasts in the test display exactly "straddle" the adapting contrast, then the task is nearly impossible. The chapter explores the implications of this strange result for our understanding of the visual computations underlying pattern perception.

Chapter 2, by Joshua A. Solomon and Isabelle Mareschal, analyzes another aspect of pattern vision. Sensory systems exaggerate feature contrasts. One classic example is the tilt illusion: When a collection of line segments surrounding an upright line segment are all tilted in the same direction, the upright segment appears to be tilted in the opposite direction. Of course, one can compensate for the tilt illusion by giving the upright line segment a slight tilt in the same direction as its neighbors. However, most people do not realize that the tilted neighbors also produce another effect for which it is impossible to compensate: They make it harder to identify the direction of small changes in the orientation of the near-vertical line segment. The question explored in this chapter is, why?

Graham and Wolfson and also Solomon and Mareschal investigate how human vision processes achromatic variations in light intensity. By contrast, Chapter 4, by Geoffrey Iverson and Charles Chubb, investigates basic questions about how human vision senses color. It is only recently in our evolutionary history that we have experienced any high-intensity illumination other than daylight. Thus, one might expect daylight to have played an important role in sculpting the properties of our visual system. It should be noted, however, that daylight itself comes in different colors: at dawn and dusk, it tends to be reddish, and then yellowish as the sun rises higher. On cloudy days, it tends to be white and moves toward blue on clear days when the sun is high. If one extracts the Commission Internationale de l'Éclairage (CIE) chromaticity coordinates of these different-colored daylights, they fall on a curved line in the CIE chromaticity diagram. Chapter 4 addresses the following questions: Why does this "daylight locus" take the form that it does, and, more generally, how are the properties of the three cone classes related to the natural variations in daylight?

Although most of the chapters concern vision, Chapter 11, by Adam Reeves, focuses instead on a mysterious phenomenon from auditory perception. As Reeves documents experimentally, if listeners concentrate their attention to detect a specific tone occurring in noise, they become more sensitive to brief tones lower in pitch than to the pitch they are listening for; thus, one should concentrate on a higher pitch than the tone one hopes to hear. Although this result seems paradoxical, Reeves explains why it occurs in terms of known properties of the auditory system.

Two of the chapters are special in introducing new experimental methodologies with a broad range of promising applications. The first of these has already been mentioned; this is Chapter 9 by Barbara A. Dosher and Zhong-Lin Lu. The methodology they introduce makes use of their *perceptual template model,* which incorporates various possible kinds of processing noise that may or may not be influenced by changes in the attention state of the participant. The special genius of their approach lies in the empirical manipulations they describe that enable them to measure the changes in the model parameters corresponding to these different types of noise.

A second new methodology called *equisalience analysis* is introduced in Chapter 5 by Charles E. Wright, Charles Chubb, Alissa Winkler, and Hal S. Stern. There is a prominent theory (Milner & Goodale, 1995) that the subsystem used to make visually controlled motor responses (e.g., reaching out to pick up a coffee cup) is distinct from the subsystem that uses visual input to make conscious judgments about people and things in the world. What's more, it seems likely that these two systems differ in their relative sensitivities to various visual properties, for example, to color versus luminance. Behavioral studies investigating this theory have yielded mixed results largely because it is difficult to compare the relative effectiveness of different stimulus properties (e.g., color vs. luminance) in controlling performance across tasks using different dependent variables (e.g., percent correct vs. movement time). Equisalience analysis is tailored to problems of this sort, and it has many potential applications in the analysis of perceptual and cognitive systems. After introducing the methodology, equisalience analysis is demonstrated in an experimental test of the theory of Milner and Goodale (1995).

Finally, three chapters present basic research that addresses real-world problems more directly than the other chapters. The first of these is Chapter 12, by Zhong-Lin Lu, Chang-Bing Huang, and Yifeng Zhou. Amblyopia, commonly known as "lazy eye," is the leading cause of visual impairment in children and affects approximately 3% to 5% of the population worldwide. It causes a spectrum of spatial vision disorders, including reduced letter acuity, loss of contrast sensitivity, visual distortions, reduced stereoacuity, and abnormal binocular interactions, in addition to higher level deficits that can hamper reading, reaching, grasping, driving, and participation in sports.

Existing treatments for amblyopia, occlusion (eye patching) and penalization (blurring eyedrops), temporarily suspend vision in the better eye, forcing the use of the amblyopic eye. However, these treatments are unsuccessful in 25% to 50% of cases and rarely restore normal binocular vision; moreover, conventional wisdom suggests that amblyopia is fully established by the time a child is 8 years old and can no longer be influenced by therapeutic interventions, so patients older than 8 are routinely left untreated. The chapter by Lu, Huang, and Zhou addresses two central questions about amblyopia: (a) Why is the amblyopic eye less sensitive than the fellow (nonamblyopic) eye? and (b) Is it possible to use perceptual learning-based interventions to treat adults with amblyopia?

The second chapter aimed at solving an important real-world problem is by Jean-Claude Falmagne (Chapter 14). Falmagne and colleagues have pioneered research in the important practical problem of how to assess a person's knowledge in some particular domain (e.g., physics, elementary algebra, statistics). In this work, a person's *knowledge state* is conceived of as the set problems from the target domain that the person can solve. As a person masters a given domain of knowledge, he or she learns to solve more types of problems. With each new problem type a person masters, he or she moves from one knowledge state to another that contains the previous knowledge state as a subset. Different learners may take different paths to mastery. Thus some learners may pass through knowledge states that other learners never visit. Roughly speaking, the *learning space* for a given target domain is the set of all knowledge states through which a learner might conceivably pass in the process of mastering the target domain. In practice, the task of assessing the knowledge state of an individual is challenging for the following reason: For real domains of knowledge, learning spaces typically comprise a vast number of knowledge states, a number that increases exponentially with the number of problem types in the target domain. To solve the problem posed by this combinatorial explosion, what is needed is a method for splitting a learning space into simpler chunks, each of which can be analyzed separately to derive the knowledge state of a given individual. In his chapter, Falmagne develops a key theoretical tool for such purposes. This is the concept of the *projection* of a learning space on a subset of the original domain of problems. Such a projection summarizes the features of the original structure much the same way as the projection of a high-dimensional shape into a lower dimensional Euclidean space summarizes that shape.

Finally, Chapter 13, by Peter Werkhoven and Jan van Erp, focuses on real-world applications of the results of basic research in the area of multi-modal perception. In our daily lives, we experience a world in which sights, sounds, and tactual impressions are bound together to create the people and things that are the actual foci of our concern. Somehow, this binding together of the information carried by the separate sensory streams is accomplished for us by our perceptual systems without any conscious effort on our part. What is the nature of the computational processes that achieve this synthesis? As Werkhoven and van Erp show, the emerging answers to this question enable startling new technologies that extend the possibilities of human experience—for example, systems to see with our skin.

This book is aimed at the reader whose imagination reaches beyond standard research in psychology toward new ways of probing the mysteries of mind, world, and action. Although the research described in these pages ranges broadly across the fields of vision, memory, and attention, as well as other areas of perception and cognition, there are common threads that draw these diverse efforts together. First, none of these scientists is content with vague characterizations of the processes they investigate; all rely heavily on formal models.

This passion for modeling reflects a commitment to the principle that genuine scientific progress requires clarity of insight that can only be certified through the use of precisely specified models that enable testable, quantitative predictions. Second, these scientists share a flair for invention; the work described here represents the cutting edge of innovation in perceptual and cognitive science. Although two chapters were highlighted here for introducing new methods with broad potential applications, the reader will discover that all of the chapters in this volume are groundbreaking both in the questions they pose and the methods they use to answer them. Finally, all of the authors collected herein are enthralled by questions that reach to the source of human existence: What processes operate within us to crystallize this welter of sound and light into the world as we experience it, persisting as it does beyond us in time and space, and how do these processes produce the stream of our ongoing action?

References

Craik, F. I., & Lockhart, R. S. (1972). A framework for memory research. *Journal of Verbal Learning & Verbal Behavior, 11,* 671–684. doi:10.1016/S0022-5371(72)80001-X

James, W. (1890). *The principles of psychology* (Vol. 1). New York, NY: Henry Holt.

Jones, P. D., & Holding, D. H. (1975). Extremely long-term persistence of the McCollough effect. *Journal of Experimental Psychology: Human Perception and Performance, 1,* 323–327. doi:10.1037/0096-1523.1.4.323

McCollough, C. (1965, September 3). Color adaptation of edge-detectors in the human visual system. *Science, 149,* 1115–1116. doi:10.1126/science.149.3688.1115

Milner, A. D., & Goodale, M. A. (1995). *The visual brain in action.* New York, NY: Oxford University Press.

Posner, M. I. (1980). Orienting of attention. *The Quarterly Journal of Experimental Psychology, 32,* 3–25. doi:10.1080/00335558008248231

Sperling, G. (1960). The information available in brief visual presentations. *Psychological Monographs: General and Applied, 74*(11, Whole No. 498), 1–29.

Part I ——————————————————————

Vision

1

Two Visual Contrast Processes: One New, One Old

Norma Graham and S. Sabina Wolfson

In everyday life, we occasionally look at blank, untextured regions of the world around us—a blue unclouded sky, for example. Most of the time, however, our eyes see regions occupied by spatial patterning, by texture, form, or patterns, as when looking at a person to whom we are talking or at the text on this page. Furthermore, there is constant temporal change as well as spatial patterning, if only as a result of eye movements. Thus, the eye is usually looking at a visual scene, where different parts of the scene are characterized by different levels of visual contrast, and, from moment to moment, the contrast at any point on the retina is changing. (*Visual contrast* in any region of the scene is the difference between the lightest and darkest parts of that region, relative to some measure of overall intensity in that region.) Therefore, one might wonder how the spatial patterning an observer has just seen affects the visual processing of the spatial patterning that an observer sees now. More specifically, one might wonder how the visual contrast one has just seen in a region affects the processing of visual contrast there now.

The first part of this chapter is about an effect of contrast adaptation discovered rather recently, nicknamed *Buffy adaptation*. For the origin of the nickname, see Graham and Wolfson (2007). We are using the term *adaptation* here only to mean the effect of preceding contrast on the processing of subsequent visual contrast. Our procedure, which is described in Figure 1.1, might also be called *masking* or *a procedure to study temporal processing*. This recently discovered effect of contrast adaptation dramatically increases the visibility of some contrast-defined patterns and dramatically decreases that of others. The second part of the chapter briefly places this new effect in the context of a previously known effect (called the *old effect* here), which exhibits more conventional Weber law–like behavior.

DOI: 10.1037/14135-002
Human Information Processing: Vision, Memory, and Attention, C. Chubb, B. A. Dosher, Z.-L. Lu, and R. M. Shiffrin (Editors)

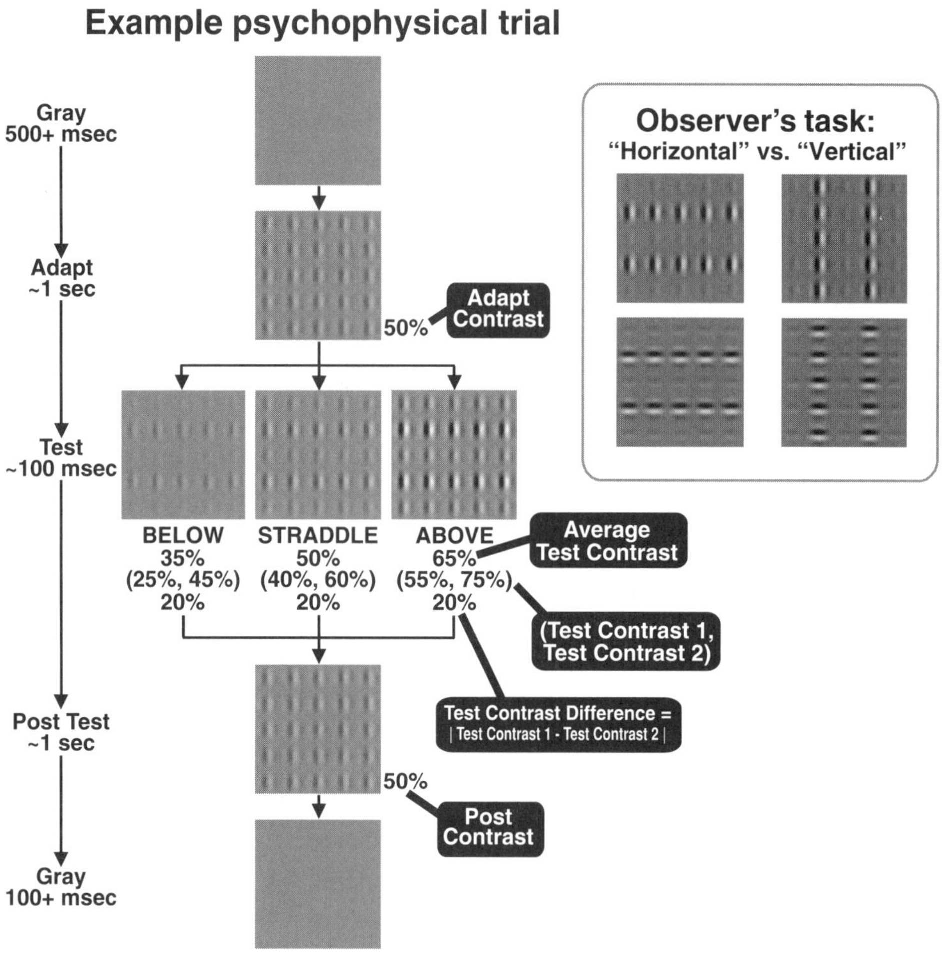

Example psychophysical trial

Figure 1.1 illustration content:

Gray
500+ msec

Adapt
~1 sec

Adapt Contrast
50%

Test
~100 msec

BELOW	STRADDLE	ABOVE
35%	50%	65%
(25%, 45%)	(40%, 60%)	(55%, 75%)
20%	20%	20%

Average Test Contrast

(Test Contrast 1, Test Contrast 2)

Test Contrast Difference = | Test Contrast 1 - Test Contrast 2 |

Post Test
~1 sec

Post Contrast
50%

Gray
100+ msec

Observer's task:
"Horizontal" vs. "Vertical"

Figure 1.1. A typical trial from the experiments is shown here. The experimental setup is described further in Wolfson and Graham (2007). The conditions shown in this figure are referred to as the standard conditions, and exceptions are explicitly noted when they occur. Note that only one Test pattern is shown on any trial, but three example Test patterns are shown on this figure. The right half illustrates the task of the observer. On each trial, the observer indicates whether the contrast-defined stripes are horizontal or vertical. Two examples of patterns corresponding to each of these responses are shown.

The New Effect and Hypothesized Process

Figure 1.1 shows a typical trial from the experiments reported here. The observer looks at a gray screen briefly and then sees a pattern we call the *Adapt* pattern. The duration of the Adapt pattern is approximately 1 s except where noted. Then, for an even briefer time, approximately 100 ms except where noted, the observer sees a *Test* pattern, which can be one of a number of possibilities, depending on the experiment. Three possibilities are illustrated in Figure 1.1.

The Test pattern is followed by a *Posttest* pattern that here is exactly the same as the Adapt pattern. The screen then returns to gray. (The mean luminance of the screen stays constant throughout the experiment.)

The Adapt pattern is a grid of Gabor patches all of the same contrast. The images in Figure 1.1 show 5×5 grids of Gabor patches, but the experiments reported here used either 15×15 or 2×2 grids. The Test pattern on any trial here is exactly like the Adapt pattern except that the contrasts of the Gabor patches will generally differ between Adapt and Test. Each Test pattern is composed of two potentially different contrasts of Gabor patches (which vary from trial to trial); the Gabor patches are arranged so that the two contrast values define a striped pattern.

For the experiments reported here, the spatial frequency of the sinusoidal fluctuation in the Gabor patches is two cycles per degree; there is approximately one full cycle in each patch. In the grid, there is one row of patches per degree of visual angle and one column per degree of visual angle. The Gabor patches are either all vertical or all horizontal, changing randomly from trial to trial. The contrast values shown in the figure are illustrative only, and those for each study are specified separately. (Each contrast value is the contrast of a Gabor patch, expressed as one-half the difference between peak and trough luminances divided by the mean luminance underneath the Gaussian window of the Gabor patch.) The contrast of the Adapt pattern remains constant throughout a block of trials, but the test contrasts vary from trial to trial.

The observer's response is to indicate whether the contrast-defined stripes in the Test pattern are "horizontal" or "vertical," as illustrated in the right half of Figure 1.1. Feedback is provided as to the correctness of the response.

After responding, the observer initiates the next trial with a key press, so the duration of gray on the screen between one trial's Posttest pattern and the next trial's Adapt pattern is significantly longer than the 600 ms required by the trial's characteristics. The gray screens were at the same mean luminance as the patterns.

The New Result: The Straddle Effect

Figures 1.2 and 1.3 show the results of a study with trials like those in Figure 1.1, with the following contrast choices: the contrast of the Adapt pattern could be 35%, 50%, or 65%; the two contrasts in the Test pattern always differ by 10% for the results shown here, but their average varies. For further details of the study, see the figure legends and Wolfson and Graham (2007).

Figure 1.2 shows the results from several observers for a subset of three kinds of trials. In all three, the Adapt pattern's contrast is 50%, and the difference between the two contrasts in the Test pattern is 10%. However, the two test contrasts vary (values are shown in the parentheses) and can be above the adapt contrast (top row), can straddle it (middle row), or can be below it (bottom row). The performance was much worse for the Straddle test pattern (53%, 57%, and 61% correct) than for the Above or Below test pattern (between 86% and 99% correct).

According to one common point of view, the function of adaptation (e.g., light adaptation) along a dimension (e.g., light intensity) is to re-center the operating

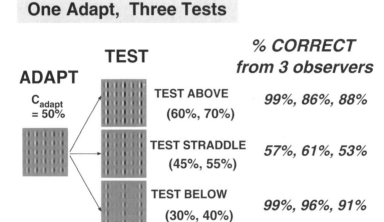

One Adapt, Three Tests

ADAPT   **TEST**   **% CORRECT** *from 3 observers*

C_{adapt} = 50%

TEST ABOVE (60%, 70%)   *99%, 86%, 88%*

TEST STRADDLE (45%, 55%)   *57%, 61%, 53%*

TEST BELOW (30%, 40%)   *99%, 96%, 91%*

Figure 1.2. Results from one Adapt pattern followed by each of several Test patterns, a subset of the results in Figure 1.3. Performance is given as percent correct identification of the orientation of the contrast-defined stripes, where each percentage is from approximately 50 trials of a given trial type (15×15 grids; spatial characteristics and timing are standard as in Figure 1.1 and accompanying test. Three observers: AG, CG, and CT.)

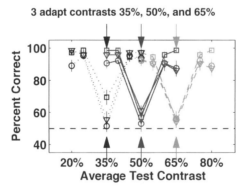

Figure 1.3. The results of adapting to different contrasts 35%, 50%, and 65% (identified by arrows on the upper and lower horizontal axes) are shown by three different line types. The three observers are represented by different symbol types. The difference between the two contrasts in the Test pattern is always 10%. From the same study as Figure 1.2.

range of the system to be at or near the current adaptation level (the recent time-averaged level on the dimension). This re-centering is done so that the system can respond near optimally in the current environment, responding best for values near the current adaptation level and worse for values farther away. On this point of view, there is something surprising about the results in Figure 1.2. The observers perform worse on the *Straddle* test pattern, which is the Test pattern with contrast values nearest the adapt contrast level. They do better on the *Above* and *Below* test patterns, and those are patterns that contain contrast values farther away from the adapt contrast level. This is exactly opposite to what is expected from the common point of view mentioned earlier. Also, the effect is large, a point that is developed further in the next two figures.

Figure 1.3 shows the results for all three adapting contrasts, each paired with many Test patterns. The difference between the two test contrasts was always 10%. As is clear from the V-shaped curves, for any adapt contrast, performance is lowest when the average test contrast equals the adapt contrast (that is, when the test contrasts straddle the adapt contrast). Also, performance is much better when the average test contrast is substantially above or substantially below the adapt contrast (within the range shown).

In another study (Graham & Wolfson, 2007), we measured contrast-difference thresholds rather than just measuring performance for a fixed test contrast difference. Some results from this study are replotted in a new manner in Figure 1.4. Each panel shows the results for one observer with one duration of Test pattern (82 ms in the left column and 35 ms in the right column). The adapt contrast was always 50%. Each point shows the results from trials in which the average test contrast was constant at some value in the range of 37.5% to 62.5%, and the difference between the two contrasts varied. The threshold was that contrast difference leading to criterion performance correct for the identification of the orientation of contrast-defined stripes, the task shown on the right of Figure 1.1. As expected from the percent correct performances in the study shown in Figures 1.2 and 1.3, the thresholds measured in this study for the Straddle test pattern (center point on each curve) are substantially higher than those for the Above or Below test patterns. This finding can be represented numerically by the ratio of the Straddle threshold to the other thresholds' average, and this number is indicated on each panel as "*th. ratio.*" The highest threshold ratio was 5.7, and even the lowest ratio was above 2.0. (The black lines are fitted to the data points in each panel, and the values of k and g are from a model that is discussed later.)

Explanations That Do Not Work for the Straddle Effect

Consider three patterns, which, like those in Figures 1.2 and 1.3, have a difference between test contrasts of 10%. In the Straddle test pattern (composed of 45% and 55% contrasts), the magnitude (absolute value) of the difference between the adapt contrast and either test contrast is only 5%. In the Above pattern composed of (50%, 60%) and the Below pattern composed of (40%, 50%), the magnitude of one of the differences between one test contrast (50%) and the adapt contrast (50%) is zero, but the other is 10% (i.e., |60%–50%| or |40%–50%|), much larger

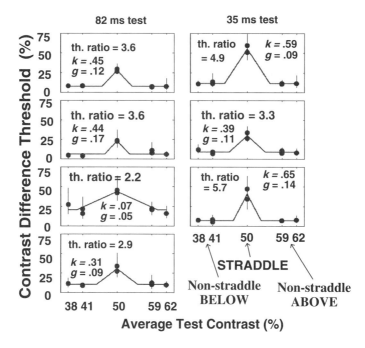

Figure 1.4. Contrast-difference thresholds as a function of average test contrast. The adapt contrast was 50% contrast. The mean ± 2 standard errors across sessions is plotted at each point. This full set of thresholds is unpublished but done under the same conditions as those in Graham and Wolfson (2007). See text for description of the threshold ratio *th. ratio* and the parameters *k* and *g* used to produce the model fit to the data points (black lines). The observer was KF for both panels in the top row. The other three observers at the longer test duration (left column) were JW, EG, and AG from the second panel down. The other two observers at the shorter duration (right column) were KN and SH from the second panel down.

than the 5% differences in the Straddle pattern. A number of people have asked us whether these larger change magnitudes (let's refer to them as *transients*) that occur in the Above and Below cases relative to the Straddle case account for the better performance on the Above and Below test patterns. The answer to that question, by a straightforward empirical test, turns out to be no. Again using an adapt contrast of 50%, consider the following set of three test patterns, constructed so that this change magnitude is always 10%: The contrast values in the Below test pattern are (40%, 50%), in the Straddle pattern are (40%, 60%), and in the Above pattern are (50%, 60%). As it turns out, empirically, performance in the Straddle case is still substantially worse than in the Above and Below cases. We have now collected results from many such sets of three patterns, or *constant-transient trios*, and they consistently show much worse performance on the Straddle case. See Figure 3 of Wolfson and Graham (2007) and Figure 7 of Wolfson and Graham (2009).

A nonlinear transducer (monotonic function applied locally) also cannot account for the new effect. This is true even if the transducer is shaped to produce so-called pedestal effects for both increments and decrements in contrast. The discussion is lengthy, so we do not include it here. The interested reader can see "Appendix A1: Shifting Monotonic Transducer" in Wolfson and Graham (2009).

An Explanation of the Straddle Effect: Shifting, Rectifying, Contrast Comparison

How can one make sense of the experimental results? It is as if, within whatever system is responsible for the observer's performance in these experiments,

1. adaptation to contrast resets some comparison level to represent the recent time-average contrast seen at each place in the visual field,
2. the current contrast at each spatial position pattern is evaluated relative to that comparison level, and
3. with increases and decreases in contrast being equally salient but quite confusable with each other (within whatever system is doing this perceptual task).

This idea is diagrammed as the comparison process illustrated in Figure 1.5. The core of this idea is that there exists something in the visual system that acts like a rectification function on the contrast dimension. This rectification makes it hard to perceive a Straddle test pattern correctly because, when the Straddle test pattern appears after the Adapt pattern, the increase in contrast

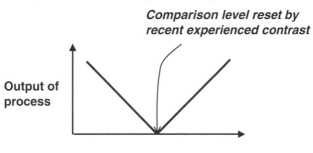

A possible comparison process

Figure 1.5. Diagram of a process that rectifies with a shifting "zero point," the comparison level, that adapts to equal the average of its recent input (the average recent local contrast). The output of this possible comparison process (at any particular position) is proportional to the unsigned difference between the current input contrast and the comparison level. Thus, under suitable temporal conditions, the output is proportional to the magnitude of the change from the Adapt pattern to the Test pattern, but it ignores the direction of the change.

produces the same output as the decrease. Thus, it is difficult for observers to identify the orientation of the contrast-defined stripes in the Straddle test pattern. Indeed, if the rectification function were a full-wave function, like that in Figure 1.5, then increases and decreases of the same magnitude would produce identical outputs from this comparison process and thus be totally confusable by the subsequent stages of visual processing. The full-wave rectification function shown is too extreme to quantitatively fit our results because it would predict that an observer's performance would be at chance on all Straddle test patterns, no matter how large the difference between the two contrasts. We have never seen an observer quite that extreme. This aspect of Figure 1.5 is modified below.

Conventional second-order (complex, *FNF,* non-Fourier) channels are composed of two linear-filter stages with a rectification-type nonlinearity between the two stages. These channels can be described informally as structures in which neurons with small receptive fields feed into neurons with large receptive fields with a pointwise rectification in between. Thus, these channels are selectively sensitive to both the first-order spatial-frequency and orientation content (determined primarily by individual Gabor patches) and the second-order spatial-frequency and orientation (determined by overall arrangement of contrast in the grid of Gabor patches). These second-order channels are a useful addition to the previously suggested simple (first-order, Fourier) channels and can account for many aspects of human pattern perception, as has been shown by many different investigators in a large number of studies (see Graham, 2011, for a recent overview of this work, with many references).

In Graham and Wolfson (2007), Figures 2.22 and 2.23 with accompanying text present a channel model that is modified from the conventional second-order channel model. The modified channel contains, in addition to the components of the conventional channel, a process with behavior like that in Figure 1.5. To explain the experimental results for any observer we have yet studied, we cannot use a strict full-wave rectification for that process as mentioned earlier. We need some compromise between a half-wave and a full-wave rectification in this channel model. We embody this compromise in our current model by using pairs of channels. The rectification functions in any pair of channels are mirror-symmetric, each somewhere between a full-wave and a half-have rectification, so that one channel is more sensitive to contrast increases and the other more sensitive to contrast decreases. The degree of compromise between a half- and a full-wave rectification function can be represented by a parameter k, which varies from 0 for half-wave to 1 for full-wave. More completely, its value equals the absolute value of the ratio of the slope of the rectification function's shallower side to the slope of its steeper side.

An alternate approach would be to consider mixtures of channels, some having strict full-wave and some having strict half-wave rectification functions (e.g., Sperling, 1989; Sperling, Chubb, Solomon, & Lu, 1994). We have not tried this yet, but we suspect that the predictions from a mixture model would look similar to those presented here and that the parameter k values here would be monotonic with the ratios of full-wave to half-wave channels in the best-fitting mixture model's predictions.

Let's look at the threshold results in Figure 1.4 again. The black lines fitted to the data points show best-fitting predictions from a model including adaptable complex channels. The simple model we used to generate these predictions and produce the fits here assumes that all stages of visual processing were deterministic (there was no noise in the responses). It also assumes that the channel with the maximum output determined the observer's response. Finally, it is a static model (there is no explicit representation of time), but the assumption is made that Adapt pattern duration is long enough to make the comparison level equal to the adapt contrast (see Graham, 2011, for the equations). What is represented by the rectification function on the contrast dimension in this simple static model might well be unpacked in a dynamic model to be something that came from the temporal processing of contrast transients (or perhaps even of luminance transients, although that seems unlikely to be true in the visual system).

The model predictions (black lines) fitted to the data points in Figure 1.4 result from a 2-parameter fit: k is the ratio of slopes referred to before, and g is an overall gain parameter. The fit is excellent.

There are individual differences in both parameters. The sensitivity parameter g varies substantially among observers, which is not surprising. It is determined in the fits by the thresholds to the Above and Below test patterns (the thresholds on the horizontal line segments at the left and right ends of the predicted curves). The parameter k is more interesting. It varies substantially among data sets. It was determined in the fits by the threshold ratio "*th. ratio*" (the ratio of straddle thresholds to the above and below thresholds). A value of $k = 0$ (half-wave rectification) corresponds to a threshold ratio of 2. Something close to this value occurs for one data set. A value of $k = 1$ (strict full-wave) corresponds to a threshold ratio of infinity (the threshold for the Straddle would be infinitely high) and did not occur in our results. The highest values of this parameter k were near 0.6 and indicate rectification functions middling between half- and full-wave.

The Old Effect and Hypothesized Process

We switch now to a situation that does not show the new Straddle effect that we have been discussing so far. Instead, this situation shows an old effect that is an example of generalized Weber law behavior. All the results shown so far in this chapter involved middle-range adapt contrasts and middle-range average test contrasts. On the basis of our own previous work (e.g., Graham & Sutter, 2000; Wolfson & Graham, 2005) and of extrapolations from others' work, we already knew a great deal about the effects of one other, extreme adapt contrast—namely, the effect of an adapt contrast of 0%.

The Old Result: Weber Law Behavior

Adapting to 0% contrast means adapting to a steady homogeneous gray field with no Gabor patches in it. Such a condition is often called *no adaptation* or *before adaptation* and may be the condition most often used in experiments on pattern perception. We have studied this condition a great deal ourselves in the past and have referred to it this way. We no longer view it in this manner for reasons we hope will be clear by the end of this chapter.

Let's look at some results of adapting to 0% contrast. For this study (done recently to replicate the older results but with the current observers), we used test patterns in which the test contrast difference was 10%, and the average test contrast took on closely spaced values from 10% to 90%. This is almost, but not quite, the full range possible. The smallest and largest possible average test contrasts for patterns characterized by a 10% test contrast difference are 5% and 95%, respectively. (There is no Test pattern that can straddle an Adapt pattern of 0% contrast or one of 100% contrast.) As shown in the top part of Figure 1.6, performance after adapting to 0% contrast is good for the lowest average test contrasts used—that is, for test contrasts near the adapt contrast. Performance then drops monotonically (within the limits of experimental variability) as the average test contrast gets far away from the adapt contrast. This decrease in performance is reminiscent of many effects seen in perception. It and its close relatives have been much studied. We refer to this behavior as *Weber law–like behavior,* or just Weber behavior for short, for the reason indicated in the bottom part of Figure 1.6. The leftmost of the three example Test patterns there has an average test contrast of 10% and contains two contrasts of 15% and 5%, producing a contrast ratio of 3. The Test pattern in the middle is composed of 55% and 45%, and the contrast ratio is 1.2. The Test pattern on the right has a still smaller contrast ratio. Thus, in general, performance gets worse as the ratio of the higher contrast to the lower contrast in the Test pattern gets smaller. In previous, more extensive

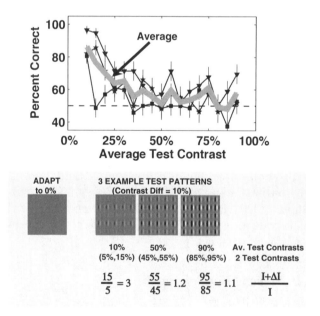

Figure 1.6. The top shows performance after adapting to 0% contrast for Test patterns in which the contrast difference was 10%. Results are shown for average test contrasts from 10% to 90%. Patterns were 2×2 grids of Gabor patches. Three observers are indicated by different symbols: MM (stars), RK (squares), and VR (upside-down triangles).

experiments, we have further shown that, after adaptation to 0% contrast, it is indeed this ratio that predicts performance over a large part of the range. For example, if you considered another Test pattern with the same ratio, that is, 60% and 20% compared with 15% and 5%, then the observer's performance would likely be similar on both (e.g., Graham & Sutter, 2000; Wolfson & Graham, 2005). Dependence on the ratio of intensities occurs on many dimensions (here the dimension is contrast) and is a generalization of the behavior described in Weber's law.

As it turns out, the Weber behavior in this situation cannot be explained by a nonlinear monotonic function applied locally (e.g., Fechner). For brevity's sake, we do not describe this here. (An interested reader could consult Graham & Sutter, 2000, or Wolfson & Graham, 2009.)

An Explanation of the Weber Behavior: Inhibition Among Channels in a Normalization Network

A model that can account for the Weber law–like behavior after adaptation to 0% contrast includes inhibitory interconnections among simple (linear) and complex (second-order) spatial-frequency and orientation-selective channels. The inhibitory interactions are in a form often called normalization, a form of divisive suppression in which the response of each neuron is divided by (normalized by, has its contrast gain set by) the total output of a pool of neurons. This kind of model provides an excellent fit for a wide variety of visual patterns. (Recent discussions of this kind of normalization process can be found in Reynolds & Heeger, 2009, and Graham, 2011.) In particular, this kind of model correctly predicts the Weber-like behavior after adaptation to 0% contrast for a large range of patterns like those used here (e.g., Graham & Sutter, 2000).

The Old and the New Together

What happens for those combinations of adapt and test contrasts that we have not yet discussed? In particular, what happens when you adapt to middling contrasts and test with very low or very high average contrasts? What happens when you adapt to very high contrasts? Figure 1.7 shows the results of an experiment (Wolfson & Graham, 2009) with five adapt contrasts ranging from 0% (in the bottom panels) to 100% (in the top panels) and pairs of test contrasts that varied from the lowest possible to the highest possible (their average is plotted on the horizontal axis). The difference between the test contrasts was always 10%.

Adaptation to 0% (bottom panels) replicates earlier results (e.g., Figure 1.6). There are individual differences in sensitivity; SYP (on left) is a very sensitive observer (highest performing for a given contrast difference), whereas RK (on right) is less sensitive.

What happens after adaptation to a middle contrast for the full range of average test contrasts (e.g., 50% in the middle row of Figure 1.7)? We again see the bad performance on the Straddle test patterns, with good performance

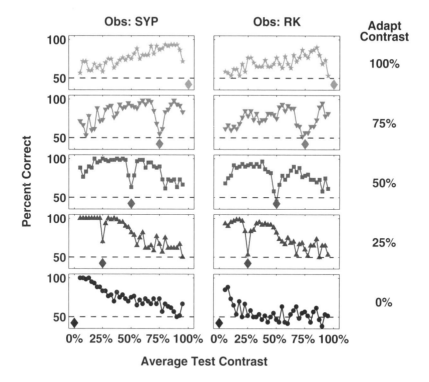

Figure 1.7. Results of experiment covering the full range of adapt and test contrasts. The five different adapt contrasts are marked in the right side and indicated by diamond symbols on the horizontal axis. They range from 0% (in the bottom panels) to 100% (in the top panels). The difference between the test contrasts was always 10%, and the average varied from 5% to 95% (the lowest possible to the highest possible). The patterns were 2 × 2 grids. These data are from two of the three observers shown in Wolfson and Graham (2009).

for Above and Below test patterns of contrasts somewhat outside the Straddle range (as in Figure 1.3). However, we now also see bad performance for Test patterns at the ends of these curves, having contrasts far above or far below the adapt contrast. To put it another way, the observers' best performance overall is for test contrasts at an intermediate distance from the adapt contrast.

As you look from the top panel of Figure 1.7 (adapt contrast of 100%) down to the bottom panel (adapt contrast of 0%), you can see the movement of the region of peak performance from right to left, following the adapt contrast, where this region of peak performance has a notch at the adapt contrast itself. (This is clearest for the three intermediate curves, where it is possible to have an average test contrast equal to the adapt contrast, but the notch is also clear at an adapt contrast of 100%.) Therefore, the range of contrast patterns that are perceived best, at least in the sense of the perception required in our experimental task, generally shifts to regions near the adapting contrast. This shift is consistent with a frequently suggested function of adaptation: that of moving the operating range to suit the current conditions. The exception to the general shift is the poor performance on the Straddle test patterns, which are patterns with average test contrasts right in the middle of the good-performance region.

We suspect that these curves in Figure 1.7 result from the interaction of two processes across the full range of contrasts but dominating in different ranges. The adaptable contrast-comparison-level process (nicknamed the *Buffy adaptation*) is the primary cause of the bad performance for the Straddle. The normalization process produces the Weber-like behavior, where the dimension is the unsigned difference between the test contrast and the adapt contrast. Thus it occurs both for increments and decrements in contrast (both for average test contrasts substantially above and for those substantially below the adapt contrast).

We have recently started some fitting of these results with predictions from a model that combines the normalization model we used previously for adapting to 0% (instantiated in simple equations) and the contrast-comparison process (also instantiated in simple equations). The results are encouraging (Graham, 2011).

We have been interested in studying the dynamics of both the Straddle effect and the Weber behavior to help uncover the properties of the presumed processes (contrast comparison and normalization), their neural substrate, and also their functionality in human vision. We have been doing two kinds of study. The first kind used flickering Adapt patterns of various temporal frequencies (Graham & Wolfson, 2007). The second kind used different durations of Adapt patterns in the situation of Figure 1.1 here. Results for one observer in one version of this second kind of study are shown in Figure 1.8.

The results of both kinds of dynamic experiment suggest the following conclusions, which should be held tentatively, given the absence to date of any modeling of these dynamics: The resetting of the comparison level in the new process may happen largely if not completely within 50 to 100 ms; the temporal integration of the contrast-gain control in the old normalization process takes a second or longer.

Discussion

The duration of a typical eye fixation is approximately 200 to 250 ms, and the duration of a typical saccade is approximately 50 to 70 ms. Thus, the hypothesized resetting of the contrast-comparison level might well occur within an eye fixation or even within a saccade. Such fast adaptation may be important because "eye movements are frequently large enough that there will be little correlation in the contrast or luminance on a receptive field from one fixation to the next, and thus rapid contrast and luminance gain control are essential" (Frazor & Geisler, 2006, p. 1585).

Is the perceiving of changes (perceiving the change in contrast between the Adapt and Test patterns in the experiments here) so desirable that loss of direction-of-change information (loss which leads to bad performance on Straddle test patterns in the experiments here) can persist as a side effect throughout the course of evolution? Furthermore, unless it is positively advantageous to perform badly in Straddle situations, which seems unlikely, the

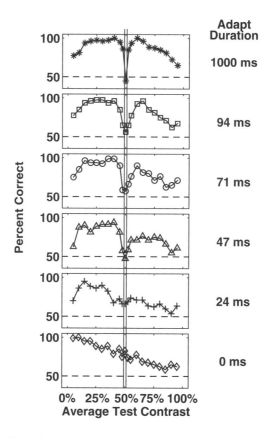

Figure 1.8. The effect of varying the Adapt pattern duration between 0 and 1,000 ms (shown by the right-hand labels) when adapting to 50% contrast (indicated by double vertical line). The duration of the test pattern was 82 ms. The Posttest pattern duration equaled that of the Adapt pattern. The duration of the gray screens (the first and last events in the trial as shown in Figure 1.1) were such that the total length of the trial was the same for all adapt durations. The difference between the two contrasts in a Test pattern was always 10%. The patterns were 2×2 grids. Observer was SYP.

following question arises: Could the visual system perfectly track the sign of the change as well as the fact of the change? If the answer is yes, why doesn't the visual system do so here? If the answer is no, why? We are beginning to suspect that there is some design reason why it is best (fastest, easiest, cheapest) to detect changes in a way that partially loses information about sign (direction of change). Perhaps the design constraint has something to do with some difficulty neural networks have in responding stably to rapid changes (transients) because large imbalances from different parts of the network are likely to occur at transients. Other possible design constraints are suggested in recent studies that ask whether some features of adaptation (in particular, orientation-selective adaptation) may occur as a reaction to changes in an organism's internal state rather than to changes in the external environment. They consider factors such as sparseness and variance of cortical spike trains, and they explore these factors' implications for optimal processing at different time scale. Perhaps some such design constraint could help explain the puzzling loss of direction-of-change information in the Straddle effect here.

References

Frazor, R. A., & Geisler, W. S. (2006). Local luminance and contrast in natural images. *Vision Research, 46,* 1585–1598. doi:10.1016/j.visres.2005.06.038

Graham, N., & Sutter, A. (2000). Normalization: Contrast-gain control in simple (Fourier) and complex (non-Fourier) pathways of pattern vision. *Vision Research, 40,* 2737–2761. doi:10.1016/S0042-6989(00)00123-1

Graham, N., & Wolfson, S. S. (2007). Exploring contrast-controlled adaptation processes in human vision (with help from Buffy the Vampire Slayer). In L. R. M. Harris & M. R. Jenkin (Eds.), *Computational vision in neural and machine systems* (pp. 9–47). Cambridge, England: Cambridge University Press.

Graham, N. V. (2011). Beyond multiple pattern analyzers modeled as linear filters (as classical V1 simple cells): Useful additions of the last 25 years. *Vision Research, 51,* 1397–1430. doi:10.1016/j.visres.2011.02.007

Reynolds, J. H., & Heeger, D. J. (2009). The normalization model of attention. *Neuron, 61,* 168–185. doi:10.1016/j.neuron.2009.01.002

Sperling, G. (1989). Three stages and two systems of visual processing. *Spatial Vision, 4,* 183–207. doi:10.1163/156856889X00112

Sperling, G., Chubb, C., Solomon, J. A., & Lu, Z.-L. (1994). Full-wave and half-wave rectification in motion and texture. In G. R. Bocke & J. A. Goode (Eds.), *Higher-order processing in the visual system, No. 184 Ciba Symposium* (pp. 287–308). Chichester, England: Wiley.

Wolfson, S. S., & Graham, N. (2005). Element-arrangement textures in multiple objective tasks.

Wolfson, S. S., & Graham, N. (2007). An unusual kind of contrast adaptation: Shifting a contrast comparison level. *Journal of Vision, 7*(8), 12.

Wolfson, S. S., & Graham, N. (2009). Two contrast adaptation processes: Contrast normalization and shifting, rectifying contrast comparison. *Journal of Vision, 9*(4), 30.1–23.

2

The Incompatibility of Feature Contrast and Feature Acuity

Joshua A. Solomon and Isabelle Mareschal

Orientation Contrast

Repulsion is ubiquitous in the visual system. For example, gray things seem darker in a bright context, and objects with zero disparity seem closer when flanked by more distant objects. We studied repulsion in the orientation domain, where it is popularly known as the *tilt illusion:* When tilted objects are nearby, an upright object appears to be tilted in the other direction. The goal of our research was to determine why a tilted context also reduces the consistency of apparent orientation.

Gibsonian Normalization

Gibson (1937) used the term *orientation contrast* for both a property in some visual stimuli (see Figure 2.1a) and the visual system's exaggeration of that property. In this chapter, we reserve the term for the former definition. We refer to the latter as the *tilt illusion*. Figure 2.2a is a cartoon of Gibson's explanation for the tilt illusion. Essentially, he suggested that the label for "vertical" shifts from the mechanism preferring this orientation to another, which is better aligned with the surround.

A more general but formally equivalent idea is Gilbert and Wiesel's (1990) description of orientation preferences that shift toward the surround's orientation. This is depicted in Figure 2.2b. Both Gilbert and Wiesel and Dragoi, Sharma, and Sur (2000) looked for evidence of a shift like this. Instead, their data (from cat V1) suggest, if anything, that orientation preferences shift away from the surrounding orientation.

DOI: 10.1037/14135-003

Human Information Processing: Vision, Memory, and Attention, C. Chubb, B. A. Dosher, Z.-L. Lu, and R. M. Shiffrin (Editors)

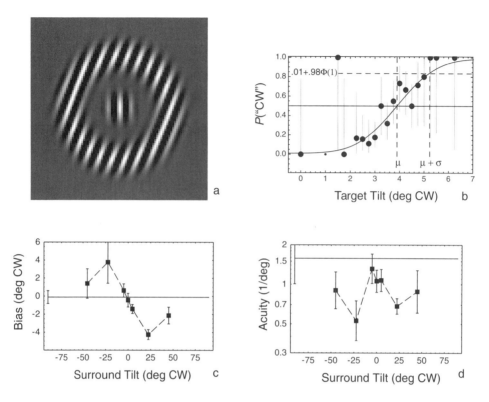

Figure 2.1. Stimulus and aggregated results from Solomon and Morgan (2009). An annularly windowed grating produces the illusion of tilt in a vertical Gabor pattern (a). This illusion was measured by asking observers whether a slightly tilted Gabor was clockwise (CW) or counterclockwise (CCW) of vertical. Observer AT's CW response probabilities for this 22.5° surround form a Gaussian function (b) of target tilt t, i.e., $P(\text{"CW"}) = 0.01 + 0.98\Phi(t;\mu,\sigma^2)$. Two summary statistics are derived from this psychometric function: bias ($-\mu$) and acuity ($1/\sigma$). All biases (c) effectively exaggerated the difference between target and surround. Acuities (d) were particularly poor with the same ($\pm 22.5°$) surrounds that produced the maximum biases. In panels b, c, and d, CCW tilts are negative, horizontal lines represent a no-surround condition, and error bars contain 95% confidence intervals or 4 standard errors of the mean. From "Strong Tilt Illusions Always Reduce Orientation Acuity," by J. A. Solomon and M. J. Morgan, 2009, *Vision Research, 49*, 819–824. Copyright 2009 by Elsevier Science. Adapted with permission.

Lateral Inhibition Within a Neural Population

Today, the most popular models of the tilt illusion are based on the concept of gain control. The earliest of these models (Blakemore, Carpenter, & Georgeson, 1970) featured inhibition between neurons preferring dissimilar orientations. If the target and surround had sufficiently different orientations, this inhibition would further separate the two peaks in the response of a population sensitive to both target and surround. That is, this population would naturally

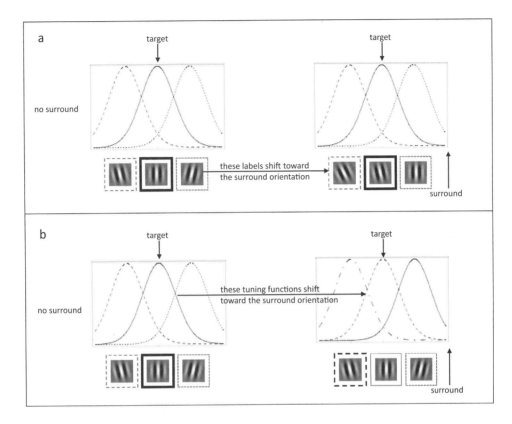

Figure 2.2. Normalization theories. In Gibson's (1937) version (a), a vertical target will always stimulate the same neuron, whereas in Gilbert and Wiesel's (1990) version (b), the surround influences which neurons receive maximum stimulation from the target. However, in both versions, when a CW surround is present, the maximally stimulated neuron will be labeled with a CCW tilt.

exaggerate orientation contrast. On the other hand, a similarly oriented target and surround would only produce one peak in the response of this population (Solomon, Felisberti, & Morgan, 2004). Orientation contrast would not be exaggerated; it would be eliminated.

Crowding

Although Blakemore et al.'s (1970) model predicts a much more dramatic effect, there certainly are situations in which the visual system attenuates orientation contrast. For example, in parafoveal vision, it can be much more difficult to tell whether a particular Gabor pattern is tilted clockwise or counterclockwise of vertical when it is flanked by perfectly vertical Gabors (Parkes, Lund, Angelucci, Solomon, & Morgan, 2001).

Flank-induced orientation uncertainty is now known as *crowding*. It was first demonstrated using a Landolt ring (Flom, Weymouth, & Kahneman, 1963), which is like the letter *C* in one of four orientations. It is much harder to identify the orientation of a Landolt ring when it is surrounded by four line segments, unless that ring appears at fixation (Jacobs, 1979). Vernier acuity shows a similar pattern of results (Levi, Klein, & Aitsebaomo, 1985), suggesting that crowding is relatively weak at the fovea.

Parafoveal tilt discrimination was first studied by Andriessen and Bouma (1976). They found it to be particularly difficult when the target line segment was surrounded by similarly oriented segments. When the target was surrounded by roughly perpendicular segments, the task was not so difficult. Our own measurements (Solomon et al., 2004) confirm this result, and, like Vernier alignment and the Landolt task, the introduction of similarly oriented flanks has little influence on tilt discrimination at the fovea (Solomon & Morgan, 2006). However, we also found that the introduction of obliquely oriented flanks nearly doubled the size of a just-noticeable tilt (i.e., they halved acuity). If crowding is weak at the fovea, why do oblique flanks impair tilt discrimination there?

Squishing

Before we discuss potential mechanisms for this context-induced acuity loss, we need a name for it. Because it occurs in the center of the visual field, it may not be crowding. Nor does it require particularly small target-flanker separations. Levi, Klein, and Hariharan (2002) reported that flanks could elevate the contrast threshold for detecting a Gabor pattern at the fovea, as long as they were no further than 3σ from the target. In our experiments, the target-flank separation was a minimum of 6σ. Therefore, we do not want to use their term *foveal crowding* either. For now, we are calling it *squishing*. Squishing may not be particularly euphonious, but it is much easier to say than "the context-induced acuity loss for tilt that occurs in central vision," which is how we define it.

Squishing is often accompanied by a large tilt illusion (Solomon & Morgan, 2009; relevant methods and results appear in Figure 2.1a–2.1d). Consequently, we wondered whether any contemporary models of the tilt illusion might also explain squishing. Blakemore et al.'s (1970) gain-control model is inadequate because it relies on a single population, which is sensitive to both target and flanks. As discussed earlier, a population like this would effectively attenuate the orientation contrast between similar-but-not-identical stimuli, and although there is some of this "small-angle assimilation" in the visual periphery, there is none at the fovea (Solomon & Morgan, 2006).

Lateral Inhibition Between Neural Populations

Because a gain control that spreads across orientation preference does not seem sufficiently versatile to cause both a large tilt illusion and no small-angle assimilation, we next consider a gain control that spreads across orientation preference and space. Figure 2.3 shows one way this might work. If divisive

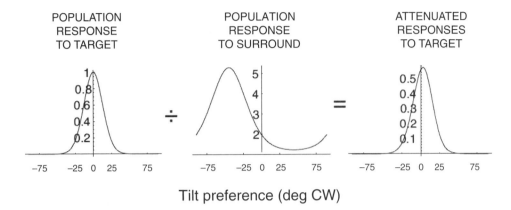

POPULATION RESPONSE TO TARGET   POPULATION RESPONSE TO SURROUND   ATTENUATED RESPONSES TO TARGET

Tilt preference (deg CW)

Figure 2.3. Gain control: The population excited by an untilted target gets divisively inhibited by nearby populations. These latter are excited by stimuli having a –45° (i.e., counterclockwise) tilt. Consequently, both the mean and the mode of the target population are shifted clockwise (CW).

inhibition were strongest between neighboring neurons of similar orientation preference, then the introduction of a tilted surround would shift responses in the target population away from the surround's tilt. It would also cause an overall attenuation of response to the target.

Several authors have expressed dissatisfaction with this model because the putatively attenuated response does not manifest as dramatically impaired visibility (Snowden & Hammett, 1998; Solomon & Morgan, 2006). However, this may not be a serious problem. Visibility is thought to be governed by the ratio of signal strength to visual noise (Green & Swets, 1966). If the source of noise that limited visibility were relatively early, then any downstream gain-control would attenuate this noise as well as any signal. That way, the signal-to-noise ratio would remain unchanged, and target visibility could escape unscathed.

Contrast Contrast

To look for the effects of gain control on visibility, we need a paradigm in which visual noise does not matter. Chubb, Sperling, and Solomon's (1989) seems to fit the bill. Just as the visual system exaggerates the orientation contrast between center and surround, Chubb et al. found that it exaggerates the contrast contrast as well (compare Figure 2.4a and 2.4b). However, mere gain-control models for apparent contrast are necessarily incomplete. They cannot explain why regions of uniform contrast actually appear to be uniform, despite having contrast contrast at their boundaries. There must be some relatively high-level mechanism for "filling in," which equalizes the apparent contrast within a contrast–contrast boundary.

The influence of boundaries is often demonstrated with the Craik–Cornsweet–O'Brien effect (Figure 2.4c), which works to some degree for contrast as well (Lu & Sperling, 1996; Figure 2.4d). Exactly how and to what

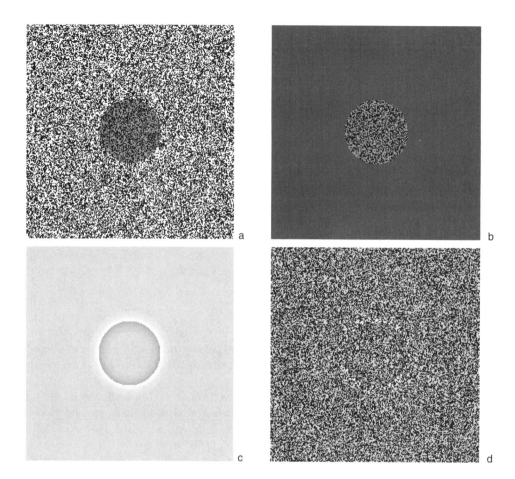

Figure 2.4. Contrast contrast. The centers in panels a and b are identical, but they appear to have different contrasts. Like the tilt illusion, this contrast-domain analogue can be ascribed to the lateral spread of divisive inhibition. The contrast-domain analogue (d) of the Craik–Cornsweet–O'Brien effect (c) demonstrates the large influence that edges have on apparent contrast. From "Second-Order Illusions: Mach Bands, Chevreul, and Craik–O'Brien–Cornsweet," by Z.-L. Lu & G. Sperling, 1996, *Vision Research, 36,* 559–572. Adapted with permission.

extent apparent intensities are governed by edge information remains a matter of debate. However, it must be noted that we are by no means the first to suggest that tilt boundaries are primarily responsible for the tilt illusion.

Separating Target and Surround

Tolhurst and Thompson (1975) made such a claim. Their evidence was that the tilt illusion decreased when a small gap was placed between center and surround. Similar results have been reported at least twice (Durant & Clifford, 2006; Wenderoth & Johnstone, 1988). In all studies, a gap of 1°

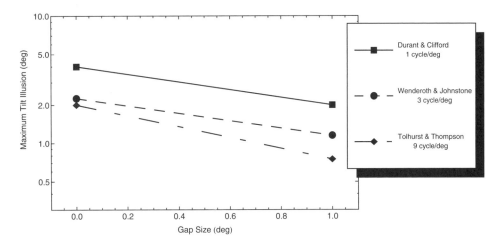

Figure 2.5. How separating target from surround affects the tilt illusion. These data originate from the studies shown in the figure legend. Regardless of spatial frequency, a 1° gap roughly halves the maximum tilt illusion, which is invariably obtained with orientation contrasts between 10° and 25°.

roughly halved the maximum tilt illusion. Moreover, Figure 2.5 suggests that the spread of the tilt illusion is probably better discussed in terms of visual angle, rather than in terms of wavelength. Another noteworthy aspect of this graph is its suggestion that the tilt illusion is strongest with low spatial frequencies.

If a gap were placed between center and surround and the observer moved away from the stimulus, the frequency would increase and the angular extent of the gap would decrease. However, our own data (see Figure 2.6) suggest these two effects would not balance. Having a smaller gap seems to be more important than having a lower spatial frequency. Also noteworthy in this figure is the effect of viewing eccentricity. The tilt illusion is maximized when observers do not look straight at the target (Over, Broerse, & Crassini, 1972). Elsewhere (Mareschal et al., 2010), we have argued that it is not really the gap size in degrees that matters; it is the gap size in cortical distance.

So what we have here seems to be a relatively weak gain control process that can spread over 1° of visual field to the fovea. This gain control does not seem to affect contrast discrimination, so it probably attenuates noise as well as signal. Furthermore, its effects can be modified by downstream processes, which overemphasize featural differences at the boundary between the target and its immediate surroundings.

Mechanisms for Squishing

Our primary concern is how this gain control could cause squishing. According to the simple model in Figure 2.3, there are two possibilities. Squishing could result from either the shift or the attenuation of responses to the target. We

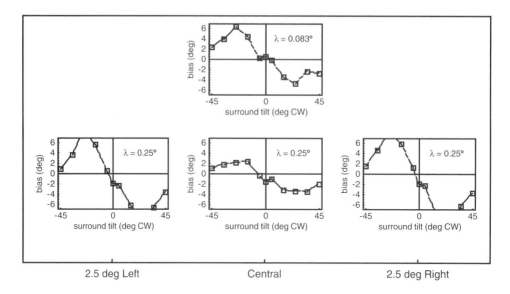

2.5 deg Left   Central   2.5 deg Right

Figure 2.6. How the tilt illusion varies with scale and eccentricity. The methods are described in Figure 2.1, Observer JAS. Here, wavelength (λ) is confounded with gap size. The two "Central" stimuli were identical, merely fixated from different viewing distances. CW = clockwise.

have made a step toward distinguishing these possibilities by measuring the effects of surrounds that are expected to attenuate, but not skew, the population responses to the target. These surrounds appear in Figure 2.7. Both the bull's eyes and the rings contain power at all orientations. Therefore, they can be expected to produce a lateral inhibition that is evenly spread across orientation. Our results clearly show that this inhibition does not reduce orien-

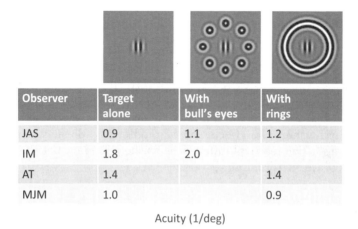

Observer	Target alone	With bull's eyes	With rings
JAS	0.9	1.1	1.2
IM	1.8	2.0	
AT	1.4		1.4
MJM	1.0		0.9

Acuity (1/deg)

Figure 2.7. No squishing from isotropic surrounds. Although both the bull's eyes and the rings have the same center frequency as the target, neither produces a substantial reduction in orientation acuity.

tation acuity. Therefore, we conclude that isotropic surrounds do not squish. Orientation contrast seems to be required.

Whether through lateral inhibition, a shift of neural preferences, or some as-yet-unidentified mechanism, orientation contrast is exaggerated. Elsewhere (Solomon & Morgan, 2006), we championed normalization (Figure 2.2) and proposed that it could vary from trial to trial. As a result of this *stochastic recalibration,* psychometric functions for orientation identification (Figure 2.1b) would flatten out, and acuities inferred from these functions would be lowered.

Normalization could be wrong. As described earlier, gain-control models of the tilt illusion remain viable. Perhaps it is this gain control that is inconsistent. It, too, could shift the population response by a different amount on every trial. The result would be the same: Whenever there was a tilt illusion, there would also be squishing. Moreover, we have no reason to believe that the tilt illusion is special. Any feature contrast may be exaggerated at a boundary, and that exaggeration may be stochastic. If so, then acuity for that feature will necessarily suffer.

References

Andriessen, J. J., & Bouma, H. (1976). Eccentric vision: Adverse interactions between line segments. *Vision Research, 16,* 71–78. doi:10.1016/0042-6989(76)90078-X

Blakemore, C., Carpenter, R. H. S., & Georgeson, M. A. (1970, October 3). Lateral inhibition between orientation detectors in the human visual system. *Nature, 228,* 37–39. doi:10.1038/228037a0

Chubb, C., Sperling, G., & Solomon, J. A. (1989). Texture interactions determine perceived contrast. *Proceedings of the National Academy of Sciences of the United States of America, 86,* 9631–9635. doi:10.1073/pnas.86.23.9631

Dragoi, V., Sharma, J., & Sur, M. (2000). Adaptation-induced plasticity of orientation tuning in adult visual cortex. *Neuron, 28,* 287–298. doi:10.1016/S0896-6273(00)00103-3

Durant, S., & Clifford, C. W. G. (2006). Dynamics of the influence of segmentation cues on orientation perception. *Vision Research, 46,* 2934–2940. doi:10.1016/j.visres.2006.02.027

Flom, M. C., Weymouth, F. W., & Kahneman, D. (1963). Visual resolution and contour interaction. *Journal of the Optical Society of America, 53,* 1026–1032. doi:10.1364/JOSA.53.001026

Gibson, J. J. (1937). Adaptation, after-effect, and contrast in the perception of tilted lines. II. Simultaneous contrast and the areal restriction of the after-effect. *Journal of Experimental Psychology, 20,* 553–569. doi:10.1037/h0057585

Gilbert, C. D., & Wiesel, T. N. (1990). The influence of contextual stimuli on the orientation selectivity of cells in primary visual cortex of the cat. *Vision Research, 30,* 1689–1701. doi:10.1016/0042-6989(90)90153-C

Green, D. M., & Swets, J. A. (1966). *Signal detection theory and psychophysics.* New York, NY: Wiley.

Jacobs, R. J. (1979). Visual resolution and contour interaction in the fovea and periphery. *Vision Research, 19,* 1187–1195. doi:10.1016/0042-6989(79)90183-4

Levi, D. M., Klein, S. A., & Aitsebaomo, A. P. (1985). Vernier acuity, crowding and cortical magnification. *Vision Research, 25,* 963–977. doi:10.1016/0042-6989(85)90207-X

Levi, D. M., Klein, S. A., & Hariharan, S. (2002). Suppressive and facilitatory spatial interactions in foveal vision: Foveal crowding is simple contrast masking. *Journal of Vision, 2,* 140–166.

Lu, Z.-L., & Sperling, G. (1996). Second-order illusions: Mach bands, Chevreul, and Craik–O'Brien–Cornsweet. *Vision Research, 36,* 559–572. doi:10.1016/0042-6989(95)00139-5

Mareschal, I., Morgan, M. J., & Solomon, J. A. (2010). Cortical distance determines whether flankers cause crowding or the tilt illusion. *Journal of Vision, 10*(8), 1–14.

Over, R., Broerse, J., & Crassini, B. (1972). Orientation illusion and masking in central and peripheral vision. *Journal of Experimental Psychology, 96,* 25–31. doi:10.1037/h0033470

Parkes, L., Lund, J., Angelucci, A., Solomon, J., & Morgan, M. (2001). Compulsory averaging of crowded orientation signals in human vision. *Nature Neuroscience, 4,* 739–744. doi:10.1038/89532

Snowden, R. J., & Hammett, S. T. (1998). The effects of surround contrast on contrast thresholds, perceived contrast and contrast discrimination. *Vision Research, 38,* 1935–1945. doi:10.1016/S0042-6989(97)00379-9

Solomon, J. A., Felisberti, F. M., & Morgan, M. J. (2004). Crowding and the tilt illusion: Toward a unified account. *Journal of Vision, 4,* 500–508. doi:10.1167/4.6.9

Solomon, J. A., & Morgan, M. J. (2006). Stochastic re-calibration: Contextual effects on perceived tilt. *Proceedings of the Royal Society of London, Series B. Biological Sciences, 273,* 2681–2686. doi:10.1098/rspb.2006.3634

Solomon, J. A., & Morgan, M. J. (2009). Strong tilt illusions always reduce orientation acuity. *Vision Research, 49,* 819–824. doi:10.1016/j.visres.2009.02.017

Tolhurst, D. J., & Thompson, P. G. (1975). Orientation illusions and after-effects: Inhibition between channels. *Vision Research, 15,* 967–972. doi:10.1016/0042-6989(75)90238-2

Wenderoth, P., & Johnstone, S. (1988). The different mechanisms of the direct and indirect tilt illusions. *Vision Research, 28,* 301–312. doi:10.1016/0042-6989(88)90158-7

3

The Analysis of Visual Motion and Smooth Pursuit Eye Movements

Miriam Spering and Karl R. Gegenfurtner

Pursuit eye movements are closely connected to motion perception and have been studied extensively to gain a better understanding of how visual motion signals control motor behavior. Ultimately, it is the goal of this line of research to shed light on the cortical interaction between sensory and motor systems. This chapter outlines the properties of smooth pursuit eye movements and describes the visual signals that are used to control motion perception and smooth pursuit eye movements. We review studies that have compared motion perception and pursuit, particularly those that used stimuli resembling requirements in complex and natural visual situations.

The development of pursuit eye movements was made necessary by the evolvement of the fovea, the retinal area with the greatest visual acuity. As early as in 1903, Raymond Dodge provided a comprehensive description of the function and characteristics of smooth pursuit eye movements: "If we wish to see a moving object . . . , a more or less continuous movement of the eyes will be necessary in order to keep the line of regard congruent with the line of interest" (Dodge, 1903, p. 317). These movements mainly serve to compensate for object motion to track a moving visual object of interest and enhance high-acuity vision of the object (Carpenter, 1988; Leigh & Zee, 2006). Other visually driven continuous tracking movements, the initial ocular following response (OFR) and the optokinetic nystagmus (OKN), are reflexive and differ from pursuit in a number of properties (Miles, Kawano, & Optican, 1986). Both OFR and OKN are best elicited by brief, unexpected motion of large patterns, whereas pursuit can be evoked by a variety of small and large stimuli from single dots to random-dot kinematograms (see Visual Context later in the chapter).

DOI: 10.1037/14135-004

Human Information Processing: Vision, Memory, and Attention, C. Chubb, B. A. Dosher, Z.-L. Lu, and R. M. Shiffrin (Editors)

Stimulus for Pursuit

When observers are asked to track the motion of their index finger, they will engage in continuous, slow tracking eye movements—smooth pursuit. However, tracking an imagined trajectory of the finger can only be achieved by a combination of pursuit and saccadic eye movements. From this, it was concluded that pursuit could only be elicited in response to a visual, physical motion stimulus. Although visual motion signals are clearly the main input for pursuit, reliable pursuit can be elicited and maintained in the absence of a physical motion, that is, without retinal motion, provided that the observer perceives motion: "the fundamental requirement for pursuit is the appreciation of an object in motion with respect to the observer irrespective of retinal stimulation, and . . . irrespective of the sense modality through which motion is assessed" (Steinbach, 1976, p. 1371). Steinbach attached two light-emitting diodes on the opposite sides of a wheel riding along a horizontal track in front of an observer sitting in the dark. Observers not only perceived a rolling wheel but were also able to track its imagined center smoothly with their eyes. Therefore, the relevant motion signal for pursuit is a representation of motion, or perceptual motion, rather than the retinal image motion itself. More recent experiments have provided additional evidence that pursuit can be evoked in the absence of retinal image motion by apparent motion of illusory contours or imaginary targets and by the motion aftereffect (see Illusory Motion later in the chapter).

Pursuit Characteristics

Pursuit latencies are fast: on the order of 80 to 150 ms in humans and 65 to 120 ms in monkeys (Carl & Gellman, 1987; Lisberger, Morris, & Tychsen, 1987; Robinson, 1965; Tavassoli & Ringach, 2010). Human observers can track a target moving in the range of 1 to 100 deg/s. However, pursuit is often too slow with respect to the target, especially when target velocity exceeds 30 deg/s. To compensate for retinal image slip, smooth motion is often supported by catch-up saccades (de Brouwer, Yuksel, Blohm, Missal, & Lefèvre, 2002; Rashbass, 1961).

The pursuit response is usually separated into an open-loop (initiation) and a closed-loop or steady-state (maintenance) phase (Lisberger et al., 1987; Tychsen & Lisberger, 1986). During the open-loop phase—approximately the first 140 ms of the eye movement before a catch-up saccade is made—pursuit is primarily driven by the retinal image velocity of the target, because an internal feedback signal on the retinal error between eye and target motion is not yet available to the system. In the earliest phase (0–40 ms) of initiation, the eye starts to accelerate in the direction of the target, and in the later phase (~40–100 ms), eye velocity is adjusted to target velocity (see Figure 3.1).

During the closed-loop phase, pursuit is maintained by an internal signal, and velocity errors are corrected by reducing retinal image slip (Robinson, Gordon, & Gordon, 1986), indicating a close relationship between pursuit eye movements and retinal image motion signals (Lisberger et al., 1987; Tychsen & Lisberger, 1986; Robinson, 1965).

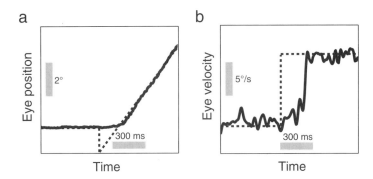

Figure 3.1. Eye movement position (A) and velocity (B) responses to a target moving to the right. Solid lines: eye movement traces. Dotted lines: target motion. The target initially steps 1.8° to the left of a central fixation position (step) and then moves to the right at 11 deg/s, crossing the central fixation position (ramp). This "step-ramp procedure" (Rashbass, 1961) is known to prevent early catch-up saccades. The eye does not respond to the retinal position error created by the target step but follows the smooth motion to the right after a latency of approximately 100 ms. The eye reaches steady-state velocity after 150 to 200 ms, marking the beginning of the closed-loop phase of the pursuit response. During this phase, eye velocity oscillates around target velocity at a frequency of approximately 2 Hz.

Visual Motion Signals for Smooth Pursuit Eye Movements

With the exception of the earliest open-loop response—approximately the first 40 ms of pursuit—which seems to be largely unaffected by stimulus features other than motion direction (Lisberger et al., 1987; Rashbass, 1961), pursuit eye movements depend on the visual properties of the stimulus (Lisberger & Westbrook, 1985; Tychsen & Lisberger, 1986). The characteristics of a smooth pursuit eye movement—namely, its initial acceleration, steady-state velocity, and latency—are closely related to target motion features such as target velocity, position, direction, and acceleration. Pursuit is also influenced by relative target contrast, color, size, and shape and by features of the visual context.

Velocity

Behavioral studies in humans and monkeys have generally shown an excellent agreement between perceptual judgments of motion direction or velocity and smooth pursuit eye movements (Beutter & Stone, 1998, 2000; Gegenfurtner, Xing, Scott, & Hawken, 2003; Stone & Krauzlis, 2003; Watamaniuk & Heinen, 2003). Motion perception and pursuit seem to be limited by the same source of noise, and similar thresholds for discriminating speed changes were found for both behaviors.

   These psychophysical studies are in line with neurophysiological evidence linking neuronal activity in the primate's middle temporal area (MT) and middle superior temporal area (MST) to both the perception of visual motion

(Ilg & Churan, 2004; Newsome, Britten, & Movshon, 1989; Rudolph & Pasternak, 1999; Salzman, Murasugi, Britten, & Newsome, 1992) and the control of smooth pursuit eye movements (Dürsteler & Wurtz, 1988; Ilg & Thier, 2003; Keller & Heinen, 1991; Krauzlis, 2004).

Classical evidence for the use of velocity error rather than position error comes from a series of ingenious experiments by Rashbass (1961). In a step-ramp paradigm (Figure 3.1a), the fixation spot jumps away from the fixation position (the step) and instantly starts to move into the opposite direction to the step toward the fovea at a constant velocity (the ramp). Rashbass observed that the pursuit response went in the direction of the ramp movement, rather than to the step position, and was often initiated before the target crossed the fovea. This so-called step-ramp paradigm is often used to study the open-loop pursuit phase because the paradigm usually produces a saccade-free pursuit initiation.

Open- and closed-loop pursuit velocity are related to target speed: Velocity increased and pursuit latency decreased with increasing target speeds (range 2.5–30 deg/s; Movshon, Lisberger, & Krauzlis, 1990), but increasing target speed also caused a higher number of saccades (Rashbass, 1961). Furthermore, pursuit velocity precision sensitively reflected changes in target velocity (Gegenfurtner et al., 2003; Kowler & McKee, 1987). These studies found that discrimination was relatively poor during open-loop pursuit, indicating that influences other than pure stimulus motion were operating to initiate pursuit. Others have studied the variability of open-loop pursuit and suggested that even the early pursuit response provides a faithful, and almost online, account of motion information that is as efficient as perceptual judgments. These studies imply that the variability of pursuit velocity might depend more on variability in the sensory than in the motor system (Osborne, Lisberger, & Bialek, 2005; Rasche & Gegenfurtner, 2009).

Position

Pursuit eye movements are driven mainly by velocity signals. However, position information can also directly influence pursuit. Small target jumps during ongoing pursuit can modulate eye velocity in the monkey (Krauzlis & Miles, 1996; Morris & Lisberger, 1987; Segraves & Goldberg, 1994) and in human observers (Carl & Gellman, 1987; Pola & Wyatt, 1980). Segraves and Goldberg (1994) introduced target steps during steady-state pursuit of a horizontally moving target, which was stabilized on the retina. The direction of the step (i.e., the position error) could be in either the same or opposite direction to the target's initial motion direction. After the step, a continuous retinal velocity error of the target, slower (negative) or faster (positive) than the original target motion, was introduced, with the effect being that the target moved toward or away from the fovea after the step. When position and velocity error went in the same direction as initial pursuit, eye velocity was not affected. When position and velocity error went in the opposite direction to initial pursuit, eye velocity decreased substantially. For opposite-sign errors (e.g., a position error to the left and velocity error to the right), eye velocity slowed down to near zero and then began to accelerate in the direction of the retinal slip error. These observations imply that target offset relative to the fovea, i.e., position error, affects pursuit velocity. By changing the sign of position and velocity errors, the direction of pursuit can be reversed. Note, however, that even stabilized targets produce percepts of visual motion. The evidence from studies with stabilized targets for the use of position signals is therefore not conclusive.

Lisberger and Westbrook (1985) demonstrated the effect of initial target eccentricity on the open-loop pursuit response in monkeys. Initial eye acceleration increased linearly with decreasing eccentricity of the target relative to the fovea. For a given eccentricity, higher acceleration values were achieved for objects moving toward the fovea than for objects moving away from it. Target position has also been shown to affect pursuit deceleration and termination. When a target jumped ahead during the steady-state pursuit phase and remained stationary without being fixed on the retina, pursuit decelerated quickly. When the target was stabilized on the retina, pursuit decelerated more slowly, depending on the position error (Pola & Wyatt, 2001). However, in all paradigms reported here, position and velocity errors were not separated, because the position stimulus always contained a retinal velocity component, even if attempts were made to stabilize the stimulus on the retina.

Blohm, Missal, and Lefèvre (2005) provided the first direct evidence for a separate influence of position error signals on pursuit. During ongoing pursuit, a salient stimulus was briefly flashed in the periphery of the tracked target. Upon appearance of the flashed stimulus, observers had to make a saccade to the flash or ignore it. In a typical saccade trial, before the saccade to the flash was initiated, observers generated a pursuit eye movement in the direction of the flash. Pursuit velocity was proportional to the size of the position error.

In summary, the pursuit system clearly uses position signals to control eye movement initiation and maintenance, and these signals seem to be used separately from velocity error signals. However, despite their strong modulating effect, position error signals cannot be the sole driving signal for a smooth pursuit eye movement.

Acceleration

Many studies have implied that the perceptual sensitivity to continuous changes in target speed (acceleration) is less pronounced than sensitivity to step changes in target speed (Snowden & Braddick, 1991). Because individual MT neurons are not tuned to acceleration (Lisberger & Movshon, 1999), the pursuit system can be expected to show a similar lack of sensitivity to acceleration than the perceptual system.

Two studies have systematically tested effects of acceleration on pursuit: One study focused on open-loop pursuit (Krauzlis & Lisberger, 1994), and the other on the sensitivity of closed-loop pursuit to changes in acceleration (Watamaniuk & Heinen, 2003). In human observers, acceleration discrimination during the late open-loop and early closed-loop pursuit phase was poorer than pursuit speed discrimination (Watamaniuk & Heinen, 2003). On a neuronal level, these findings imply that acceleration signals cannot be directly extracted from activity in individual neurons in the motion-sensitive middle temporal cortex (area MT). Acceleration seems to be coded by a population of speed-sensitive neurons, rather than acceleration-sensitive neurons, in area MT (Lisberger & Movshon, 1999; Price, Ono, Mustari, & Ibbotson, 2005). These findings hold for accelerations during ongoing pursuit.

However, there is also evidence that the pursuit system can discriminate acceleration. Krauzlis and Lisberger (1994) tested monkeys with targets accelerating gradually or with a stepwise change, with varied motion onset delay. When a target step change in velocity from 0 to values ranging between 2.5 and 30 deg/s was introduced, initial eye acceleration in the interval 40 to 100 ms after pursuit onset was graded linearly with target speed, but the early pursuit phase (0–40 ms) was not affected. For gradual changes in target speed (smooth acceleration) in the first 125 ms of target motion, however, initial acceleration was graded with target speed starting in the interval 0 to 40 ms after pursuit onset. In smooth acceleration trials, pursuit latency was longer than in trials with step changes in target speed. The authors further showed that the graded response to smooth target acceleration was not due to preceding step changes in target velocity. Therefore, to drive the early pursuit response, the smooth pursuit system does have access to smooth changes in target speed.

When an accelerating target for smooth pursuit eye movements was occluded after varying exposure time to the accelerating target before the blank, predictive eye velocity during the blank was affected by the rate of acceleration, but only if exposure time was longer than 200 ms (Bennett, Orban de Xivry, Barnes, & Lefèvre, 2007). This study provides further evidence for the use of acceleration signals for predictive smooth pursuit.

Higher Order Motion

To account for the complexity of the visual environment where motion cues are not derived from luminance changes alone and to understand the stages of motion processing accomplished for motion perception and pursuit generation, psychophysical studies have used stimuli that require higher level motion processing (Masson, 2004). Simple luminance- or color-defined motion stimuli (first-order motion stimuli) can be fully described by a spatiotemporal energy model (Adelson & Bergen, 1985) and can be decoded by an elementary motion detector (Reichardt, 1987). In second-order motion stimuli, on the other hand, local motion is based on derived stimulus attributes such as texture contrast or flicker and can go in the opposite direction to the object's global motion (Chubb & Sperling, 1988). Hawken and Gegenfurtner (2001) compared observers' pursuit eye movements to first- and second-order motion stimuli and found pursuit velocity gain to be reduced for second-order motion stimuli, especially at slow stimulus speed. Similarly, it has been shown that second-order motion stimuli can elicit an ocular following response, albeit with a longer latency than first-order motion stimuli (Benson & Guo, 1999; Masson, 2004). Second-order motion information alone cannot elicit an optokinetic response reliably (Harris & Smith, 1992) but can modulate OKN responses to first-order motion (Harris & Smith, 2000). Butzer, Ilg, and Zanker (1997) showed that observers' steady-state pursuit followed the direction of the perceived object motion (Churan &

Ilg, 2001), rather than the local retinal image motion. Pursuit initiation, however, was dominated by first-order motion signals and followed the direction of the local motion (Lindner & Ilg, 2000).

Illusory Motion

There has been some debate over the years whether pursuit correlates better with physical or perceived stimulus motion. When physical and perceived motions are different, the oculomotor system mostly follows the percept rather than the physical stimulus (Beutter & Stone, 1998, 2000; Biber & Ilg, 2008; Hafed & Krauzlis, 2006, 2010; Ilg & Thier, 2003; Madelain & Krauzlis, 2003; Ringach, Hawken, & Shapley, 1996; Steinbach, 1976; Wyatt, Pola, Fortune, & Posner, 1994). One particularly interesting case of perceived motion is the illusory motion caused by the motion aftereffect (MAE) in which there is no physical motion at all. Braun, Pracejus, and Gegenfurtner (2006) showed that after adaptation to a moving stimulus, pursuit eye movements were elicited to the illusory motion of a physically stationary stimulus that was perceived to move into the direction opposite to the adaptation stimulus. Conversely, the eyes remained stationary in response to a physically moving stimulus that was perceived to be stationary (Watamaniuk & Heinen, 2007). These results show that the neural mechanisms of motion adaptation for perception and pursuit are linked (Gardner, Tokiyama, & Lisberger, 2004).

Contrast

Human motion perception is strongly influenced by contrast. A low-contrast stimulus moving at a given speed is perceived to move more slowly than a high-contrast stimulus moving at the same speed (Stone & Thompson, 1992; Thompson, 1982; Weiss, Simoncelli, & Adelson, 2002). A corresponding phenomenon to perceptual slowing was demonstrated in the pursuit response in humans (Spering, Kerzel, Braun, Hawken, & Gegenfurtner, 2005) and monkeys (Priebe & Lisberger, 2004). Smooth pursuit eye velocity gain increased as a function of contrast. In humans, the increase was linear for slowly moving targets (< 1 deg/s). For targets moving at a higher velocity, velocity gain first increased steeply up to contrast values of two to three times threshold, and then saturated (Spering et al., 2005). Similarly, Hawken and Gegenfurtner (2001) found a reduction in eye velocity with decreasing contrast for first-order motion targets but only for slow targets moving at 1 deg/s. Pursuit latency was markedly reduced with increasing target luminance in the monkey (Lisberger & Westbrook, 1985) and in human subjects (O'Mullane & Knox, 1999; Spering et al., 2005). Stimulus contrast, therefore, influences motion perception and pursuit eye movements in a similar way. Note that the finding of perceptual slowing holds for relatively slow speeds only. For higher speeds, a paradoxical increase of perceived speed has been observed at low contrast (Thompson, Brooks, & Hammett, 2006), but a corresponding effect has not yet been shown for pursuit.

Motion Signals From Color Stimuli

Isoluminant stimuli (which have the same luminance as the background and differ from it only in color) are often perceived to move up to 50% slower than luminance stimuli that move at the same physical speed (Cavanagh, Tyler, & Favreau, 1984; Gegenfurtner et al., 1994) or even perceived to stand still (Lu, Lesmes, & Sperling, 1999), especially at low temporal frequencies (Gegenfurtner & Hawken, 1995). The perception of color- and luminance-defined stimuli has also been shown to be qualitatively different with regard to the influence of contrast and temporal frequency (Gegenfurtner & Hawken, 1996). Braun, Mennie, Rasche, Hawken, and Gegenfurtner (2008) compared speed judgments to luminance and isoluminant targets during fixation and pursuit and measured the effects of isoluminant stimuli on pursuit characteristics. Speed judgments of isoluminant targets generally showed a substantial slowing by up to 30% during fixation. The strongest effect of isoluminant stimuli on pursuit was found during the initiation phase. Pursuit latency to isoluminant stimuli was delayed by 50 ms, and initial eye acceleration was reduced. Only a small but significant difference was observed for steady-state pursuit velocity. Interestingly, pursuit was also impaired for stimuli moving at higher speeds (up to 10.3 deg/s), whereas perceptual impairments were usually only observed for slow stimuli (< 4 deg/s). Motion signals from color stimuli, therefore, seem to be weaker in driving both perception and pursuit eye movements.

Visual Context

Most studies reported so far have looked at eye movements in response to a single moving stimulus. With the aim of using stimuli that more closely resemble the demands of natural viewing conditions, Heinen and Watamaniuk (1998) asked observers to track random-dot kinematograms that were composed of multiple coherently moving dots. With increasing number of dots, pursuit latency decreased and initial acceleration increased. When dot motion was coherent, the number of catch-up saccades was reduced (Watamaniuk & Heinen, 1999). These findings imply that the spatial integration of motion information improves the extraction of a target velocity signal for smooth pursuit initiation.

However, in our natural environment, it can be even more demanding to track a moving object. Often, a single object of interest is embedded in a richly structured dynamic visual context. In order to extract a target motion signal for the initiation and maintenance of pursuit, the moving object has to be segregated from the visual context. The extracted target motion signal is likely to be affected by motion signals from the visual context. The effect of a moving visual background on motion perception has first been reported by Gestalt psychologist Karl Duncker (1929). In the *Duncker illusion,* a stationary, fixated target object appeared to move into the opposite direction to a second object, which moved in the periphery of the first object. This type of induced or apparent motion can also influence eye movements (Spering & Gegenfurtner, 2008). In a study by Pola and Wyatt (1980), an initial target step was followed by sinusoidal ramp motion, during which the target was stabilized on the retina. A sinusoidally moving frame, inducing apparent motion, surrounded the target. Although the physically moving stimulus did not elicit a velocity signal on the retina, the eye velocity response was in phase with induced motion.

Generally, spatial integration of target and context motion signals has been studied by having observers track a pursuit target in the presence of a second moving object or in front of a stationary or moving textured background. When observers were presented with two possible pursuit targets without an instruction regarding which stimulus to track, most studies found that pursuit initially followed the vector average of the two resulting motion signals (Lisberger & Ferrera, 1997). The eye movement was shifted in favor of one or the other stimulus, when observers were asked to attend to or were cued in one direction (Ferrera & Lisberger, 1995; Garbutt & Lisberger, 2006). However, when observers were instructed to track one stimulus and ignore the other, the oculomotor system compensated for the irrelevant stimulus, and the eye vertically curved away from it (Spering, Gegenfurtner, & Kerzel, 2006).

Pursuit of a small object on a stationary textured background was generally found to be impaired, and initial acceleration and steady-state velocity were reduced (Collewijn & Tamminga, 1984; Kimmig, Miles, & Schwarz, 1992; Masson, Proteau, & Mestre, 1995; Niemann & Hoffmann, 1997; Schwarz & Ilg, 1999; Spering & Gegenfurtner, 2007a). For moving backgrounds, some studies provide evidence for a spatial summation of motion signals (motion assimilation). A background moving into the same direction as the pursuit target increased pursuit velocity, whereas a background moving into the opposite direction decreased eye velocity (Masson et al., 1995). Similarly, a brief background perturbation evoked a transient increase in eye velocity into the direction of the perturbation (Kodaka, Miura, Suehiro, Takemura, & Kawano, 2004; Lindner, Schwarz, & Ilg, 2001; Miura, Kobayashi, & Kawano, 2009; Schwarz & Ilg, 1999; Spering & Gegenfurtner, 2007a; Suehiro et al., 1999), when the background was moving in the same direction as the target. Pursuit was not affected by background perturbations when the background moved opposite to the pursuit target. Other results are more in line with the idea that relative motion signals (motion contrast) are relevant for controlling pursuit in the presence of a moving background. When the background moved into the direction opposite to the pursuit target, an increase in initial acceleration and steady-state velocity were reported (Niemann & Hoffmann, 1997; Spering & Gegenfurtner, 2007a). Motion contrast also seems to drive pursuit to a horizontal target in response to brief background perturbations in the vertical direction (Spering & Gegenfurtner, 2007a).

Effects of Pursuit on Motion Perception

Numerous studies have investigated the effect of eye movements on the perceived motion of a pursuit target and of other objects, moving or stationary. It has been known since the work of Aubert (1886) and von Fleischl (1882) that a moving target can appear slower when it is pursued than when the eyes are stationary. At the same time, stationary objects can appear to move in the direction opposite to pursuit. This is known as the Filehne-illusion (Haarmeier & Thier, 1998; Wertheim, 1987). Both effects are compatible with the idea that the gain of a reafferent signal is not perfect (Souman, Hooge, & Wertheim, 2005). A simple Bayesian model, based on the general idea that prior expectations increasingly influence perceptual decisions as sensory signals become uncertain, might be able to explain these misperceptions (Freeman, Champion, & Warren, 2010). The finding that stimulus speed is more difficult to discriminate during pursuit than during fixation would then be due to the expectation that the world is stationary (implying a prior probability distribution for motion centered at zero), both for stimulus motion and eye movements. Here, we discuss the effects of pursuit on perception of motion and other features such as color.

Context Effects

Most of the studies reported so far underlined the close relationship between motion perception and pursuit eye movements. Spering and Gegenfurtner (2007b) tested whether perception and pursuit also correlate when a moving target is tracked in the presence of a dynamic context. Motion perception and pursuit eye movements in human observers were analyzed in response to step changes in target and context velocities. In each trial, pursuit target and visual context were independently perturbed simultaneously to briefly increase or decrease in velocity. Observers had to track a moving target and estimate whether its velocity had increased or decreased. Pursuit eye movements followed the vector average of target and context motion (Figure 3.2a). The perceptual response was clearly different from the pursuit response: When target velocity remained unchanged, and the context briefly moved faster, eye velocity increased (vector average or motion assimilation), but target velocity was judged to be slower than before the perturbation (motion contrast). Observers systematically underestimated target velocity when context velocity increased, and overestimated target velocity when context velocity decreased (Figure 3.2b). This experiment shows that perception and pursuit can differ when a moving target is surrounded by a dynamic visual context. Here, perception was driven by a relative velocity signal (motion contrast), whereas pursuit was driven by an average velocity signal (motion assimilation; Figure 3.2c).

A series of control experiments (Spering & Gegenfurtner, 2007b, 2008) showed that, in contrast to what has been shown for the Filehne illusion (Haarmeier & Thier, 1998), the opposing effects in pursuit and perception were not due to an inability to compensate for eye movements.

Despite the strong evidence for shared motion processing systems for perception and pursuit, there are some situations in which both types of behavior differ (Boström & Warzecha, 2010; Tavassoli & Ringach, 2010). The opposing effects of a dynamic context reflect the different needs for perception and pursuit. For the perceptual system, the most important task is to isolate and segment a moving object from the background. This can be done by accentuating speed differences and calculating the relative velocity difference between object and

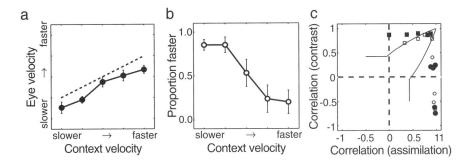

Figure 3.2. Mean pursuit and perceptual responses to speed perturbations in target and context. (A) Eye velocity responses to five context speed perturbations at fixed target speed (11.3 deg/s). Individual data points are means ± SEM. Dashed black line: prediction of the assimilation model. (B) Perceived target velocity (proportion faster) for same conditions as in panel A. (C) Scatter plot of correlations between model predictions for assimilation and contrast and pursuit velocity (circles) and perceived velocity (squares) for 100 ms (open symbols) and 250 ms (filled symbols) perturbation intervals. Class boundaries divide the plot into zones in which responses are classified as assimilation-type or contrast-type responses. Correlation coefficients for these data points were significantly different. Data points falling in between boundaries are considered as unclassified, meaning that responses are well predicted by both models (correlation coefficients not significantly different).

background. Information about the absolute speed is not relevant for this task. For smooth pursuit eye movements, in contrast, the most immediate demand is to extract a precise velocity signal to initiate and maintain an accurate eye movement. Integrating over a larger spatial region will generally improve this calculation, unless the relevant context contains a different motion signal.

Motion Prediction

Large voluntary eye movements, such as pursuit eye movements, challenge the visual system. The visual system has to update the changing visual input constantly. Moreover, self-motion generally produces movement-induced retinal image motion, which has to be disentangled from the target's retinal image motion. When the system fails to compensate for movement-induced image motion, misperceptions such as the Aubert-Fleischl phenomenon or the Filehne illusion arise, and numerous examples have been reported during pursuit. However, there is also evidence for a perceptual performance benefit during pursuit versus fixation. In the study by Spering, Schütz, Braun, and Gegenfurtner (2011), observers judged whether a moving target (ball) would have hit or missed a stationary vertical line (goal). Ball and goal were presented briefly for 100 to 500 ms, and both disappeared from the screen before the perceptual judgment was prompted. Observers either pursued the ball or fixated on different locations (e.g., the goal). Results show that perceptual performance was significantly better during pursuit than during fixation, regardless of fixation position. The performance difference between pursuit and fixation has to be due to extraretinal motion direction information gained from the pursuit response, possibly through an efference copy signal as well as the pursuit direction error (the angular velocity difference between eye and ball). Pursuit, even if it is not perfectly accurate, can, therefore, aid the prediction of visual motion in space.

Perception of Color During Pursuit

It was mentioned earlier that moving colored targets appear to slow down or even stand still (Lu et al., 1999). Although pursuit to these colored targets is imperfect, Braun et al. (2008) observed that the eye movements in this case actually improved perceptual judgments of speed. Surprisingly, in contrast to speed judgments during fixation, speed judgments of moving isoluminant stimuli during pursuit were veridical. More recently, Schütz, Braun, Kerzel, and Gegenfurtner (2008) measured detection thresholds for horizontally oriented lines that were modulated either in color or luminance and briefly flashed extrafoveally. During pursuit, sensitivity to luminance lines was impaired, but the sensitivity to colored stimuli was unexpectedly improved by 16% during pursuit compared with during fixation. These findings show that pursuit can lead to the selective boosting of a whole processing system—here, the parvocellular pathway, which is sensitive to red and green stimuli as well as to high spatial-frequency patterns. Accordingly, sensitivity to high-spatial frequency patterns was shown to be higher during pursuit than during fixation. Schütz, Braun, and Gegenfurtner (2009) also reported improved sensitivity to colored targets during OKN but not during the vestibuloocular reflex, which is only partially driven by visual signals.

Conclusion

The results presented in this chapter show that there is a rich variety of interactions between smooth pursuit eye movements and the perception of visual motion. There is typically an excellent agreement between pursuit and perception. However, there are some complex situations in which pursuit affects the perception of motion quite substantially. In the case of isoluminant targets, eye movements can improve motion perception. For complex context stimuli, eye movements and motion perception can follow different patterns of behavior.

References

Adelson, E. H., & Bergen, J. R. (1985). Spatiotemporal energy models for the perception of motion. *Journal of the Optical Society of America A: Optics and Image Science, 2,* 284–299. doi:10.1364/JOSAA.2.000284

Aubert, H. (1886). Die Bewegungsempfindung [The sensation of motion]. *Pflugers Archiv, 39,* 347–370. doi:10.1007/BF01612166

Bennett, S. J., Orban de Xivry, J.-J., Barnes, G., & Lefèvre, P. (2007). Target acceleration can be extracted and represented within the predictive drive to ocular pursuit. *Journal of Neurophysiology, 98,* 1405–1414. doi:10.1152/jn.00132.2007

Benson, P. J., & Guo, K. (1999). Stages in motion processing revealed by the ocular following response. *NeuroReport: For Rapid Communication of Neuroscience Research, 10,* 3803–3807. doi:10.1097/00001756-199912160-00015

Beutter, B. R., & Stone, L. S. (1998). Human motion perception and smooth eye movements show similar directional biases for elongated apertures. *Vision Research, 38,* 1273–1286. doi:10.1016/S0042-6989(97)00276-9

Beutter, B. R., & Stone, L. S. (2000). Motion coherence affects human perception and pursuit similarly. *Visual Neuroscience, 17,* 139–153. doi:10.1017/S0952523800171147

Biber, U., & Ilg, U. J. (2008). Initiation of smooth pursuit eye movements by real and illusory contours. *Vision Research, 48,* 1002–1013. doi:10.1016/j.visres.2008.01.021

Blohm, G., Missal, M., & Lefèvre, P. (2005). Direct evidence for a position input to the smooth pursuit system. *Journal of Neurophysiology, 94,* 712–721. doi:10.1152/jn.00093.2005

Boström, K. J., & Warzecha, A. K. (2010). Open-loop speed discrimination performance of ocular following response and perception. *Vision Research, 50,* 870–882. doi:10.1016/j.visres.2010.02.010

Braun, D. I., Mennie, N., Rasche, C., Hawken, M. J., & Gegenfurtner, K. R. (2008). Smooth pursuit eye movements to isoluminant targets. *Journal of Neurophysiology, 100,* 1287–1300. doi:10.1152/jn.00747.2007

Braun, D. I., Pracejus, L., & Gegenfurtner, K. R. (2006). Motion aftereffect elicits smooth pursuit eye movements. *Journal of Vision, 6,* 671–684. doi:10.1167/6.7.1

Butzer, F., Ilg, U. J., & Zanker, J. M. (1997). Smooth-pursuit eye movements elicited by first-order and second-order motion. *Experimental Brain Research, 115,* 61–70. doi:10.1007/PL00005686

Carl, J. R., & Gellman, R. S. (1987). Human smooth pursuit: Stimulus-dependent responses. *Journal of Neurophysiology, 57,* 1446–1463.

Carpenter, R. H. S. (1988). *Movements of the eyes.* London, England: Pion.

Cavanagh, P., Tyler, C. W., & Favreau, O. E. (1984). Perceived velocity of moving chromatic gratings. *Journal of the Optical Society of America A: Optics and Image Science, 1,* 893–899. doi:10.1364/JOSAA.1.000893

Chubb, C., & Sperling, G. (1988). Drift-balanced random stimuli: A general basis for studying non-Fourier motion perception. *Journal of the Optical Society of America A: Optics and Image Science, 5,* 1986–2007. doi:10.1364/JOSAA.5.001986

Churan, J., & Ilg, U. J. (2001). Processing of second-order motion stimuli in primate middle temporal area and medial superior temporal area. *Journal of the Optical Society of America A: Optics, Image Science, and Vision, 18,* 2297–2306. doi:10.1364/JOSAA.18.002297

Collewijn, H., & Tamminga, E. P. (1984). Human smooth pursuit and saccadic eye movements during voluntary pursuit of different target motions on different backgrounds. *The Journal of Physiology, 351,* 217–250.

de Brouwer, S., Yuksel, D., Blohm, G., Missal, M., & Lefèvre, P. (2002). What triggers catch-up saccades during visual tracking? *Journal of Neurophysiology, 87,* 1646–1650.

Dodge, R. (1903). Five types of eye movement in the horizontal meridian plane of the field of regard. *American Journal of Physiology, VIII,* 307–329.

Duncker, K. (1929). Über induzierte Bewegung: Ein Beitrag zur Theorie optisch wahrgenommener Bewegung [On induced motion: A contribution to the theory of optically perceived motion]. *Psychologische Forschung, 12,* 180–259.

Dürsteler, M. R., & Wurtz, R. H. (1988). Pursuit and optokinetic deficits following chemical lesions of cortical areas MT and MST. *Journal of Neurophysiology, 60,* 940–965.

Ferrera, V. P., & Lisberger, S. J. (1995). Attention and target selection for smooth pursuit eye movements. *The Journal of Neuroscience, 15,* 7472–7484.

Freeman, T. C. A., Champion, R. A., & Warren, P. A. (2010). A Bayesian model of perceived head-centered velocity during smooth pursuit eye movement. *Current Biology, 20,* 757–762. doi:10.1016/j.cub.2010.02.059

Garbutt, S., & Lisberger, S. J. (2006). Directional cuing of target choice in human smooth pursuit eye movements. *The Journal of Neuroscience, 26,* 12479–12486. doi:10.1523/JNEUROSCI.4071-06.2006

Gardner, J. L., Tokiyama, S. N., & Lisberger, S. G. (2004). A population decoding framework for motion aftereffects on smooth pursuit eye movements. *The Journal of Neuroscience, 24,* 9035–9048. doi:10.1523/JNEUROSCI.0337-04.2004

Gegenfurtner, K. R., & Hawken, M. J. (1995). Temporal and chromatic properties of motion mechanisms. *Vision Research, 35,* 1547–1563. doi:10.1016/0042-6989(94)00264-M

Gegenfurtner, K. R., & Hawken, M. J. (1996). Perceived velocity of luminance, chromatic and non-Fourier stimuli: Influence of contrast and temporal frequency. *Vision Research, 36,* 1281–1290. doi:10.1016/0042-6989(95)00198-0

Gegenfurtner, K. R., Kiper, D. C., Beusmans, J., Carandini, M., Zaidi, Q., & Movshon, J. A. (1994). Chromatic properties of neurons in macaque MT. *Visual Neuroscience, 11,* 455–466. doi:10.1017/S095252380000239X

Gegenfurtner, K. R., Xing, D., Scott, B. H., & Hawken, M. J. (2003). A comparison of pursuit eye movement and perceptual performance in speed discrimination. *Journal of Vision, 3,* 865–876. doi:10.1167/3.11.19

Haarmeier, T., & Thier, P. (1998). An electrophysiological correlate of visual motion awareness in man. *Journal of Cognitive Neuroscience, 10,* 464–471. doi:10.1162/089892998562870

Hafed, Z. M., & Krauzlis, R. J. (2006). Ongoing eye movements constrain visual perception. *Nature Neuroscience, 9,* 1449–1457. doi:10.1038/nn1782

Hafed, Z. M., & Krauzlis, R. J. (2010). Interactions between perception and smooth pursuit eye movements. In U. J. Ilg & G. S. Masson (Eds.), *Dynamics of visual motion processing: Neuronal, behavioral, and computational approaches* (pp. 189–211). New York, NY: Springer.

Harris, L. R., & Smith, A. T. (1992). Motion defined exclusively by second-order characteristics does not evoke optokinetic nystagmus. *Visual Neuroscience, 9,* 565–570. doi:10.1017/S0952523800001802

Harris, L. R., & Smith, A. T. (2000). Interactions between first- and second-order motion revealed by optokinetic nystagmus. *Experimental Brain Research, 130,* 67–72. doi:10.1007/s002219900232

Hawken, M. J., & Gegenfurtner, K. R. (2001). Pursuit eye movements to second-order motion targets. *Journal of the Optical Society of America A: Optics, Image Science, and Vision, 18,* 2282–2296. doi:10.1364/JOSAA.18.002282

Heinen, S. J., & Watamaniuk, S. N. J. (1998). Spatial integration in human smooth pursuit. *Vision Research, 38,* 3785–3794. doi:10.1016/S0042-6989(97)00422-7

Ilg, U. J., & Churan, J. (2004). Motion perception without explicit activity in areas MT and MST. *Journal of Neurophysiology, 92,* 1512–1523. doi:10.1152/jn.01174.2003

Ilg, U. J., & Thier, P. (2003). Visual tracking neurons in primate area MST are activated by smooth-pursuit eye movements of an "imaginary" target. *Journal of Neurophysiology, 90,* 1489–1502. doi:10.1152/jn.00272.2003

Keller, E. L., & Heinen, S. J. (1991). Generation of smooth-pursuit eye movements: Neuronal mechanisms and pathways. *Neuroscience Research, 11,* 79–107. doi:10.1016/0168-0102(91)90048-4

Kimmig, H. G., Miles, F. A., & Schwarz, U. (1992). Effects of stationary textured backgrounds on the initiation of pursuit eye movements in monkeys. *Journal of Neurophysiology, 68,* 2147–2164.

Kodaka, Y., Miura, K., Suehiro, K., Takemura, A., & Kawano, K. (2004). Ocular tracking of moving targets: Effects of perturbing the background. *Journal of Neurophysiology, 91,* 2474–2483. doi:10.1152/jn.01079.2003

Kowler, E., & McKee, S. P. (1987). Sensitivity of smooth eye movement to small differences in target velocity. *Vision Research, 27,* 993–1015. doi:10.1016/0042-6989(87)90014-9

Krauzlis, R. J. (2004). Recasting the smooth pursuit eye movement system. *Journal of Neurophysiology, 91,* 591–603. doi:10.1152/jn.00801.2003

Krauzlis, R. J., & Lisberger, S. G. (1994). Temporal properties of visual motion signals for the initiation of smooth pursuit eye movements in monkeys. *Journal of Neurophysiology, 72,* 150–162.

Krauzlis, R. J., & Miles, F. A. (1996). Transitions between pursuit eye movements and fixation in the monkey: Dependence on context. *Journal of Neurophysiology, 76,* 1622–1638.

Leigh, R. J., & Zee, D. S. (2006). *The neurology of eye movements* (4th ed.). New York, NY: Oxford University Press.

Lindner, A., & Ilg, U. J. (2000). Initiation of smooth-pursuit eye movements to first-order and second-order motion stimuli. *Experimental Brain Research, 133,* 450–456. doi:10.1007/s002210000459

Lindner, A., Schwarz, U., & Ilg, U. J. (2001). Cancellation of self-induced retinal image motion during smooth pursuit eye movements. *Vision Research, 41,* 1685–1694. doi:10.1016/S0042-6989(01)00050-5

Lisberger, S. G., & Ferrera, V. P. (1997). Vector averaging for smooth pursuit eye movements initiated by two moving targets in monkeys. *The Journal of Neuroscience, 17,* 7490–7502.

Lisberger, S. G., Morris, E. J., & Tychsen, L. (1987). Visual motion processing and sensory-motor integration for smooth pursuit eye movements. *Annual Review of Neuroscience, 10,* 97–129. doi:10.1146/annurev.ne.10.030187.000525

Lisberger, S. G., & Movshon, J. A. (1999). Visual motion analysis for pursuit eye movements in area MT of macaque monkeys. *The Journal of Neuroscience, 19,* 2224–2246.

Lisberger, S. G., & Westbrook, L. E. (1985). Properties of visual inputs that initiate horizontal smooth pursuit eye movements in monkeys. *The Journal of Neuroscience, 5,* 1662–1673.

Lu, Z. L., Lesmes, L. A., & Sperling, G. (1999). Perceptual motion standstill in rapidly moving chromatic displays. *Proceedings of the National Academy of Sciences of the United States of America, 96,* 15374–15379. doi:10.1073/pnas.96.26.15374

Madelain, L., & Krauzlis, R. J. (2003). Pursuit of the ineffable: Perceptual and motor reversals during the tracking of apparent motion. *Journal of Vision, 3,* 642–653. doi:10.1167/3.11.1

Masson, G., Proteau, L., & Mestre, D. R. (1995). Effects of stationary and moving textured backgrounds on the visuo-oculo-manual tracking in humans. *Vision Research, 35,* 837–852. doi:10.1016/0042-6989(94)00185-O

Masson, G. S. (2004). From 1D to 2D via 3D: Dynamics of surface motion segmentation for ocular tracking in primates. *Journal of Physiology, Paris, 98,* 35–52. doi:10.1016/j.jphysparis.2004.03.017

Miles, F. A., Kawano, K., & Optican, L. M. (1986). Short-latency ocular following responses of monkey. I. Dependence on temporospatial properties of visual input. *Journal of Neurophysiology, 56,* 1321–1354.

Miura, K., Kobayashi, Y., & Kawano, K. (2009). Ocular responses to brief motion of textured backgrounds during smooth pursuit in humans. *Journal of Neurophysiology, 102,* 1736–1747. doi:10.1152/jn.00430.2009

Morris, E. J., & Lisberger, S. G. (1987). Different responses to small visual errors during initiation and maintenance of smooth-pursuit eye movements in monkeys. *Journal of Neurophysiology, 58,* 1351–1369.

Movshon, J. A., Lisberger, S. G., & Krauzlis, R. J. (1990). Visual cortical signals supporting smooth pursuit eye movements. *Cold Spring Harbor Symposia on Quantitative Biology, 55,* 707–716. doi:10.1101/SQB.1990.055.01.066

Newsome, W. T., Britten, K. H., & Movshon, J. A. (1989, September 7). Neuronal correlates of a perceptual decision. *Nature, 341,* 52–54. doi:10.1038/341052a0

Niemann, T., & Hoffmann, K. P. (1997). The influence of stationary and moving textured backgrounds on smooth-pursuit initiation and steady state pursuit in humans. *Experimental Brain Research, 115,* 531–540. doi:10.1007/PL00005723

O'Mullane, G., & Knox, P. C. (1999). Modification of smooth pursuit initiation by target contrast. *Vision Research, 39,* 3459–3464. doi:10.1016/S0042-6989(99)00099-1

Osborne, L. C., Lisberger, S. G., & Bialek, W. (2005). A sensory source for motor variation. *Nature, 437,* 412–416. doi:10.1038/nature03961

Pola, J., & Wyatt, H. J. (1980). Target position and velocity: The stimuli for smooth pursuit eye movements. *Vision Research, 20,* 523–534. doi:10.1016/0042-6989(80)90127-3

Pola, J., & Wyatt, H. J. (2001). The role of target position in smooth pursuit deceleration and termination. *Vision Research, 41,* 655–669. doi:10.1016/S0042-6989(00)00280-7

Price, N. S. C., Ono, S., Mustari, M. J., & Ibbotson, M. R. (2005). Comparing acceleration and speed tuning in macaque MT: Physiology and modeling. *Journal of Neurophysiology, 94,* 3451–3464. doi:10.1152/jn.00564.2005

Priebe, N. J., & Lisberger, S. G. (2004). Estimating target speed from the population response in visual area MT. *The Journal of Neuroscience, 24,* 1907–1916. doi:10.1523/JNEUROSCI.4233-03.2004

Rasche, C., & Gegenfurtner, K. R. (2009). Precision of speed discrimination and smooth pursuit eye movements. *Vision Research, 49,* 514–523. doi:10.1016/j.visres.2008.12.003

Rashbass, C. (1961). The relationship between saccadic and smooth tracking movements. *The Journal of Physiology, 159,* 326–338.

Reichardt, W. (1987). Evaluation of optical motion information by movement detectors. *Journal of Comparative Physiology A: Neuroethology, Sensory, Neural, and Behavioral Physiology, 161,* 533–547. doi:10.1007/BF00603660

Ringach, D. L., Hawken, M. J., & Shapley, R. (1996). Binocular eye movements caused by the perception of three-dimensional structure from motion. *Vision Research, 36,* 1479–1492. doi:10.1016/0042-6989(95)00285-5

Robinson, D. A. (1965). The mechanics of human smooth pursuit eye movement. *The Journal of Physiology, 180,* 569–591.

Robinson, D. A., Gordon, J. L., & Gordon, S. E. (1986). A model of the smooth pursuit eye movement system. *Biological Cybernetics, 55,* 43–57. doi:10.1007/BF00363977

Rudolph, K., & Pasternak, T. (1999). Transient and permanent deficits in motion perception after lesions of cortical areas MT and MST in the macaque monkey. *Cerebral Cortex, 9,* 90–100. doi:10.1093/cercor/6.6.814

Salzman, C. D., Murasugi, C. M., Britten, K. H., & Newsome, W. T. (1992). Microstimulation in visual area MT: Effects on direction discrimination performance. *The Journal of Neuroscience, 12,* 2331–2355.

Schütz, A. C., Braun, D. I., & Gegenfurtner, K. R. (2009). Chromatic contrast sensitivity during optokinetic nystagmus, visually enhanced vestibulo-ocular reflex, and smooth pursuit eye movements. *Journal of Neurophysiology, 101,* 2317–2327. doi:10.1152/jn.91248.2008

Schütz, A. C., Braun, D. I., Kerzel, D., & Gegenfurtner, K. R. (2008). Improved visual sensitivity during smooth pursuit eye movements. *Nature Neuroscience, 11,* 1211–1216. doi:10.1038/nn.2194

Schwarz, U., & Ilg, U. J. (1999). Asymmetry in visual motion processing. *NeuroReport: For Rapid Communication of Neuroscience in Research, 10,* 2477–2480. doi:10.1097/00001756-199908200-00008

Segraves, M. A., & Goldberg, M. E. (1994). Effect of stimulus position and velocity upon the maintenance of smooth pursuit eye velocity. *Vision Research, 34,* 2477–2482. doi:10.1016/0042-6989(94)90291-7

Snowden, R. J., & Braddick, O. J. (1991). The temporal integration and resolution of velocity signals. *Vision Research, 31,* 907–914. doi:10.1016/0042-6989(91)90156-Y

Spering, M., & Gegenfurtner, K. R. (2007a). Contextual effects on smooth pursuit eye movements. *Journal of Neurophysiology, 97,* 1353–1367. doi:10.1152/jn.01087.2006

Spering, M., & Gegenfurtner, K. R. (2007b). Contrast and assimilation in motion perception and smooth pursuit eye movements. *Journal of Neurophysiology, 98,* 1355–1363. doi:10.1152/jn.00476.2007

Spering, M., & Gegenfurtner, K. R. (2008). Contextual effects on motion perception and smooth pursuit eye movements. *Brain Research, 1225,* 76–85. doi:10.1016/j.brainres.2008.04.061

Spering, M., Gegenfurtner, K. R., & Kerzel, D. (2006). Distractor interference during smooth pursuit eye movements. *Journal of Experimental Psychology: Human Perception and Performance, 32,* 1136–1154. doi:10.1037/0096-1523.32.5.1136

Spering, M., Kerzel, D., Braun, D. I., Hawken, M. J., & Gegenfurtner, K. R. (2005). Effects of contrast on smooth pursuit eye movements. *Journal of Vision, 5,* 455–465. doi:10.1167/5.5.6

Spering, M., Schütz, A. C., Braun, D. I., & Gegenfurtner, K. R. (2011). Keep your eyes on the ball: Smooth pursuit eye movements enhance the prediction of visual motion. *Journal of Neurophysiology, 105,* 1756–1767. doi:10.1152/jn.00344.2010

Steinbach, M. J. (1976). Pursuing the perceptual rather than the retinal stimulus. *Vision Research, 16,* 1371–1376. doi:10.1016/0042-6989(76)90154-1

Stone, L. S., & Krauzlis, R. J. (2003). Shared motion signals for human perceptual decisions and oculomotor actions. *Journal of Vision, 3,* 725–736. doi:10.1167/3.11.7

Stone, L. S., & Thompson, P. (1992). Human speed perception is contrast dependent. *Vision Research, 32,* 1535–1549. doi:10.1016/0042-6989(92)90209-2

Souman, J. L., Hooge, I. T. C., & Wertheim, A. H. (2005). Perceived motion direction during smooth pursuit eye movements. *Experimental Brain Research, 164,* 376–386. doi:10.1007/s00221-005-2261-6

Suehiro, K., Miura, K., Kodaka, Y., Inoue, Y., Takemura, A., & Kawano, K. (1999). Effects of smooth pursuit eye movement on ocular responses to sudden background motion in humans. *Neuroscience Research, 35,* 329–338. doi:10.1016/S0168-0102(99)00098-X

Tavassoli, A., & Ringach, D. L. (2010). When your eyes see more than you do. *Current Biology, 20,* R93–R94. doi:10.1016/j.cub.2009.11.048

Thompson, P. (1982). Perceived rate of movement depends on contrast. *Vision Research, 22,* 377–380. doi:10.1016/0042-6989(82)90153-5

Thompson, P., Brooks, K., & Hammett, S. T. (2006). Speed can go up as well as down at low contrast: Implications for models of motion perception. *Vision Research, 46,* 782–786. doi:10.1016/j.visres.2005.08.005

Tychsen, L., & Lisberger, S. G. (1986). Visual motion processing for the initiation of smooth-pursuit eye movements in humans. *Journal of Neurophysiology, 56,* 953–968.

von Fleischl, E. (1882). Physiologisch-optische Notizen. *Sitzungsbericht der Akademie der Wissenschaften Wien, 3,* 7–25.

Watamaniuk, S. N., & Heinen, S. J. (1999). Human smooth pursuit direction discrimination. *Vision Research, 39,* 59–70. doi:10.1016/S0042-6989(98)00128-X

Watamaniuk, S. N., & Heinen, S. J. (2003). Perceptual and oculomotor evidence of limitations on processing accelerating motion. *Journal of Vision, 3,* 698–709. doi:10.1167/3.11.5

Watamaniuk, S. N., & Heinen, S. J. (2007). Storage of an oculomotor motion aftereffect. *Vision Research, 47,* 466–473. doi:10.1016/j.visres.2006.09.030

Weiss, Y., Simoncelli, E. P., & Adelson, E. H. (2002). Motion illusions as optimal percepts. *Nature Neuroscience, 5,* 598–604. doi:10.1038/nn0602-858

Wertheim, A. H. (1987). Retinal and extraretinal information in movement perception: How to invert the Filehne illusion. *Perception, 16,* 299–308. doi:10.1068/p160299

Wyatt, H. J., Pola, J., Fortune, B., & Posner, M. (1994). Smooth pursuit eye movements with imaginary targets defined by extrafoveal cues. *Vision Research, 34,* 803–820. doi:10.1016/0042-6989(94)90218-6

4 _____

The Analytic Form
of the Daylight Locus

Geoffrey Iverson and Charles Chubb

It is an interesting computational exercise to take the full collection of Munsell chips, including the grays, illuminate them all with a standard source such as D_{65} or a flat equal energy source, present the reflected lights to three receptors following the spectral absorption profiles of human cones, integrate to produce receptor excitation 3-vectors, one vector per chip, and plot the totality of excitation vectors on a computer screen. What does one see?

Not much at first: a blob, a splotch with no apparent structure. However, as one zooms in on the blob and rotates appropriately, a structure appears. The excitation vectors corresponding to the same Munsell value (gray scale) fall in parallel planes, and within any such plane, the colors form nested chromatic loops (roughly, "ovoids"), each loop being distinguished by a different value of chroma (saturation). Qualitatively, the overall structure resembles a double-cone, just as one would expect if Munsell reflectances were well represented by the simplest Fourier basis 1, sin, cos.

What happens to this structure when one changes the illuminant? If the illuminants are the different phases of daylight, and the receptors are based on the Commission Internationale de l'Éclairage (CIE) 2deg color matching functions (Stockman & Sharpe, 2000; Stockman, Sharpe, & Fach, 1999), the constant (gray) reflectance moves along a three-dimensional curve, which when replotted in CIE chromaticity coordinates (x, y) is the *daylight locus*. This locus is known (Wyszecki & Stiles, 1982) to be well fit by a quadratic equation,

$$y_D = -3x_D^2 + 2.87x_D - 0.275.$$

In Figure 4.1 the circles represent, in CIE chromaticity coordinates, 12 phases of daylight equally spaced in reciprocal correlated color temperature (mired scale). The extreme points correspond to $T_c = 4{,}000$ K (upper right) and $T_c = 25{,}000$ K (lower left). The curve represented by the continuous line

DOI: 10.1037/14135-005
Human Information Processing: Vision, Memory, and Attention, C. Chubb, B. A. Dosher, Z.-L. Lu, and R. M. Shiffrin (Editors)

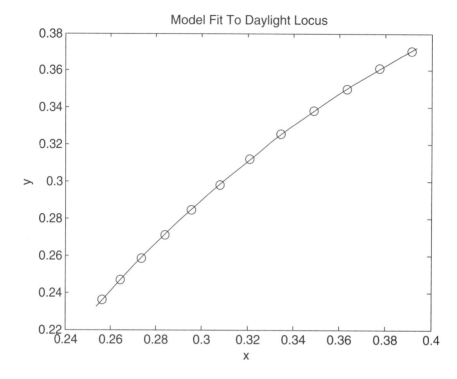

Figure 4.1. Twelve phases of daylight interpolated by an analytic function predicted to follow from a property of visual receptors. This property, which we call *similarity,* is discussed in detail later in the chapter.

interpolating these 12 daylights does *not* follow the empirically fit CIE quadratic but instead is a rather complicated implicit function of the form

$$x(u)=\frac{a+bu+cu^{\vartheta}}{A+Bu+Cu^{\vartheta}}, y(u)=\frac{a'+b'u+c'u^{\vartheta}}{A+Bu+Cu^{\vartheta}}, \quad (4.1)$$

where a, b, c, a', b', c', A, B, C and ϑ are all *known* constants, and u is the running coordinate of the locus; u is a positive number varying over an interval.

The curve expressed by Equation 4.1 is not an empirical template with 10 free parameters to be estimated from some fitting procedure. Rather, the 10 constants in Equation 4.1 are fixed by an underlying theory, developed later in the chapter, that is expressed most naturally not in CIE coordinates but in terms of cone excitations. Equation 4.1 looks relatively complicated only because the passage from cone excitations to the projective CIE chromaticity coordinates introduces that complexity. In contrast, when expressed in terms of ratios of cone excitations, the daylight locus is a simple power function, with an exponent that is determined by the wavelength of maximum sensitivity of each of the cones.

It seems a bit limp to expend so much effort on understanding the daylight locus as a curve in cone-excitation coordinates. Can we extend our theory of a gray surface to chromatically selective surfaces? The answer is yes, and we briefly consider the extension in our concluding remarks. Although our theoretical developments are concentrated on a white surface, similar considerations apply to all Munsell chips.

To develop the theoretical basis for Equation 4.1, we proceed through a sequence of increasingly more realistic models for receptor excitations produced by daylights shining on a white surface. The simplest model we consider assumes narrowband photoreceptor sensitivities. Despite the obvious shortcomings of the narrowband assumption, it generates simple predictions that, to a surprising degree, are preserved in more realistic models. The narrow-band assumption yields a special case of the theoretically important *diagonal* model (Finlayson, Drew, & Funt, 1994; Forsyth, 1994), which predicts that surface ratios of these narrowband receptor excitations are invariant over changes in the illuminant spectral power distribution.

Now it turns out that to a good approximation, human cone excitation ratios are similarly invariant (Foster & Nascimento, 1994). Who would have anticipated this? We argue that the reason predictions of the narrowband model carry over to the broadband sensitivities characteristic of vertebrate photoreceptors resides in the similarity in shape of those receptor sensitivities (Lamb, 1995, 1999; Mansfield, 1985).

It is useful to consider in detail the predictions of a model that involves light from Wien illuminants absorbed by realistic photoreceptors (next section). In all of our calculations, we have used Stockman and Sharpe's (2000) estimates of the 2° human cone sensitivities. By *Wien illuminants,* we mean the family of spectral power distributions

$$W_T(\lambda) = c_1 \lambda^{-5} \exp\left(-\frac{c_2}{\lambda T}\right). \qquad (4.2)$$

Wien illuminants are close relatives of Planck (blackbody) radiators; the physical constants c_1 and c_2 are taken identical to those of the Planck radiation law (Wyszecki & Stiles, 1982); λ denotes wavelength (nm), and T denotes temperature (K). In calculations, we usually take in the range 4,000 K to 25,000 K to match the range of correlated color temperatures characteristic of daylights. However, the theory developed in the next section holds for a much larger range of temperatures, for example, $\infty \geq T \geq 3,000$ K.

Let us fix the notation that is in use throughout. We denote an arbitrary illuminant spectral power distribution by $E(\lambda)$. Special illuminants are given special notation: daylights are referred to by the notation $D_T(\lambda)$ and, as in Equation 4.2, Wien illuminants are written $W_T(\lambda)$. A general surface spectral reflectance function is denoted $R(\lambda)$. The daylight locus involves illuminating a surface whose reflectance spectrum is uniform, that is, $R(\lambda) = $ constant, and the majority of our theoretical developments might seem to be irrelevant to colored surfaces. However, as already mentioned, our developments do, in fact, extend to colored surfaces (see the Conclusion section of this chapter).

Photoreceptor absorption spectra are denoted $S_k(\lambda)$, $k = L, M, S$; these are assumed to be normalized to take the value 1 at their maxima, which occur at wavelengths λ_k, $k = L, M, S$. Photoreceptor excitations, denoted q_k, and produced by light reflected from a matte surface R lit by an illuminant E are given by

$$q_k(E, R) = \int_0^\infty E(\lambda) R(\lambda) S_k(\lambda) d\lambda, \; k=L,M,S \qquad (4.3)$$

We will often take logarithms of photoreceptor sensitivities. When we do so, we find it convenient to write $Q_k = \ln q_k$.

Narrowband Photoreceptors

In a simple model (Finlayson et al., 1994; Finlayson & Hordley, 2001; Marchant & Onyango 2001; Marchant & Onyango, 2002), it is assumed that photoreceptors are so narrowband as to be well represented by delta functions, that is, $S_k = \delta(\lambda - \lambda_k)$. In terms of the photoreceptor excitations given in Equation 4.3, the narrowband assumption entails that $q_k(E, R) = E(\lambda_k)R(\lambda_k)$. In vector notation, this model couples the excitation 3-vectors $\boldsymbol{q}(E, R)$ and $\boldsymbol{q}(E', R)$ by a diagonal matrix with nonzero elements that contain the ratios $E(\lambda_k)/E'(\lambda_k)$. This is the diagonal model referred to earlier. For future reference, we note here that the diagonal model is simple to interpret in logarithmic coordinates: under a change in illumination, $E \rightarrow E'$, all logarithmic excitation vectors $\boldsymbol{Q} = \log \boldsymbol{q}$ undergo a common rigid translation: $\boldsymbol{Q} \rightarrow Q' = Q + \boldsymbol{t}$ where $t_k = \log\left(\dfrac{E'(\lambda_k)}{E(\lambda_k)}\right)$. For a spectrally flat reflectance function—an ideal white surface—the kth photoreceptor excitation value is proportional to $E(\lambda_k)$, the value of the illuminant spectral power distribution evaluated at the peak wavelength λ_k of S_k.

When the illuminants are chosen from a one-parameter family such as Planck (blackbody) radiators, Wien illuminants, or Daylights, the excitations q_k trace out a space curve that is characteristic of the class of illuminants. In the special case of the Wien family of illuminants given by Equation 4.2, the coordinates of the Wien curve $T \mapsto (q_L(T), q_M(T), q_S(T))$ take on the especially simple form

$$q_k(T) = c_1 \lambda_k^{-5} \exp\left(-\frac{c_2}{\lambda_k T}\right). \qquad (4.4)$$

It is evident from Equation 4.4 that color temperature T can be eliminated, allowing any two photoreceptor excitations to be expressed in terms of a third. In particular we have, for all excitations q_k on the Wien curve,

$$q_k = \rho_k \rho_L^{-\beta_k} q_L^{\beta_k} \text{ for } k = L, M, S, \qquad (4.5)$$

in which we have written $\rho_k = c_1 \lambda_k^{-5} = \lim\limits_{T \rightarrow \infty} q_k(T)$ and $\beta_k = \lambda_L/\lambda_k$. Thus, on the Wien curve, the M-cone excitation value is a power function of the L-cone excitation value; the exponent $\beta_M = \lambda_L/\lambda_M$ of this power function is the ratio of the peak wavelengths of the two types of cones. Similarly, the S-cone excitation value is a power function of the L-cone excitation value, with exponent $\beta_M = \lambda_L/\lambda_S$.

It is useful to introduce projective coordinates $v = q_S/q_L$ and $u = q_M/q_L$ because these are independent of the intensity of illumination. A little algebra reveals that

$$v = \rho_L^{\vartheta-1}\rho_M^{-\vartheta}\rho_S u^\vartheta, \quad (4.6)$$

in which the exponent ϑ is given by

$$\vartheta = \left(\frac{\lambda_L}{\lambda_S}-1\right)\bigg/\left(\frac{\lambda_L}{\lambda_M}-1\right) = \left(\frac{1}{\lambda_S}-\frac{1}{\lambda_L}\right)\bigg/\left(\frac{1}{\lambda_M}-\frac{1}{\lambda_L}\right). \quad (4.7)$$

A useful alternative form of Equation 4.6 uses logarithmic coordinates. Recalling the definition of u and v, and taking logarithms in Equation 4.6, we have the *linear* equation

$$Q_S - Q_L = \eta + \vartheta(Q_M - Q_L), \quad (4.8)$$

in which the slope ϑ and intercept η are dimensionless constants; ϑ is given in Equation 4.7, and $\eta = 5(\vartheta\ln(\lambda_M/\lambda_L) - \ln(\lambda_S/\lambda_L))$.

Alternative coordinates to are provided by the *chromaticities* introduced by MacLeod and Boynton (1979)—namely, $x = q_L/(q_L + q_M)$ and $y = q_S/(q_L + q_M)$. In these coordinates, the power function in Equation 4.5 becomes

$$y = Cx^{1-\vartheta}(1-x)^\vartheta, \quad (4.9)$$

in which the constant $C = \rho_L^{\vartheta-1}\rho_M^{-\vartheta}\rho_S$.

This toy model, with its unrealistic photoreceptors, provides a poor basis for biological color vision. Nevertheless, we shall see later that its predictions are met, with surprising precision, under more realistic assumptions on photoreceptoral sensitivities. For future reference, we record here the value of the exponent ϑ assuming realistic photoreceptors. For human cones, Sharpe, Stockman, Jägle, and Nathans (1999) estimated $\lambda_L = 559.1\ nm, \lambda_M = 530.6\ nm$ and $\lambda_S = 420.8\ nm$. Using Equation 4.7, these values give $\vartheta = 6.12$. That value of ϑ is used to evaluate our prediction Equation 4.1 for the CIE daylight locus. We justify this numerical value for ϑ outside of the limitations of the narrowband model.

Photoreceptors With a Common Shape

The predictions expressed in Equations 4.6 through 4.9 of the narrowband model are, to an excellent approximation, preserved in a more realistic model using photoreceptors with mutually overlapping bandwidths, as is the case for vertebrate photoreceptors. This agreeable circumstance is a consequence of the

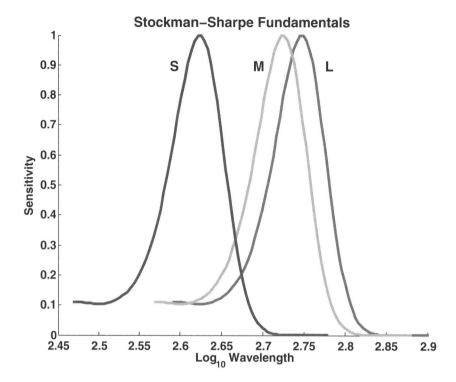

Figure 4.2. Stockman-Sharpe (Stockman & Sharpe, 2000) cone sensitivities plotted as functions of log wavelength. That these sensitivities are simple translations of one another means that they are similar in the sense of Equation 4.10 and footnote 1.

assumption that the photoreceptor sensitivities appear to be based on a *common* template. Specifically, we assume that as functions of log wavelength the photoreceptor sensitivities differ only in the values of their peak wavelengths. In other words,

$$S_k(\lambda) = S_{k'}(\lambda(\lambda_{k'}/\lambda_k)) \text{ for any indices } {}_{k,k'\in\{L,M,S\}}. \quad (4.10)$$

The similarity[1] of photoreceptors formalized in Equation 4.10 is a striking feature of vertebrate photoreceptor sensitivities, including, of course, those of human rods and cones (Lamb, 1995; Mansfield, 1985). It is the similarity of cone sensitivities that allows the excitations of one class of cone to be related to those of any other class (cf. Equation 4.5), as we now show. The Stockman and Sharpe (2000) cone sensitivities are pictured in Figure 4.2. As functions of log wavelength, they are merely translations of one another.

---

[1]Let $\mathsf{F} = \{f_j(x) \mid j = 1, 2, \ldots, J\}$ be a finite collection of real-valued functions defined on the positive reals. We say that the collection F is *similar,* or equivalently that the functions $f_1, f_2, \ldots, f_J$ are mutually similar, if there are positive constants a_j, b_j and a function g such that $f_j(x) = a_j g(b_j x)$. If a family F is similar, it follows that all members of F can be expressed in terms of any single member, f_i, say, as follows: $f_j(x) = (a_j/a_i) f((b_j/b_i)x)$.

Excitations produced by shining a Wien illuminant on the photoreceptors are given by

$$q_k(T) = c_1 \int_0^\infty \lambda^{-5} \exp\left(-\frac{c_2}{\lambda T}\right) S_k(\lambda)\, d\lambda. \quad (4.11)$$

We combine Equations 4.10 and 4.11 to express the excitations of the *M* and *s* photoreceptors in terms of those of the *L* receptors. It is enough to carry out the argument explicitly for the *M* excitations:

$$q_M(T) = c_1 \int_0^\infty \lambda^{-5} \exp\left(-\frac{c_2}{\lambda T}\right) S_M(\lambda)\, d\lambda$$

$$= c_1 \int_0^\infty \lambda^{-5} \exp\left(-\frac{c_2}{\lambda T}\right) S_L(\lambda \beta_M)\, d\lambda,$$

where $\beta_M = \lambda_L/\lambda_M$. By a simple change of variable, we obtain

$$q_M(T) = \beta_M^4 c_1 \int_0^\infty \lambda^{-5} \exp\left(-\frac{c_2}{\lambda T/\beta_M}\right) S_L(\lambda)\, d\lambda,$$

and we see that

$$q_M(T) = \beta_M^4 q_L(T/\beta_M). \quad (4.12a)$$

In the same way, we have

$$q_S(T) = \beta_S^4 q_L(T/\beta_S), \quad (4.12b)$$

where $\beta_S = \lambda_L/\lambda_S$. The ratios β_S and β_M are in constant use subsequently.

Equation 12a and 12b allow the Wien space curve $T \mapsto (q_L(T), q_M(T), q_S(T))$ to be expressed solely in terms of the excitations of any one of the photoreceptors, say, the *L*-cones. Put another way, the mutual similarity of photoreceptors as functions of wavelength λ is reexpressed (via the integration in Equation 4.11) as mutual similarity of the excitations q_k as functions of the Wien temperature T.[2]

By studying the function $T \mapsto q_L(T)$ in further detail, it is possible to develop an analogue of the system of Equation 4.5. Consider the *L*-excitations. We have[3]

---

[2]This transfer of similarity from functions of wavelength to functions of color temperature is not restricted to Wien illuminants. It holds as well for Planck blackbody radiators and in fact for any family of illuminants of the form $E(\lambda, T) = \lambda^{-\gamma} G(\lambda T)$.

[3]The existence of the function $T \mapsto \Lambda_L(T)$ arising in the second line of Equation 4.13 follows from the fact (an integral form of the mean-value theorem of the calculus) that for any functions f and g on a bounded open real interval I, f everywhere positive and g continuous on I, there exists $c \in I$ such that $\int_I g(x) f(x)\, dx = g(c) \int_I f(x)\, dx$.

$$q_L(T) = c_1 \int_0^\infty \lambda^{-5} \exp\left(-\frac{c_2}{\lambda T}\right) S_L(\lambda) d\lambda$$

$$= \exp\left(-\frac{c_2}{\Lambda_L(T)T}\right) c_1 \int_0^\infty \lambda^{-5} S_L(\lambda) d\lambda \quad (4.13)$$

$$= \exp\left(-\frac{c_2}{\Lambda_L(T)T}\right) \rho_L.$$

In the last line of Equation 4.13, we have written $\rho_L = c_1 \int_0^\infty \lambda^{-5} S_L(\lambda) d\lambda = \lim_{T\to\infty} q_L(T)$. A graph of the function $T \mapsto \Lambda_L(T)$ (assuming the $S_L(\lambda)$ are the 2° spectral sensitivities of human L-cones given by Stockman and Sharpe, 2000) is shown in Figure 4.3 (top panel).

From Equation 4.13, we have

$$q_L(T/\beta_M) = \rho_L \exp\left(-\frac{c_2 \beta_M}{\Lambda_L(T/\beta_M)T}\right)$$

$$= \rho_L \left[\exp\left(-\frac{c_2}{\Lambda_L(T)T}\right)\right]^{\alpha_M(T)}$$

$$= \rho_L^{1-\alpha_M(T)} q_L^{\alpha_M(T)}.$$

The exponent $\alpha_M(T)$ is given by

$$\alpha_M(T) = \beta_M \frac{\Lambda_L(T)}{\Lambda_L(T/\beta_M)}. \quad (4.14a)$$

From Equation 4.12a, we thus obtain

$$q_M(T) = \beta_M^4 \rho_L^{1-\alpha_M(T)} q_L(T)^{\alpha_M(T)}. \quad (4.15a)$$

In the same way, we have

$$q_S(T) = \beta_S^4 \rho_L^{1-\alpha_S(T)} q_L(T)^{\alpha_S(T)}, \quad (4.15b)$$

in which the exponent $\alpha_S(T)$ is given by

$$\alpha_S(T) = \beta_S \frac{\Lambda_L(T)}{\Lambda_L(T/\beta_S)}. \quad (4.14b)$$

The Equations 4.15a and 4.15b correspond to the relations given in Equation 4.5 for $k = M, S$, respectively. The major difference, of course, between the two systems of Equations 4.5 and 4.15a–4.14b is that for the latter system, the exponents $\alpha_M(T)$ and $\alpha_S(T)$ depend on T through the factors

$$\frac{\Lambda_L(T)}{\Lambda_L(T/\beta_M)} \text{ and } \frac{\Lambda_L(T)}{\Lambda_L(T/\beta_S)}. \text{ However, these factors vary but little in } T \text{ for}$$

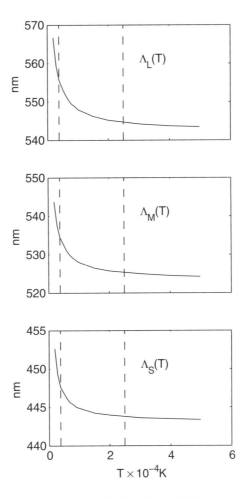

Figure 4.3. Characteristic wavelength functions $\Lambda_k(T)$, $k = L, M, S$ for a white surface. See the text for details, especially Equations 4.13 and 4.16. Notice that these functions are roughly constant except for small values of T (note the vertical scale in each plot). That these functions are mutually similar is established in Equation 4.18 and is also visually apparent. The dashed vertical lines delineate the set of Wien illuminants, $4{,}000 \leq T \leq 25{,}000$.

$T \geq 4000$ K (see Figure 4.3); and, to a good first approximation, they can be taken as constants. In turn, this means that taking logarithms in Equations 4.15a and 4.15b should produce nearly linear plots of Q_M vs. Q_L and Q_S vs. Q_L with respective slopes α_M and α_S. That this is, indeed, the case is shown in Figure 4.4.

An alternative path connecting Equations 4.12a and 4.12b and 4.15a and 4.15b proceeds by defining individual characteristic wavelength functions $\Lambda_k(T)$, one for each cone type:

$$q_k(T) = \rho_k \exp\left(-\frac{c_2}{\Lambda_k(T)T}\right), \quad (4.16)$$

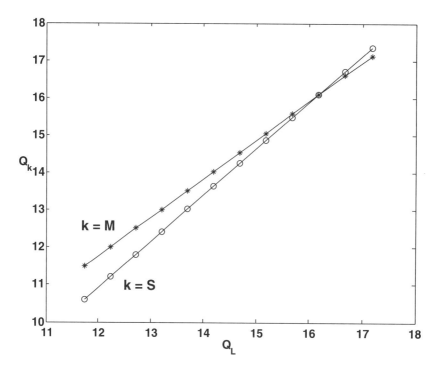

Figure 4.4. Log-excitation of M and S cones versus log-excitation of L cones. Variation in cone excitation is caused by variation in the temperature T of Wien illuminants shone on a white surface.

where $\rho_k = \lim_{T \to \infty} q_L(T)$. It follows that

$$q_k(T) = \rho_k \left(q_L(T)/\rho_L\right)^{\frac{\Lambda_L(T)}{\Lambda_k(T)}}. \quad (4.17)$$

Comparing Equations 4.15a–4.15b and 4.17, we obtain

$$\Lambda_k(T) = \beta_k^{-1}\Lambda_L(T/\beta_k),_{k=L,M,S}. \quad (4.18)$$

Thus, the mutual similarity of the cone sensitivities is again reflected in the mutual similarity of a different collection of functions—namely, the $\Lambda_k(T)$; compare Equations 4.18 and 4.12a–4.12b.

The Daylight Locus

Let us acknowledge two limitations of the foregoing developments that might conceivably have a negative impact on the conclusions of the previous section.[4]

---

[4]This section can be skipped at a first reading. The effects of optic media and the high frequency tail of daylight spectra on our theoretical developments are, in a sense, mere distractions.

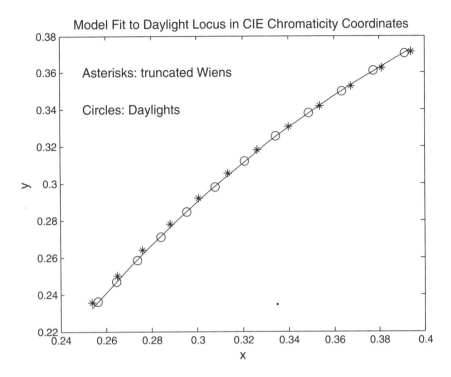

Figure 4.5.   The daylight locus (open circles) and the locus of truncated Wien illuminants (asterisks).

On the one hand, we are interested in the daylight locus, and Wien illuminants are not identical to daylights. On the other hand, we have ignored the fact that the similarity property Equation 4.9 holds well for cones in vitro and not so well for corneal cone sensitivities; to deal with the latter, we need to take into account the optic media of the eye, primarily the macular pigment and the lens.

Fortunately, neither of these complications turns out to have important qualitative implications for the results established in the previous section. If one plots both the daylight locus and the corresponding Wien locus using coordinates $\ln(q_S/q_L) = Q_S - Q_L$ and $\ln(q_M/q_L) = Q_M - Q_L$, both loci plot as nearly parallel lines displaced from one another by approximately 0.1 log units. To make these loci more nearly superimpose, we alter the Wien illuminants so that they better approximate daylights. We do this by truncating the Wien spectra at short wavelengths.

Figure 4.5 is a plot in chromaticity coordinates of the daylight locus and the locus of truncated Wien illuminants; the two loci are now nearly coincident. That is, truncated Wien illuminants approximate daylights, and what has been shown analytically to hold for Wien illuminants carries over to the more complex daylight spectra.

To extend the theory in the previous section to incorporate the joint effects of the optic media and the truncation of the Wien illuminants, we note that these two effects are of a similar nature. Each involves multiplication of the in vitro cone sensitivities by a wavelength transmittance function that is constant for wavelengths at or above 600 nm, decreasing to zero at short wavelengths. We can incorporate the effects of the optic media and the truncation of the Wien illuminants as a single transmittance $t(\lambda)$ rising from zero at or below 400 nm, and saturating with value 1 at approximately 600 nm. The appropriate generalization of Equation 4.10 is thus

$$q_k(T) = c_1 \int_0^\infty t(\lambda)\lambda^{-5}\exp\left(-\frac{c_2}{\lambda T}\right)S_k(\lambda)d\lambda. \quad (4.19)$$

By the mean value theorem, the function $t(\lambda)$ can be taken out from the integral in Equation 4.19, and we have

$$q_k(T) = t(w_k(T))c_1 \int_0^\infty \lambda^{-5}\exp\left(-\frac{c_2}{\lambda T}\right)S_k(\lambda)d\lambda.$$

The theoretical developments of the chapter's previous section now apply unchanged to the ratios $q_k(T)/t(w_k(T))$. We see that

$$q_k(T) = \left(t(w_k(T))/t(w_L(T))^{\alpha_k(T)}\right)\beta_k^4\rho_L^{1-\alpha_k(T)}q_L^{\alpha_k(T)} \quad (4.20)$$

$$= B_k(T)q_L(T)^{\alpha_k(T)}.$$

The functions $B_k(T)$ and $\alpha_k(T)$ are slowly varying in T, and, to a good approximation, each is effectively constant over the range of values of T that define the daylight locus—namely, $4{,}000\ \mathrm{K} \le \mathrm{T} \le 25{,}000\ \mathrm{K}$. To a good approximation, the conclusions of the chapter's previous section are unchanged by the additional complications of the optic media.

Conclusion

We have shown that in appropriately chosen coordinates, for example, $(Q_M - Q_L, Q_S - Q_L)$, the daylight locus plots as a straight line. Moreover, the parameters of this line, and its direction in particular, are found to be determined by the peak sensitivities of the photoreceptors. This occurs because the cones are similar to one another in spectral shape. Because of this similarity, the cones behave in important respects as though they were narrowband receptors.

We have focused on the cone excitations produced by shining one-parameter families of illuminants (daylights, Wien illuminants, blackbody radiators) on a "white," spectrally flat piece of paper. This invites the following question: What happens if we replace our white piece of paper next to a colored one with a nontrivial reflectance spectrum $R(\lambda) \ne$ const. ? Suppose a member of the Wien family of illuminants is reflected from a surface with reflectance $R(\lambda)$, and the reflected light is absorbed by each cone type. The excitations produced are

$$q_k(R,T)=c_1\int_0^\infty \lambda^{-5}\exp\left(-\frac{c_2}{\lambda T}\right)R(\lambda)S_k(\lambda)d\lambda,$$

and we can write this integral as

$$q_k(R,T)=\bar{R}_k(T)c_1\int_0^\infty \lambda^{-5}\exp\left(-\frac{c_2}{\lambda T}\right)S_k(\lambda)d\lambda$$

$$=\bar{R}_k(T)q_k(1,T),$$

where $\bar{R}_k(T)$ is an average value characteristic of the surface and the illuminant temperature T. Taking logarithms, we see that

$$Q_k(R,T)=\log \bar{R}_k(T)+Q_k(1,T).$$

It is clear that information about colored surfaces is carried by deviations from the white surface:

$$\Delta Q_k(R,T)=Q_k(R,T)-Q_k(1,T)=\log \bar{R}_k(T).$$

In Figure 4.6, we have plotted the loci of a chromatic loop of Munsell chips of the same saturation (chroma). We see that as illuminant temperature varies, each chip travels on a line with parameters that are characteristic of the color of the chip. Figure 4.6 is consistent with the idea that the vector of log excitations for any colored surface and any illuminant temperature T with $T_0 \le T \le T_1$, linearly interpolates between two standard "views," corresponding to (arbitrarily chosen) extreme color temperatures T_0 and T_1:

$$Q_k(R,T)=\phi(T)Q_k(R,T_0)+(1-\phi(T))Q_k(R,T_1), \quad (4.21)$$

with $0 \le \phi(T) \le 1$ and $\phi(T_0)=1$. Evidently, the relative coordinates $\Delta Q_k(R,T)$ carrying chromatic information also satisfy Equation 4.21. This model is different from but closely related to the diagonal model (Finlayson et al., 1994; Forsyth, 1994; Foster & Nascimento, 1994). In addition, MacLeod and Golz (2003) presented an interesting Gaussian world that provides linear coordinates when expressed in logarithmic receptor excitation space, although in that world the motion of a white surface under changing illumination is along a quadratic curve rather than a line.

In logarithmic form, the diagonal model reads

$$Q_k(R,T)=A_k(R)+B_k(T). \quad (4.22)$$

As we mentioned earlier, the defining property of the diagonal model is that it separates the effect of surface spectra R from the effect of the illuminant temperature T. The effect of changing illuminant temperature from T to T' is thus to translate all log-excitation vectors Q to new positions Q', and the translation vectors $Q'-Q$ do not depend on the surface reflectance spectrum R.

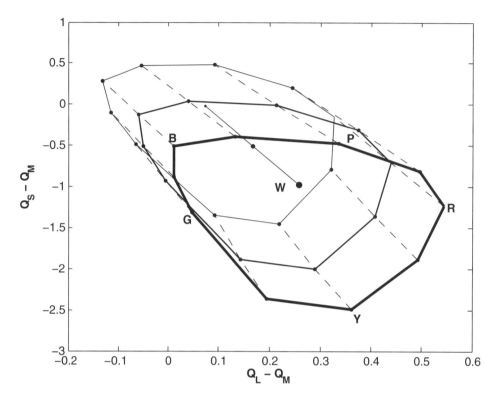

Figure 4.6. In logarithmic coordinates Munsell chips vary linearly with Wien temperature T. The larger chromatic loop closest to the viewer corresponds to $T = 4000$ K, the middle loop is for $T = 6,000$ K, and the smallest loop is for $T = 15,000$ K. The daylight locus is shown by the line connecting solid dots at the "center" of each loop.

The mixture weights $\phi(T)$ in Equation 4.21 can be expressed as

$$\phi(T) = \frac{Q_k(R, T_1) - Q_k(R, T)}{Q_k(R, T_1) - Q_k(R, T_0)}. \qquad (4.23)$$

That the ratio on the right-hand term of Equation 4.23 is independent of surface R and of cone type constitutes a remarkable prediction of the model expressed in Equation 4.21. This prediction is tested in Figure 4.7 and, as can be seen, it is well supported. Note, however, that dilatation (a noticeable "shrinking") with increasing T is evident in Figure 4.6. This dilatation is enough to rule out the diagonal model Equation 4.22.

We do not pursue any further in this chapter a more complete description of the transformations that move the gamut of Munsell chips along the daylight locus. We do note, however, that a prediction of Golz and MacLeod (2002) and MacLeod and Golz (2003) is obtained as a by-product of a more detailed description of our analysis: *As the light gets redder, the reds get lighter.* That this prediction is borne out in perception is easy to demon-

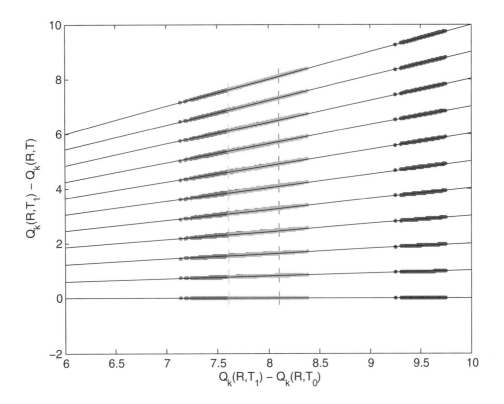

Figure 4.7.   A test of the prediction contained in Equation 4.23. According to this equation, the coordinate pairs $(Q_k(R, T_1) - Q_k(R, T_0), Q_k(R, T_1) - Q_k(R, T))$ should, for *all* chips and *all* cone types, fall on a line whose slope depends only on the temperature T of the illuminant, the value of which is that of the function ϕ defined in Equation 4.23. In the figure, we have plotted these log-excitation coordinates for every Munsell chip, over temperatures spaced equally on the mired scale from $T_0 = 4000$ K to $T_1 = 100,000$ K. As one would expect, the coordinate pairs for L-cones overlap with those of the M-cones (as delineated by the dashed lines). In contrast, the S-cone coordinate pairs are well separated.

strate with a light source, a red filter, and a 1970s map of the New York City subway system (http://www.nycsubway.org/perl/caption.pl?/img/maps/system_1972.jpg).

References

Finlayson, G. D., Drew, M. S., & Funt, B. F. (1994). Color constancy: Generalized diagonal transforms suffice. *Journal of the Optical Society of America A: Optics, Image Science, and Vision, 11,* 3011–3019. doi:10.1364/JOSAA.11.003011

Finlayson, G. D., & Hordley, S. D. (2001). Color constancy at a pixel. *Journal of the Optical Society of America A: Optics, Image Science, and Vision, 18,* 253–264. doi:10.1364/JOSAA.18.000253

Forsyth, D. A. (1994). Colour constancy. In A. Blake & T. Troscianko (Eds.), *AI and the eye* (pp. 201–228). Chichester, England: Wiley.

Foster, D. H., & Nascimento, S. M. C. (1994). Relational color constancy from invariant cone-excitation ratios. *Proceedings. Biological Sciences, 257,* 115–121. doi:10.1098/rspb.1994.0103

Golz, J., & MacLeod, D. I. A. (2002, February 7). Influence of scene statistics on color constancy. *Nature, 415,* 637–640. doi:10.1038/415637a

Lamb, T. D. (1995). Photoreceptor spectral sensitivities: Common shape in the long-wavelength region. *Vision Research, 35,* 3083–3091. doi:10.1016/0042-6989(95)00114-F

Lamb, T. D. (1999). Photopigments and the biophysics of transduction in cone photoreceptors. In K. R. Gegenfurtner & L. T. Sharpe (Eds.), *Color vision* (pp. 89–101). New York, NY: Cambridge University Press.

MacLeod, D. I. A., & Boynton, R. M. (1979). Chromaticity diagram showing cone excitation by stimuli of equal luminance. *Journal of the Optical Society of America A: Optics and Image Science, 69,* 1183–1186.

MacLeod, D. I. A., & Golz, J. (2003). A computational analysis of colour constancy. In R. Mausfeld & D. Heyer (Eds.), *Color perception: Mind and the physical world* (pp. 205–242). Oxford, England: Oxford University Press. doi:10.1093/acprof:oso/9780198505006.003.0007

Mansfield, R. J. W. (1985). Primate photopigments and cone mechanisms. In A. Fein & J. S. Levine (Eds.), *The visual system* (pp. 89–106). New York, NY: Liss.

Marchant, J. A., & Onyango, C. M. (2001). Color invariant for daylight changes: Relaxing the constraints on illuminants. *Journal of the Optical Society of America A: Optics, Image Science, and Vision, 18,* 2704–2706. doi:10.1364/JOSAA.18.002704

Marchant, J. A., & Onyango, C. M. (2002). Spectral invariance under daylight illumination changes. *Journal of the Optical Society of America A: Optics, Image Science, and Vision, 19,* 840–848. doi:10.1364/JOSAA.19.000840

Sharpe, L. T., Stockman, A., Jägle, H., & Nathans, J. (1999). Opsin genes, cone photopigments, color vision, and color blindness. In K. R. Gegenfurtner & L. T. Sharpe (Eds.), *Color vision* (pp. 3–51). Cambridge, England: Cambridge University Press.

Stockman, A., & Sharpe, L. T. (2000). Spectral sensitivities of the middle- and long-wavelength sensitive cones derived from measurements in observers of known genotype. *Vision Research, 40,* 1711–1737. doi:10.1016/S0042-6989(00)00021-3

Stockman, A., Sharpe, L. T., & Fach, C. (1999). The spectral sensitivity of the human short-wavelength cones derived from thresholds and color matches. *Vision Research, 39,* 2901–2927. doi:10.1016/S0042-6989(98)00225-9

Wyszecki, G., & Stiles, W. S. (1982). *Color science: Concepts and methods, quantitative data and formulae* (2nd ed.). New York, NY: Wiley.

Part II

Memory and
Information Processing

5

Equisalience Analysis: A New Window Into the Functional Architecture of Human Cognition

Charles E. Wright, Charles Chubb,
Alissa Winkler, and Hal S. Stern

Different dimensions of visual sensitivity play different roles in visual processing. We see this neurophysiologically in the specialization of brain regions for various sorts of visual information. For example, as discussed in this chapter, the magnocellular layers of the lateral geniculate nucleus (LGN) convey information about achromatic luminance variations of low spatial and high temporal frequency, whereas the parvocellular layers carry information about both chromatic and achromatic variations of high spatial and low temporal frequency (Livingstone & Hubel, 1987, 1988). Psychophysics also reveals that different sorts of visual information play different roles in visual processing. Consider that acuity for luminance modulations is much higher than acuity for either (a) equiluminant, chromatic modulations (e.g., Mullen, 1985) or (b) modulations of texture contrast (Sutter, Sperling, & Chubb, 1995). Apparently, variations in light intensity (compared with variations in color or in texture contrast) have special status in conveying information about fine detail in the visual scene. By contrast, Chaparro, Stromeyer, Huang, Kronauer, and Eskew (1993) investigated detection of briefly flashed, small (between 5′ and 15′ of arc) foveally presented spots; spots could differ from the background either in color (either redder or greener than the yellow background) or in luminance (either brighter or darker than the background). Over the range of spot sizes and durations tested, participants were generally more sensitive to chromatic than to luminance differences, leading Chaparro et al. to claim in their title that "Colour is what the eye sees best" (p. 348). They also concluded, based on differences in temporal and spatial summation, that different signal processing streams are used to produce the luminance and chromatic judgments.

These considerations suggest that to understand human visual processing, we need to understand what sorts of visual information (which dimensions of

DOI: 10.1037/14135-006
Human Information Processing: Vision, Memory, and Attention, C. Chubb, B. A. Dosher, Z.-L. Lu, and R. M. Shiffrin (Editors)

visual sensitivity) are used for what computational purposes. The main goal of this chapter is to introduce equisalience analysis (EA), a psychophysical method to address this question, likely to find applications in diverse areas of human perception and cognition. To motivate and explain the approach, we have chosen an example that has generated substantial recent interest: characterizing the differences in visual what-and-where processing.

The idea that visual processing splits into anatomically and functionally distinct dorsal and ventral streams originates with Ungerleider and Mishkin (1982), who called them the *where* and *what* streams because they thought the function of the dorsal stream was to localize things in space whereas that of the ventral stream was to identify things. They also pointed out that these streams receive their primary input from different subcortical pathways. Although both streams receive input from the magnocellular layers of the LGN, the ventral stream alone also receives input from the parvocellular layers.

These two subcortical streams carry different sorts of information (Livingstone & Hubel, 1988). Neurons in the parvocellular layers tend to be color-selective and sluggish with small receptive fields. By contrast, magnocellular neurons tend to be insensitive to color and fast (sensitive to rapid transients) with large receptive fields. These observations suggest that dorsally mediated functions might be less sensitive to color variations than ventral functions.

Since Ungerleider and Mishkin's (1982) original what-and-where theory, alternative theories of ventral–dorsal visual processing have been proposed. The most influential of these is the *what-and-how* theory of Milner and Goodale (1995), who argued that the ventral stream is specialized "to permit the formation of perceptual and cognitive representations that embody the enduring characteristics of objects and their significance," whereas the dorsal stream "mediate(s) the control of goal-directed movements" using primarily "instantaneous and egocentric features of objects" (p. 66). Others (e.g., Creem & Proffitt, 2001) have argued for a hybrid *what–where–how* theory that locates the *where* system in the inferior parietal lobule and the *how* system in the superior parietal lobule.

Many studies have attempted to demonstrate a functional difference in the processing of visual information by tasks thought to be primarily "dorsal" versus "ventral." One approach has been to look for evidence of visual "illusions" in ventrally mediated judgment tasks and the relative absence of such illusions in dorsally mediated pointing or grasping tasks (e.g., Aglioti, Goodale, & DeSouza, 1995; Brown, Moore, & Rosenbaum, 2002; Haffenden & Goodale, 1998, 2000; Haffenden, Schiff, & Goodale, 2001). However, as witnessed by the debate over this issue (Franz, 2001; Franz, Buelthoff, & Fahle, 2003; Franz, Fahle, Buelthoff, & Gegenfurtner, 2001; Franz, Gegenfurtner, Buelthoff, & Fahle, 2000; Smeets & Brenner, 2006), these studies have failed to provide comparisons that compellingly demonstrate a functional difference. In a recent review of this and other related lines of evidence, Cardoso-Leite and Gorea (2010) suggested that this distinction may be impossible to "test" definitively because of "pervasive methodological problems relating precisely to the empirical (im)possibility of 'strictly matching' perceptual and motor tasks" (p. 133). An important part of this problem is that the tasks being compared have different dependent measures. Even using tasks with dependent variables that have the same units (e.g., the latency of a judgment and the duration of a movement, both measured in milliseconds) does not solve the underlying "apples and oranges" problem.

We propose EA as a way to overcome these inherent problems in comparing the relative sensitivity of two or more tasks to visual stimulation. We present EA first conceptually and then with a set of illustrative, but real, data.

Equisalience Analysis

To appreciate the issues involved in comparing data across tasks, consider a thought experiment modeled after one of the experiments that we have actually run. (We present some actual, illustrative data later.) This thought experiment includes two blocked tasks: a speeded identification task and a masked location task. (Under the what-and-where theory, one might expect the identification and location tasks to selectively engage the ventral and dorsal streams, respectively.) The stimuli for both tasks are identical: an isosceles triangle pointing in one of four directions—up, down, right, or left—presented at one of four locations. In the masked location task, the stimulus is masked after a brief display, and the participant presses one of four keys to indicate the location of the triangle. In the speeded identification task, the stimulus remains visible, and the participant presses one of four keys as quickly as possible to indicate which way the triangle is pointing.

In each task, the target can be defined in either of two ways: It can be gray and brighter than the background, or it can be green and equiluminant to the background. In either case, the target also varies from trial to trial in intensity—that is, in luminance for gray targets or in saturation for green targets. In the masked location task, the dependent variable is proportion of correct responses; in the speeded identification task, it is response time.

Under the what-and-where theory, one might expect the identification task to draw mainly on ventral and the location task on dorsal processes. If so, then one might expect the two tasks to have roughly equal sensitivity to luminance variations (both streams get magnocellular input); however, because only the ventral stream gets parvocellular input, one might expect the identification task to be more sensitive to equiluminant green variations than the location task.[1] This leads the what-and-where theorist to predict that these two tasks differ in their relative sensitivity to luminance versus green saturation. The choice of two tasks with very different dependent variables will help to illustrate the strengths of the EA method.

For any given task, T, the gray-to-green equisalience function f_T maps any gray-intensity x onto the green-intensity $y = f_T(x)$ that yields the same level of performance as x. This concept is illustrated for the masked location task, Task 1 on left side of Figure 5.1. The two curves show hypothetical psychometric functions

---

[1]It should be noted that the equiluminant green stimuli are expected to activate both the parvocellular and koniocellular channels of the LGN. Koniocellular neurons seem to be sensitive primarily to S-cone activations (see Hendry & Reid, 2000, for a review). At the risk of oversimplifying the discussion, we ignore possible complications resulting from the koniocellular channel.

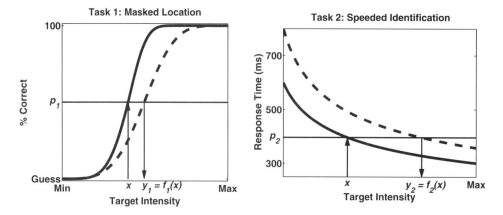

Figure 5.1. Hypothetical data from two tasks. In both panels, task performance is related to target intensity. For Task 1, in the left panel, performance is measured by percent correct; for Task 2, in the right panel, performance is measured by reaction time. In both panels, the solid curve gives performance as a function of target luminance, and the dashed curve gives performance as a function of equiluminant green target saturation. In Task 1, the green saturation value y_1 yields the same level of performance, p_1, in the masked location task as does luminance x. This means $y_1 = f_1(x)$, where f_1 is the gray-to-green equisalience function for the masked location task; that is, x and y_1 are equisalient for this task. In Task 2, the green saturation value y_2 yields the same level of performance, p_2, in the masked location task as does luminance x; that is, x and y_2 are equisalient for this Task 2.

from this task, one for gray intensities (solid line) and one for green (dashed line). The horizontal line indicates the performance level p_1 yielded by gray-intensity x. This line intersects the green psychometric function at point $y_1 = f_1(x)$, for f_1, the gray-to-green equisalience function for the masked location task.

Analogous, hypothetical, speeded identification task data are shown for Task 2 on the right side of Figure 5.1. Notice that the dependent measure is different from that of Task 1; nonetheless, we can define the gray-to-green equisalience function f_2 just as we defined f_1. That is, gray-intensity x maps to a performance level p_2, which maps to the corresponding green-intensity $y_2 = f_2(x)$.

Figure 5.2 makes it clear that the location and identification tasks differ. Here the circle and square mark the equisalient points in a coordinate system with gray intensity on the horizontal and green on the vertical axis: the circle marks the equisalient point from Task 1 (x, y_1), the location task, and the square marks the equisalient point from Task 2 (x, y_2), the identification task. In this hypothetical example, levels of gray and green intensity that yield identical location task performance (x and y_1) yield different identification-task performance: A higher green intensity (y_2) is required to produce the same identification-task performance as x. This difference, which we call a *task-related contrast in sensitivity,* is important because we might suppose that, if two tasks with the same information requirements are informed by the same data stream, then any manipulation of the input that influences the quality of the data available in that stream should analogously influence performance in both tasks, in

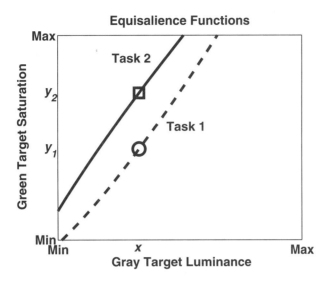

Figure 5.2. Hypothetical equisalient points and functions of luminance and saturation for two tasks. The two points, marked by a circle and a square, are equisalience points. Each indicates the level of green target saturation (y_1 for Task 1, the masked location identification task, and y_2 for Task 2, the speeded shape identification task) that produces the same level of performance as a gray target luminance level, x. The two curves are equisalience functions that generalize the relationship indicated by the equisalience points across the range of gray target luminance levels. The dashed line is for Task 1. The solid line is for Task 2.

which case we would have observed the same equisalient point for both tasks. Figure 5.2 contradicts this expectation for manipulations of gray and green across the location and identification tasks, suggesting either that they have different information requirements or that they do not reside in the same data stream.

EA is an elaboration of the procedure just described for comparing equisalient points. A minimal application of EA involves two dimensions of stimulus intensity, X and Y (e.g., luminance and green saturation), and two tasks, $Task_1$ and $Task_2$ (e.g., the speeded identification and masked location tasks). The first step is to collect data using various levels of each of X and Y in each of tasks $Task_1$ and $Task_2$. We then use standard models to fit the X-data in $Task_1$, the Y-data in $Task_1$, the X-data in $Task_2$ and the Y-data in $Task_2$, in each case deriving a parametric function relating stimulus intensity to performance. In the foregoing example, data would be collected to fit the four functions shown in Figure 5.1. Then for each of $k = 1$ and 2, we use the parameters from the fits of X-data and Y-data in $Task_k$ to derive the $Task_k$, X-to-Y equisalience function f_k. To reiterate, for any X-intensity x, $f_k(x)$ gives the Y-intensity that yields the same level of performance as x in $Task_k$. The two lines in Figure 5.2 are the equisalience functions for the masked location and speeded identification tasks, the psychophysical functions of which are shown in Figure 5.1. Importantly, the X-to-Y equisalience function for a task does not depend on the measure of performance used in the task.

As shown in Figure 5.2, visual comparison of the equisalience functions strengthens the impression that variations of X = gray and Y = green intensities influence performance differently in the two tasks. However, for EA to be a useful tool, it is important that we go beyond visual impressions and provide a statistical test of the null hypothesis that the X-to-Y equisalience functions of the two tasks are equal. Here, if one makes standard assumptions about the relation of stimulus intensity to performance, the equisalience functions for both forced-choice and speeded tasks turn out to be power functions. That is, for either sort of task, the X-to-Y equisalience function takes the form $f(x) = \gamma x^\phi$, where the parameters γ and ϕ can be computed from the parameters used to fit the X- and Y-data from that task. This result enables a straightforward likelihood-ratio test of the null hypothesis that the X-to-Y equisalience functions of the two tasks are identical, that is, they have the same values of γ and ϕ.

To summarize, EA is a new method for testing whether cognitive processes have similar access to or make equivalent use of different sorts of sensory information. This method requires (a) two (or more) to-be-compared tasks,[2] in each of which performance depends on the sensory strength of the stimulus information; (b) two (or more) sensory stimulus dimensions; and (c) an invertible function relating intensity to performance for each task, such that the resulting equisalience function can be parameterized with the same function, here a power function. EA does not replace psychometric functions as an important way to understand performance with different tasks and stimulus dimensions. What the method provides is a systematic way to compare the relative sensitivity of different tasks to different dimensions of stimulus intensity.

Equisalience Functions Versus Equisalience Points

A reasonable question at this point is whether it is necessary to develop full equisalience functions to make these comparisons. After all, in our development of equisalience functions, we alluded to drawing the inferences of interest simply by comparing equisalience points. As described later, we have found the concept of equisalience functions has helped to clarify this issue.

An approach based on the analysis of equisalient points seems particularly plausible as an extension of a technique often used to compare psychophysical data across conditions. A nice example of this technique is a paper by Pestilli and Carrasco (2005) that looked at the effect of valid, neutral, and invalid cues (which we can think of as three different tasks) on the discrimination of the orientation of Gabor patches at two eccentricities. To make these comparisons, they used a staircase procedure to estimate the stimulus contrast needed to achieve 82% correct responses (so contrast at Eccentricity 1 plays the role of x, and contrast at Eccentricity 2 plays the role of y). If the valid-cue task is Task 1 and the invalid-cue task is Task 2, then this procedure yields equisalient pairs (x_1, y_1) for Task 1 and (x_2, y_2) for Task 2. The panels of Figure 5.3 illustrate pairs

---

[2]For convenience and brevity, we have chosen always to describe these comparisons as being between "tasks." However, there is nothing in the logic of EA that prohibits it from being used to compare salience across what might be considered "conditions" within a single task.

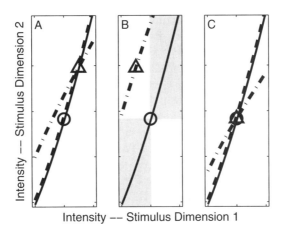

Figure 5.3. Three possible outcomes for an experiment with only one equisalient point for each task.

of equisalient points from three possible outcomes from such an experiment and several equisalience functions consistent with each outcome. The horizontal and vertical axes in Figure 5.3 represent stimulus intensity on each of two stimulus dimensions. The circle, in each panel, indicates the equisalient point for Task 1, that is, the pair of intensities that produced criterion performance in this task. The triangle indicates the equisalient point for Task 2.

Panel A of Figure 5.3 illustrates a plausible outcome in which the equisalient points differ, on both stimulus dimensions. The solid line is an equisalience function (one of many) consistent with the equisalient point for Task 1. The two broken lines are both consistent with the equisalient point for Task 2. The figure makes the ambiguity in this outcome obvious: These two equisalient points can arise either when there truly is a task-related contrast in sensitivity or when there is not such a difference. In the first case, the equisalience function for Task 2 might be the broken line with the dot-dash pattern. If there is no difference, the equisalience function for Task 2 must be the dashed line that is collinear with the solid line that is the equisalience function for Task 1.

One clear difference between the outcome illustrated in Panel A of Figure 5.3 and that of Figure 5.2 is that the procedure for generating the equisalient points in Figure 5.2 included steps designed to ensure that the same stimulus intensity level was used to generate the data on one of the stimulus dimensions (the one represented by the horizontal axis in Figure 5.2) for both tasks. As a result, both equisalient points were constrained to fall on a single vertical line. Perhaps this constraint is necessary to produce results that can be interpreted without ambiguity.

Panel B of Figure 5.3 shows that it is possible, however, to obtain equisalient points that can be interpreted unambiguously with a less restrictive constraint. In Panel B, the equisalient points again differ. However, because equisalience functions are power functions and must be monotonically increasing, there is no equisalience function that can pass through both of these two equisalient points, and thus there is no ambiguity: They must reflect a task-related contrast in sensitivity. We can reach this same conclusion (up to the limits of statistical reliability) if the equisalient point for Task 2 lies anywhere in the unshaded region of Panel B. This shows that a single pair of equisalient points can suffice to demonstrate the existence of a task-related contrast.

By contrast, however, Panel C of Figure 5.3 makes it clear that a single pair of equisalient points can never refute the existence of a task-related contrast. In this case, the equisalient points for the two tasks lie on top of one another. This is the case when the criterion performance level is produced by the same pair of stimulus intensities in Task 1 and Task 2. In the discussion of Figure 5.2, we implied that this outcome was consistent with the absence of a task-related contrast. However, as the three equisalience functions in Panel C make clear, this result is ambiguous: If the solid line is the equisalience function for Task 1, the equisalience function for Task 2 can be either collinear (the dashed line) or not (the broken line with the dot-dash pattern). Resolution of this ambiguity requires data defining at least two separated equisalient points for each task. Although it might be marginally more efficient to limit one's data to just that necessary to satisfy this requirement, in fact, the data required to fit both full psychometric functions for each task, and thus to determine the equisalience functions, is not that much more extensive than the data required to precisely estimate two equisalient points for each task.

Treatment of Actual Data

Tasks and Stimuli

To illustrate the application of EA, this section briefly describes an actual experiment that builds on the thought experiment described in the previous section. In this experiment, data from three tasks using the same stimuli, and six levels each of gray luminance and green saturation were collected for each of eight trained participants over five daily, 1-hour sessions (following 4 days of practice). The stimulus on each trial was one of four isosceles triangles (Figure 5.4b shows an upward gray version) displayed at one of four parafoveal locations about a fixation mark (Figure 5.4a).

In the speeded location task, participants pressed one of four keys as quickly as possible to indicate target location (Figure 5.4b); the stimulus stayed on until the response. The masked location task was similar except that the screen was masked 116 ms after stimulus onset, and participants guessed target location without worrying about speed. In the speeded identification task, participants pressed a key (Figure 5.4c) to indicate which way the target triangle was pointing; there was no mask. For both speeded tasks, errors were excluded from the analysis.

The target on a given trial differed from the gray background (CIE coordinates $Y = 23.4$ cd/m^2, x = .293, y = .303) in either luminance or color. Based on results during the practice days, six levels of gray target luminance ($24.3 \leq x \leq 25.4$) and equiluminant green target variation ($.328 \leq y \leq .371$) were chosen for each participant to yield performance ranging from 30% to 95% correct in the masked location task. It should be noted that although the primary variation in the green target is in its saturation, it also varies in hue.

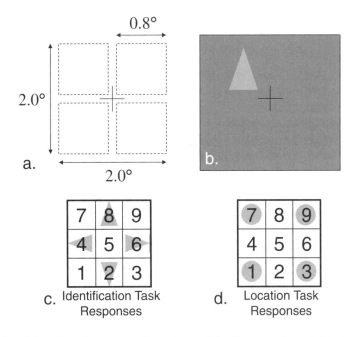

a. 0.8° 2.0° 2.0° b.

c. Identification Task Responses

d. Location Task Responses

Figure 5.4. Stimuli and response layouts used in the experiment. Part a shows the dimensions of the array containing four possible stimulus locations. Part b shows possible stimulus, illustrating a single level of location, shape, luminance, for a gray target (not shown saturation of green targets). Part c shows how stimulus shape was mapped to response keys in the identification task. Part d shows how stimulus location was mapped to the response keys in the location task.

Rationale

The what-and-where theory predicts that the two location tasks should rely on dorsal mechanisms, whereas under the what-and-how theory, the judgments required in the location tasks are of allocentric position and thus should be ventrally mediated, although perhaps localized in the inferior parietal lobule. Under both theories, speeded identification should be ventrally mediated. Thus, the what-and-how theory predicts that the gray-to-green equisalience functions of all three tasks will be the same; however, the what-and-where theory predicts that the gray-to-green equisalience function for the identification task will differ from those of the two location tasks. In any case, if (as seems likely) the masked and speeded location tasks are mediated by one mechanism, then their gray-to-green equisalience functions should be the same.

Results

Figure 5.5 shows, for one participant, three equisalience functions with the fitted data, one for each of the tasks. For any level p of performance in a given task, T, there exists a unique luminance $x(p)$ and saturation $y(p) = f_T(x(p))$, that yield performance p. Each of the three equisalience functions in Figure 5.5

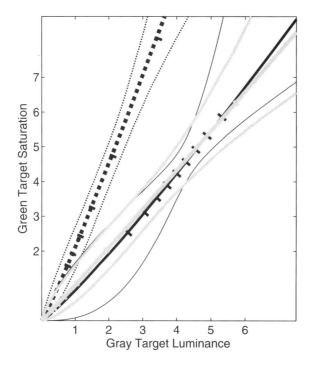

Figure 5.5. Equisalience functions of green saturation versus luminance for three tasks from one participant. The dotted black line is the equisalience function for the speeded, shape identification task. The solid black line is the equisalience function for the speeded location task. The solid gray line is the equisalience function for the masked location task. The tick marks along the gray line (masked location task) mark nine equisalience points that range from a proportion correct of 0.325, at the lower to 0.925, on the upper right, in steps of 0.075. The tick marks along the solid black (speeded shape) and dotted black (speeded location) lines mark six equisalience points that range from a reaction time of 1000 ms, on the lower left, to 500 ms, on the upper right, in 100 ms increments.

plots the locus of points $(x(p), y(p))$ for a task. Notice that the dependent measure, p, has no explicit representation in Figure 5.5, although we could label every point on any equisalience function with the corresponding value of p. As indicated in the figure caption, tick marks on each equisalience function locate specific, arbitrary performance levels.

The implicit representation of p creates a problem; it makes it difficult to indicate the dispersion of the actual data around the model predictions. This problem is solved in Figure 5.5 by contour lines surrounding each equisalience function marking 95% credible intervals obtained using a Bayesian procedure.

Note that for this participant (a) the equisalience functions for the speeded location (solid black line) and masked location (solid gray line) tasks are nearly identical, whereas (b) the equisalience function for the identification task (dotted black line) differs strongly from those for the two location tasks. As shown in Table 5.1, this pattern reflects a general tendency observed across our participants. Specifically, for six of our eight observers, a likelihood ratio

Table 5.1. Summaries of Two Paired-Task Comparisons

| Subject | Speeded location vs. masked location | | | Speeded identification vs. masked location | | |
| | Likelihood ratio test | | Log$_{10}$ Bayes factor | Likelihood ratio test | | Log$_{10}$ Bayes factor |
	χ^2	p		χ^2	p	
1	1.38	.502	1.544	52.86	.000	−4.014
2	0.18	.938	1.908	90.94	.000	−10
3	9.34	.009	−0.911	64.11	.000	−4.706
4	2.34	.309	1.465	62.54	.000	−3.954
5	8.43	.014	−0.003	27.74	.000	−2.038
6	2.66	.265	1.978	122.37	.000	−10
7	4.35	.113	1.819	72.86	.000	−3.233
8	0.43	.808	2.034	104.86	.000	−10

test (method described later) fails to reject the null hypothesis that the equisalience functions for the masked and speeded versions of the location task are different. (Consonant with this result, Bayes factors strongly favor equality of the equisalience functions for the two location tasks.) By contrast, for all eight observers, likelihood ratio tests decisively reject the null hypothesis that the equisalience functions for the identification task and masked location task are equal ($p < .0001$ in all cases, and all of the log-Bayes factors are less than −2).

Discussion

The finding that the equisalience functions are similar for the masked and speeded location tasks confirms our expectation that, despite the change in dependent variable associated with the change from a speeded- to an accuracy-based procedure, these two tasks are mediated by the same processes. The result that equisalience functions are different for the masked location versus the identification task might be taken to confirm the what-and-where theory in favor of the what-and-how theory of ventral–dorsal processing. However, as Cardoso-Leite and Gorea (2010) so persuasively argued, the results from any single EA experiment are unlikely to support conclusions as strong as this. An alternative account of the current results, for example, proposes that the identification task makes use of higher spatial frequency information than do the location tasks (because high spatial frequencies are required to discriminate the tip of the isosceles triangle from the other vertices). Therefore, because high spatial frequency information is carried more efficiently by luminance than by equiluminant chromatic variations, the identification task is relatively less sensitive to saturation versus luminance than the location tasks. Additional EA experiments are needed to determine exactly why the equisalience functions for the identification and location tasks differ, but this is an ambiguity inherent in understanding a complex system, not a problem of the method.

Testing the Hypothesis that Two Tasks Share
the Same Equisalience Function

In the previous section, we reported p values for two tests of the null hypothesis that two equisalience functions are identical. This section explains how the equisalience functions and these p values were obtained.

The Models for the Forced-Choice and Response-Time Tasks

We first derive the equisalience functions for the two psychometric models used to address performance in the tasks of interest: the model for a four-alternative forced-choice (4-AFC) task (e.g., the masked location task) and the model for a response-time task (e.g., the speeded location or the speeded identification task). For concreteness, we continue to use x for target luminance and y for equiluminant green target saturation; however, x and y could be variable intensities of any sensory properties.

We model 4-AFC task performance using Weibull functions (Mortensen, 2002; Quick, 1974):

$$\Psi(u|\alpha,\beta) = .25 + .75\left(1 - e^{-\left(\frac{u}{\alpha}\right)^{\beta}}\right). \quad (5.1)$$

For some α_L, β_L, α_S, and β_S, probability correct is assumed to be $\Psi(x \mid \alpha_L, \beta_L)$ for a gray target of luminance x and $\Psi(y \mid \alpha_S, \beta_S)$ for a green target of saturation y. Under these assumptions, the equisalience function for the 4-AFC task is

$$f_1(x) = \Psi_S^{-1}(\Psi_L(x)) = \gamma_1 x^{\phi_1}, \quad (5.2)$$

where

$$\gamma_1 = \frac{\alpha_S}{\alpha_L^{\left(\frac{\beta_L}{\beta_S}\right)}} \quad \text{and} \quad \phi_1 = \frac{\beta_L}{\beta_S}. \quad (5.3)$$

When viewed in the form of Equation 5.2, the equisalience function approach can be seen to be related to the quantile-comparison function used to compare two probability distributions (Lehmann, 1974).

To fit the data from a response-time task, we assume that, for a given target luminance (or equiluminant green saturation) u, response times w conform to a delay-shifted Wald density:

$$g(w|u,\kappa,\eta,\rho,\delta) = \frac{\rho}{\sqrt{2\pi(w-\delta)^3}} \exp\left[-\left(\frac{(\rho - \kappa u^{\eta}(w-\delta))^2}{2(w-\delta)}\right)\right]. \quad (5.4)$$

Variants of the Wald distribution are commonly used to model response times (Heathcote, 2004; Luce, 1986). With $\delta = 0$, the Wald distribution reflects the distribution of first-passage times through level ρ of a homogeneous Wiener diffusion process with initial value 0, drift κu^{η}, and variance 1. The idea is that response time depends on a process of information-accrual that can be mimicked by such a diffusion process. Setting $\delta > 0$ introduces a fixed delay reflecting factors such as sensory transduction and response production. We assume that for a gray target with luminance x, response times have density $g(w|x, \kappa_L, \eta_L, \rho, \delta)$, whereas for a green target with saturation y, response times have density $g(w|y, \kappa_S, \eta_S, \rho, \delta)$. The boundary ρ and delay δ are assumed to be the same for green and gray targets.

Note that $g(w|y, \kappa_S, \eta_S, \rho, \delta) = g(w|x, \kappa_L, \eta_L, \rho, \delta)$ if and only if $\kappa_S y^{\eta_S} = \kappa_L x^{\eta_L}$, implying that

$$f_2(x) = \gamma_2 x^{\phi_2}, \quad (5.5)$$

where

$$\gamma_2 = \left(\frac{\kappa_L}{\kappa_S}\right)^{\frac{1}{\eta_S}} \text{ and } \phi_2 = \frac{\eta_L}{\eta_S}. \quad (5.6)$$

Modeling the Equality of Two Equisalience Functions

Equations 5.2 and 5.5 show that for both the forced-choice and response-time models the equisalience functions are power functions. Our unconstrained model allows all parameters from both tasks to vary freely. However, our constrained model requires that $f_1 = f_2$, implying that

$$\gamma_1 = \gamma_2 = \gamma \text{ and } \phi_1 = \phi_2 = \phi, \quad (5.7)$$

yielding a new parameterization that replaces η_S, β_S, κ_S, and α_S with γ and ϕ by setting

$$\eta_S = \frac{\eta_L}{\phi}, \beta_S = \frac{\beta_L}{\phi}, \kappa_S = \frac{\kappa_L}{\gamma^{\eta_S}} = \frac{\kappa_L}{\gamma^{\left(\frac{\eta_L}{\phi}\right)}}, \text{ and } \alpha_S = \gamma \alpha_L^{\phi}. \quad (5.8)$$

Thus, the unconstrained model has separate α, β, η, κ parameters for the two tasks, whereas in the constrained model the α, β, η, κ parameters for saturation are derived from ϕ, γ and the parameters for luminance using Equation 5.8.

The 4-AFC Task Likelihood Functions

For any luminance x, let N_x be the number of trials in which the target had luminance x, and let k_x be the number of those N_x trials in which the observer responded correctly. Define N_y and k_y analogously for any green saturation y. Then the 4-AFC task, gray-target-trial, likelihood function is

$$\Lambda_1^L(\alpha_L, \beta_L) = \prod_x \Psi(x|\alpha_L, \beta_L)^{k_x} (1 - \Psi(x|\alpha_L, \beta_L))^{N_x - k_x}, \quad (5.9)$$

where the product in Equation 5.9 is over all luminances x used to define targets in the task. Similarly, the green-target-trial likelihood function is

$$\Lambda_1^S(\alpha_S,\beta_S) = \prod_y \Psi(y|\alpha_S,\beta_S)^{k_y}(1-\Psi(y|\alpha_S,\beta_S))^{N_y-k_y}, \quad (5.10)$$

where the product in Equation 5.10 is over all saturations y used to define green targets in the task.

The Response-Time Task Likelihood Functions

Let w_t be the response time on trial t in the response-time task; if the target on trial t was gray, let x_t be its luminance; if green, let y_t be its saturation. Then the gray- and green-target-trial likelihood functions are

$$\Lambda_2^L(\kappa_L,\eta_L,\rho,\delta) = \prod_{\text{gray-target trials } t} g(w_t|x_t,\kappa_L,\eta_L,\rho,\delta), \quad (5.11)$$

and

$$\Lambda_2^S(\kappa_S,\eta_S,\rho,\delta) = \prod_{\text{green-target trials } t} g(w_t|y_t,\kappa_S,\eta_S,\rho,\delta). \quad (5.12)$$

The Likelihood Functions for Both Tasks

For any α_L, β_L, α_S, β_S, κ_L, η_L, κ_S, η_S, ρ, and δ, the likelihood function for the results of both tasks is

$$\Lambda_{Unconstrained}(\alpha_L,\beta_L,\alpha_S,\beta_S,\kappa_L,\eta_L,\kappa_S,\eta_S,\rho,\delta) =$$

$$\Lambda_1^L(\alpha_L,\beta_L)\Lambda_1^S(\alpha_S,\beta_S)\Lambda_2^L(\kappa_L,\eta_L,\rho,\delta)\Lambda_2^S(\kappa_S,\eta_S,\rho,\delta). \quad (5.13)$$

In the constrained model,

$$\Lambda_{Constrained}(\phi,\gamma,\alpha_L,\beta_L,\kappa_L,\eta_L,\rho,\delta) =$$

$$\Lambda_{Unconstrained}(\alpha_L,\beta_L,\alpha_S,\beta_S,\kappa_L,\eta_L,\kappa_S,\eta_S,\rho,\delta), \quad (5.14)$$

where the values of η_S, β_S, κ_S and α_S appearing on the right are given by Equation 5.8.

As is well known (e.g., Hoel, Port, & Stone, 1971), if the null hypothesis that $f_1 = f_2$ is true, then the statistic

$$X = -2\ln\left(\frac{\max(\Lambda_{Constrained})}{\max(\Lambda_{Unconstrained})}\right) \quad (5.15)$$

is asymptotically distributed as chi-square with two degrees of freedom (for the two additional parameters used in the unconstrained model).

Bayesian Elaborations of Equisalience Analysis

We have described traditional likelihood-based inference for equisalience functions; however, a Bayesian approach offers important benefits. First, one can incorporate previous information about the parameters used for the tasks and properties being compared. Although investigators are unlikely to impose strong prior constraints, they may wish to provide upper or lower bounds (or both) on model parameters based on results in the literature. Second, the Bayesian approach frees us from large sample inference. Modern, simulation-based (Markov chain Monte Carlo) methods enable accurate posterior inferences for any sample size, providing posterior intervals for individual psychophysical model parameters. Also, because the equisalience function parameters are functions of the psychophysical model parameters, posterior inference is available for the equisalience functions as well. Finally, the Bayesian approach facilitates hierarchical modeling to accommodate multiple subjects in a single analysis.

In the current study, we used Bayesian parameter estimation (Markov chain Monte Carlo simulation) to generate credible intervals around equisalience function plots in Figure 5.5. This provides a convenient (if indirect) way of indicating the dispersion of the data around model estimates. In addition, we use the Savage–Dickey (e.g., Verdinelli & Wasserman, 1995) method to derive Bayes factors (Columns 3 and 6 of Table 1) comparing the constrained model requiring equisalience functions to be equal to the unconstrained model. For purposes of comparing these Bayes factors to the results of the likelihood ratio tests, note that any Bayes factor whose log (base 10) is greater than 1.0 (–1.0) is typically taken as strong evidence in favor of the constrained (unconstrained) model. It is easy to see that the Bayesian tests return results that are highly consonant with the likelihood ratio tests.

Summary of Fitting Procedures

In this example, different models are appropriate to summarize the data yielded by response-time and 4-AFC tasks (Wald vs. Weibull distributions). Nonetheless, these two models both yield equisalience functions of the same form (power functions). Consequently, the null hypothesis that two tasks of either type share the same equisalience function nests within the general model in which all parameters vary freely. This enables a comparison of these hypotheses that can be done, as we have spelled out, using likelihood ratio test or a Bayes factor.

We emphasize that EA can be used to compare any two tasks, provided that their equisalience functions are both of the same form. Thus, the method is straightforward if the dependent variables of the two tasks are identical. However, as illustrated here, the method can often be applied to compare tasks with different dependent variables.

Summary

EA is a new method for analyzing the functional architecture of human perception and cognition. EA allows one to compare the relative sensitivity of two or more perceptual–cognitive tasks to two or more dimensions of stimulus intensity.

For a given task T, and two dimensions X and Y of stimulus intensity that can be used to control performance in T (e.g., X might be luminance and Y equiluminant green saturation), the X-to-Y equisalience function f_T maps any intensity x of X onto the intensity $y = f_T(x)$ of Y that yields the same level of performance in task T. Here we have shown how to test statistically whether two tasks (possibly with different dependent variables) share the same X-to-Y equisalience function. This question is of interest because, if two tasks with the same information requirements are found to have different equisalience functions, then the tasks probably reside in different processing streams. There are two primary ways of using EA to make scientific progress. First, by discovering tasks with different equisalience functions, we can begin to analyze cognitive processing into different functional streams. Second, by enlarging families of tasks that all share the same equisalience function, we can delineate the functional boundaries between those streams.

References

Aglioti, S., Goodale, M. A., & DeSouza, J. F. X. (1995). Size-contrast illusions deceive the eye but not the hand. *Current Biology, 5,* 679–685. doi:10.1016/S0960-9822(95)00133-3

Brown, L. E., Moore, C. M., & Rosenbaum, D. A. (2002). Feature-specific perceptual processing dissociates action from recognition. *Journal of Experimental Psychology: Human Perception and Performance, 28,* 1330–1344. doi:10.1037/0096-1523.28.6.1330

Cardoso-Leite, P., & Gorea, A. (2010). On the perceptual/motor dissociation: A review of concepts, theory, experimental paradigms and data interpretations. *Seeing and Perceiving, 23,* 89–151. doi:10.1163/187847510X503588

Chaparro, A., Stromeyer, C. F., III, Huang, E. P., Kronauer, R. E., & Eskew, R. T. (1993). Color is what the eye sees best. *Nature, 361,* 348–350. doi:10.1038/361348a0

Creem, S. H., & Proffitt, D. R. (2001). Defining the cortical visual systems: "What," "where," and "how." *Acta Psychologica, 107,* 43–68. doi:10.1016/S0001-6918(01)00021-X

Franz, V. H. (2001). Action does not resist visual illusions. *Trends in Cognitive Sciences, 5,* 457–459. doi:10.1016/S1364-6613(00)01772-1

Franz, V. H., Buelthoff, H. H., & Fahle, M. (2003). Grasp effects of the Ebbinghaus illusion: Obstacle avoidance is not the explanation. *Experimental Brain Research, 149,* 470–477.

Franz, V. H., Fahle, M., Buelthoff, H. H., & Gegenfurtner, K. R. (2001). Effects of visual illusions on grasping. *Journal of Experimental Psychology: Human Perception and Performance, 27,* 1124–1144. doi:10.1037/0096-1523.27.5.1124

Franz, V. H., Gegenfurtner, K. R., Buelthoff, H. H., & Fahle, M. (2000). Grasping visual illusions: No evidence for a dissociation between perception and action. *Psychological Science, 11,* 20–25. doi:10.1111/1467-9280.00209

Haffenden, A. M., & Goodale, M. A. (1998). The effect of pictorial illusion on prehension and perception. *Journal of Cognitive Neuroscience, 10,* 122–136. doi:10.1162/089892998563824

Haffenden, A. M., & Goodale, M. A. (2000). Independent effects of pictorial displays on perception and action. *Vision Research, 40,* 1597–1607. doi:10.1016/S0042-6989(00)00056-0

Haffenden, A. M., Schiff, K. C., & Goodale, M. A. (2001). The dissociation between perception and action in the Ebbinghaus illusion: Nonillusory effects of pictorial cues on grasp. *Current Biology, 11,* 177–181. doi:10.1016/S0960-9822(01)00023-9

Heathcote, A. (2004). Fitting Wald and ex-Wald distributions to response time data: An example using functions for the S-PLUS package. *Behavior Research Methods, Instruments & Computers, 36,* 678–694. doi:10.3758/BF03206550

Hendry, S. H. C., & Reid, R. C. (2000). The koniocellular pathway in primate vision. *Annual Review of Neuroscience, 23,* 127–153. doi:10.1146/annurev.neuro.23.1.127

Hoel, P. G., Port, S. C., & Stone, C. J. (1971). *Introduction to statistical theory.* Boston, MA: Houghton-Mifflin.

Lehmann, E. L. (1974). *Statistical methods based on ranks*. San Francisco, CA: Holden-Day.

Livingstone, M., & Hubel, D. (1988, May 6). Segregation of form, color, movement, and depth: Anatomy, physiology, and perception. *Science, 240,* 740–749. doi:10.1126/science.3283936

Livingstone, M. S., & Hubel, D. H. (1987). Psychophysical evidence for separate channels for the perception of form, color, movement and depth. *The Journal of Neuroscience, 7,* 3416–3468.

Luce, R. D. (1986). *Response times*. New York, NY: Oxford University Press.

Milner, A. D., & Goodale, M. A. (1995). *The visual brain in action*. Oxford, England: Oxford University Press.

Mortensen, U. (2002). Additive noise, Weibull functions and the approximation of psychometric functions. *Vision Research, 42,* 2371–2393. doi:10.1016/S0042-6989(02)00195-5

Mullen, K. T. (1985). The contrast sensitivity of human colour vision to red-green and blue-yellow chromatic gratings. *The Journal of Physiology, 359,* 381–400.

Pestilli, F., & Carrasco, M. (2005). Attention enhances contrast sensitivity at cued and impairs it at uncued locations. *Vision Research, 45,* 1867–1875. doi:10.1016/j.visres.2005.01.019

Quick, R. F. (1974). A vector-magnitude model of contrast detection. *Kybernetik, 16,* 65–67. doi:10.1007/BF00271628

Smeets, J. B. J., & Brenner, E. (2006). 10 years of illusions. *Journal of Experimental Psychology: Human Perception and Performance, 32,* 1501–1504. doi:10.1037/0096-1523.32.6.1501

Sutter, A., Sperling, G., & Chubb, C. (1995). Measuring the spatial frequency selectivity of second order texture mechanisms. *Vision Research, 35,* 915–924. doi:10.1016/0042-6989(94)00196-S

Ungerleider, L. G., & Mishkin, M. (1982). Two cortical visual systems. In D. J. Ingle, M. A. Goodale, & R. J. Mansfield (Eds.), *Analysis of visual behavior* (pp. 549–586). Cambridge, MA: MIT Press.

Verdinelli, I., & Wasserman, L. (1995). Computing Bayes factors using a generalization of the Savage-Dickey density ratio. *Journal of the American Statistical Association, 90,* 614–618. doi:10.1080/01621459.1995.10476554

6

On the Nature of Sensory Memory

Michel Treisman and Martin Lages

The Memory Trace

Aristotle (350 BCE/2007) believed that when a stimulus is presented, we form a "presentation" of it that is "something like an impression or picture" (para. 8). Memory was "the state of a presentation, related as a likeness to that of which it is a presentation" (para. 12). This construct is now generally known as a *memory trace*. This trace is believed to represent the original experience and make it available for later comparison; it is fixed and unchanging except for the inevitable damage wrought by decay and interference. We refer to these rather general ideas as *fixed memory trace theory* (FMTT). They have provided a popular basis for accounts of memory for a long time and still dominate our understanding of memory in psychophysics. Orban and Vogels (1998), for example, discussed "the three processes underlying temporal comparison: (1) sensorial representation of visual stimuli, (2) maintaining a trace of the preceding stimulus, and (3) comparison of the incoming stimulus with that trace" (p. 117), and many other authors have offered similar accounts.

The notion that information retention is accomplished by making and preserving a representation or copy of the original stimulus has rarely been critically challenged, perhaps because it may seem intuitively obvious. An alternative does exist, however. Here we review work on psychophysical decision making, which offers a different account of sensory information retention, and test this against the implications of FMTT.

Criterion Setting Theory

Signal detection theory (SDT; Green & Swets, 1966) assumes that psychophysical decisions use a criterion that is fixed, at least for the length of the session, but there are difficulties with this. In the real world, discrimination takes place under conditions that may vary unpredictably. An efficient discrimination system should be able to adjust the criterion to match changing conditions.

DOI: 10.1037/14135-007

Human Information Processing: Vision, Memory, and Attention, C. Chubb, B. A. Dosher, Z.-L. Lu, and R. M. Shiffrin (Editors)

Criterion setting theory (CST) is an extension of SDT that addresses this problem (Lages &Treisman, 1998; Treisman, 1984a, 1984b, 1985, 1987; Treisman & Faulkner, 1984a, 1984b, 1985, 1987; Treisman, Faulkner, Naish, & Rosner, 1995; Treisman & Williams, 1984). It rests on the following principles: (a) The sensory processes have evolved to optimize performance; (b) to achieve this, a criterion setting mechanism (CSM) adjusts the decision criterion on each trial to bring it nearer the optimum; (c) to estimate the current optimal value, it draws on any source of useful information; and (d) A simple mechanism combines information from different sources to approximate the optimal criterion.

Mechanisms that provide this information are discussed later in the chapter. Here we consider a discrimination task using the *method of single stimuli* (MSS), in which a single presentation of the reference stimulus is followed by a series of test stimuli. However, CST applies to any procedure using a criterion.

Criterion Stabilization Mechanism

It is fortunate if the flux of sensory inputs generated on the sensory decision axis, E, by a set of test stimuli is centered on the current decision criterion: Maximum information transmission occurs when HIGH and LOW responses are equally likely. (RESPONSES are written in upper case, *stimuli* in lower case.) If the sensory inputs fall mainly above the criterion, say, so that the latter is too low, most responses will be HIGH, conveying little information. However, the primary imperative for a sensory mechanism is to transmit information. To ensure that it does so, the stabilization mechanism acts to maintain the criterion near the mean of the current sensory inputs.

This is illustrated in Figure 6.1 for four trials of a discrimination experiment. An initial reference criterion value, E_o, is selected, based on previous experience, relevant knowledge, or the initial stimuli. Over trials, each of the randomly presented test stimuli generates a normal distribution of sensory inputs on the decision axis. Probability density functions are shown for test stimuli s_n and s_n+1. On Trial 1, the current value of the criterion $E_c(1)$ is set equal to the criterion reference value E_o. A test stimulus is presented and generates the sensory input, E_1, shown falling to the right of $E_c(1)$; this indicates that the criterion is most likely too low and should move to the right. This information is stored as a stabilization indicator trace, shown on the right as an arrow whose magnitude and direction indicate the needed rightward criterion shift. This magnitude is $\Delta_s (E_1 - E_c(1))$, where Δ_s is a weighting constant.

On Trial 2, $\Delta_s (E_1 - E_c(1))$ (if positive) has been reduced to $\Delta_s (E_1 - E_c(1)) - \delta_s$, where δ_s is a constant decrement (or if it was negative, incremented by δ_s). Thus, the absolute value of the indicator trace decreases on each trial; when it reaches zero, it disappears. Decrementation reflects the decreasing relevance of past observations to the current situation. If conditions change rapidly, δ_s should be large; if they are constant, δ_s should be small or zero. On Trial 2, the current criterion becomes $E_c(2) = E_o + \Delta_s (E_1 - E_c(1)) - \delta_s$ (for a positive trace). The stimulus input, E_2, falls to the right of $E_c(2)$, giving the response HIGH, so a right-pointing indicator trace is generated, $\Delta_s (E_2 - E_c(2))$. On Trial 3, both indicator traces are decremented, but neither reaches zero, so $E_c(3)$ is given by $E_o + \Delta_s (E_1 - E_c(1)) - 2\delta_s + \Delta_s (E_2 - E_c(2)) - \delta_s$. On Trial 3, E_3 falls to the left of $E_c(3)$, so the indicator trace, $\Delta_s(E_3 - E_c(3)) < 0$, prescribes a shift to the left.

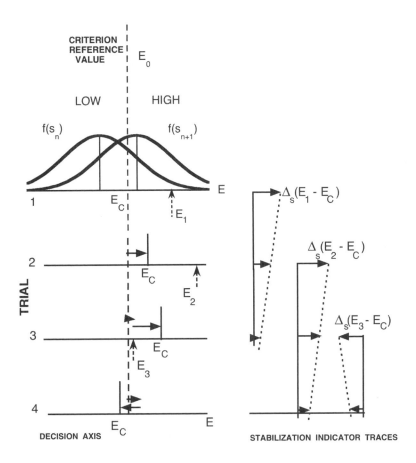

Figure 6.1. Effects of stabilization on the decision criterion. From "A Criterion Setting Theory of Discrimination Learning That Accounts for Anisotropies and Context Effects", by M. Lages and M. Treisman, 2010, *Seeing and Perceiving, 23,* p. 405. Copyright 2010 by Brill. Reprinted with permission.

If a majority of inputs fall above (or below) the current criterion, this mechanism moves the criterion upward (or downward), reducing the imbalance. These trial-to-trial adjustments manifest as sequential dependencies in the data. Thus, if the input on trial i falls above the criterion (more likely with a *high* stimulus, and giving the response HIGH), an indicator trace is produced that will raise the criterion on subsequent trials, reducing the probability of repeating HIGH. This fall in P(HIGH) following a *high* stimulus is known as contrast or a negative sequential dependency (Treisman & Williams, 1984).

Probability Tracking Mechanism

The probability tracking mechanism uses a different source of information, the current best estimate of the probability of the signal. In the real world, because targets tend to persist through time, our best guides to current probabilities are our previous responses; negative or positive detections should lower or raise the estimated probability of the target. If this probability rises, the criterion should be lowered accordingly. The corresponding mechanism resembles that for stabilization except that it uses positive feedback: A HIGH response lowers the criterion, making HIGH responses more likely (a positive sequential dependency). Tracking indicator traces have a constant initial absolute value Δ_r and their absolute values decrease by $\delta_r \geq 0$ on each trial until they reach zero and disappear.

Feedback From External Sources

Feedback from external sources offers a further source of information (Treisman & Williams, 1984). CST assumes that feedback may be handled by a mechanism similar to that for probability tracking, with parameters Δ_f and δ_f. However, because feedback was not used in the experiments that follow, this is not discussed further here.

      We assume that the system can adjust the magnitude parameters, Δ_s and Δ_r, to reflect the informativeness of the corresponding traces, and it can adjust the decrementation parameters, δ_s and δ_r, to ensure that traces reduce at the rate at which their relevance to current judgments decreases. If these parameters are set to zero, past experience may be preserved indefinitely. To integrate the different information sources, on each trial the CSM simply sums all the indicator traces currently in store to determine the net criterion shift.

Fixed Memory Traces Versus Criterion Setting: Conflicting Predictions

If fixed memory traces (FMTs) that behave like "high-fidelity" copies of the visual input, photographic in their accuracy, mediate sensory memory (Magnussen, 2000; Magnussen & Dyrnes, 1994), a number of predictions follow.

FMTT-1

According to FMTT, a comparison between two neural representations, the FMTs of the reference and test stimuli, determines discrimination. If a psychometric function is fitted to data obtained with the MSS or method of constant stimuli (MCS), the 50% point, traditionally known as the *point of subjective equivalence* (PSE), will correspond to the FMT of the reference stimulus. The PSE should remain stable at this value whatever changes to the number or location of test stimuli may occur.

FMTT-2

With the MSS, accuracy of discrimination depends on the delay between the reference stimulus and the test stimuli, as the FMT may decay during this interval. Consequently, the life of the memory trace can be studied by increasing this delay until discrimination fails.

FMTT-3

In this model, the outcome of the current trial is unrelated to events on preceding trials, so it offers no scope for effects of context. Apparent dependencies between successive trials must be attributable to noise and be random in form. CST makes contrasting predictions.

CST-1

Consider a delayed discrimination MSS experiment. This uses a range of test stimuli, $R(m)$, where m is the midpoint of the range. The range is customarily symmetrical, centered approximately at the reference stimulus value. A positive asymmetrical range, $R(m^+)$, would have more than half its stimulus values lying above the reference stimulus, a negative range, $R(m^-)$, more than half below it. If different test stimulus ranges are used, what will CST predict? Test stimuli that lie mainly above the reference stimulus will usually produce sensory inputs that fall above the current criterion, and these will generate stabilization indicator traces that tend to shift E_c upward. Similarly, if the range is symmetrical, E_c will remain near E_0, and a negative asymmetrical range will lower E_c. Thus, over trials, the momentary effective criterion E_c, and the PSE, which estimates it, will come to lie near the midpoint of the range used, m^+, m_0, or m^-. This is the PSE shift prediction. Predictions FMTT-1 and CST-1 are illustrated in Figure 6.2, upper panel.

CST-2

Magnussen and Dyrnes (1994), using the MSS with a delay interval of 50 hr, obtained unimpaired discrimination. They claimed this shows that an FMT can be retained with perfect fidelity for long periods. This implicitly assumes that if no reference stimulus were presented, there would be no basis of comparison for the test stimulus, and performance would break down; the authors reported an experiment they believe supports this. Under CST, if there is no reference stimulus, an initial criterion will be selected when the first test stimuli are presented. The accumulation of indicator traces over subsequent trials will shift E_c toward the range midpoint. The slope of the psychometric function depends on sources of noise, such as the physical noise in the stimulus, and variance due to criterion setting; whether or not a reference stimulus is presented, the noise will be similar. Thus, CST predicts similar psychometric function slopes whether or not a reference stimulus is presented.

CST-3

Each stimulus presentation and each response produces an indicator trace, which while it lasts will affect criterion values, producing dependencies. We consider the effect of the stimulus or response on trial i on the criterion $E_c(k)$ on an index trial k coming n trials after i, that is, at lag $n = k - i$. Thus, to examine the effect of the response HIGH on the criterion for trials following at lag n, we

PSE Shift Prediction (CST)

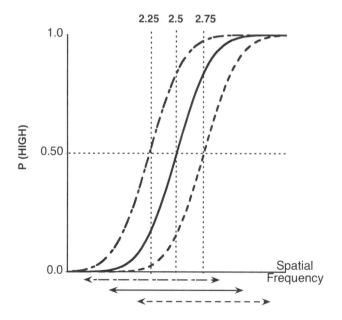

PREDICTED DEPENDENCIES

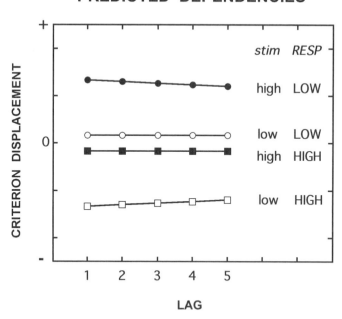

Figure 6.2. Upper panel: Point of subjective equivalence shift predictions for three stimulus ranges (criterion setting theory). From "Spatial Frequency Discrimination: Visual Long-Term Memory or Criterion Setting?", by M. Lages and M. Treisman, 1998, *Vision Research, 38,* p. 561. Copyright 1998 by Elsevier. Adapted with permission. Lower panel: Dependencies on preceding stimulus-response combinations predicted by (CST-3). From "A Criterion Setting Theory of Discrimination Learning That Accounts for Anisotropies and Context Effects", by M. Lages and M. Treisman, 2010, *Seeing and Perceiving, 23,* p. 412. Copyright 2010 by Brill. Reprinted with permission.

find the PSE for the subset of trials, each of which follows n trials after a HIGH: Subset(n, HIGH). This PSE estimates the corresponding criterion position.

$\bar{E}_c$, the mean of the E_c values for a block of trials, represents the net effect of all preceding stimulus presentations and responses on subsequent criteria. Let $\bar{E}_c = 0$; this corresponds to the PSE. For any trial j in Subset(n, HIGH), the preceding trials in the session, excluding trial j–n, should tend to place $E_c(j)$ at 0. However, trial j–n has always given the response HIGH and, therefore, always generated the tracking trace $-\Delta_r$, which will have decreased to $-(\Delta_r - n\delta_r)$ on the index trial (or reached 0 and disappeared). Thus, the preceding HIGH responses will shift the mean criterion for trials in Subset(n, HIGH) downward, as compared with $\bar{E}_c = 0$, for n not too great; similarly, LOWs will shift it up—a positive dependency on past responses. Similarly, a *high* stimulus n trials back will tend to raise the criterion for Subset (n, *high*), a negative dependency on past stimuli.

The two dependencies are opposite in direction, but any cancellation is incomplete because the two processes have different parameters. However, attempts to calculate either dependency alone give results that may be difficult to interpret. Examining different combinations of a past stimulus and response is more informative. The predictions for such combinations are illustrated in the lower panel of Figure 6.2. For example, as both a *high* stimulus and a LOW response tend to move the criterion upward, the criterion contingent on a preceding (*high* LOW) combination shows the highest positive values. For the (*low* LOW) and (*high* HIGH) combinations, the curves are intermediate; their relative positions are arbitrary because they depend on the exact parameter values.

Tests of FMTT and CST Predictions

These and other predictions have been tested by Lages and Treisman (1998, 2010) and Treisman and Lages (2010), in which further references, significance tests, and experimental detail can be found. In Lages and Treisman (1998, Experiment 1), subjects discriminated the spatial frequencies (SF) of vertical sine-wave gratings using MSS. In one condition, a 2.5-cpd reference SF stimulus was presented initially for 10 s, followed by a 30-s delay. A block of test stimuli was then given. Three test stimulus ranges, R(2.25), R(2.5), and R(2.75), were used, in separate sessions. Experiment 2 was similar, except that the reference stimulus was omitted.

The upper panel of Figure 6.3 shows psychometric functions for the three test stimulus ranges in Experiment 1. Their midpoints are indicated by vertical lines. The answers to the questions raised by predictions CST-1 and CST-2 are unambiguous. In the upper panel (Experiment 1), the psychometric function shifts upward when R(2.75) is used and downward when R(2.25) is used, confirming the PSE shift prediction and refuting the FMTT stability prediction. Functions for the three ranges in Experiment 2 are shown in the lower panel. Despite the omission of the reference stimulus, the accuracy of discrimination is strikingly unimpaired. These results again support CST and reject FMTT. They invalidate Magnussen and Dyrnes's (1994) claim to have shown that a sensory memory may be retained with perfect fidelity for 50 hr. The criterion

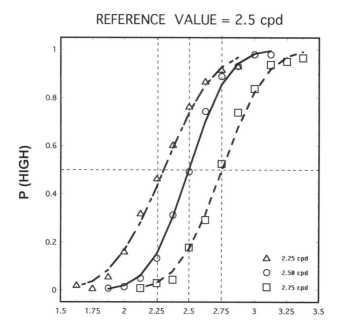

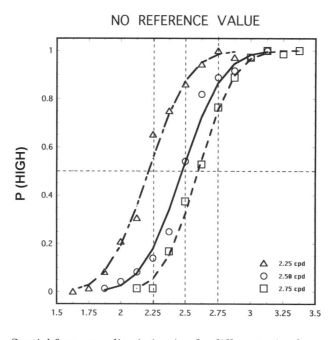

Figure 6.3. Spatial frequency discrimination for different stimulus ranges, with or without a reference stimulus. From "Spatial Frequency Discrimination: Visual Long-Term Memory or Criterion Setting?", by M. Lages and M. Treisman, 1998, *Vision Research, 38,* pp. 561 and 564. Copyright 1998 by Elsevier. Adapted with permission.

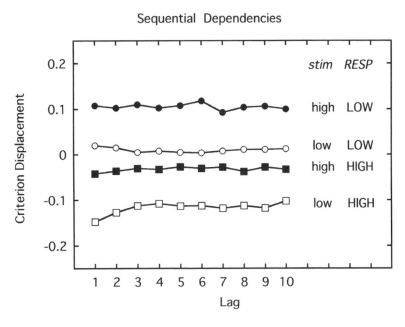

Figure 6.4. Sequential dependencies for spatial frequency discrimination. From "Spatial Frequency Discrimination: Visual Long-Term Memory or Criterion Setting?", by M. Lages and M. Treisman, 1998, *Vision Research, 38,* p. 563. Copyright 1998 by Elsevier. Adapted with permission.

setting effects of the test stimuli despite the absence of a reference are sufficient to explain their results.

Magnussen and Dyrnes (1994) reported that an experiment without a reference showed "that guessing is random, except for the extreme test frequencies." To our eyes, their data could be fitted by a psychometric function with an increased threshold. This poorer performance, in contrast to our results, could be due to a difference in the number of trials (four per point for their subjects vs. 24 here), although, when Lages and Treisman (1998) analyzed only the first four responses for each point, they obtained similar slopes to the full data, with or without a reference. Possibly, there was a disruptive effect of Magnussen and Dyrnes's (1994) instructions, which described the required behavior as "guessing."

The sequential dependencies in Figure 6.4 show PSE values contingent on preceding stimulus-response combinations, plotted against lag (Lages & Treisman 1998, Experiment 1). They match the pattern predicted in Figure 6.2 (lower panel). Prediction CST-3 is supported; prediction FMTT-3 is not.

Discrimination Learning, Context, Anisotropies

The FMT hypothesis explains only one feature of sensory processing, the retention of information; however, discrimination demonstrates a number of interconnected features, such as PSE shifts, contextual effects, and improvement with practice, which call for an integrated explanation. CST offers an approach to modeling such phenomena (Lages & Treisman, 2010).

The criterion setting process relies on the intrinsic context provided by indicator traces accumulated from trials presented earlier in the session. If, in addition, traces from past sessions can persist and contribute to setting the current criterion, we have a mechanism that allows past experience to improve current performance. This provides a mechanism for discrimination learning.

It follows that if a particular value on a physical dimension is discriminated exceptionally frequently, and δ_s is set low so that traces persist, the greater accumulation of traces for the corresponding criterion should make discrimination more accurate at that location, thus setting up an anisotropy. For example, our need to stay erect requires constantly determining body orientation relative to the direction of gravity, which may provide a basis for enhanced discrimination of the vertical. Criteria for such highly practiced values may be described as *permanent* because they are maintained over time by a persisting residue of traces preserved from past discriminations. In contrast, a novel task such as discriminating departures from an arbitrary reference value will require setting up a corresponding ad hoc criterion that lacks such accumulated support.

In addition to this intrinsic context, surround stimuli provide an extrinsic context for the test stimuli. Information from some of these stimuli, the *effective extrinsic context,* may be used in setting the test stimulus criterion. CST hypothesizes that effective context may include stimuli in the same modality that are "isodiscriminal" to the test stimuli in that they are subject to discrimination on the same dimension for a similar range of values.

Such stimuli are assumed to act on E_c(test) through a process we refer to as *projection.* Latent or overt discriminations of stimuli varying on the isodiscriminal dimension generate indicator traces. These are copied, their parameters may be modified, and the copies are transferred or projected to CSM(test), which adds them to its store of intrinsic traces. The projected extrinsic traces are summed with the intrinsic indicator traces to determine the current value of E_c(test). This model of discrimination learning and context effects leads to additional predictions.

CST-4

Permanent criteria, supported by larger samples of traces, produce steeper psychometric functions than ad hoc criteria.

CST-5

Faced with the PSE shifts in Figure 6.3, FMTT theorists might argue, as a fallback position, that even if the ad hoc criteria used in SF discrimination can be shifted, anisotropies must depend on FMTs that are especially strong and so can ensure rigidly fixed PSEs. In CST, however, permanent and ad hoc criteria differ only in the size of the indicator trace sample, and therefore both types of criterion should show PSE shifts.

CST-6

Asymmetric ranges should produce larger PSE shifts for ad hoc than for permanent criteria because the effect of the current asymmetrically distributed traces on the latter should be diluted by the greater number of accumulated traces stabilizing permanent criteria.

A measure of the PSE shift is given by the regression of PSE values onto the range midpoints. For a 45° reference and asymmetric ranges R(43°) and R(47°), for example, the magnitude of the PSE shift would be

$$Span = (PSE(R(47°)) - PSE(R(43°))/(47° - 43°). \quad (6.1)$$

FMTT predicts $Span = 0$. CST predicts (a) $0 < Span \leq 1$, and (b) $Span(ad\ hoc) > Span$(permanent). Thus, for any intermediate value of $Span$, such as $Span = 0.50$, values of $Span$(permanent) are relatively more likely to fall below it, and values of $Span(ad\ hoc)$ are relatively more likely to fall above it.

CST-7

CST predicts that extrinsic context may affect the position of the criterion. To examine this, we use the following design. Consider orientation discrimination in relation to a reference stimulus at m°. We randomly divide the n trials in a block into two subsets, Subset$_A$ and Subset$_B$, each with $n/2$ trials. We randomly assign the stimuli in an asymmetric test range to the trials in Subset$_A$. The discrimination judgments made of these stimuli will be analyzed to determine their PSE; we refer to these stimuli as the Judged Range (JR). It is centered either at $m^+ > m°$, or at $m^- < m°$, and the stimuli are 2 cpd gratings. Similarly, we assign stimuli from a different test stimulus range to the $n/2$ trials in Subset$_B$; these stimuli will act as context and are referred to as the *contextual range* (CR). The contextual stimuli are isodiscriminal with the JR but are distinguished from the low SF (2 cpd) JR stimuli by their high SF, 10 cpd.

CST predicts that the CR stimuli will project traces to CSM(JR), and these may affect the location of the criterion, E_c(2 cpd). If the JR and CR are concordant, that is, both centered at m^+, or both centered at m^-, the CR will not affect the location of E_c(2 cpd). However, if the two test stimulus ranges are discordant, one centered at m^+ and the other at m^-, and if the assumption that isodiscriminal stimuli may provide effective context is correct, then the PSE shift produced by the JR will be partly or wholly cancelled out by indicator traces from the CR.

Because all trials are conducted in the same way, we can also reanalyze the data with 10 cpd (h) stimuli defined as JR, and 2 cpd (l) stimuli as CR, to see whether the location of E_c(10 cpd) is affected by the 2-cpd CR stimuli.

CST-8

If the effective extrinsic context operates by projecting indicator traces to CSM(JR), these should produce trial-by-trial variations in the JR criterion as a function of preceding contextual stimuli and responses. Thus, 2 cpd criterion estimates should show sequential dependencies not only on preceding 2 cpd trials but also on preceding 10 cpd trials (and the reverse), in the pattern predicted in Figure 6.2 and confirmed in Figure 6.4.

Figure 6.5 shows data from Lages and Treisman (2010, Experiment 1). Orientation was discriminated using an oblique reference orientation (45° [right oblique], or 135° [left oblique], data pooled, upper panel), or a vertical (90°) reference stimulus (lower panel). Two asymmetrical test stimulus ranges were used for each reference stimulus, with midpoints at 43° or 47° (or 133° or 137°) for the oblique reference, 88° or 92° for the vertical. The range midpoints and reference stimulus are indicated by vertical lines. Psychometric functions are plotted for JR–CR pairs with JR = 2 cpd, CR = 10 cpd. (Thus, "192 h88" specifies a 2-cpd JR centered on 92° intermingled with a 10-cpd CR with 88° midpoint.)

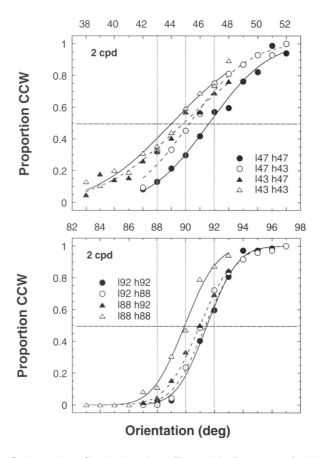

Figure 6.5. Orientation discrimination. From "A Criterion Setting Theory of Discrimination Learning That Accounts for Anisotropies and Context Effects", by M. Lages and M. Treisman, 2010, *Seeing and Perceiving, 23,* p. 417. Copyright 2010 by Brill. Reprinted with permission.

Steeper functions were predicted for permanent criteria (CST-4). The greater steepness of the vertical data, compared with the relatively ad hoc obliques is evident. Larger values of *Span* were predicted for ad hoc criteria (CST-6). The separation between positive concordant and negative concordant curves (filled circles and empty triangles) for the obliques at the 50% response level appears greater than for the vertical data. The latter shifts confirm prediction CST-5. CST-7 predicted that discordant JR-CR pairs (plotted as dashed lines) would show reduced PSE shifts. In both panels, these curves are intermediate between the concordant pairs.

Figure 6.6 shows sequential dependencies from the same experiment. The upper panel shows criterion displacements following preceding test stimuli from the same range, and the lower panel shows criterion displacements for the 10 cpd JR at different lags following 2-cpd CR stimuli. These results conform with the predictions in Figure 6.2 and confirm prediction CST-8.

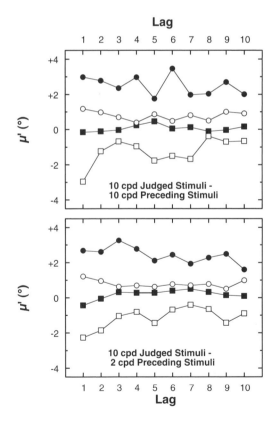

Figure 6.6. Sequential dependencies in orientation. From "A Criterion Setting Theory of Discrimination Learning That Accounts for Anisotropies and Context Effects", by M. Lages and M. Treisman, 2010, *Seeing and Perceiving, 23,* p. 422. Copyright 2010 by Brill. Reprinted with permission.

Cross-Modal Sensory Integration

We have seen that the test stimulus criterion can be modified by isodiscriminal contextual stimuli differing on a single orthogonal dimension. Can less similar extrinsic contextual stimuli, isodiscriminal stimuli differing on multiple dimensions, also be effective? Taking this further, can nonisodiscriminal stimuli affect the test criterion? There is evidence for this; cue combination in depth perception, for example, may combine inputs on different dimensions (Landy, Maloney, Johnston, & Young, 1995), speech perception may integrate hearing and visual perception of the face (Dodd & Campbell, 1987), and posture affects the visual vertical (e.g., Mittelstaedt, 1983).

To account for such findings, we introduce the concept of *functional linkage:* dimensions of discrimination are functionally linked when decisions made on either dimension can affect the same behavioral decision. For example, the distance of an object and its size are not isodiscriminal, but they are functionally linked in that distance and retinal size vary inversely, so information from one source may be relevant to judging the other, and variation on either dimension may have the same implications for function. Thus, it could be advantageous for retinal size inputs to contribute to setting criteria for distance judgments, or the reverse. We now extend CST by adding the assumption that if different stimuli vary on functionally linked dimensions, either stimulus type may act as effective extrinsic context for the other.

This allows us to construct a theory of cross-modal sensory integration based on CST. For example, alignment of the body with the direction of gravity is functionally relevant to the discrimination of departures from the vertical in vision because proprioceptive or visual detection of a deviation from the direction of gravity (which defines the visual vertical) requires a similar corrective response to maintain the organism's posture. This linkage is the condition for kinesthetic discrimination of body position to project indicator traces to the CSM for the visual vertical: CSM(vis, vertical). It follows that anisotropies may be supported not only by past judgments of test stimuli and isodiscriminal contextual stimuli but also by discriminations of functionally related stimuli in the same or different modalities. This leads to additional predictions.

CST-9

Isodiscriminal visual contextual stimuli that differ from the test stimuli on more than one orthogonal dimension may act as effective extrinsic context.

CST-10

If stimulus set B acts as effective context for an anisotropic criterion $E_c(A', \alpha)$ where α is a value on dimension A' of stimulus set A, then suppressing discrimination of the functionally relevant dimension B' of the B stimuli will reduce the anisotropy at α, increasing the variance of the psychometric function.

CST-11

The need to stay erect requires kinesthetic discrimination of the direction of gravity and the slope of the ground, and visual discrimination of vertical and horizontal, making these discriminations in each modality functionally relevant to the other. However, the same necessity does not exist for obliques. Thus, kinesthetic inputs may contribute to setting criteria for the visual cardinal orientations but should have little effect on obliques.

CST-12

Let source B and source C both act as effective context for test stimuli A, so that depriving CSM(A′, α) of input from either source impairs discrimination at α. Then suppressing information from both B and C should have a greater effect.

These predictions were tested using visual orientation discrimination (Treisman & Lages, 2010). Sine-wave gratings were presented on a computer screen in central vision in a dimly lit cubicle. MSS was used, and the reference stimuli were positioned at 45°, 90°, 135°, or 180° and followed after a 10-s delay by a block of randomly intermingled 2-cpd and 10-cpd test stimuli. An asymmetric test stimulus range was used for each reference stimulus, with midpoints at 43°, 88°, 133°, and 178°. Viewing was unrestricted (V+ condition), or a black tube and goggles allowed only the center of the screen to be seen (V–). The subjects either sat (S) or lay supine (L). They were tested under each combination of posture and viewing condition.

Two types of extrinsic context were studied: (a) peripheral visual stimuli and (b) covert postural discriminations. The peripheral visual stimuli were not formally part of the experimental stimulus presentation. These were mainly the edges of the table and apparatus and the junction lines where walls and ceiling meet. These stimuli are aligned mainly with the cardinal directions, being then isodiscriminal with the cardinal test stimuli, but they differ from them on numerous dimensions such as color, size, shape, SF, location, and duration. The covert postural discriminations have two relevant functions. When the observer sits erect (S condition) facing a vertical screen, the direction of a vertical feature on the display was closely aligned with the direction of gravity acting on the observer's body. Thus, kinesthetic discriminations serving to maintain body posture in relation to gravity could project indicator traces to CSM(vis, vertical) and CSM(vis, horizontal); we refer to these as *gravity inputs*. When subjects lying on their backs (L condition) judged stimuli on a visual display held horizontally above their heads, the relation between the gravitational vertical and the visually defined vertical on the screen was removed because gravity was then orthogonal to the display and to the long axis of the body. However, a second function of kinesthesia remains, that of monitoring changes in the relations between the parts of the body to maintain a body schema and to relate it to a schema for the immediate environment. An important component of the body schema is the long axis of the trunk and head; discriminations in relation to this may contribute to defining criteria for the cardinal axes.

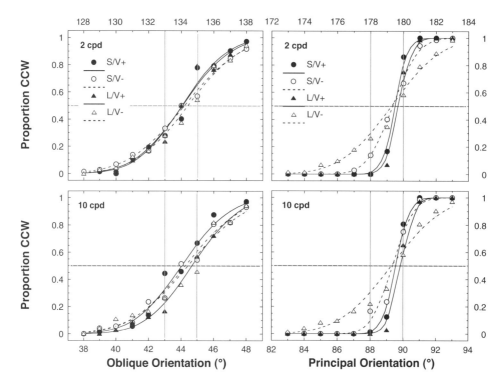

Figure 6.7. Counterclockwise (CCW) orientation responses. From "Sensory Integration Across Modalities: How Kinaesthesia Integrates With Vision in Visual Orientation Discrimination", by M. Treisman and M. Lages, 2010, *Seeing and Perceiving, 23,* p. 446. Copyright 2010 by Brill. Reprinted with permission.

Figure 6.7 shows normal curves fitted to proportions of counterclockwise responses. In each panel, the right vertical line is the reference value, and the left line is the midpoint of the test stimulus range. Filled and empty symbols of the same shape contrast the effects of displaying or occluding peripheral visual stimulation. Comparing circles and triangles (both filled or both empty) illustrates the effect of reducing kinesthetic input.

The data conform with the PSE shift prediction CST-1 and with CST-5. For both oblique and cardinal reference values, the 50% point has shifted toward the range midpoint. CST-6 predicted larger shifts for ad hoc than for permanent criteria. Thus, *Half-Span* = (PSE − reference orientation) / (Range midpoint − Reference orientation) should be greater for oblique than cardinal orientations. In every comparison, this is the case. CST-4 is also confirmed: The curves are steeper for cardinal orientations.

The results of revealing or hiding the peripheral visual stimuli accord with prediction CST-9. The differences in the right-hand panels between the S/V+ and S/V− conditions and between the L/V+ and L/V− conditions show that occluding these stimuli considerably increased the variances of the psychometric functions for the cardinal axes. However much isodiscriminal contextual stimuli may differ on other dimensions, it seems that perception can abstract the presence of the test dimension and use information from this in maintaining the criterion. Nonetheless, removing the peripheral visual stimuli, which were mainly oriented at or near the cardinal directions, did not detectably affect the curves for the obliques.

The effects on the data for the cardinal orientations conform with the prediction CST-10 that if discrimination on a dimension that contributes indicator traces to E_c(test) is suppressed, the variance of the psychometric functions will increase. This prediction is tested for kinesthetic inputs by the difference between the sitting and lying conditions. It is supported for the cardinal axes in the V– condition by the flatter slopes of the psychometric functions for L/V– than for S/V–, but it is not supported for V+; this is discussed later. In conformity with prediction CST-11, this effect is not shown by the oblique data.

It was also predicted CST-12 that the effects of removing both kinesthetic and peripheral visual information would be greater than for either alone, but this is confirmed only in part. For the cardinal axes, the comparisons between S/V+ and S/V–, and between S/V– and L/V– show this effect: The loss of postural information in the second case adds to the loss of visual information in the first. However, there is no variance increase when we go from S/V+ to L/V+: With peripheral visual stimulation present, the loss of postural information is tolerated. This last finding was not anticipated, but otherwise the results support the predictions well.

We are led to the following interpretation. We have noted that kinesthetic inputs may serve two goals. First, kinesthetic (including vestibular) inputs may provide measures of the alignment of the body with the direction of gravity, to allow us to maintain this alignment. These inputs may be used to stabilize kinesthetic criteria for the principal axes, which are defined in relation to gravity, for example, E_c(kin, vertical). Second, kinesthesia may also maintain a body schema and relate it to a schema for the immediate environment, important for understanding the lying condition. A main component of the body schema is the long axis of the trunk and head, the direction which in this experiment corresponded to the vertical on the display screen; kinesthetic inputs would be used to maintain a criterion E_c(kin, long axis) defining the general lie of the body, and this would need to be related to the visual criteria for the principal directions of space. Even in weightlessness, information about the relation of the body to the surroundings is retained.

Of the information sources that may determine the visual criteria, normal vision has the highest resolution; measures based on gravity are likely to benefit from the acuity of the vestibular system while defining the long axis of the body, mobile and flexible as it is, in relation to the other contents of space may be least precise. The CSMs for the visual cardinal criteria should weight traces from different sources in accordance with their informativeness; when a more reliable source is available, it may be advantageous to suppress those less reliable (Treisman, 1998). Our data show the lowest variances for the cardinal axes under V+ conditions. This illustrates that the peripheral visual context is here most effective in maintaining the visual criterion; the similar acuity for L/V+ and S/V+ strongly suggests that with this context present, kinesthetic inputs were given low weights or not used. Cardinal axis performance deteriorated from V+ to V–: With peripheral visual stimuli occluded, kinesthetic inputs may have been used to improve stabilization of the visual criteria. The clear advantage of S/V– over L/V– suggests that the gravity inputs available when sitting were more reliable than the body schema inputs available when subjects lay supine.

In contrast to the cardinal axes, the four combinations of viewing condition and posture produce remarkably similar results for oblique discriminations. The relatively ad hoc oblique criteria appear to gain little benefit from information relating to the cardinal axes, whether from peripheral visual or gravity-related kinesthetic sources, suggesting that no useful interpolation from cardinals to obliques is available. This result suggests that body schema kinesthetic inputs may provide a basis for consistent oblique judgments.

CST-6 predicted that PSE shifts would be larger for ad hoc than for permanent criteria. With the range of *Span* values divided, for convenience, at its midpoint, this suggests we might generally find $0 < Span(\text{permanent}) \le 0.5$, and $0.5 \le Span(\text{ad hoc}) \le 1$. Data from several experiments that bear on this prediction are plotted in Figure 6.8.

SF and ocular vergence discrimination should use ad hoc criteria; we expect *Span* to be large. The values for binocular disparity and the cardinal

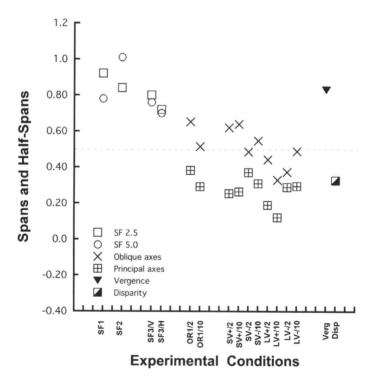

Figure 6.8. Span is plotted for three spatial frequency discrimination experiments. From "Sensory Integration Across Modalities: How Kinaesthesia Integrates With Vision in Visual Orientation Discrimination", by M. Treisman and M. Lages, 2010, *Seeing and Perceiving, 23,* p. 451. Copyright 2010 by Brill. Reprinted with permission.

axes relate to permanent criteria and should be small. Although less salient than the cardinal axes, the oblique orientations sometimes have a special place in perception and so may benefit from a smaller residue of traces. This places them intermediate between the cardinal axes and a randomly chosen unfamiliar orientation, suggesting their *Span* values should be intermediate.

If we take *Span* = 0.5 as an arbitrary point of division between "large" and "small," the *Span* values for SF (mean of 8 points, 0.82) and vergence (0.83) are all large. For the moderately salient oblique orientations, the mean is 0.49. The 10 points for the cardinal axes average 0.28 and binocular disparity is 0.33. Every result supports the theory: The 9 points predicted to be large fall above *Span* = 0.5, and the 11 points predicted to be small fall below it. The probability of this occurring by chance is $p = 2^{-20} < .000001$.

Conclusion

Recent developments in the understanding of psychophysical decision making as modeled by CST have been reviewed. The CST account of how sensory information is retained and used in sensory decision making offers an alternative to the traditional belief that sensory memory in delayed discrimination is based on comparing a current input with an internal copy of a stimulus or object, the FMT.

CST proposes that the location of the criterion, and therefore the PSE, may be affected by context. In FMTT, discrimination is determined only by the relation between the current sensory input and the FMT, the fixity of which should protect the PSE from contextual influences. We have shown that the psychometric function may shift if the test stimulus distribution shifts and that shifts may also be induced by intrinsic and extrinsic context. CST introduces a distinction between permanent and ad hoc criteria and predicts that the former should show smaller PSE shifts than the latter. FMTT implies that PSEs, like memory traces, should be fixed. Our evidence supports the CST predictions and rejects FMTT. Criterion setting predicts sequential dependencies and explains the patterns they should show. FMTT can only attribute them to random error. The CST predictions were confirmed here, including the existence of dependencies on contextual stimuli (see also Lages & Treisman, 1998, 2010; Treisman & Lages, 2010).

The implications of FMTT for psychophysics have not been adequately examined in the past, perhaps because FMTT was taken to be intuitively obvious. Therefore, in some cases, we have had to derive predictions from FMTT to investigate the theory. However, these predictions, we believe, are natural and difficult to avoid.

Magnussen and Dyrnes (1994) claimed to have demonstrated perfect retention of a "stored representation of a reference stimulus" for up to 50 hr. However, we have shown that equally good performance can be obtained in the absence of a reference stimulus, as predicted by CST, refuting this claim (Figure 6.3). Magnussen and Greenlee (1999) claimed that our findings merely demonstrate that criterion setting is a "confounding factor" in that "subjects might solve the task by a strategy of guessing" (p. 90) rather than by comparison with the memory trace. This is an interpretation we neither offered nor accept. Magnussen, Greenlee, Aslaksen, and Kildebo (2003) presented a reference stimulus for 5 s, followed either 5 s or 24 hr later by a test stimulus. They used a large number of subjects, each responding only once, and obtained similar results for both delay intervals. Magnussen et al. believed this design excludes criterion setting and, therefore, confirms that long-term memory image storage occurs.

We consider their argument to be mistaken. Under CST, exposure to the initial reference stimulus would generate one or more indicator traces, and these would determine an initial criterion value. This would be available when the first test stimulus is presented. Indicator traces can be preserved for long intervals by setting δ at or near zero, allowing performance to be similar at both short and long delay intervals. Thus, their experiment does not distinguish between the theories. Lages and Paul (2006) replicated their experiment but controlled for the effects of stimuli that were presented in training (which were centered on the reference in the original experiment) and failed to confirm the claimed "high-fidelity" sensory memory.

CST provides a new understanding of the role of context: This is used as an information source that contributes to maximizing sensory performance by optimizing the current value of the criterion. Effective context includes past exposures to stimuli of the type being judged, in the same or earlier sessions, and it includes extrinsic context, whether isodiscriminal or not, similar or not, in the same modality or not, provided the contextual stimuli are functionally linked to the stimuli undergoing discrimination and so can provide relevant information. CST offers a basis for understanding discrimination learning, sequential dependencies, different contextual effects, and anisotropies. It offers a model of cross-modal sensory integration that may help us understand how the perceptual processes align the spatial frameworks constructed by different modalities to produce the coordinated whole, which is the basis of integrated perception. Application of the model to orientation anisotropy in vision has provided evidence that this is at least partly determined by integration of information from covert postural and peripheral visual orientation judgments.

An alternative to traditional memory trace theory was put forward by Bartlett (1932), who rejected the idea that remembering was accomplished by "the re-excitation of innumerable fixed, lifeless and fragmentary traces." Memory was not "reduplicative" but a "construction" based on "a whole, active mass of organized past reactions or experience" (p. 213), continually modified by new experiences, which he referred to as a schema. However, Bartlett did not offer a model of the processes underlying the schema or explain how it arose. CST proposes and the present results support a model for information retention that is similar in spirit to Bartlett's proposed flexibly modifiable schemata, but that is anchored in the need to optimize discrimination performance.

We have shown that CST can provide an account of the role of memory in determining successful performance of psychophysical procedures such as discrimination. The same principles may offer a basis for developing accounts of the operation of procedural memory in other and more complex skills.

References

Aristotle. (350 BCE/2007). On memory and reminiscence. (J. I. Beare, Trans.). Retrieved from http://ebooks.adelaide.edu.au/a/aristotle/memory

Bartlett, F. (1932). *Remembering: A study in experimental and social psychology*. London, England: Cambridge University Press.

Dodd, B., & Campbell, R. (Eds.). (1987). *Hearing by eye: The psychology of lip-reading*. Hillsdale, NJ: Erlbaum.

Green, D. M., & Swets, J. A. (1966). *Signal detection theory and psychophysics*. New York, NY: Wiley.

Lages, M., & Paul, A. (2006). Visual long-term memory for spatial frequency? *Psychonomic Bulletin & Review, 13*, 486–492. doi:10.3758/BF03193874

Lages, M., & Treisman, M. (1998). Spatial frequency discrimination: Visual permanent memory or criterion setting? *Vision Research, 38*, 557–572. doi:10.1016/S0042-6989(97)88333-2

Lages, M., & Treisman, M. (2010). A criterion setting theory of discrimination learning that accounts for anisotropies and context effects. *Seeing and Perceiving, 23*, 401–434. doi:10.1163/187847510X541117

Landy, M. S., Maloney, L. T., Johnston, E. B., & Young, M. (1995). Measurement and modeling of depth cue combination: In defense of weak fusion. *Vision Research, 35*, 389–412. doi:10.1016/0042-6989(94)00176-M

Magnussen, S. (2000). Low-level memory processes in vision. *Trends in Neurosciences, 23*, 247–251. doi:10.1016/S0166-2236(00)01569-1

Magnussen, S., & Dyrnes, S. (1994). High-fidelity perceptual permanent memory. *Psychological Science, 5*, 99–102. doi:10.1111/j.1467-9280.1994.tb00638.x

Magnussen, S., & Greenlee, M. W. (1999). The psychophysics of perceptual memory. *Psychological Research, 62*, 81–92. doi:10.1007/s004260050043

Magnussen, S., Greenlee, M. W., Aslaksen, P. M., & Kildebo, O. O. (2003). High-fidelity perceptual long-term memory revisited and confirmed. *Psychological Science, 14*, 74–76. doi:10.1111/1467-9280.01421

Mittelstaedt, H. (1983). A new solution to the problem of the subjective vertical. *Naturwissenschaften, 70*, 272–281. doi:10.1007/BF00404833

Orban, G. A., & Vogels, R. (1998). The neuronal machinery involved in successive orientation discrimination. *Progress in Neurobiology, 55*, 117–147. doi:10.1016/S0301-0082(98)00010-0

Treisman, M. (1984a). Contingent aftereffects and situationally coded criteria. *Annals of the New York Academy of Sciences, 423*, 131–141. doi:10.1111/j.1749-6632.1984.tb23423.x

Treisman, M. (1984b). A theory of criterion setting: An alternative to the attention band and response ratio hypotheses in magnitude estimation and cross-modality matching. *Journal of Experimental Psychology: General, 113*, 443–463. doi:10.1037/0096-3445.113.3.443

Treisman, M. (1985). The magical number seven and some other features of category scaling: Properties of a model for absolute judgment. *Journal of Mathematical Psychology, 29*, 175–230. doi:10.1016/0022-2496(85)90015-X

Treisman, M. (1987). Effects of the setting and adjustment of decision criteria on psychophysical performance. In: E. E. Roskam & R. Suck (Eds.), *Progress in mathematical psychology* (Vol. 1, pp. 253–297). Amsterdam, the Netherlands: Elsevier Science.

Treisman, M. (1998). Combining information: Probability summation and probability averaging in detection and discrimination. *Psychological Methods, 3*, 252–265. doi:10.1037/1082-989X.3.2.252

Treisman, M., & Faulkner, A. (1984a). The effect of signal probability on the slope of the receiver operating characteristic given by the rating procedure. *British Journal of Mathematical and Statistical Psychology, 37*, 199–215. doi:10.1111/j.2044-8317.1984.tb00800.x

Treisman, M., & Faulkner, A. (1984b). The setting and maintenance of criteria representing levels of confidence. *Journal of Experimental Psychology: Human Perception and Performance, 10*, 119–139. doi:10.1037/0096-1523.10.1.119

Treisman, M., & Faulkner, A. (1985). Can decision criteria interchange locations? Some positive evidence. *Journal of Experimental Psychology: Human Perception and Performance, 11*, 187–208. doi:10.1037/0096-1523.11.2.187

Treisman, M., & Faulkner, A. (1987). Generation of random sequences by human subjects: Cognitive operations or psychophysical process? *Journal of Experimental Psychology: General, 116,* 337–355. doi:10.1037/0096-3445.116.4.337

Treisman, M., Faulkner, A., Naish, P. L. N., & Rosner, B. S. (1995). Voice-onset time and tone-onset time: The role of criterion-setting mechanisms in categorical perception. *The Quarterly Journal of Experimental Psychology, 48,* 334–366.

Treisman, M., & Lages, M. (2010). Sensory integration across modalities: How kinaesthesia integrates with vision in visual orientation discrimination. *Seeing and Perceiving, 23,* 435–462. doi:10.1163/187847510X541126

Treisman, M., & Williams, T. C. (1984). A theory of criterion setting with an application to sequential dependencies. *Psychological Review, 91,* 68–111. doi:10.1037/0033-295X.91.1.68

7

Short-Term Visual Priming Across Eye Movements

Stephen E. Denton and Richard M. Shiffrin

The perceptual system has evolved to interpret rapid sequences of events. Processing events takes time, so perceptual information must persist long enough to allow it to be assessed (Sperling, 1960). Persistence combined with a continuous flow of sensory input poses challenges caused by the likely prospect of confusions between perceptual features. Thus, in general, the perceptual system, and the visual system in particular, must carry out probabilistic inference to determine the origin of perceived information. Examples of visual inference abound, from the apparent clarity of the visual world despite apparent defects in the retina (e.g., blind spots and unevenly spaced receptors) producing nonuniform visual acuity (O'Regan, 1992) to the many examples of change blindness (Rensink, 2002; Simons & Ambinder, 2005). Sperling's research contains a number of examples of visual inference, including the way motion is perceived by first-, second-, and particularly third-order (attentional) processes (Lu & Sperling, 1995, 2001).

Huber, Shiffrin, Lyle, and Ruys (2001) explored the way the visual system performs inference in the face of successive perceptual inputs using a direct and simple task: visual priming. A prime is presented before a brief target flash, and the features of the prime and target become confused. The *responding optimally to unknown sources of evidence* (ROUSE) model proposed by Huber et al. (2001) explains the inference processes that allow perceived features to be assigned evidence values and hence allow a decision about the target to be made. Their research was restricted to static perceptual conditions, without eye movements. In life generally, and in such situations such as reading, the eyes are moving many times per second. In this chapter, we present primes in one location and cue the eyes to move to another relatively distant location where the target appears, asking whether similar feature confusions and inference processes operate. In part because reading is important, we use words as stimuli (Huber et al., 2001), although the conclusions should apply generally.

DOI: 10.1037/14135-008

Human Information Processing: Vision, Memory, and Attention, C. Chubb, B. A. Dosher, Z.-L. Lu, and R. M. Shiffrin (Editors)

Short-Term Visual Priming

A first stimulus, the *prime,* influences perception of an immediate following stimulus, the *target.* Early theories posited the existence of *spreading activation* because it was thought that activation spread from the prime to target, thereby speeding responding (Collins & Loftus, 1975; McNamara, 1992, 1994). However, priming sometimes slowed responding (Hochhaus & Johnston, 1996), results elaborated in the research by Huber and colleagues, whose research provided convincing evidence for an alternative account based on feature confusions between prime and target and the use of inference processes. In a visual identification task, Huber et al. (2001) presented two prime words, of variable duration, followed by a flashed and postmasked target word. The target flash was followed by two choice words: the target and a foil. The primes could match the target only (target-primed condition), the foil only (foil-primed condition), neither (neither-primed condition), or both (both-primed condition).[1] When primes appeared for short durations (< 400 ms), there was a positive priming preference—a tendency to select whatever choice had been primed, whether correct or incorrect. When primes appeared for longer durations, this preference reversed: There was a tendency to select the choice that had not been primed. The dependence on prime duration argued against spreading activation accounts and led to an alternative Bayesian-inspired inference model termed *ROUSE.* This model accounts for these and many other, often counterintuitive findings (Huber, Shiffrin, Quach, & Lyle, 2002; Weidemann, Huber, & Shiffrin, 2005, 2008).

ROUSE has two key components: The *source confusion* portion of the model posits that the perceived features following the target flash are a mixture of target and prime features, without source information identifying which is which. This factor alone tends to produce positive priming, because the presence of prime features will tend to increase the match between the precept and any choice that shares prime features. The second component, a *discounting* mechanism in the model, tends to counteract and can even reverse this preference, because this component posits that perceived features are used as evidence for one choice or the other, and feature evidence is discounted (lowered) when known to have come from the prime. If the degree of feature intrusions from primes were known, a normative Bayesian decision process could assign an amount of discounting that would eliminate any positive or negative priming effect. However, ROUSE assumes that the amount of feature intrusions from primes is not known exactly and must be estimated. Furthermore, and most critically, this estimate is assumed to be a little lower than the actual degree of intrusions for short primes, resulting in positive priming, and a little

---

[1]In most priming experiments, the mix of conditions is such that the primes are truly irrelevant to performance on average and are just as likely to indicate the incorrect choice as the correct choice. Furthermore, participants are informed that the primes are irrelevant, and trial-by-trial feedback demonstrates this to be the case.

higher than the actual degree of intrusions for long primes, resulting in negative priming. Note that it is the difference between the actual intrusion rate and the estimated intrusion rate that produces positive or negative priming. The actual rate could be quite low for brief or subliminal primes and much higher for long primes.

A critical temporal component of priming is the interstimulus interval (ISI) between prime and target. For example, an ISI greater than 250 ms disrupts and diminishes priming (Hochhaus & Marohn, 1991), consistent with processing of prime and target as separate events. An eye movement between prime and target, as in the present research, mandates a certain minimum ISI that will somewhat reduce effect size compared with the previous static studies.

Feature Carryover Across Eye Movements

Eye movements (*saccades*) are made mainly to bring important visual features of the environment into the high acuity part of the visual field. Visual information is extracted during the *fixations* when the eye is still between saccades. We ask whether features from primes migrate to a target percept when an eye movement separates the two, whether their source is known, and whether the evidence they supply is discounted. In our critical conditions, the prime occurs at fixation, and the eyes move to a relatively distant location (10° visual angle) where the target appears. If prime features do transfer across saccades, the different spatial locations of features coming from the prime and target might either prevent confusions or change the degree of discounting.

Experiment 1: Priming Across Eye Movements

The standard priming condition had prime and target words in the same spatial location; the experimental condition had prime and target words spatially separated. The prime word was presented in the center of the screen for either 50 or 1,000 ms. The prime word was identical to the target, the foil, or neither. The target word was flashed in the center of the display on half the trials and on the other half it appeared equally often in one of four locations: above, below, left, or right of center (all at an eccentricity of 10°). We did not directly measure eye movements, but an eye movement was necessary to perform the task in the eye-movement conditions given that visual acuity drops to roughly 25% (of central vision) at a visual eccentricity of 10° (Low, 1951). Following the target flash and mask, the target and a foil were presented (at the location at which the target was flashed), and the participant's task was to choose which was the target. A schematic of two example trials is presented in Figure 7.1.

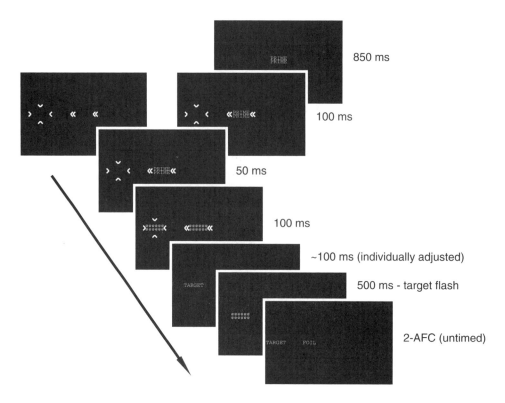

850 ms

100 ms

50 ms

100 ms

~100 ms (individually adjusted)

500 ms - target flash

2-AFC (untimed)

Figure 7.1. An example sequence of events in the present experiments.

Participants

Fifty-one undergraduate students volunteered to participate for partial credit in an introductory psychology course at Indiana University.

Materials and Apparatus

We used two pools of 1,100 five-letter and 1,600 six-letter words with a written-language frequency of at least three per millions as defined by Kučera and Francis (1967). All words were presented in uppercase using the fixed-width Courier Bold 17-point font. Stimulus words were sampled randomly without replacement with the only constraint being that five- and six-letter words never appeared together in the same block of trials. All masking was done with two rows of six "@" signs presented in Arial Narrow Bold 13-point font. This ensured dense coverage of the prime and target. Stimulus words were presented in white against a black background.

All stimuli were displayed on 16-in. (40.6 cm) PC CRT monitors with vertical refresh rates of 120 Hz and a screen resolution of 800 × 600 pixels. The experiment was programmed using the Vision Egg library for the Python programming language (Straw, 2008). The display was synchronized to the vertical refresh of the monitor providing display increments of 8.33 ms. Participant responses were collected using a standard computer keyboard.

Procedure

The eye movement and control conditions were matched on a variety of possible contaminating factors, including certain critical elements of timing. A 10° saccade takes less than 50 ms to complete once initiated but takes more than 150 ms to plan and initiate (Irwin, Brown, & Sun, 1988). Thus, a masked target flash appearing in the periphery immediately after the prime would not be visible because it would be gone before the eyes arrived. We therefore provided an advance cue for the target location at the central (prime) location, with timing such that the eyes remained at fixation during prime presentation yet arrived at the distant target location before the target was flashed. The same timing was used in the control conditions.

Participants sat individually in a dimly lit, ventilated, sound-dampened booth. Participants were asked to sit up straight to keep the distance from their eyes to the monitor at approximately 50 cm, but no head restraint was used to enforce this viewing distance. This viewing distance ensured that peripheral targets would appear at a minimum of 10° visual angle away from the center of the screen.

On each trial, a fixation cross appears in the center of the screen for 500 ms. Then (as in prior research), the prime is displayed twice, one directly above the other (Figure 7.1). In long prime conditions, the prime is presented for 1,000 ms. Starting 150 ms before the end of this 1-s period, the target position indicator is added (depicted in the first three frames of the right sequence in Figure 7.1). In peripheral target conditions, the target position indicator provides a cue to initiate a saccade, which will take roughly 150 ms to plan. The prime is replaced by a mask immediately after the initial 1,000 ms period expires. The position indicator and the mask appear together for 100 ms. This 100-ms masking period provides a long window to complete a saccade, which should have only taken participants roughly 50 ms to perform. The target then appears in the indicated location for a short period (individually adjusted but approximately 100 ms for the average participant, as discussed later). In the peripheral conditions, it is unlikely that the target will be seen at all if the saccade to the target location is not completed during the 100-ms masking period. The target is followed by a 500-ms mask in the same location and then by two choice words to the right and left of the target location. There are two location indicators for a peripheral target: central arrows pointing toward the peripheral location and four carets bracketing the target location. In the central target condition, there is just one indicator, four carets bracketing the central location. In trials with short prime durations, the target indicator appears first by itself for 100 ms, then the prime and the target indicator appear together for 50 ms. The subsequent trial events are the same as for the long prime condition. Once again, the target position indicator provides the cue to initiate a saccade. Participants should not have been able to plan and initiate a saccade in less than 100 ms, ensuring that the prime would be viewed before the saccade was performed; thus, the prime was "snuck in" before the eyes had a chance to move. As in the long prime condition, the eyes would land on the peripheral target location before the target was flashed there. Note that central target trials had the same timing as peripheral target trials.

Each participant had 672 priming trials, broken into seven blocks of 96. The participant identified the target word by pressing the F or J key to choose the left or right alternative, respectively. Once a selection was made, feedback was provided. The first 32 trials were neither-primed practice trials with long target durations (150 ms). There were then 64 neither-primed calibration trials. Target word durations were individually adjusted for each subject such that accuracy was roughly 75% on neither-primed conditions. This calibration was done separately for the center and peripheral target locations using a staircase method. As with previous studies (Huber et al., 2001; Weidemann et al., 2005), there were large individual differences. For center target trials, target flash times ranged from 25 to 91.7 ms, with a median of 50 ms. For peripheral targets, flash times ranged from 33.3 ms to 200 ms (the maximum allowed), with a median of 91.7 ms. The increase in flash times and their variability for peripheral locations is likely due to individual differences in saccade latency layered on top of individual differences in target processing time.

Results and Discussion

Data from all peripheral target locations were combined. Trials with RTs less than 100 ms or more than 3,000 ms were eliminated (roughly 1% of the data). Statistical analysis used a $3 \times 2 \times 2$ (Priming Condition × Prime Duration × Target Location) repeated-measures analysis of variance.

There were large main effects of prime condition, $F(2, 100) = 167.6, p < .001$, and prime duration, $F(1, 50) = 135.5, p < .001$. Also, these two variables interacted, $F(2, 100) = 121.37, p < .001$. Although the main effect of target location was not significant, this variable had a significant interaction with both prime condition, $F(2, 100) = 20.43, p < .001$, and prime duration, $F(1, 50) = 8.637, p < .005$. Finally, there was a significant three-way (Priming Condition × Prime Duration × Target Location) interaction, $F(2, 100) = 48.57, p < .001$.

Average accuracy is shown in Figure 7.2. The dots in the figure give ROUSE model predictions (discussed later). For short primes, there is a strong positive priming effect that replicates prior research; that is, there is a tendency to select the primed choice. The effect appears in both central and peripheral conditions, although the magnitude is smaller in the peripheral conditions. For long primes, this pattern shifted considerably, but not as dramatically as in prior research. In previous research, negative priming occurred in the long prime conditions, whereas the present long prime results for both central and peripheral conditions showed neutral priming. These less dramatic shifts with long primes are likely due to the delay that had to be introduced in both central and peripheral conditions to allow eye movements to be made to a peripheral target. Note that the data show higher neither-primed performance for long than for short prime durations, a result found in prior research. We assume the

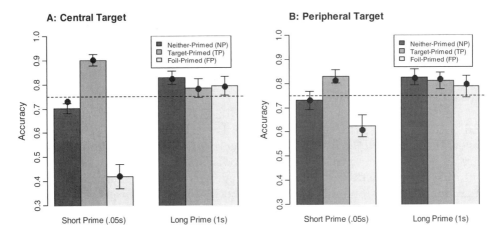

Figure 7.2. Forced choice performance for Experiment 1 and corresponding similarity ROUSE predictions (represented by the dots). The bar heights show the mean proportions of correct target identification choices within each condition (error bars show ± 95% confidence intervals). Panel A shows accuracy for centrally located targets. Panel B shows accuracy when the target was presented in a peripheral location. Each panel is subdivided by prime duration and priming condition. The dashed horizontal line indicates 75% performance; the accuracy participants should roughly achieve on neither-primed trials due to the target duration calibration procedure.

effect is due to extra perceptual noise introduced when primes are short and incorporate this assumption in the ROUSE model presented and discussed in the following section.

The ROUSE Model

For a detailed exposition of ROUSE, the reader is referred to Huber et al. (2001) for the original stochastic version and Huber (2006) for a later analytic version. Choice words and the perceived target word, the percept, are represented as vectors of 20 binary features, features thought to be mostly orthographic in the present context. The features of the target and foil choice words are matched against the current target percept, with matching features providing evidence for that choice alternative and mismatching features providing evidence against that choice alternative. The percept is the result of stochastic feature activation from the prime, with probability α; the target, with probability β; and noise, with probability γ. The percept features are not labeled by source, so the prime features that join the percept (due to α), if not counteracted, will lead to a preference for whichever choice alternative is primed.

This positive priming preference is counteracted by a *discounting* process that assigns lower levels of evidence to features that might have been activated by the prime word (i.e., discounting). Optimal discounting would require knowledge of the "true" probabilities α, β, and γ, but ROUSE assumes these are not known and must be estimated: The estimates are termed α', β', and γ'. Estimates of β and γ are theorized to be close to their true values. However, α varies with the conditions of any visual setting, and its estimates are not assumed to match the true values. A wide range of results are explained by assuming that the estimate is a little high ($\alpha' > \alpha$: too much discounting) for primes presented longer and attended more, and a little low ($\alpha' < \alpha$: too little discounting) for primes presented briefly and attended less.

Feature evidence takes the form of a likelihood ratio specifying the probability that a feature is from the target word over the probability the feature is part of the foil, given the feature's current activation state and whether the feature appeared in the prime. Assuming conditional independence between the features, feature evidence can be multiplied together across all word features to produce an overall likelihood that the choice word is the target. The optimal response selects the choice word with the larger likelihood (guessing for ties).

A final important parameter of the model is ρ, representing the similarity between a prime and a given choice (i.e., the proportion of features in a target or foil choice option that match the prime and therefore could conceivably be activated by it). When the prime and choice are the same, ρ is set to 1.0. Experiment 1 (as with many previous studies) used primes that are random with respect to a foil choice, thereby allowing chance letter overlaps, but for simplicity, ρ was set to 0.0 (this confound is controlled in Experiment 2). When primes and choices vary in similarity, as in some past studies and in our Experiment 2, then ρ is allowed to vary accordingly.

Applying the ROUSE Model to Experiment 1

ROUSE was fit to the data using published algorithms (Huber, 2006). The model is applied in its normal form, with one exception: Because neither-primed performance is better for longer primes, noise (the γ parameter) was allowed to be higher for shorter primes. This change uniformly lowers performance for shorter primes. In principle, the actual feature intrusion probabilities from primes might well vary with prime duration. However, the predictions are determined almost entirely by the relative magnitude of the actual intrusion rate and the estimated intrusion rate. The actual rate was therefore set to a single value that did not differ with prime duration, and only the estimated intrusion values were allowed to vary. Following the precedents set in earlier modeling (Huber et al., 2001; Weidemann et al., 2005), it is assumed that estimates of feature activations due to targets and noise are equal to the actual values (i.e., $\beta' \equiv \beta$ and $\gamma' \equiv \gamma$) and that the similarity of a prime and a prime choice word when both appear at the same central location is fixed at identity (i.e., $\rho_C = 1.0$).

These stipulations being fixed, we compared versions of ROUSE that differed in the parameters allowed to vary between the central and peripheral (eye-movement) conditions. Here we report only models that allowed α, α', and ρ to vary. The various restrictions have different conceptual justifications. The most restricted model varied none of these parameters and, not surprisingly, could not fit well. The most general model, termed *unrestricted*, allowed each of these parameters to differ. This version, of course, does well and serves as a benchmark to which the restricted models can be compared. The models were assessed with nested model comparisons. Fitting the *unrestricted* ROUSE model involves estimating the following 10 parameters:

1. the probability that a choice word feature is activated by the prime located in the same central location (α_C),
2. the probability that a choice word feature is activated by a prime that is located at a previous fixation location (α_P),
3. the estimated probability that a feature is activated by a short prime when the prime and target are located in the center ($\alpha'_{S.C}$),
4. the estimated probability that a feature is activated by a long prime located in the center ($\alpha'_{L.C}$),
5. the estimated probability that a feature is activated by a short prime from a previous fixation ($\alpha'_{S.P}$),
6. the estimated probability that a feature is activated by a long prime from a previous fixation ($\alpha'_{L.P}$),
7. the probability that a feature is activated due to the target flash (β),
8. the probability that a feature is activated due to noise given a short prime presentation (γ_S),
9. the probability that a feature is activated due to noise given a long prime duration (γ_L), and
10. the proportion of features that are shared between a prime and a prime choice option when the target appears at the periphery, ρ_P.

There are four restricted models fit to the data: (a) the baseline no-variation model assumes that the parameters do not change between central and peripheral conditions, (b) the prime intrusion probability is the same (i.e., $\alpha_C = \alpha_P = \alpha$), (c) the estimates of these probabilities within each prime duration condition are the same (i.e., $\alpha'_{S.C} = \alpha'_{S.P} = \alpha'_S$ and $\alpha'_{L.C} = \alpha'_{L.P} = \alpha'_L$), and (d) prime similarity to the primed choice word is the same (i.e., $\rho_P = \rho_C = \rho = 1.0$). Given these constraints, the *restricted* model has six free parameters. There are three partially restricted models: (a) When the "true" prime intrusion probability is allowed to vary between central and peripheral target conditions, the model is termed differential *source confusion;* (b) when the estimates of the prime feature intrusion probabilities for both short and long prime durations are allowed to vary, the model is termed differential *discounting;* and (c) when the similarity is allowed to drop for the peripheral conditions, representing the possibility that prime features may be lost during the execution of an eye movement, the model is termed differential *similarity.*

Each of the five models was fit to 12 independent data values from Experiment 1 (shown in Figure 7.2), and the resulting best fit values are presented in Table 7.1. The *similarity* model provides the best quantitative fit to the data out of the nested models. Furthermore, the *similarity* model's fit is not significantly different from the *unrestricted* model given that the difference in fit ($G_{similarity} - G_{unrestricted} = 1.52$) is far less than expected difference ($\chi^2(\alpha = .05$, $df = 3) = 7.81$). The quite good predictions of the *similarity* model are shown in Figure 7.2. The best fitting parameters for this model are: $\alpha = .233$, $\alpha'_S = .0534$, $\alpha'_L = .234$, $\beta = .146$, $\gamma_S = .347$, $\gamma_L = .163$, and $\rho_P = .510$.

Table 7.1. Model Goodness-of-Fit Values

Model	No. of free parameters	Experiment 1 fit (G)	Experiment 2 fit (G)
Restricted	6	295.5	543.5
Source confusion	7	41.15	264.9
Discounting	8	33.33	199.3
Similarity[a]	7	20.07	132.4
Unrestricted	10	18.56	132.2

Note. [a]The fits of the similarity model are presented in Figures 7.2 and 7.3.

The *similarity* model assumes that eye movements cause an effective loss of features from the prime. Several justifications for this loss are conceivable. Features activated by the prime could be suppressed, misinterpreted, or otherwise lost before they have a chance to join the target precept. Saccades could differentially suppress low-level features (see the final discussion at the end of the chapter). Spatial distortions with eye movements could distort some features. Peripheral target signals may have diverted attention and reduced processing of the prime features. These and other possibilities cannot be distinguished on the basis of the present studies. Whatever the cause, the loss of prime features in the eye-movement condition in effect makes prime and matching choice word nonidentical. Source confusion and discounting operate similarly in the central and peripheral target conditions but over a reduced proportion of prime activated features in the peripheral condition. To test the idea that eye movements affect similarity while leaving source confusion and discounting processes largely unaltered, we performed a second experiment with added conditions that explicitly manipulated similarity between prime and choice.

Experiment 2: Similarity Variation

If similarity between prime and a primed choice word is reduced when there is an intervening eye movement, then such an effect could be mimicked by an explicit similarity manipulation. Following Huber, Shiffrin, Lyle, and Quach (2002), who varied orthographic similarity and verified a priori ROUSE predictions, we varied the number of letters kept the same between words but used central and peripheral priming as in Experiment 1. If prime similarity is altered by an eye movement, then the peripheral condition results should be an offset version of the central conditions.

Experiment 2 was much the same as Experiment 1: The novel manipulation was the addition of six similarity conditions. The six similarity conditions correspond to the letter overlap (in the same position) between the prime and the primed choice word (either the target or the foil). The six orthographic similarity conditions were 0, 1, 2, 3, 4, or all letters different (0 is the repetition priming condition and all letters different is the neither-primed condition from Experiment 1).

Participants

Seventy-nine undergraduate students volunteered to participate for partial credit in an introductory psychology course at Indiana University. Of these 79 participants, five did not complete the experiment, and an additional nine were discarded because they responded in less than 100 ms on more than 10% of their trials.

Materials and Apparatus

All materials and equipment (word sets, experiment software, monitors, etc.) were the same as those in Experiment 1. Both the five- and six-letter word sets from Experiment 1 were used. For five-letter words, the six similarity conditions correspond 5, 4, 3, 2, 1, and 0 letters the same (and in the same position) between prime and primed choice word. For the six-letter words, the six conditions correspond to 6, 5, 4, 3, 2, and 0 letters the same. For each participant, the words were extensively sorted into triads at the beginning of the experiment. The first two words in each triad were chosen to have a particular number of overlapping letters in the same position and no incidental letter overlap otherwise. These two words were used as the prime and the primed choice word (either target or foil) with letter overlap specified by similarity condition. The third word in each triad was chosen such that there was no letter overlap, in position or otherwise, between it and the first two words of the triad. This word was used as the unprimed choice word, and, as such, it was always the case that the two choice words appearing at the end of each trial had no letter overlap.

Procedure

The procedure used in Experiment 2 is also much the same as in Experiment 1. The eye-movement manipulation, with a target indicator cue and masking, was unaltered. The timing of individual trials (fixation duration, ISI, etc.) was also the same, except that long duration primes now appeared for 2 s, which meant that the prime appeared in duplicate for 1,850 ms and then appeared together with the target indicator for an additional 150 ms.

There were 864 priming trials, broken into nine blocks of 96. The first block had 32 practice trials, followed by 64 calibration trials with separate calibrations for center and peripheral trials. For center target trials, target flash times ranged from 16.7 to 117 ms, with a median of 41.7 ms. For peripheral targets, flash times ranged from 16.7 to 192 ms, with a median of 83.3 ms. Four subsequent blocks used five-letter words, and four used six-letter words.

Results and Discussion

Data from all peripheral target locations were combined. Trials with responses less than 100 ms or more than 3,000 ms were eliminated (< 1% of the data).

Table 7.2. Experiment 2: Statistical Test Results

Effect	(df_N, df_D)	F
Similarity	(5, 320)	6.241****
Priming condition	(1,64)	127.6****
Prime duration	(1,64)	361.0***
Target location	(1,64)	14.66****
Similarity × Priming Condition	(5, 320)	24.51****
Similarity × Prime Duration	(5, 320)	2.868**
Priming Condition × Prime Duration	(1,64)	203.8****
Similarity × Target Location	(5, 320)	1.110
Priming Condition × Target Location	(1,64)	75.48****
Prime Duration × Target Location	(1,64)	11.49***
Similarity × Priming Condition × Prime Duration	(5, 320)	44.22****
Similarity × Priming Condition × Target Location	(5, 320)	8.212****
Similarity × Prime Duration × Target Location	(5, 320)	2.036*
Priming Condition × Prime Duration × Target Location	(1,64)	77.76****
Similarity × Priming Condition × Prime Duration × Target Location	(5, 320)	8.877****

Note. $*p < .1.$ $**p < .05.$ $***p < .01.$ $****p < .001.$

The data were analyzed with a $6 \times 2 \times 2 \times 2$ (Similarity × Priming Condition × Prime Duration × Target Location) repeated measures analysis of variance (see Table 7.2). Average accuracy is presented in Figure 7.3.

The results reproduce and extend those from Experiment 1. For short primes, the data for the central condition (Panel A1) show the usual strong bias to select the choice that matched the prime, an effect that gradually diminished as the dissimilarity between the two increased. The data for the peripheral condition (Panel B1) are similar but the magnitude of the effect is smaller. When the prime was presented for a longer duration (Figure 7.3, Panels A2 and B2), this prime preference disappeared.

Applying the ROUSE Model to Experiment 2

The ROUSE models used for Experiment 1 were fit with new parameter values to Experiment 2, with the addition that the prime similarity parameter, ρ, was varied by decreasing its value linearly for each letter different between the prime and the primed target word. For the central conditions, ρ_C went from 1 to 0 in increments of 0.2. For the peripheral conditions, ρ_P, the initial repetition priming similarity estimate, was similarly reduced to zero in increments of 20%.

The resultant models were each fit to the 48 independent data values from Experiment 2 (shown in Figure 7.3), and the resulting goodness-of-fit values are presented in Table 7.1. As seen in Table 7.1, the *similarity* model once again provides the best quantitative fit to the data and greatly outperforms both the *source confusion* and *discounting* models. Furthermore, it is only ever

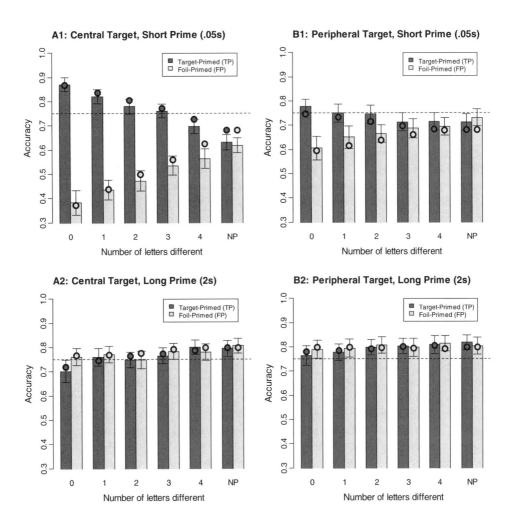

Figure 7.3. Forced choice performance for Experiment 2 and corresponding similarity ROUSE model predictions (represented by the dots). The bar heights show the mean proportions of correct target identification choices (error bars show ± 95% confidence intervals) within each condition. Panel A1 shows accuracy across priming and similarity conditions when the target is centrally located and the prime duration is short. Panel A2 shows accuracy when the prime is long and the target is centrally located. Panels B1 and B2 present the accuracy for short and long prime durations, respectively, when the target appears at the periphery. The last two bars labeled "NP" in each figure panel correspond to two experimentally equivalent neither-primed conditions (i.e., target and foil priming with zero letter overlap). The bars were left separate only so that each bar shown is based on approximately the same number of observations in the 6 × 2 (similarity × prime condition) experimental design.

so slightly worse than the *unrestricted* model. The parameters used to generate the similarity model predictions seen in Figure 7.3 are as follows: $\alpha = .380$,
$\alpha'_S = .177$, $\alpha'_L = .414$, $\beta = .107$, $\gamma_S = .329$, $\gamma_L = .106$, and $\rho_P = .275$.

General Discussion

We showed that prime features migrate across an eye movement of substantial
size (10°) and join the target percept at the new fixation location. However, the
similarity of prime to choice words is reduced by the eye movement, reducing
the number of shared features between a prime and a matching choice word.
The inference processes that then operate on the features in the percept are the
same for both the central and eye-movement conditions: Because the features are
not identified as to their source, discounting mechanisms are used to reduce the
evidentiary value of features known to be in primes. The discounting depends on
an estimate of the actual intrusion probability, and this estimate is too low for
short primes. In previous research without a delay between prime and target, the
results for long primes reversed, and negative priming was observed; hence, the
estimated intrusion probability for long primes was set to be to be higher than
the actual probability. However, in the present research, with a delay between
prime and target, the priming effect did not reverse for long primes and only
disappeared. Thus, in our modeling, for longer primes, the estimated intrusion
rate and the actual rate were about equal. In sum, the perceptual and inference
processes in visual priming are much the same with and without eye movements
between prime and target, with only the magnitudes differing, probably due to
changes in timing.

Irwin (1992) showed that saccades effectively erase iconic memory (Sperling,
1960). A few visual items (three or four) are retained from one eye fixation to
the next in what is termed transsaccadic memory (Irwin, 1992; Prime, Tsotsos,
Keith, & Crawford, 2007), which is a short-term visual memory store that
has a limited capacity compared with iconic memory but a longer duration
(Hollingworth, Richard, & Luck, 2008; Melcher & Colby, 2008; Rayner, 2009).
Because an eye movement effectively masks low-level visual features in iconic
memory from the previous fixation, subsequent inference must be based on
higher level features (that are more likely to be location-independent or at least
more transferable across eye movements). If source confusion and discounting
operate with such features, then an eye movement would not eliminate priming effects. This hypothesis is consistent with the findings of Huber et al. (2001)
and particularly Sanborn, Malmberg, and Shiffrin (2004), who showed that the
use of pattern post masks after a brief target makes subsequent visual inference depend on high-level rather than low-level visual features. Nonetheless,
if some residual inference relies on lower level features despite the presence of
a mask, and these are purged during the execution of a saccade (due to either
suppression or distortion), that could help explain why eye movements slightly
degrade the effectiveness of priming (i.e., partial feature loss as supposed by
the *similarity* model). Alternatively, if some prime features are insufficiently

encoded due to a presaccadic shift of attention away from the prime location, this would provide a similar explanation for the degradation of priming effects across eye movements that, in the present context, would be indistinguishable from the feature loss explanation provided by the similarity model.

References

Collins, A. M., & Loftus, E. F. (1975). Spreading activation theory of semantic processing. *Psychological Review, 82,* 407–428. doi:10.1037/0033-295X.82.6.407

Hochhaus, L., & Johnston, J. C. (1996). Perceptual repetition blindness effects. *Journal of Experimental Psychology: Human Perception and Performance, 22,* 355–366. doi:10.1037/0096-1523.22.2.355

Hochhaus, L., & Marohn, K. M. (1991). Repetition blindness depends on perceptual capture and token individuation failure. *Journal of Experimental Psychology: Human Perception and Performance, 17,* 422–432. doi:10.1037/0096-1523.17.2.422

Hollingworth, A., Richard, A. M., & Luck, S. J. (2008). Understanding the function of visual short-term memory: Transsaccadic memory, object correspondence, and gaze correction. *Journal of Experimental Psychology: General, 137,* 163–181. doi:10.1037/0096-3445.137.1.163

Huber, D. E. (2006). Computer simulations of the ROUSE model: An analytic simulation technique and comparison between the error variance-covariance and bootstrap methods for estimating parameter confidence. *Behavior Research Methods, 38,* 557–568. doi:10.3758/BF03193885

Huber, D. E., Shiffrin, R. M., Lyle, K. B., & Quach, R. (2002). Mechanisms of source confusion and discounting in short-term priming 2: Effects of prime similarity and target duration. *Journal of Experimental Psychology: Learning, Memory, and Cognition, 28,* 1120–1136. doi:10.1037/0278-7393.28.6.1120

Huber, D. E., Shiffrin, R. M., Lyle, K. B., & Ruys, K. I. (2001). Perception and preference in short-term word priming. *Psychological Review, 108,* 149–182. doi:10.1037/0033-295X.108.1.149

Huber, D. E., Shiffrin, R. M., Quach, R., & Lyle, K. B. (2002). Mechanisms of source confusion and discounting in short-term priming: 1. Effects of prime duration and prime recognition. *Memory & Cognition, 30,* 745–757. doi:10.3758/BF03196430

Irwin, D. E. (1992). Memory for position and identity across eye movements. *Journal of Experimental Psychology: Learning, Memory, and Cognition, 18,* 307–317. doi:10.1037/0278-7393.18.2.307

Irwin, D. E., Brown, J. S., & Sun, J.-S. (1988). Visual masking and visual integration across saccadic eye movements. *Journal of Experimental Psychology: General, 117,* 276–287. doi:10.1037/0096-3445.117.3.276

Kučera, H., & Francis, W. (1967). *Computational analysis of present-day American English.* Providence, RI: Brown University Press.

Low, F. N. (1951). Peripheral visual acuity. *Archives of Ophthalmology, 45,* 80–99. doi:10.1001/archopht.1951.01700010083011

Lu, Z.-L., & Sperling, G. (1995). The functional architecture of human visual motion perception. *Vision Research, 35,* 2697–2722. doi:10.1016/0042-6989(95)00025-U

Lu, Z.-L., & Sperling, G. (2001). Three-systems theory of human visual motion perception: Review and update. *Journal of the Optical Society of America A: Optics, Image Science, and Vision, 18*(9), 2331–2370. doi:10.1364/JOSAA.18.002331

McNamara, T. P. (1992). Theories of priming: I. Associative distance and lag. *Journal of Experimental Psychology. Learning, Memory, and Cognition, 18,* 1173–1190. doi:10.1037/0278-7393.18.6.1173

McNamara, T. P. (1994). Theories of priming: II. Types of primes. *Journal of Experimental Psychology: Learning, Memory, and Cognition, 20,* 507–520. doi:10.1037/0278-7393.20.3.507

Melcher, D., & Colby, C. L. (2008). Trans-saccadic perception. *Trends in Cognitive Sciences, 12,* 466–473. doi:10.1016/j.tics.2008.09.003

O'Regan, J. K. (1992). Solving the "real" mysteries of visual perception: The world as an outside memory. *Canadian Journal of Psychology, 46,* 461–488. doi:10.1037/h0084327

Prime, S. L., Tsotsos, L., Keith, G. P., & Crawford, J. D. (2007). Visual memory capacity in transsaccadic integration. *Experimental Brain Research, 180,* 609–628. doi:10.1007/s00221-007-0885-4

Rayner, K. (2009). Eye movements and attention in reading, scene perception, and visual search. *The Quarterly Journal of Experimental Psychology: Human Experimental Psychology, 62,* 1457–1506. doi:10.1080/17470210902816461

Rensink, R. A. (2002). Change detection. *Annual Review of Psychology, 53,* 245–277. doi:10.1146/annurev.psych.53.100901.135125

Sanborn, A. N., Malmberg, K. J., & Shiffrin, R. M. (2004). High-level effects of masking on perceptual identification. *Vision Research, 44,* 1427–1436. doi:10.1016/j.visres.2004.01.004

Simons, D. J., & Ambinder, M. S. (2005). Change blindness. *Current Directions in Psychological Science, 14,* 44–48. doi:10.1111/j.0963-7214.2005.00332.x

Sperling, G. (1960). The information available in brief visual presentations. *Psychological Monographs: General and Applied, 74*(11, Whole No. 498).

Straw, A. D. (2008). Vision egg: An open-source library for realtime visual stimulus generation. *Frontiers in Neuroinformatics, 2*(4), 1–10. doi:10.3389/neuro.11.004

Weidemann, C. T., Huber, D. E., & Shiffrin, R. M. (2005). Confusion and compensation in visual perception: Effects of spatiotemporal proximity and selective attention. *Journal of Experimental Psychology: Human Perception and Performance, 31,* 40–61. doi:10.1037/0096-1523.31.1.40

Weidemann, C. T., Huber, D. E., & Shiffrin, R. M. (2008). Prime diagnosticity in short-term repetition priming: Is primed evidence discounted, even when it reliably indicates the correct answer? *Journal of Experimental Psychology: Learning, Memory, and Cognition, 34,* 257–281. doi:10.1037/0278-7393.34.2.257

Part III

Attention

8

Strategies of Saccadic Planning

Eileen Kowler and Misha Pavel

Eye movements have to be rational. For eye movements—saccadic eye movements in particular—to provide a useful tool to support real-life tasks, the line of sight must be directed to locations that contain task-relevant information. Everyday life experiences, as well as classical and recent research, confirm this fundamental characteristic of saccades (Epelboim & Suppes, 2001; Land & Hayhoe, 2001; Suppes, Cohen, Laddaga, Anliker, & Floyd, 1983; Yang & McConkie, 2001; Yarbus, 1967). In general terms, rational behavior will optimize task-relevant outcomes, for example, minimizing the expected time to find a target, but what does it mean for saccadic planning to be rational? In particular, what happens if the effort needed to determine the best saccadic landing location is excessive and threatens to interfere with other concurrent activities? Or, in decision-theoretic terms, what if the computation or execution of the optimal strategy is itself too costly?

Questions about strategies and mechanisms of saccadic planning can be addressed through visual search tasks. In visual search, cues that reveal the likely location of targets, including contextual cues that are woven into global characteristics of a scene, have been shown to influence the choices people make about where to direct saccades (Eckstein, Drescher, & Shimozaki, 2006; Einhäuser, Rutishauser, & Koch, 2008; Neider & Zelinsky, 2006; Pomplun, 2006; Torralba, Oliva, Castelhano, & Henderson, 2006).

Yet despite such support for sensible strategies of saccadic planning, sometimes people fail to use vivid and easily discernible cues to guide the line of sight to important or useful locations. These failures are interesting because of their implications for the underlying processes that govern saccadic planning. They reveal what may be an inherent preference, rooted in characteristics of the saccadic system itself, for rapidly generated, as opposed to more carefully planned, saccadic paths.

DOI: 10.1037/14135-009
Human Information Processing: Vision, Memory, and Attention, C. Chubb, B. A. Dosher, Z.-L. Lu, and R. M. Shiffrin (Editors)

Local Cues and Saccadic Decisions

Studies of where people look during visual search through natural scenes have typically focused on the spatial distributions of fixation positions, obtained by pooling over successive saccades and often across observers. These studies, as noted earlier, supported the view that people are sensitive to cues (e.g., scene layout) that indicate the likely location of a target. Much of this work on the effects of these so-called top-down cues on saccadic landing positions was seen as presenting evidence against the notion that eye movements are drawn to locations solely on the basis of physical variables, such as local feature contrast (Peters, Iyer, Itti, & Koch, 2005). Thus, the emphasis was on showing that the cues could be effective, rather than the question of whether viewers took full advantage of the information provided to guide their saccades.

Hints about limitations in the use of visual cues to guide saccades emerged from the oculomotor community and, in particular, from those dedicated to using behavioral studies of saccades to infer the underlying control machinery of the saccadic system. A tradition in this line of work, dating back to Raymond Dodge (1903) in the early part of the 20th century, was to present simple tasks and sparse stimuli and not to expect too much thinking on the part of the human subjects. For example, a single target point would be presented that jumped rapidly from one portion of the field to another. The job of the subject was to use a saccade to track the motion of the point as quickly and as accurately as possible.

This basic "step-tracking" task has lent itself to many variations, but the one that concerns us here is the presentation of distractor stimuli surrounding the designated target, distractors that subjects were instructed to ignore. It turned out that ignoring these distractors was not so easy. Instead of landing on the designated target, saccadic landing positions deviated toward the center of the entire configuration (Coren & Hoenig, 1972; Findlay, 1982). The shorter the latency of the saccade, the larger these "center of gravity" effects (Coëffè & O'Regan, 1987; Ottes, Van Gisbergen, & Eggermont, 1985).

Center-of-gravity saccades were initially greeted with considerable surprise. Oculomotorists had been accustomed to expect a lot from the saccadic machinery. If you present a target, the saccades should certainly be able to reach it accurately. What had gone wrong?

The experiments on center-of-gravity saccades, using targets presented among distractors, created a situation that was not different from traditional visual search (Findlay, 1997; He & Kowler, 1989).[1] From this perspective, the source of the difficulty leading to the center of gravity saccades was not the saccadic system itself but the search process leading up to the saccades. People were launching their saccades before they knew where they were going. They landed somewhere in the middle, and then, having reduced retinal eccentricity and

---

[1]In a separate line of research, center-of-gravity saccades have also been studied using single, spatially extended targets. These saccades land near the target centroid with a level of precision comparable to that achieved with single target points and may be important for ensuring accurate saccadic localization of shapes and objects in natural scenes (Cohen, Schnitzer, Gersch, Singh, & Kowler, 2007; Melcher & Kowler, 1999; Vishwanath & Kowler, 2004).

bought a little more time, they found the target with a second saccade (Coëffé & O'Regan, 1987; Rao, Zelinsky, Hayhoe, & Ballard, 2002). Although the visual information was available that would have allowed an initial saccade to reach the target accurately, the preference was instead to view the entire configuration as the "target" and avoid having to make what was an attainable, but perhaps resource intensive, selection.

The reluctance to use spatially local, eccentric cues to guide saccades, which was observed in the center-of-gravity tasks, was demonstrated more directly in an interesting series of experiments by Hooge and Erkelens (1996, 1998, 1999). In their studies, people had to saccade through orderly arrays of characters (Landolt Cs varying in width and gap size) to find the target, a circle with no gap. Hooge and Erkelens did everything they could to try to help their subjects find the target. They arranged things so that the gaps in the Cs pointed to the target circle, or they peppered the arrays of distractors with Cs of a width easily distinguishable from that of the target. These clues helped guide the saccades to some extent, but they were not nearly as useful as they should have been. Even worse, when subjects finally fixated the target, they often kept going, only to have to look back a saccade or two later. Hooge and Erkelens concluded that the problem was the duration of the fixation pause. People do not pause between saccades long enough to take advantage of the information provided and produce the best search performance. They prefer to race ahead even when they are not sure where they are going.

Two-Location Search

To further explore the role of cues in saccadic planning, Araujo, Kowler, and Pavel (2001) developed a two-location search task. They constructed the task to pit two factors against each other: the distance of a potential target location from the line of sight and the probability that this location would contain the target. A sensible and rational strategy, one minimizing the expected time to find a target, would send the saccade to the location most likely to contain the target. However, mechanisms responsible for programming the saccade might prefer the location closer to the line of sight.

In the Araujo et al. (2001) task, observers had to report the orientation of a small letter T that was contained in one of two dense clusters of characters located at various distances to the right or to the left of fixation (see Figure 8.1). The dense array of characters surrounding the target letter T ensured that the orientation judgment could not be made on the basis of eccentric vision. The task could be done accurately if there were enough time to make a saccade to each cluster in sequence, but Araujo et al. kept the display presentations brief (.5 s), leaving time for inspection of only one cluster. A visual cue, a fourfold difference in intensity, signaled which cluster had the greater likelihood (80% probability) of containing the T. Because the trials were too brief to allow sequential examination of each cluster, the only strategy that could guarantee successful identification of the orientation of the target on the majority of the trials would be to take note of the intensity cue and direct the saccade to the cluster with the higher probability level. Easy enough.

Figure 8.1. Sample display from the experiment of Araujo, Kowler, and Pavel (2001). The critical display frame contained a single target letter T, the orientation of which had to be reported at the end of each trial. The T could be located in either the left-hand or right-hand clusters. From "Eye Movements During Visual Search: The Costs of Choosing the Optimal Path," by C. Araujo, E. Kowler, and M. Pavel, 2001, *Vision Research, 41,* p. 3615. Copyright 2001 by Elsevier. Reprinted with permission.

Remarkably, only one of the six subjects tested used this sensible and easily attainable strategy consistently. Figure 8.2 shows that this subject (FF) almost always looked in the direction of the higher probability cluster, regardless of its distance from fixation. Subjects BB and CC, in contrast, showed the complementary pattern: They ignored the probability cue and instead directed the first saccade to the less eccentric location. The remaining three subjects, interesting because of their ambivalence, planned their saccades according to both eccentricity and probability level. Their performance shows that they understood the significance of the cue, but for whatever reason did not always use it.

Was it so difficult to take the cue into account? Using the cue was costly, in that the latency of the initial saccade made to the high probability cluster was increased by 20 to 50 ms when the cue was used. Finding that additional saccadic planning time was needed to take note of the cue was not surprising. What was surprising was to find that people were not willing to wait just that little bit of extra time to make a better saccade (why, after all, spend hundreds of trials getting the wrong answer if a delay of less than 1/20th of a second could change the outcome dramatically?). The performance in our task, in the laboratory, was revealing something about the way in which people plan saccades out of the laboratory, in everyday life.

A further clue to the reasons for this seemingly peculiar strategy was revealed by examining performance beyond the initial saccade. Most trials contained a pair of consecutive saccades, one to each cluster, with some separated by extremely brief (< 100 ms) pauses (see Figure 8.3). With intersaccadic pauses this brief, the planning of the second saccade had to have begun before the first was completed (Becker & Jürgens, 1979; McPeek & Keller, 2002; McPeek, Skavenski, & Nakayama, 2000; Viviani & Swensson, 1982; Zingale & Kowler, 1987). However, a strategy of making two saccades in succession could never succeed because trials were too short to allow each cluster to be processed. Nevertheless, despite the futility of the strategy, the attempts to make two saccades remained an attractive option.

Additional experimental manipulations (detailed trial-by-trial feedback or tangible rewards) could have succeeded in altering the strategy in Araujo et al.'s (2001) two-location search task, encouraging all subjects to take their time and select a sensible saccadic goal. The interesting question from the point of view of understanding saccadic mechanisms and saccadic planning is why a short latency response, leading to saccades to a useless location and requiring a second, corrective movement, would ever be a preferable option.

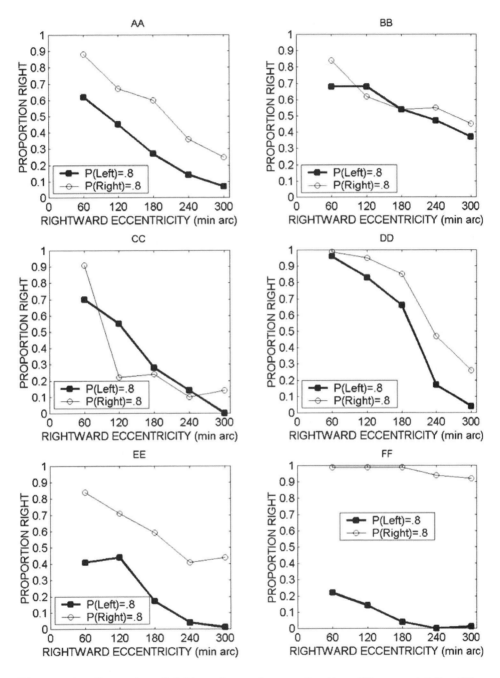

Figure 8.2. Proportion of rightward saccades as a function of the eccentricity of the right-hand cluster for six subjects (AA–FF). The two functions in each graph come from blocks of trials in which the target letter T was located in either the left-hand or right-hand cluster with probability = .8. From "Eye Movements During Visual Search: The Costs of Choosing the Optimal Path," by C. Araujo, E. Kowler, and M. Pavel, 2001, *Vision Research, 41,* p. 3617. Copyright 2001 by Elsevier. Reprinted with permission.

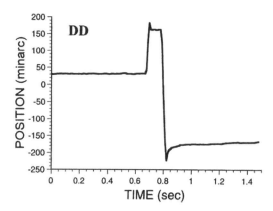

Figure 8.3. Sample eye trace of Subject DD in the two-location search task of Araujo et al. (2001) showing a short intersaccadic pause (<100 ms). From "Eye Movements During Visual Search: The Costs of Choosing the Optimal Path," by C. Araujo, E. Kowler, and M. Pavel, 2001, *Vision Research, 41,* p. 3621. Copyright 2001 by Elsevier. Reprinted with permission.

More Locations to Search

We recently extended this work to displays containing more clusters, a wider range of probability levels, and a more vivid probability cue. The displays contained six clusters, half red, half green, located at randomly selected positions within a 7×5 matrix. The single target letter T was once again presented in one of the clusters, and, as was the case in the two-location task, its orientation had to be reported at the end of each trial. During any block of 100 trials, the probability of the T occurring in a cluster of one color was higher ($p = .6, .8,$ or 1) than the probability of it appearing in the other. We also tested an equal probability condition ($p = .5$) in which cluster color became irrelevant. The trial length was increased to 1 s to allow time for at least two useful saccades per trial.

The probability cue again proved to have modest influence on the first saccade (see Figure 8.4a). Two of the four subjects (JF and MG) took the probability cue into account (albeit imperfectly) in planning the initial saccade, with approximately 80% of the first saccades landing on clusters with the higher probability of containing the target. For the other two subjects, the cue was less important; approximately 60% of initial saccades landed on the high probability cluster.

Saccades to high probability clusters tended to have longer latencies (Figure 8.4b), showing once again the cost of taking the cue into account. For some subjects, latencies decreased when the decision load was reduced by making the target T equally likely to appear in either color cluster ($p = .5$; subjects JF, MJ) or when the uncertainty (and effective set size) was reduced by setting $p = 1$ (JF, MG, and MJ). (One subject, SK, showed a latency pattern that was opposite to these two trends.)

The bias to favor looking at clusters at smaller eccentricities appeared once again in this six-location task. Saccades to high probability clusters were usually larger, indicating a willingness to travel a bit farther to reach a better

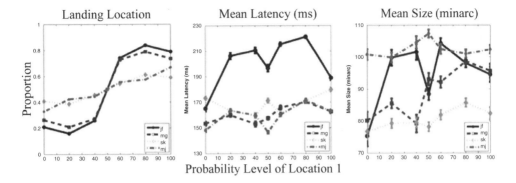

Figure 8.4.   Properties of the initial saccades in the six-location search task as a function of probability level of the targeted cluster. Data for four subjects in each graph. Left: Proportion of saccades directed to a cluster location; center: mean latency of initial saccades; right: mean size of initial saccades. SEs, except where shown, are smaller than plotting symbols.

location, although the effects were not monotonic, and there were substantial differences in average saccade sizes among the subjects (Figure 8.4c).

As was the case in the two-location search, the interesting question at this point was not what we would have to do to induce a strategy of more careful saccadic planning but rather what was so attractive about launching so many early, yet useless, saccades.

A partial answer to this question is shown in Figure 8.5a, in which the duration of the pause following the first saccade is shown as a function of the

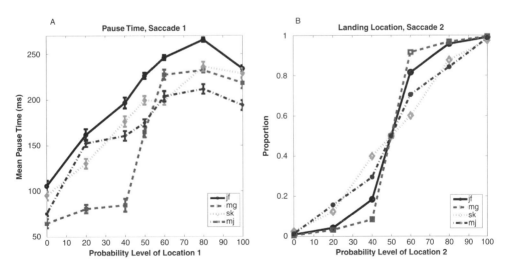

Figure 8.5.   Results from the six-location search task. (A) Average fixation pause time on a cluster following the initial saccade as a function of the probability level of the cluster. Bars show ± 1 SE. (B) Proportion of second saccades directed to clusters of different probability levels.

probability level of the fixated cluster. Unlike the small effects of probability on saccadic latency, there were large effects of probability on pause duration. Average pause durations varied from values near 100 ms for the lowest probability levels to 250 ms for the highest levels. Thus, although probability did not have large effects on whether a cluster would be fixated with the initial saccade, it did play a significant role in determining how long the line of sight would remain on the cluster. Given that many of the pauses between first and second saccades were short (< 100 ms, as in the two-location search), it is reasonable to conclude that the planning of many of these more sensible second saccades was underway before the first saccade was completed (Caspi, Beutter, & Eckstein, 2004; McPeek & Keller, 2002; McPeek et al., 2000).

Thus, the eye may have initially arrived at a useless location, but it quickly found its way out. Where it went is shown in Figure 8.5b, which plots the proportion of second saccades landing on clusters of different probability. Although individual differences persisted, all subjects did a much better job of targeting high-probability clusters with the second saccade than with the initial saccade. There was a cost, in terms of the total time needed to reach the high-probability cluster, in making the initial useless saccades, but evidently people preferred the extra saccade rather than engaging in a more difficult selection of the initial saccadic target.

The pattern of results was the much same for a 10-location version of the task. In the 10-location task, we compared performance on two types of clusters: clusters that were either all red or all green, or clusters whose color was mixed, either predominantly red or predominantly green. The mix of colors was produced by setting the color of seven of the nine characters making up the cluster to one color (red or green), and the remaining two characters to the other. The difference between these mixed-color clusters, although less salient than the difference between the single-color clusters, could, nevertheless, be discerned regardless of the fixation position within the display.

Two new subjects were tested. Figure 8.6a shows that although subject EC aimed more of his initial saccades to the high-probability cluster than did subject GT, both were less sensitive to the probability cue with the mixed-color clusters than with the single-color clusters. The latency of the initial saccades did not vary appreciably across these two types of clusters (Figure 8.6b), showing that neither subject was inclined to delay saccades to improve the accuracy of selection. As with the six-location task, the duration of the pause following the initial saccade increased with the probability level of the landing location (Figure 8.6c). The effects of location probability on selectivity of the saccades, in particular, the differences between performance with the single-color and mixed-color clusters (Figure 8.7a), and the effects of probability on pause time (Figure 8.7b) persisted even for the more selective second saccades.

Reading

Although this chapter has been about saccades during visual search, the strategy of making saccades quickly, before the best endpoint has been selected, can be connected to a recent study of eye movements during reading.

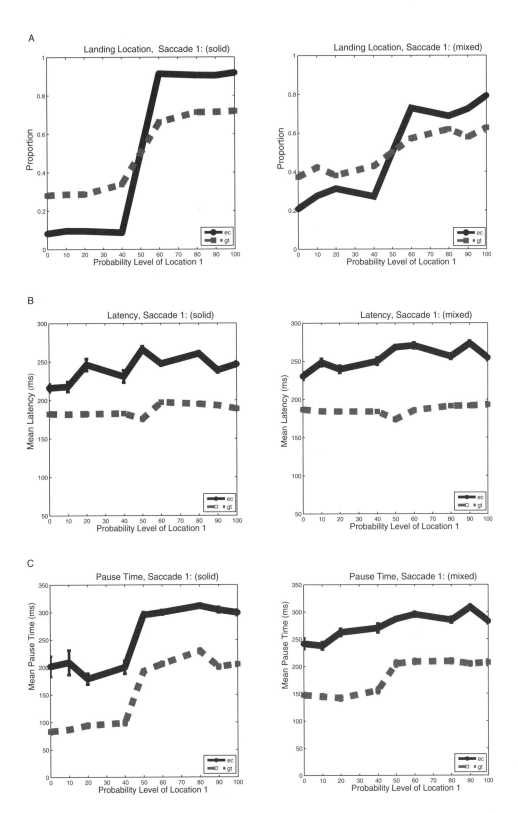

Figure 8.6. Results from a 10-location search task for two subjects. (A) Proportion of initial saccades landing on a given cluster location. (B) Mean latency of initial saccades. (C) Pause time following initial saccades, as a function of the probability level of the cluster. Left: solid clusters. Right: Mixed colors. SEs except where shown are smaller than plotting symbols.

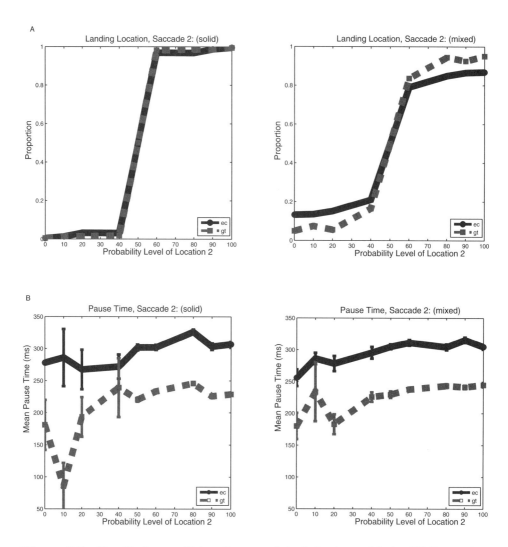

Figure 8.7.   Results from a 10-location search task for two subjects. (A) Proportion of second saccades landing on a given cluster location. (B) Pause time following second saccades as a function of the probability level of the cluster. Left: solid clusters. Right: Mixed colors. SEs except where shown are smaller than plotting symbols.

Schnitzer and Kowler (2006) had their subjects read the same four passages, of approximately 60 words each, 44 times. Repeated reading has not often been studied, yet it is something people do, particularly when a premium is placed on comprehension and memory (e.g., when studying for exams, editing or reviewing manuscripts, or deciphering instructional manuals). In the Schnitzer and Kowler study, no passage was read more than four times on any given day, and never twice in succession. Repeated texts were interspersed with other texts that were read only once. Comprehension questions and a change-detection task were also used to help maintain attention to the texts despite the repetition.

During repeated reading of the same text, the saccadic landing positions fell into clusters, showing that there were preferred landing locations dictated by the content of the passages or by characteristics of the text.

The finding that was of most relevance to the theme of this chapter is that with repeated reading, changes to forward (rightward) saccades, either their size or intersaccadic pause durations, were modest and inconsistent across readers. However, all readers showed the same proportional reduction in the rate of regressive (leftward) saccades made to look back along a line of text. Regressions became less frequent with repeated reading because of the greater certainty of the content. This raises the question of why make regressions at all.

Schnitzer and Kowler (2006) argued that when reading a text for the first time, the presence of regressions is a sign that the reader is moving too quickly. Regressions could, in principle, be avoided, or at least be reduced in frequency, by slowing the pace of reading. However, it seems that the option to proceed at a brisk pace (so brisk that even 40+ readings did not lead to much change) and use regressive saccades, as needed, is preferred.

From the perspective of saccadic planning, it may be easier (less effortful or computationally expensive) to make corrective saccades or regressions than to slow the rate of saccadic production. Making saccades at a high rate is not too harmful if, as we have seen already in visual search, the saccadic system is configured to facilitate the production of new saccades quickly, with little additional processing load.

What's the Hurry?

The evidence summarized in this chapter supports a pervasive strategy, observed in at least three tasks—"center-of-gravity" saccadic tasks, visual search, and reading—to issue saccades at a brisk rate, including some with short latencies and short intersaccadic pauses, even if the goal locations prove to be useless and require immediate corrections. Why is this option chosen so often?

From the perspective of decision theory, answering this question requires specifying the costs of the computations needed to determine the best (i.e., most informative) places to look (for related examples involving different motor tasks, see Chittka, Dyer, Bock, & Dornhaus, 2003; Dean, Wu, & Maloney, 2007; Gallistel et al., 2007). One obvious cost of determining the best saccadic landing site is the diversion of visual resources to extrafoveal locations to identify and evaluate the relevant display characteristics or the cues that could be useful in guiding saccades. These computations take time and occur at the expense of the processing of foveal details. Such decision-related costs are reduced when saccades are made within highly structured and familiar environments, where the visual cues available to guide saccades are vivid and predictable. Costs are also reduced under conditions in which scanning the same environment continues over several seconds, allowing factors such as learning to supplement online visual analyses. Under all these conditions, saccades by and large follow useful paths to task-relevant locations (e.g., Epelboim et al., 1995; Land & Hayhoe, 2001). The usefulness of the chosen saccadic paths under such conditions, where multiple factors cooperate to support saccadic planning, can obscure the underlying costs associated with making choices about where to look.

The costs were apparent in the saccadic, search, and reading tasks we described, where the displays were unfamiliar and available scanning time was short. Yet even under these conditions, it would seem to be preferable to wait until the relevant computations were completed rather than make quickly planned, but ultimately useless, saccades. The costs of the useless saccades would appear to be greater than the cost of waiting because of the extra time and effort invested in the corrections (imagine if people drove cars with the same preferences they displayed during visual search).

We suspect that a complete understanding the reasons behind the difference in costs between the two options, issuing saccades frequently versus planning saccades carefully, requires not only consideration of the visual and cognitive demands of finding the best landing positions (as discussed earlier) but also consideration of aspects of the saccadic system itself, in particular characteristics that both encourage rapid saccadic planning and facilitate prompt corrections.

Rapid saccadic planning is encouraged by mechanisms that set global rates of saccadic production. Neurophysiologic studies have shown that saccades are initiated when the activity levels of single neurons in areas such as frontal eye field reach a threshold (Hanes & Schall, 1996). Within a given saccadic task, thresholds tend to remain stable. Trial-by-trial variability in saccadic latencies is due to fluctuations in the rate of rise to threshold, not to variation in the threshold itself (Hanes & Schall, 1996). Although thresholds can be adjusted (Reddi, Asrress, & Carpenter, 2003), adjustments on a saccade-by-saccade basis may be computationally costly (Hooge & Erkelens, 1996). Given the option to set global rates of saccadic production, it would seem preferable to gamble on a relatively high rate. A rate that is too slow will result in the line of sight often having to linger at a location after the useful visual information has been extracted, clearly not the best use of time.

This brings us to the second relevant aspects of saccades—namely, the ability to make corrections quickly. Oculomotor research has shown that the selection of a saccadic target, and the initial stages in the preparation of a given saccade, can begin before a prior saccade is completed (Becker & Jürgens, 1979; McPeek & Keller, 2002; Viviani & Swensson, 1982). The option to plan saccades concurrently reduces the need to inhibit every errant saccade to a useless location. Errors can be corrected by new saccades for which planning has started well before the erroneous or useless saccade is over. The ability to issue corrective saccades quickly and to plan multiple saccades concurrently has been linked to the role played by spatial attention in guiding saccades (Gersch, Kowler, Schnitzer, & Dosher, 2008, 2009).

We have argued that the saccadic mechanisms that set global rates of saccadic production, as well as those that facilitate rapid corrections, support the frequent occurrence of saccades to useless locations and contribute to reducing the costs in effort and time of inspecting visual scenes. But what about the effects of these useless saccades on vision? Frequent saccades to useless locations would be a serious problem for vision if we were obligated to attend to and remember everything we look at. We would overload the system with use-less details. However, we do not remember everything we look at. For the past few years, groups of investigators have followed the classical work of Sperling (1960) and found a host of experimental tasks that show how surprisingly little of the visual world is remembered from a single glance (e.g., Rensink, 2000; Simons, 2000). This failure to remember is often portrayed as a problem for vision, a limitation correctable only by frequent saccades made to pick up the lost and forgotten details.

We believe there really is no problem. The occurrence of frequent saccades to useless locations implies that having strict limitations on what we remember from a single glance is actually quite fortunate. It means that the filtering of what we take from a scene does not have to be imposed at the level of saccadic planning (which would, as we have seen, be difficult and costly) but rather at the level of visual memory. We can look wherever the saccadic system takes us with little risk, as long as we remember only the details we choose to attend. The compatibility between the properties of saccadic planning and the selectiv-ity of attention and memory is surely not a coincidence and contributes to the adoption of optimal strategies of saccadic planning in natural visual tasks.

References

Araujo, C., Kowler, E., & Pavel, M. (2001). Eye movements during visual search: The costs of choos-ing the optimal path. *Vision Research, 41,* 3613–3625. doi:10.1016/S0042-6989(01)00196-1

Becker, W., & Jürgens, R. (1979). An analysis of the saccadic system by means of double step stimuli. *Vision Research, 19,* 967–983. doi:10.1016/0042-6989(79)90222-0

Caspi, A., Beutter, B. R., & Eckstein, M. P. (2004). The time course of information accrual guiding eye movement decisions. *Proceedings of the National Academy of Sciences of the United States of America, 101,* 13086–13090. doi:10.1073/pnas.0305329101

Chittka, L., Dyer, A. G., Bock, F., & Dornhaus, A. (2003, July 24). Psychophysics: Bees trade off foraging speed for accuracy. *Nature, 424,* 388. doi:10.1038/424388a

Coëffé, C., & O'Regan, J. K. (1987). Reducing the influence of nontarget stimuli on saccades accu-racy: Predictability and latency effects. *Vision Research, 27,* 227–240. doi:10.1016/0042-6989 (87)90185-4

Cohen, E. H., Schnitzer, B. S., Gersch, T. M., Singh, M., & Kowler, E. (2007). The relationship between spatial pooling and attention in saccadic and perceptual tasks. *Vision Research, 47,* 1907–1923. doi:10.1016/j.visres.2007.03.018

Coren, S., & Hoenig, P. (1972). Effect of non-target stimuli upon length of voluntary saccades. *Perceptual and Motor Skills, 34,* 499–508.

Dean, M., Wu, S. W., & Maloney, L. T. (2007). Trading off speed and accuracy in rapid, goal-directed movements. *Journal of Vision, 7,* 10.1–12.

Dodge, R. (1903). Five types of eye movement in the horizontal meridian plane of the field of regard. *The American Journal of Psychology, 8,* 307–327.

Eckstein, M. P., Drescher, B. A., & Shimozaki, S. S. (2006). Attentional cues in real scenes, saccadic targeting, and Bayesian priors. *Psychological Science, 17,* 973–980. doi:10.1111/ j.1467-9280.2006.01815.x

Einhäuser, W., Rutishauser, U., & Koch, C. (2008). Task-demands can immediately reverse the effects of sensory-driven saliency in complex visual stimuli. *Journal of Vision, 8(2):2,* 1–19. doi:10.1167/8.2.2

Epelboim, J., & Suppes, P. (2001). The role of eye movements in solving geometry problems. *Vision Research, 41,* 1561–1574. doi:10.1016/S0042-6989(00)00256-X

Epelboim, J. L., Steinman, R. M., Kowler, E., Edwards, M., Pizlo, Z., Erkelens, C. J., & Collewijn, H. (1995). The function of visual search and memory in sequential looking tasks. *Vision Research, 35,* 3401–3422. doi:10.1016/0042-6989(95)00080-X

Findlay, J. M. (1982). Global visual processing for saccadic eye movements. *Vision Research, 22,* 1033–1045. doi:10.1016/0042-6989(82)90040-2

Findlay, J. M. (1997). Saccadic target selection during visual search. *Vision Research, 37,* 617–631. doi:10.1016/S0042-6989(96)00218-0

Gallistel, C. R., King, A. P., Gottlieb, D., Balci, F., Papachristos, E. B., Szalecki, M., & Carbone, K. S. (2007). Is matching innate? *Journal of the Experimental Analysis of Behavior, 87,* 161–199. doi:10.1901/jeab.2007.92-05

Gersch, T. M., Kowler, E., Schnitzer, B. S., & Dosher, B. (2008). Visual memory during pauses between successive saccades. *Journal of Vision, 8,* 15.1–18. doi:10.1167/8.16.15

Gersch, T. M., Kowler, E., Schnitzer, B. S., & Dosher, B. (2009). Attention during sequences of saccades along marked and memorized paths. *Vision Research, 49,* 1256–1266. doi:10.1016/j.visres.2007.10.030

Hanes, D. P., & Schall, J. D. (1996, October 18). Neural control of voluntary movement initiation. *Science, 274,* 427–430. doi:10.1126/science.274.5286.427

He, P., & Kowler, E. (1989). The role of location probability in the programming of saccades: Implications for "center-of-gravity" tendencies. *Vision Research, 29,* 1165–1181. doi:10.1016/0042-6989(89)90063-1

Hooge, I. T. C., & Erkelens, C. J. (1996). Control of fixation duration in a simple search task. *Perception & Psychophysics, 58,* 969–976. doi:10.3758/BF03206825

Hooge, I. T. C., & Erkelens, C. J. (1998). Adjustment of fixation duration in visual search. *Vision Research, 38,* 1295–1302, IN3–IN4. doi:10.1016/S0042-6989(97)00287-3

Hooge, I. T. C., & Erkelens, C. J. (1999). Peripheral vision and oculomotor control during visual search. *Vision Research, 39,* 1567–1575. doi:10.1016/S0042-6989(98)00213-2

Land, M. F., & Hayhoe, M. M. (2001). In what ways do eye movements contribute to everyday activities? *Vision Research, 41,* 3559–3565.

McPeek, R. M., & Keller, E. L. (2002). Superior colliculus activity related to concurrent processing of saccade goals in a visual search task. *Journal of Neurophysiology, 87,* 1805–1815.

McPeek, R. M., Skavenski, A. A., & Nakayama, K. (2000). Concurrent processing of saccades in visual search. *Vision Research, 40,* 2499–2516. doi:10.1016/S0042-6989(00)00102-4

Melcher, D., & Kowler, E. (1999). Shape, surfaces and saccades. *Vision Research, 39,* 2929–2946. doi:10.1016/S0042-6989(99)00029-2

Neider, M. B., & Zelinsky, G. J. (2006). Searching for camouflaged targets: Effects of target-background similarity on visual search. *Vision Research, 46,* 2217–2235. doi:10.1016/j.visres.2006.01.006

Ottes, F. P., Van Gisbergen, J. A., & Eggermont, J. J. (1985). Latency dependence of colour-based target vs. nontarget discrimination by the saccadic system. *Vision Research, 25,* 849–862.

Peters, R. J., Iyer, A., Itti, L., & Koch, C. (2005). Components of bottom-up gaze allocation in natural images. *Vision Research, 45,* 2397–2416. doi:10.1016/j.visres.2005.03.019

Pomplun, M. (2006). Saccadic selectivity in complex visual search displays. *Vision Research, 46,* 1886–1900. doi:10.1016/j.visres.2005.12.003

Rao, R. P., Zelinsky, G. J., Hayhoe, M. M., & Ballard, D. H. (2002). Eye movements in iconic visual search. *Vision Research, 42,* 1447–1463. doi:10.1016/S0042-6989(02)00040-8

Reddi, B. A. J., Asrress, K. N., & Carpenter, R. H. S. (2003). Accuracy, information, and response time in a saccadic decision task. *Journal of Neurophysiology, 90,* 3538–3546. doi:10.1152/jn.00689.2002

Rensink, R. A. (2000). Seeing, sensing, and scrutinizing. *Vision Research, 40,* 1469–1487. doi:10.1016/S0042-6989(00)00003-1

Schnitzer, B. S., & Kowler, E. (2006). Eye movements during multiple readings of the same text. *Vision Research, 46,* 1611–1632. doi:10.1016/j.visres.2005.09.023

Simons, D. J. (2000). Current approaches to change blindness. *Visual Cognition, 7,* 1–15. doi:10.1080/135062800394658

Sperling, G. (1960). The information available in brief visual presentations. *Psychological Monographs: General and Applied, 74,* 1–29.

Suppes, P., Cohen, M., Laddaga, R., Anliker, J., & Floyd, H. (1983). A procedural theory of eye movements in doing arithmetic. *Journal of Mathematical Psychology, 27,* 341–369. doi:10.1016/0022-2496(83)90033-0

Torralba, A., Oliva, A., Castelhano, M. S., & Henderson, J. M. (2006). Contextual guidance of eye movements and attention in real-world scenes: the role of global features in object search. *Psychological Review, 113,* 766–786. doi:10.1037/0033-295X.113.4.766

Vishwanath, D., & Kowler, E. (2004). Saccadic localization of shapes in the presence of cues to 3-dimensional shape. *Journal of Vision, 4,* 445–458. doi:10.1167/4.6.4

Viviani, P., & Swensson, R. G. (1982). Saccadic eye movements to peripherally discriminated visual targets. *Journal of Experimental Psychology: Human Perception and Performance, 8,* 113–126.

Yang, S. N., & McConkie, G. W. (2001). Eye movements during reading: A theory of saccade initiation time. *Vision Research, 41,* 3567–3585. doi:10.1016/S0042-6989(01)00025-6

Yarbus, A. L. (1967). *Eye movements and vision.* New York, NY: Plenum Press.

Zingale, C. M., & Kowler, E. (1987). Planning sequences of saccades. *Vision Research, 27,* 1327–1341. doi:10.1016/0042-6989(87)90210-0

9

Mechanisms of Visual Attention

Barbara A. Dosher and Zhong-Lin Lu

The psychological study of attention began with the observations of the mentalists near the turn of the past century. An introspective analysis of visual attention by Wilhelm Wundt (1912) asked the observer to fixate on the "o" in the center of an array of letters (see Figure 9.1) while moving the "subjective-fixation" of attention to the "n" on the right-hand side. He observed that the letters surrounding the "n" were "perceive[d] more clearly," whereas the letters elsewhere "seem to retreat into the darker field of consciousness" (p. 21). These introspections introduced several themes that have occupied modern studies of visual attention: improved visibility of the attended object, reduced processing of distracting elements, possible changes in the perceived appearance, and the ability to shift attention away from the location of the eye. The last decade or so of research has seen major advancements and insights into these important functional properties of attention, some of which are detailed here.

Experimental Approaches to Visual Attention and Signal Detection Theory

Perhaps the first experimental assessment of the consequences of distributing attention over the visual field was by Mertens (1956), who studied the ability to detect a weak flash of light in one or in four locations. Unaware of signal detection theory, and considering only hits and not false alarms, Mertens incorrectly inferred that attention to a single location impaired detection. Posner and colleagues extended the experimental study of visual attention to response time measures (Posner, 1980; Posner, Nissen, & Ogden, 1978). Mean reaction time to a brief flash was faster than when the flash was in the precued or attended location (80% of the time) than unattended location (20%), with uncued trials in the middle. Here, too, signal detection theory is critical to correctly interpreting results.

As these two examples indicate, signal detection theory (Green & Swets, 1966) plays a critical role in the modern understanding of attention. Attention

DOI: 10.1037/14135-010
Human Information Processing: Vision, Memory, and Attention, C. Chubb, B. A. Dosher, Z.-L. Lu, and R. M. Shiffrin (Editors)

```
            t h m
        m v x w a s f
      l  g  i  c  s  f  p  d  t
    z  r  a  e  n  p  r  h  v  z  l
    r  f  u  c  t  h  f  b  n  d  s
    k  h  e  p  n  o  t  v  b  s  i
    n  z  l  u  c  r  k  m  d  g  n
    d  i  n  i  w  g  e  t  v  r  f
      s  a  t  f  l  b  p  n  k
        m  d  w  c  k  t  g
            p  a  v  e  r
```

Figure 9.1. A stimulus devised by Wundt (1912, p. 19) to illustrate that implicit attention can be moved independent of the eye and appears to improve perceptual clarity. While fixating on the central "o," attend to the letter "n" one up and four to the right. From *Perception and Cognition at Century's End: Handbook of Perception and Cognition* (p. 221), by J. Hochberg (Ed.), 1998, San Diego, CA: Academic Press. Copyright 1998 by Barbara A. Dosher. Reprinted with permission.

manipulations may cause shifts in criteria that affect performance without any changes in the perceptual strength of the stimuli. Observers may lower the criterion for sensory evidence in an expected location and raise the criterion for evidence in an unexpected one. Changes in criterion or bias count as behavioral changes due to attention potentially separate from enhancement of perceptual strength of the stimulus by attention. Criterion effects on response time (and accuracy) are now generally treated within diffusion models of decision (Ratcliff, 1978; Ratcliff & Smith, 2004; Smith & Ratcliff, 2009).

When attention to several objects is compared with attention to a single object, as in the Mertens (1956) experiment, the decision structure changes with the attention instruction. Sampling evidence from four locations rather than one of necessity incorporates more noise samples into a perceptual decision. Even if the perceptual quality and criteria are identical in the diffuse attention conditions, more false-alarm errors occur when false alarms come from four locations rather than one (see Figure 9.2). Therefore, certain decrements in discrimination in diffuse or misdirected attention situations reflect structural changes in decision noise, uncertainty losses due to changes in the task, or changes in the strategy by the observer. Showing that attention improves discrimination requires estimating and discounting decision uncertainty or eliminating it experimentally (see Dosher & Sperling, 1998; Palmer, Verghese, & Pavel, 2000).

In a broad range of visual search and detection paradigms, performance accuracy decrements due to increasing the number of items (locations) only rarely exceed the performance losses predicted by structural decision factors or uncertainty (Baldassi & Verghese, 2002; Downing, 1988; Eckstein, 1998; Graham, 1989; Morgan, Ward, & Castet, 1998; Palmer, 1994; Palmer, Ames, & Lindsey, 1993; Palmer et al., 2000; Shaw, 1980, 1984). Indeed, predictions for

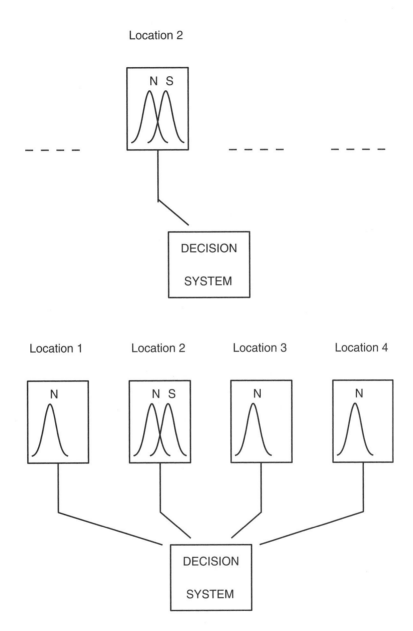

Figure 9.2. Changes in performance due to attention manipulations require analysis with signal detection theory to account for decision uncertainty or changes in criteria. Discriminating a signal (S) or noise (N) in a single location (top) has fewer sources of false alarms than cases with noise samples in several additional locations when the location of the signal is unknown. From *Perception and Cognition at Century's End: Handbook of Perception and Cognition* (p. 231), by J. Hochberg (Ed.), 1998, San Diego, CA: Academic Press. Copyright 1998 by Barbara A. Dosher. Reprinted with permission.

the decision effects on accuracy have been derived for many paradigms and a number of distinct decision rules.

Structural decision factors in the absence of any changes in perceptual quality do remarkably well at predicting the accuracy or thresholds of detection in visual search under many conditions (Palmer et al., 2000). However, attention can have important effects on the perceptual coding of the stimulus over and above these predicted changes in criterion or decision uncertainty in other situations such as with noise or masking, or under the dual-report demands of object attention.

Signatures of Attention and the Perceptual Template Model

The effects of visual attention (controlling for or discounting decision uncertainty) can be measured as a joint function of the state of attention or the task and stimulus variations such as the amount or characteristics of external noise added, and the contrast of the signal stimulus (Dosher & Lu, 2000a, 2000b; Liu, Dosher, & Lu, 2009; Lu & Dosher, 1999, 2000). A perceptual template model (PTM) of the observer creates a predictive linking function between key physical parameters of the displayed stimulus, such as signal and noise contrasts, the characteristics of the observer, and the internal distributions of a signal detection theory decision rule. External noise in the stimulus and internal limitations due to receptor sampling errors, randomness of neural responses, and loss of information during neural transmission limit the accuracy of performance. Equivalent internal noises that reduce the performance from that of a "perfect" or ideal observer are estimated by varying the amount or characteristics of the external noise. This approach is related to one of first analyses of internal noise sources introduced in early work by Sperling (1989).

The PTM is an extension of many similar models of the human observer in the literature (Burgess, Wagner, Jennings, & Barlow, 1981; Pelli & Farell, 1999) that incorporates the known qualities of the visual system (Lu & Dosher, 2008). It consists of a "template" tuned to the signal stimulus and task, with response gain β to the "signal" (matching) stimulus; a nonlinear transducer function of power γ; multiplicative internal noise with mean 0 and standard deviation determined by the base standard deviation N_m scaled proportional to the total contrast energy in the stimulus (to account for Weberlike behavior); independent additive internal noise with mean 0 and a fixed standard deviation N_a; and a decision process that operates on the noisy internal representation of the stimulus and tailored to the observer's task (i.e., detection, discrimination; see Figure 9.3). Noises are Gaussian-distributed.

Performance can be measured as d' (or percentage correct) as a function of task, attention, external noise, and contrast. Another index of performance is the contrast threshold of the signal stimulus required to achieve a given accuracy as a function of external noise, or the threshold versus (external noise) contrast (TvC) function. Figure 9.4 illustrates stimuli with varying external noise and signal contrasts for orthogonal orientation discriminations, along with an approximate equivisibility contour that is analogous to the TvC function in discrimination.

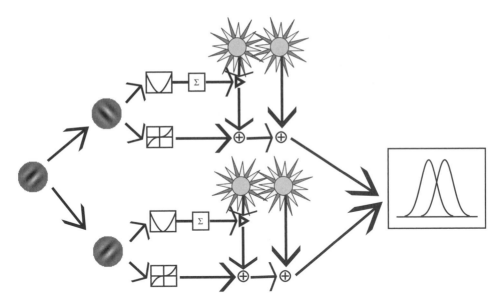

Figure 9.3. Perceptual template model of the observer. The stimulus is compared with two oriented templates. The decision reflects the difference in the two responses.

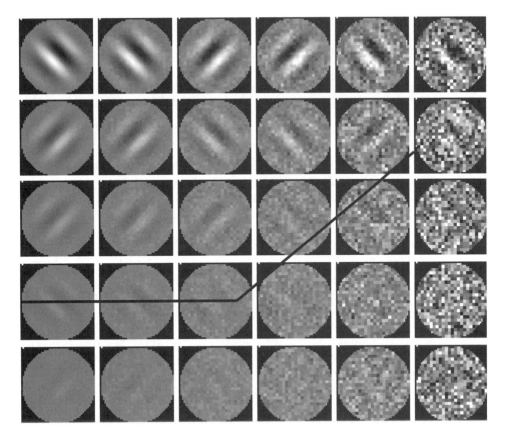

Figure 9.4. An "eye chart" shows stimulus variations with increasing external noise (left to right) and increasing signal stimulus contrast (bottom to top). The line shows an approximate threshold versus (external noise) contrast curve.

Parameters of the perceptual template model are estimated from TvCs by nonlinear estimation techniques from two or three measured threshold levels (Dosher & Lu, 1998; Lu & Dosher, 1999) or from full psychometric functions (Dosher & Lu, 2000a, 2000b; Lu & Dosher, 2008). PTM equations are in Appendix 9.1.

The mechanisms of attention—or, indeed, performance changes associated with many forms of perceptual state change—are inferred from the signature patterns of psychometric functions or TvCs for different states of attention (Figure 9.5). Attended conditions show improved performance, seen as higher accuracy in contrast psychometric functions or lower thresholds in TvC functions. Attention may operate through several distinct actions:

1. External noise exclusion reduces the effects of external noise through filtering, which improves performance only where there is significant external noise in the stimulus to filter out.
2. Stimulus enhancement improves performance through amplification of the signal stimulus, which helps to overcome internal noise in clear displays but has little effect in high external noise because the external noise and signal stimulus are amplified equally.
3. Mixtures of Points 1 and 2 improve performance in all noise levels but by an amount that scales at different criteria.
4. Multiplicative internal noise reduction squashing this noise source and/or changes in nonlinearity would affect performance in both noisy and clear displays by a different amount that changes with the criterion, although empirically this pattern is rarely observed.

Attention effects are estimated as a multiplicative gain factor A_f on external noise, A_a on internal additive noise, $A_f + A_a$ for the mixture, and A_m on internal multiplicative noise. These multipliers compare attended with unattended conditions, usually by setting the multiplier to 1 for unattended baselines, and reduce noises (< 1) for attended conditions, for which it indicates a proportional reduction in the noise source due to attention. Measuring several criterion performance levels resolves the individual contribution of each mechanism in a mixture situation (Dosher & Lu, 1999; Lu & Dosher, 1999) by testing important ratio properties in the size of effects of external noise exclusion and stimulus enhancement.

Figure 9.5 displays predictions for discrimination between (nearly) orthogonal stimuli, such as widely differing orientations (e.g., $\pm\,20°\text{--}45°$). Discriminations between highly similar stimuli, such as $\pm\,5°$ orientation judgments, depend on the difference of responses of two (near) templates (Jeon, Lu, & Dosher, 2009), yielding similar mechanism signatures, although attended and unattended conditions in this case diverge at the asymptote of the psychometric functions under most conditions (Dosher, Han, & Lu, 2010; Liu et al., 2009). These asymptotic effects of retuning in high-precision tasks may provide alternative and model-based explanations of effects along the psychometric function (Cameron, Tai, & Carrasco, 2002).

Across a substantial literature, external noise exclusion and stimulus enhancement—or filtering and amplification—are the dominant modes of atten-

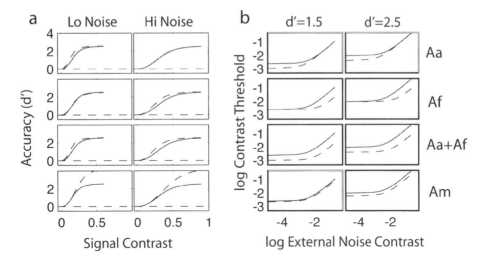

Figure 9.5. There are unique signatures of attention mechanisms for stimulus enhancement (Aa), external noise exclusion (Af), a mixture of both (Aa+Af), and multiplicative noise reduction (Am) within the perceptual template model (see text). Predictions of psychometric functions for orthogonal stimuli in low and high external noise displays (a) and for threshold versus contrast (TvC) functions at two criterion accuracies of $d' = 1.5$ and 2.5 are shown (b). Solid lines are unattended and dashed lines are attended conditions.

tion. External noise exclusion is seen in noisy or masked tests, whereas stimulus enhancement is seen in noiseless tests (Dosher & Lu, 2000a, 2000b). Recent functional magnetic resonance (fMRI) studies of visual attention (Li, Lu, Tjan, Dosher, & Chu, 2008) support these proposals by showing amplification of contrast response functions in early visual cortical areas without noise and reduced responses to masks in high noise (Lu, Li, Tjan, Dosher, & Chu, 2011).

External Noise Exclusion and Stimulus Enhancement in Visual Spatial Attention

The PTM framework provides an important taxonomy for the mechanisms of and conditions in which visual attention is important. In a series of tests of attention cued to a spatial location (Dosher & Lu, 2000a, 2000b; Han, Dosher, & Lu, 2003; Liu et al., 2009; Lu & Dosher, 2000; Lu, Lesmes, & Dosher, 2002), external noise exclusion was identified as a primary mechanism of visual attention. Stimulus enhancement, tested in clear displays, is a second mechanism that occurs in far more restricted circumstances. For example, Dosher and Lu (2000b) were the first to propose a key role for external noise exclusion in centrally cued spatial attention, finding that attended (validly precued) orientation discrimination performance exceeded unattended (invalidly precued) performance in high external noise, but not low noise, displays. Figure 9.6 shows data from the first demonstration of "pure" external noise exclusion in the

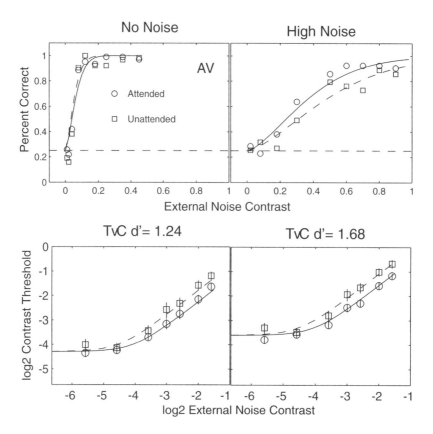

Figure 9.6. Centrally cued spatial attention improves external noise exclusion by improved filtering. AV, average data; TvC = threshold versus contrast. Data from Dosher & Lu, 2000b.

psychometric functions (0 and high noise only are shown) and in the TvC functions at two criterion levels; compare to the Af patterns in Figure 9.5.

The robust effects of attention with external noise masking create an organizing theoretical principle for understanding the inconsistency of the effects on accuracy of attention in the older literature. For example, in the absence of noise, many (Palmer et al., 1993, 2000) have found no effects of central spatial cuing beyond structural uncertainty, whereas other researchers who used masked stimuli easily found effects of central or peripheral cuing (Carrasco et al., 2000; Cheal & Lyon, 1991, 1992; Downing, 1988; Henderson, 1991, 1996; Shiu & Pashler, 1994).

Recent related claims also argue that precued spatial attention has an effect only in masked displays (Gould, Wolfgang, & Smith, 2007; Smith, Ratcliff, & Wolfgang, 2004; Smith, Wolfgang, & Sinclair, 2004) and have attributed apparent effects of attention in spatial cuing in unmasked displays (Carrasco, Penpeci-Talgar, & Eckstein, 2000), largely to uncertainty effects. However, the situations under which attention can be important may depend on factors that are only now beginning to be investigated, as are actively debated claims that attention changes the scale of visual analysis or alters the perception of objects (Carrasco, 2009; Prinzmetal, Long, & Leonhardt, 2008). One largely overlooked factor that may be especially important is the precision of judgment, which, under the PTM, may also contribute to effects of attention in the absence of noise, as seen next in the context of object attention phenomena.

Object Attention and Judgment Precision

Object attention is the organization of attended visual processing around objects rather than spatial locations. Object attention effects, when they occur, also appear to be expressed as primary effects of external noise exclusion and in some cases stimulus enhancement. Object attention tests in visual psychophysics have focused on classic dual-object report deficits, in which reporting features of two separate objects shows deficits compared with the report of a single feature or two features from the same object (Duncan, 1984, 1993a, 1993b, 1998). For example, an observer can more easily report the orientation (top tilted left or right) and phase (center black or white) of a single Gabor object than they can report the orientation of one and the phase of another (Han et al., 2003; Liu et al., 2009). In contrast, spatially cued attention is almost always tested in paradigms in which only a single report about one object is required. The limits on the ability to divide attention over objects were originally believed to be a fundamental and ineluctable limitation, one that would occur for any feature(s). Instead, the evidence suggests that object attention deficits primarily occur when the observer must use distinct features or judgment criteria about the two objects, such as the example of reporting orientation and phase, whereas reporting the same attribute, such as orientation, about both may often occur without the same costs of object attention limitations (Han et al., 2003; Liu et al., 2009).

Dual-object report deficits are robust for report of different feature dimensions, such as orientation and phase of a sine patch (Han et al., 2003). However, dual-object deficits also may be found within a single dimension, so long as the required decisions involve distinct kinds of judgments (i.e., clockwise or counterclockwise orientations about right or left diagonal implicit reference angles) and occur primarily in more demanding high-precision judgments (Liu et al., 2009; see Figure 9.7).

Object attention dual-report deficits, under the conditions where they occur, exhibit decreased accuracy or increased threshold relative to single report or dual reports from a single object. Therefore, dividing attention over two objects shows conjoint performance deficits with the dual performance for reporting from both objects below the "ideal point" for sharing without cost in which both can be reported with the same accuracy as either alone (Sperling & Dosher, 1986). However, the reductions in performance are not so great as predicted if attention capacity were strictly divided, along the lines of a sample-size sharing mode, or the even greater losses predicted by switching between reporting one attended object and guessing about the unattended object. Figure 9.8 shows asymptotic accuracy data averaged over observers (individual data were

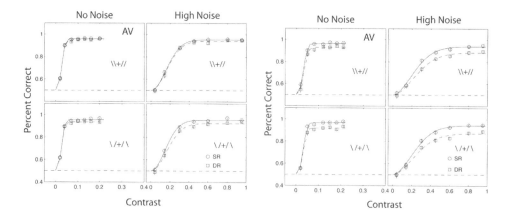

Figure 9.7. Object attention effects in low (left) and high (right) precision orientation judgments for congruent (top) and incongruent (bottom) judgments. Dual-object dual response (DR) performance is compared with single responses (SR). For incongruent judgments, orientation is judged relative to a right diagonal in one object and a left diagonal in the other (\ / or / \). AV, average data. From "The Role of Judgment Frames and Task Precision in Object Attention: Reduced Template Sharpness Limits Dual-Object Performance," by S.-H. Liu, B. A. Dosher, and Z.-L. Lu, 2009, *Vision Research, 49*, pp. 1342–1343. Copyright 2009 by Elsevier. Adapted with permission.

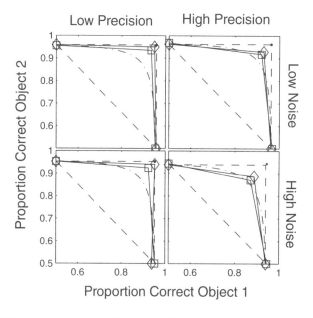

Figure 9.8. Object attention dual-report effects (on asymptotic accuracy) shown as attention operating characteristics in low (left) and high (right) precision orientation judgments in low noise (top) and high noise (bottom) tests. Data are shown for congruent (diamonds) and incongruent (squares) judgment frames. The upper right point is the *ideal point*; the diagonal dashed line is the *switching line*; the curved dashed line is the *sample size sharing* line. Data are from Liu, Dosher, and Lu (2009), Experiments 2 and 3, assumed symmetry.

similar) for the low- and high-precision tasks of Figure 9.7, projected onto an attention operating characteristic graph (Sperling & Melcher, 1978) for congruent (diamonds) and incongruent (squares) judgment frames.

The *ideal point* (small point at the upper right of the dashed square) represents capacity-free division of attention over two objects, where the dual-object responses equal the performance of single responses. The switching line (dashed diagonal) shows performance for trial-to-trial switching from one or the other single response. The sample size sharing (curved dashed) line shows the predicted losses for allocating attention across two objects for all the possible proportional assignment of sampling to one or the other of the dual-report judgments. Similar graphs would hold for 75% thresholds, although the computation of the sample size sharing is more indirect.

Dual-object performance approaches lossless performance in which each of the reports equals the accuracy achieved in single reports at the ideal point for low precision tasks and congruent judgments frames, but falls below the ideal point for high precision judgments and incongruent frames, such as judging orientation relative to different reference angles. However, the subideal performance in these cases still tends to be better than the performance predicted by sample size sharing, approaching this level of deficit only in the case of high-precision incongruent judgments. Indeed, a PTM observer analysis estimates that focal attention has better tuned templates than the templates with attention divided over objects. The attended template, composed of the relevant sensory inputs that contribute signal to the decision, narrows to improve filtering of external noise and also to reduce the response to the similar stimuli that must be recognized in high-precision discriminations.

Attention Limitations and Practice

Are these limitations seen in the division or lack of attention, in the conditions when they do occur, fundamental and unchangeable? There is increasing evidence that the answer to this is no. Continued practice in relevant tasks can both improve performance and reduce the demands of attention. The improvement of perceptual performance with practice or training is observed in many or most visual tasks (Dosher & Lu, 1998, 1999). Evidence suggests that it may also diminish the reliance on attention, a phenomenon related to early ideas of automaticity through practice (Shiffrin & Schneider, 1977). For example, a study of the effects of practice in the object attention task found reduction in dual-object–dual-report deficits (Dosher, Han, & Lu, 2010; Figure 9.8). Performance accuracy improves with practice for single-report conditions but improves even more for dual reports, reducing the size of the object attention effect. Informal analyses of a number of other attention experiments suggest to us that the reduction of attention effects is a common consequence of practice or training.

Attention and Movements of the Eye

As in Wundt's demonstration, the phenomena of spatially cued and dual-object attention described here involve focusing of attention away from the fixation of the eye. It appears, however, that similar functions of attention occur in preparation for single or sequenced saccadic movements of the eyes. Attention to a location in advance of the eye movement is crucial in controlling the visual inputs used to compute the exact position of the next fixation (Cohen, Schnitzer, Gersch, Singh, & Kowler, 2007).

Furthermore, when perceptual and saccadic performance are measured concurrently, as in the object attention experiments except that perceptual attention is to one object and the goal of a single saccade is another object, there are performance costs (Kowler, Anderson, Dosher, & Blaser, 1995). In sequences of saccades, perceptual performance is privileged at the goal location of the upcoming saccade as though attention has moved to the next location ahead of the eye (Gersch, Kowler, & Dosher, 2004; Gersch, Kowler, Schnitzer, & Dosher, 2009). In some circumstances, a spillover of improved perceptual performance is also observed for other locations that share a distinctive feature such as color with the saccadic target or targets (Gersch et al., 2009).

These examples illustrate that attention that is cued away from fixation to another location in a devised experimental manipulation operates in similar ways as a natural diversion of attention to the next location of the saccade. Similarly, a division of spatial attention between two objects at distinct locations has similar properties to the division of attention between a target object of visual scrutiny or processing and the spatial location or object of the next fixation. This, in turn, strongly suggests that the mechanisms of attention documented and understood in the laboratory are similar to those that likely occur in the process of natural purposive information-seeking behaviors, whether or not they involve movements of the eyes.

Toward a Multilevel Analysis of Visual Attention

Although increasingly sophisticated behavioral methods described here have been developed to study the functions and mechanisms of perceptual attention, attention has also emerged as a major project in physiology (Desimone & Duncan, 1995; Reynolds, Chelazzi, & Desimone, 1999) and brain imaging (Brefczynski & DeYoe, 1999; Buracas & Boynton, 2007; Li et al., 2008; Lu et al., 2011). The impact of attention on responses in early visual areas and the circuits of attention control have been of special interest. The effects of attention on cellular responses or fMRI imaging activity in visual cortex have also been interpreted in terms of gain on contrast, analogous to amplification, or differential weighting to irrelevant stimuli, or filtering. Recent analyses have examined the many reported patterns of attention (Reynolds & Heeger, 2009). Changes in responses in any given visual area altered by attention may be the precursors of changes in discrimination behavior. Documenting the changes in recorded cellular responses, or corresponding changes in measures of imaged fMRI brain activity associated with attention provides evidence of changes in one or more brain regions that together must be sufficient to underlie functional changes at the level of behavior. Specification of exactly how these changes in multiple brain regions differentially influence the altered discrimination behavior associated with attention is necessary to a true integration of these two levels of scientific description and understanding.

Appendix 9.1

The perceptual template (PTM) model is based on fundamental principles of signal and noise. The discriminability, d', reflects the signal response limited by various noises. The signal response is the gain of the template β_M for a signal stimulus times the contrast of the signal stimulus, c. The various limiting noises include external noise in the stimulus N_{ext} and two forms of internal noise, additive internal noise with standard deviation N_a that sets absolute threshold in the absence of external noise and multiplicative internal noise with base standard deviation N_m that is scaled up with the contrast in the stimulus and accounts for Weber-like behavior. Responses to contrast stimuli are affected by a non-linearity γ. Attention factors A_f, A_a, and A_m (< 1 relative to an unattended stimulus where they are set to 1) reduce the limiting noises.

$$d'\left(c, N_{ext}\right) = \frac{S_M}{\sqrt{\sigma_{Total}^2 / 2}} = \frac{\left(\beta_M c\right)^\gamma}{\sqrt{A_f^2 N_{ext}^{2\gamma} + A_m^2 N_m^2 \left[A_f^2 N_{ext}^{2\gamma} + \left(\beta_M c\right)^{2\gamma}\right] + A_a^2 N_a^2}}$$

The PTM is generalized to predict discrimination between similar stimuli by considering the difference in response between two templates, each of which respond significantly to both matching and mismatching stimuli. Indeed, for discrimination of highly similar stimuli, the gain or response of the un-matched template to a stimulus, β_U may approach the response of the matching template β_M if the stimuli to be discriminated are close, and the difference in the gain of the matched and un-matched template limits the strength of the distance between match and mismatch signal distributions (Jeon, Lu, & Dosher, 2009):

$$d'\left(c, N_{ext}\right) = \frac{S_M - S_U}{\sqrt{\left(\sigma_M^2 + \sigma_U^2\right)/2}}$$

$$= \frac{\left(\beta_M c\right)^\gamma - \left(\beta_U c\right)^\gamma}{\sqrt{\left(1 - \frac{\beta_U}{\beta_M}\right) A_f^2 N_{ext}^{2\gamma} + A_m^2 N_m^2 \left[A_f^2 N_{ext}^{2\gamma} + \frac{\left(\beta_M c\right)^{2\gamma} + \left(\beta_U c\right)^{2\gamma}}{2}\right] + A_a^2 N_a^2}}.$$

The similarity between the templates for discrimination of similar targets requires a correction for correlated responses to the same external noise sample in the matched and mismatched templates, $\sqrt{\left(1 - \frac{\beta_U}{\beta_M}\right)}$.

References

Baldassi, S., & Verghese, P. (2002). Comparing integration rules in visual search. *Journal of Vision, 2,* 559–570. Retrieved from http://journalofvision.org/2/8/3/ doi:10.1167/2.8.3

Brefczynski, J. A., & DeYoe, E. A. (1999). A physiological correlate of the "spotlight" of visual attention. *Nature Neuroscience, 2,* 370–374. doi:10.1038/7280

Buracas, G. T., & Boynton, G. M. (2007). The effect of spatial attention on contrast response functions in human visual cortex. *The Journal of Neuroscience, 27,* 93–97. doi:10.1523/JNEUROSCI.3162-06.2007

Burgess, A. E., Wagner, R. F., Jennings, R. J., & Barlow, H. B. (1981, October 2). Efficiency of human visual signal discrimination. *Science, 214,* 93–94. doi:10.1126/science.7280685

Cameron, E. L., Tai, J. C., & Carrasco, M. (2002). Covert attention affects the psychometric function of contrast sensitivity. *Vision Research, 42,* 949–967. doi:10.1016/S0042-6989(02)00039-1

Carrasco, M. (2009). Cross-modal attention enhances perceived contrast. *Proceedings of the National Academy of Sciences of the United States of America, 106*(52), 22039–22040. doi:10.1073/pnas.0913322107

Carrasco, M., Penpeci-Talgar, C., & Eckstein, M. (2000). Spatial covert attention increases contrast sensitivity across the CSF: Support for signal enhancement. *Vision Research, 40,* 1203–1215. doi:10.1016/S0042-6989(00)00024-9

Cheal, M. L., & Lyon, D. R. (1991). Central and peripheral precuing of forced-choice discrimination. *The Quarterly Journal of Experimental Psychology: Human Experimental Psychology, 43,* 859–880.

Cheal, M. L., & Lyon, D. R. (1992). Benefits from attention depend on the target type in location-precued discrimination. *Acta Psychologica, 81,* 243–267. doi:10.1016/0001-6918(92)90020-E

Cohen, E. H., Schnitzer, B. S., Gersch, T. M., Singh, M., & Kowler, E. (2007). The relationship between spatial pooling and attention in saccadic and perceptual tasks. *Vision Research, 47,* 1907–1923. doi:10.1016/j.visres.2007.03.018

Desimone, R., & Duncan, J. (1995). Neural mechanisms of selective visual attention. *Annual Review of Neuroscience, 18,* 193–222. doi:10.1146/annurev.ne.18.030195.001205

Dosher, B. A., Han, S., & Lu, Z.-L. (2010). Perceptual learning and attention: Reduction of object attention limitations with practice. *Vision Research, 50,* 402–415. doi:10.1016/j.visres.2009.09.010

Dosher, B. A., & Lu, Z.-L. (1998). Perceptual learning reflects external noise filtering and internal noise reduction through channel reweighting. *Proceedings of the National Academy of Science, 95,* 13988–13993.

Dosher, B. A., & Lu, Z.-L. (1999). Mechanisms of perceptual learning. *Vision Research, 39,* 3197–3221. doi:10.1016/S0042-6989(99)00059-0

Dosher, B. A., & Lu, Z.-L. (2000a). Mechanisms of perceptual attention in precuing of location. *Vision Research, 40,* 1269–1292. doi:10.1016/S0042-6989(00)00019-5

Dosher, B. A., & Lu, Z.-L. (2000b). Noise exclusion in spatial attention. *Psychological Science, 11,* 139–146. doi:10.1111/1467-9280.00229

Dosher, B. A., & Sperling, G. (1998). A century of human information processing theory: Vision, attention, memory. In J. Hochberg (Ed.), *Perception and cognition at century's end: Handbook of perception and cognition* (pp. 199–252). San Diego, CA: Academic Press.

Downing, C. J. (1988). Expectancy and visual-spatial attention: Effects on perceptual quality. *Journal of Experimental Psychology: Human Perception and Performance, 14,* 188–202. doi:10.1037/0096-1523.14.2.188

Duncan, J. (1984). Selective attention and the organization of visual information. *Journal of Experimental Psychology: General, 113,* 501–517. doi:10.1037/0096-3445.113.4.501

Duncan, J. (1993a). Coordination of what and where in visual attention. *Perception, 22,* 1261–1270. doi:10.1068/p221261

Duncan, J. (1993b). Similarity between concurrent visual discriminations: Dimensions and objects. *Perception & Psychophysics, 54,* 425–430. doi:10.3758/BF03211764

Duncan, J. (1998). Converging levels of analysis in the cognitive neuroscience of visual attention. *Philosophical Transactions of the Royal Society of London, Series B, 353,* 1307–1317. doi:10.1098/rstb.1998.0285

Eckstein, M. (1998). The lower visual search efficiency for conjunctions is due to noise and not serial attention processing. *Psychological Science, 9,* 111–118. doi:10.1111/1467-9280.00020

Gersch, T. M., Kowler, E., & Dosher, B. (2004). Dynamic allocation of visual attention during the execution of sequences of saccades. *Vision Research, 44,* 1469–1483. doi:10.1016/j.visres.2003.12.014

Gersch, T. M., Kowler, E., Schnitzer, B. S., & Dosher, B. (2009). Attention during sequences of saccades along marked and memorized paths. *Vision Research, 49,* 1256–1266. doi:10.1016/j.visres.2007.10.030

Gould, I. C., Wolfgang, B. J., & Smith, P. L. (2007). Spatial uncertainty explains exogenous and endogenous attentional cuing effects in visual signal detection. *Journal of Vision, 7,* 1–17. Retrieved from http://journalofvision.org/7/13/4/ doi:10.1167/7.13.4

Graham, N. (1989). *Visual pattern analyzers.* Oxford, England: Oxford University Press. doi:10.1093/acprof:oso/9780195051544.001.0001

Green, D. M., & Swets, J. A. (1966). *Signal detection theory and psychophysics.* New York, NY: Wiley.

Han, S., Dosher, B., & Lu, Z.-L. (2003). Object attention revisited: Identifying mechanisms and boundary conditions. *Psychological Science, 14,* 598–604. doi:10.1046/j.0956-7976.2003.psci_1471.x

Henderson, J. M. (1991). Stimulus discrimination following covert attentional orienting to an exogenous cue. *Journal of Experimental Psychology: Human Perception and Performance, 17,* 91–106. doi:10.1037/0096-1523.17.1.91

Henderson, J. M. (1996). Spatial precues affect target discrimination in the absence of visual noise. *Journal of Experimental Psychology: Human Perception and Performance, 22,* 780–787. doi:10.1037/0096-1523.22.3.780

Jeon, S. T., Lu, Z.-L., & Dosher, B. (2009). Characterizing perceptual performance at multiple discrimination precisions in external noise. *Journal of the Optical Society of America. A, Optics, Image Science, and Vision, 26*(11), B43–B58. doi:10.1364/JOSAA.26.000B43

Kowler, E., Anderson, E., Dosher, B. A., & Blaser, E. (1995). The role of attention in the programming of saccades. *Vision Research, 35,* 1897–1916. doi:10.1016/0042-6989(94)00279-U

Li, X., Lu, Z.-L., Tjan, B. S., Dosher, B., & Chu, W. (2008). Blood oxygenation level-dependent contrast response functions identify mechanisms of covert attention in early visual areas. *PNAS Proceedings of the National Academy of Sciences of the United States of America, 105,* 6202–6207. doi:10.1073/pnas.0801390105

Liu, S.-H., Dosher, B. A., & Lu, Z.-L. (2009). The role of judgment frames and task precision in object attention: Reduced template sharpness limits dual-object performance. *Vision Research, 49,* 1336–1351.

Lu, Z.-L., & Dosher, B. (1999). Characterizing human perceptual inefficiencies with equivalent internal noise. *Journal of the Optical Society of America A, 16,* 764–778.

Lu, Z.-L., & Dosher, B. (2000). Spatial attention: Different mechanisms for central and peripheral temporal precues? *Journal of Experimental Psychology: Human Perception and Performance, 26,* 1534–1548. doi:10.1037/0096-1523.26.5.1534

Lu, Z.-L., & Dosher, B. (2008). Characterizing observers using external noise and observer models. *Psychological Review, 115,* 44–82. doi:10.1037/0033-295X.115.1.44

Lu, Z.-L., Lesmes, L. A., & Dosher, B. (2002). Spatial attention excludes external noise at the target location. *Journal of Vision, 2,* 312–323. doi:10.1167/2.4.4

Lu, Z.-L., Li, X. R., Tjan, B., Dosher, B. A., & Chu, W. (2011). Attention extracts signal in external noise: A BOLD fMRI study. *Journal of Cognitive Neuroscience, 23,* 1148–1159.

Mertens, J. J. (1956). Influence of knowledge of a target location upon the probability of observation of peripherally observable test flashes. *Journal of the Optical Society of America, 46,* 1069–1070. doi:10.1364/JOSA.46.001069

Morgan, M. J., Ward, R. M., & Castet, E. (1998). Visual search for a tilted target: Tests of spatial uncertainty models. *The Quarterly Journal of Experimental Psychology, 51,* 347–370.

Palmer, J. (1994). Set-size effects in visual search: The effect of attention is independent of the stimulus for simple tasks. *Vision Research, 34,* 1703–1721. doi:10.1016/0042-6989(94)90128-7

Palmer, J., Ames, C. T., & Lindsey, D. T. (1993). Measuring the effect of attention on simple visual search. *Journal of Experimental Psychology: Human Perception and Performance, 19,* 108–130. doi:10.1037/0096-1523.19.1.108

Palmer, J., Verghese, P., & Pavel, M. (2000). The psychophysics of visual search. *Vision Research, 40,* 1227–1268. doi:10.1016/S0042-6989(99)00244-8

Pelli, D. G., & Farell, B. (1999). Why use noise? *Journal of the Optical Society of America A: Optics, Image Science, and Vision, 16,* 647–653. doi:10.1364/JOSAA.16.000647

Posner, M. I. (1980). Orienting of attention. *The Quarterly Journal of Experimental Psychology, 32,* 3–25. doi:10.1080/00335558008248231

Posner, M. I., Nissen, M. J., & Ogden, W. C. (1978). Attended and unattended processing modes: The role of set for spatial location. In H. I. Pick, Jr., & E. Saltzman (Eds.), *Modes of perceiving and processing information* (pp. 137–158). Hillsdale, NJ: Erlbaum.

Prinzmetal, W., Long, V., & Leonhardt, J. (2008). Attention and contrast. *Perception & Psychophysics, 70,* 1139–1150. doi:10.3758/PP.70.7.1139

Ratcliff, R. (1978). A theory of memory retrieval. *Psychological Review, 85,* 59–108. doi:10.1037/0033-295X.85.2.59

Ratcliff, R., & Smith, P. L. (2004). A comparison of sequential sampling models for two-choice reaction time. *Psychological Review, 111,* 333–367. doi:10.1037/0033-295X.111.2.333

Reynolds, J. H., Chelazzi, L., & Desimone, R. (1999). Competitive mechanisms subserve attention in macaque areas V2 and V4. *The Journal of Neuroscience, 19,* 1736–1753.

Reynolds, J. H., & Heeger, D. J. (2009). The normalization model of attention. *Neuron, 61,* 168–185. doi:10.1016/j.neuron.2009.01.002

Shaw, M. L. (1980). Identifying attentional and decision-making components in information processing. In R. S. Nickerson (Ed.), *Attention and performance VIII* (pp. 277–296). Hillsdale, NJ: Erlbaum.

Shaw, M. L. (1984). Division of attention among spatial locations: A fundamental difference between detection of letters and detection of luminance increment. In H. Bouma & D. G. Bouwhais (Eds.), *Attention and performance X* (pp. 109–121). Hillsdale, NJ: Erlbaum.

Shiffrin, R. M., & Schneider, W. (1977). Controlled and automatic human information-processing. 2. Perceptual learning, automatic attending, and a general theory. *Psychological Review, 84,* 127–190. doi:10.1037/0033-295X.84.2.127

Shiu, L., & Pashler, H. (1994). Negligible effect of spatial precuing on identification of single digits. *Journal of Experimental Psychology: Human Perception and Performance, 20,* 1037–1054. doi:10.1037/0096-1523.20.5.1037

Smith, P. L., & Ratcliff, R. (2009). An integrated theory of attention and decision making in visual signal detection. *Psychological Review, 116,* 283–317. doi:10.1037/a0015156

Smith, P. L., Ratcliff, R., & Wolfgang, B. J. (2004). Attention orienting and the time course of perceptual decisions: Response time distributions with masked and unmasked displays. *Vision Research, 44,* 1297–1320. doi:10.1016/j.visres.2004.01.002

Smith, P. L., Wolfgang, B. J., & Sinclair, A. (2004). Mask-dependent attentional cuing effects in visual signal detection: The psychometric function for contrast. *Perception & Psychophysics, 66,* 1056–1075. doi:10.3758/BF03194995

Sperling, G. (1989). Three stages and two systems of visual processing. *Spatial Vision, 4,* 183–207. doi:10.1163/156856889X00112

Sperling, G., & Dosher, B. (1986). Strategy and optimization in human information processing. In K. Boff, L. Kaufman, & J. Thomas (Eds.), *Handbook of Perception and Performance,* (Vol. 1, pp. 2.1–2.65). New York, NY: Wiley.

Sperling, G., & Melcher, M. J. (1978). The attention operating characteristic: Some examples from visual search. *Science, 202,* 315–318. doi:10.1126/science.694536

Wundt, W. (1912). *An introduction to psychology* (R. Pintner, Trans.). London, England: George Allen & Unwin.

10

Cortical Dynamics of Attentive Object Recognition, Scene Understanding, and Decision Making

Stephen Grossberg

This chapter discusses recent neural models that clarify how cortical dynamics carry out various higher level processes, such as attentive object learning and recognition, scene understanding, and decision making. These models contribute to research areas in which George Sperling has made important, indeed often seminal and pioneering, contributions, as noted subsequently. They are part of a coordinated research program aimed at developing an increasingly comprehensive model of visual intelligence.

View-Invariant Object Learning and Recognition

One model proposes how spatial and object attention are coordinated by visual surface and boundary representations to control object category learning and recognition. These processes are spread over multiple stages of the What and Where cortical processing streams. This project clarifies the following basic issues: What is an object? How does the brain learn what an object is under both unsupervised and supervised learning conditions? In particular, how does the brain learn to bind multiple views of an object into a view-invariant categorical representation of a complex object while scanning its various parts with active eye movements?

To solve this problem, one needs to face the following dilemma squarely: Suppose that, as your eyes scan a scene, two successive eye movements focus on different parts of the same object part of the time, and on different objects the rest of the time. How does the brain avoid the problem of erroneously classifying views of different objects as belonging to a single object? One cannot say that the brain does this by knowing that some views belong together whereas others do not because this can happen even before the brain has a concept of what the

DOI: 10.1037/14135-011
Human Information Processing: Vision, Memory, and Attention, C. Chubb, B. A. Dosher, Z.-L. Lu, and R. M. Shiffrin (Editors)

object is. Indeed, such scanning eye movements may be used to learn the object concept in the first place.

In addition, we take for granted the fact that our eyes seem to scan a scene intelligently, as quantified by earlier investigators such as Yarbus (1961). Why do not our saccades jump haphazardly from one part of a scene to another? How does the brain know how to direct the eyes to explore an object's surface even before it has a concept of the object?

A cortical model called ARTSCAN (see Figure 10.1) is being developed to explain how the brain uses scanning saccadic eye movements to learn view-invariant object categories (Fazl, Grossberg, & Mingolla, 2009). ARTSCAN predicts how spatial and object attention work together to direct eye movements to explore object surfaces and to enable learning of view-invariant object categories from the multiple view categories that are thereby learned. Of course, the development of ingenious experiments and modeling of the spatial and temporal characteristics of attention is a major theme in George Sperling's work, such as Reeves and Sperling (1986; see also Grossberg & Stone, 1986), Shih and Sperling (2002), and Weichselgartner and Sperling (1987). The ARTSCAN model proposes, in addition, that interactions between spatial and object attention during visual *search* are part of the brain system for visual *object learning*.

In particular, ARTSCAN predicts that spatial attention uses an *attentional shroud,* or form-fitting distribution of spatial attention, that is derived through feedback interactions with an object's surface representation. Tyler and Kontsevich (1995) introduced the concept of an attentional shroud as an alternative to the perception of simultaneous transparency and provided psychophysical evidence that only one plane is seen at a time within the perceptual moment. This concept focused on object perception. ARTSCAN proposes that an attentional shroud also plays a fundamental role in regulating object learning.

Such a shroud is proposed to persist within the Where Stream during active scanning of an object with attentional shifts and eye movements. This claim raises the basic question: How can the shroud persist during active scanning of an object if the brain has not yet learned that there is an object there? ARTSCAN proposes how a *preattentively* formed surface representation leads to activation of a shroud even before the brain can recognize the surface as representing a particular object (see Figure 10.2). Such a shroud can be formed starting with either bottom-up or top-down signals. In the bottom-up route (see Figures 10.2a and 10.2b), a surface representation (e.g., in visual cortical area V4) directly activates a shroud that conforms its shape to that of the surface, in a spatial attention cortical area (e.g., posterior parietal cortex). The shroud, in turn, can topographically prime the surface representation via top-down feedback. A *surface-shroud resonance* can hereby develop.

In the top-down route, a volitionally controlled, local focus of spatial attention (an attentional spotlight) can send a top-down attentional signal to a surface representation. This spotlight of enhanced activation can then fill in across the entire surface, being contained only by the surface boundary (Grossberg & Mingolla, 1985a). Surface filling in generates a higher level of filled-in surface activation than did the bottom-up input to the surface alone. The filling in of such a top-down attentional spotlight can hereby have an effect on the total filled-in surface activity that is similar to that caused by a higher bottom-up

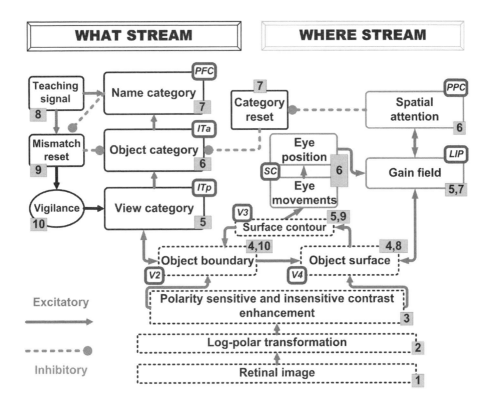

Figure 10.1. ARTSCAN model diagram. The Boundary and Surface processes have dashed borders and send input to both visual streams. The Where Stream modules have light gray borders, and the What Stream modules have black borders. The small white tabs with round edges next to each box represent the anatomical region in which the process is thought to occur. The numbers in the gray boxes next to each module box show the approximate order of first activation in that module after the retina receives an input. If there are two such numbers in a box, the second one represents the time that feedback reaches that module. Solid arrows represent excitatory connections, and dashed connections with a round head represent inhibitory ones. ITa = anterior part of inferotemporal cortex; ITp = posterior part of inferotemporal cortex; LIP = lateral intraparietal cortex; LGN = lateral geniculate nucleus; PFC = prefrontal cortex; SC = superior colliculus; V1 and V2 = primary and secondary visual areas; V3 and V4 = visual areas 3 and 4. See text for details. From "View-Invariant Object Category Learning, Recognition, and Search: How Spatial and Object Attention Are Coordinated Using Surface-Based Attentional Shrouds," by A. Fazl, S. Grossberg, and E. Mingolla, 2009, *Cognitive Psychology, 58,* p. 14. Copyright 2009 by Elsevier. Reprinted with permission.

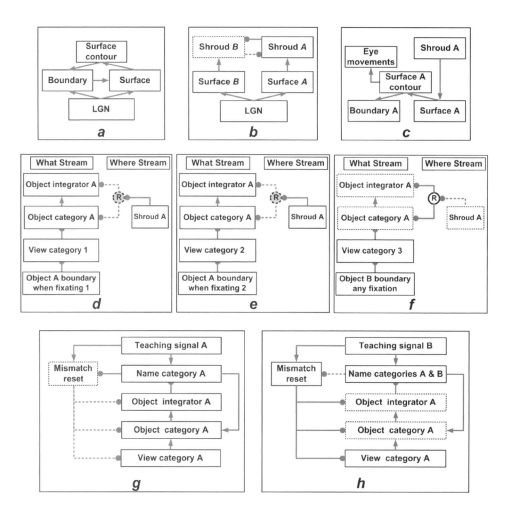

Figure 10.2. Schematic of ARTSCAN operations. (a–c): Where stream operations. (d–f): Unsupervised learning in ARTSCAN. (g–h): Supervised learning in ARTSCAN. (a) Preattentive boundary–surface interaction. The visual image represented in the lateral geniculate nucleus (LGN) input is processed by two cortical streams: boundaries and surfaces. Wherever there is a closed boundary on the boundary map, a surface will form as the result of gated diffusion on the surface map. These completed surfaces will in turn up-regulate their corresponding boundaries through feedback via surface contours. (b) Shroud formation. If there is more than one surface present, the competition between their representations on the spatial attention map results in a winner, called the attentional shroud. The coordinate transform between the retinotopic surface map and the head-centric spatial attention map in a gain field is not shown in these simplified diagrams. The attentional shroud enhances its corresponding surfaces through feedback. The circuit in panel c conveys this effect to surface contour and boundary maps. Surface contour feedback to the eye movement map increases the activity of all of the hotspots on an *attended* object, making them possible winners as the next saccade target. (d) The eyes fixate point 1 on object *A*, while the shroud has formed around that object. The feedback discussed in panels a through c has already down-regulated any other object boundary activities. This boundary activation excites View Category 1, object category neuron *A*, and its corresponding object integrator neuron. (e) If the eyes

stimulus contrast (Carrasco, Penpeci-Talgar, & Eckstein, 2000; Reynolds & Desimone, 2003). The more highly active surface representation can reactivate the spatial attention region to define a surface-form-fitting spatial locus of spatial attention, that is, a shroud. Again, the shroud is defined by a surface-shroud resonance.

Any surface in a scene can potentially sustain an attentional shroud, and surface representations dynamically compete for spatial attention (Figure 10.2b). The winner of the competition at a given moment gains activity and becomes the shroud. It has been proposed that perceptual boundaries are amodal, or invisible, within the boundary processing stream through primary visual cortical area (V1) interblobs, secondary visual area (V2) pale stripes, and V4. Visible percepts have been predicted to be surface percepts within the surface-processing stream through V1 blobs, V2 thin stripes, and V4 (Grossberg, 1994; Grossberg & Mingolla, 1985a). Earlier modeling work has also predicted that "all conscious states are resonant states" (Grossberg, 1980, 1999b, p. 1). These two streams of modeling come together in the assertion that surface-shroud resonances support conscious percepts of visible visual features. This hypothesis clarifies such phenomena as the visual neglect that occurs when a parietal lesion is made.

As saccadic eye movements explore an object's surface, the surface-induced shroud modulates object learning in the What Stream by maintaining activity of an emerging view-invariant category representation while multiple view-specific representations are linked to it through learning (Figure 10.2d and 10.2e). Output from the shroud also helps to select the boundary and surface features to which eye movements will be directed (Figure 10.2c) via a surface contour process that is predicted to play a key role in three-dimensional figure–ground

---

(Continued.) move to fixation point 2 on the same object, the new object boundary map activity might activate a different view category neuron 2, but it will activate the same object category and integrator A, because the attentional shroud is still active around the object A and inhibits the category reset neuron shown as R. (f) If the attentional shroud collapses around object A, the eyes can look at a different object, and another view category neuron will become active. Collapse of the attentional shroud disinhibits the category reset neurons, which inhibits all neurons in the two object layers, so these view category neurons will no longer be associated with object category neuron A. (g) If ARTSCAN receives the name of the object it is visiting, for example, object A, by a teaching signal A, it will associate it with the active object category and integrator neurons at that time. The activated name category neuron also inhibits the mismatch reset neuron. (h) Incorrect recall of object B's name. In the same scenario as in panel g, if the bottom-up input from object boundaries eventually excites name category A, but the teaching signal activates name B, both name category neurons A and B are activated, and, due to normalization by a shunting on-center off-surround network (see Figure 10.9), the activity of both will decrease to below a threshold such that none can inhibit the mismatch reset neuron anymore. This allows the teaching signal to activate the mismatch reset neuron and inhibit both object layers and stop learning. This also increases the vigilance parameters in the view category layer. From "View-Invariant Object Category Learning, Recognition, and Search: How Spatial and Object Attention Are Coordinated Using Surface-Based Attentional Shrouds," by A. Fazl, S. Grossberg, and E. Mingolla, 2009, *Cognitive Psychology, 58*, p. 14. Copyright 2009 by Elsevier. Reprinted with permission.

separation (Grossberg, 1994, 1997) and to be mediated via cortical area V3A (Nakamura & Colby, 2000, 2002).

The model postulates that an active shroud weakens through time due to self-inhibitory inputs at selected target locations ("inhibition of return"; Grossberg, 1978a, 1978b; Koch & Ullman, 1985), combined with chemical transmitters that habituate, or are depressed, in an activity-dependent way (Abbott, Sen, Varela, & Nelson, 1997; Francis, Grossberg, & Mingolla, 1994; Grossberg, 1968) and gate the signals that sustain the shroud. When an active shroud is weakened enough, it collapses and can no longer inhibit a reset signal (Figure 10.2f). When a reset signal is disinhibited, its tonic activity can transiently inhibit the active view-invariant object category in the What Stream, thereby preventing it from erroneously being linked to the view categories of subsequently foveated objects. Then a new shroud, corresponding to some other surface, is selected in the Where Stream, thereby inhibiting once again the reset signal, as a new object category is activated in the What Stream by the first view of the new object.

The model hereby predicts that a spatial attention shift causes a domain-independent transient reset signal that, in turn, causes a shift in categorization rules. Such a transient signal was recently reported in humans in medial superior parietal lobule by Chiu and Yantis (2009) using rapid event-related magnetic resonance imaging.

While a shroud remains active, several kinds of learning go on through time. The first kind is the bottom-up learning of a view-specific category, that is, a category that is activated by information about a specific view, or similar views, of the object (Figure 10.2d and 10.2e). The second kind of learning is top-down learning of an expectation that is activated by an active view-specific category. Such a learned expectation focuses attention on the pattern of *critical features* that are incorporated during learning into the prototype that is used to recognize variations of that particular object view. This type of top-down attention is *object attention* (Posner, 1980), and it is distinct from the *spatial attention* (Duncan, 1984) that the shroud embodies. Taken together, these bottom-up category learning and top-down expectation learning mechanisms have been predicted by adaptive resonance theory (ART) to enable the brain to rapidly learn, and stably remember, new object categories without experiencing catastrophic forgetting of previously learned object categories (Carpenter & Grossberg, 1993; Grossberg, 2003). Recent review articles summarize behavioral and neurobiological data that support all of the main ART predictions about how the brain does this, notably predictions about the role of top-down attention in regulating learning (Grossberg, 2003; Raizada & Grossberg, 2003).

These view-specific categories are, in turn, linked by associative learning to the emerging view-invariant object categories, the persistent activity of which is ensured by an active shroud (Figure 10.2d and 10.2e). In particular, even while a view-specific category is reset as the eyes move to foveate a new view of an object, the view-invariant category is protected from reset so that multiple view-specific categories of the same object can be associated with a single view-invariant object category. Surface-based spatial attention and object attention are hereby coordinated to learn view-invariant object categories and thereby to solve the view-to-object binding problem.

How does the brain move the eyes to scan different parts of an object before moving to scan other objects? Why do successive saccades not instead jump haphazardly around a scene? The ARTSCAN model traces this property to following basic design properties of the FACADE model of three-dimensional (3D) vision and figure–ground separation and its realization by laminar visual cortical circuits in the 3D LAMINART model (e.g., Cao & Grossberg, 2005; Grossberg & Yazdanbakhsh, 2005; Kelly & Grossberg, 2000). In these models, perceptual boundaries both initiate and block the filling in of surface lightness and color via *boundary-to-surface* signals, as shown in Figure 10.2a. Figure 10.2a also contains a *surface-to-boundary feedback* pathway, via a *surface contour* process (Figure 10.2c). This process was introduced in the FACADE model to ensure perceptual *consistency*: It explains how, even though boundaries and surfaces form according to *complementary* computational rules, they give rise to a *consistent* visual percept (Grossberg, 1994, 2003). Surface-to-boundary feedback ensures consistency by using the surface contours of successfully filled-in surfaces to confirm and strengthen the boundaries that triggered filling-in of these surfaces and to inhibit boundaries that do not, such as boundaries that do not surround a surface region. The FACADE model predicts that the surface-to-boundary feedback mechanism also plays a key role in 3D figure–ground separation.

This boundary–surface feedback loop is proposed to work as follows: 3D boundary signals are topographically projected from V2 Interstripes to V2 Thin Stripes. If a boundary is closed, it can contain the filling in of lightness and color within it. If the boundary has a sufficiently big gap, surface lightness and color can dissipate through the gap. The surface contour process is sensitive to the contrasts at the border of a successfully filled-in surface within a closed boundary. This contrast-sensitive process is realized by an on-center, off-surround network that detects the contours of successfully filled-in surfaces. This is a shunting on-center, off-surround network across position and within depth.

The surface contour outputs from successfully filled-in surfaces use topographic excitatory signals to strengthen the boundaries that generated these surfaces, and inhibitory signals to weaken spurious boundaries at the same positions but farther depths. This is an on-center, off-surround network within position and across depth. This surface-to-boundary feedback is predicted to arise from V2 Thin Stripes and terminate in V2 Pale Stripes.

By eliminating these spurious boundaries, surface-to-boundary feedback enables occluding surfaces and partially occluded surfaces to be separated onto different depth planes and allows partially occluded boundaries and surfaces to be amodally completed behind their occluders. Such completed representations can then be more easily recognized in the inferotemporal cortex and beyond. This sort of interaction can, for example, explain the *proximity luminance covariation* that has been described by Dosher, Sperling, and Wurst (1986). In summary, the FACADE model predicts why and how contour-sensitive surface-to-boundary feedback helps to define an object by ensuring that the correct object boundaries and surfaces are consistently bound together to form a preattentive object representation.

ARTSCAN predicts that the *same process* that preattentively defines and segregates objects in depth also regulates attentive learning of an object category. It does this by inducing sequences of scanning saccadic eye movements on an object surface, the spatial attentional shroud of which is active at any given time. Here is how that is proposed to happen.

First, the lateral geniculate nucleus (LGN) generates preattentive bottom-up inputs in response to the surfaces in a scene (Figure 10.2a). The surfaces, in turn, attempt to topographically activate spatial attention to form surface-fitting attentional shrouds (Figure 10.2b). The spatial attention network contains long-range inhibitory interactions that tend to select the strongest shroud and inhibit weaker ones, other things being equal (Figure 10.2b). The winning shroud sends topographic feedback to its generative surface, thereby activating it further (Figure 10.2c). Thus, as noted earlier, ARTSCAN predicts that surface representations receive both contrastive bottom-up inputs from areas such as the LGN and top-down spatial attention inputs from areas like the parietal cortex. Recent data support the view that attention can, in fact, increase the perceived brightness of a surface (Carrasco et al., 2000; Reynolds & Desimone, 2003) and connections from parietal areas to prestriate visual cortex are known (Cavada & Goldman-Rakic, 1989, 1991; Distler, Boussaoud, Desimone, & Ungerleider, 1993; Webster, Bachevalier, & Ungerleider, 1994).

ARTSCAN predicts that this feedback plays an important role in object learning. In particular, when the winning surface has its activation enhanced by top-down spatial attention, its contrast relative to its surround increases. As a result, *its surface contour signals increase.* As summarized in Figure 10.2c, stronger surface contour signals generate stronger eye movement target commands to the saccadic eye movement system to direct scanning eye movements to the object surface whose shroud is active. ARTSCAN hereby predicts how the views that the eyes happen to look at tend to belong to the same object surface (Theeuwes, Mathot, & Kingstone, 2010) while its spatial attentional shroud is on, and these are the views that will be learned.

Cortical area V3A is one possible brain area where such surface contour signals may get converted into eye movement target signals. Studies show that V3A is concerned with relative disparity (Backus, Fleet, Parker, & Heeger, 2001), gaze (Galletti & Battaglini, 1989), saccades (Caplovitz & Tse, 2007; Nakamura & Colby, 2000, 2002), and prehensile hand movements (Nakamura et al., 2001). This prediction clarifies how the process which helps to define separable object representations, also helps to guide our eyes to look at these object representations.

The ARTSCAN model learns with 98.1% accuracy on a letter database with letters that vary in size, position, and orientation. It does this while achieving a compression factor of 430 in the number of its category representations, compared with what would be required to learn the database without the view-invariant categories. The model also simulates reaction times (RTs) in human data about object-based attention: RTs are faster when responding to the noncued end of an attended object compared with a location outside the object, and slower engagement of attention to a new object occurs if attention has to first be disengaged from another object first (Brown & Denney, 2007; Egly, Driver, & Rafal, 1994).

ARTSCAN also provides new insights into the functional role of the *cortical magnification factor,* namely, the transformation from retinal to cortical representation is space-variant (Daniel & Whitteridge, 1961; Drasdo, 1977; Schwartz, 1977), a fact that cannot be ignored when analyzing how the eyes explore the world. These intrinsic variations in the input to the cortex, created by the combination of eye movements and cortical magnification on the same stationary object, are often larger than the extrinsic variations due to rigid transformations of the object itself. The ARTSCAN learning processes described here enable object category neurons to tolerate both *extrinsic* rigid object transformations due to movements of an object relative to an observer and *intrinsic* variations due to saccades that explore different parts of the same object.

Volitional Control of Spatial Attention Permits Multiple Shrouds to Coexist: Homologs With Working Memory Storage and Visual Imagery and Fantasy

Spatial attention need not form a shroud around only one object. Spatial attention can form over more than one object (Downing, 1988; Eriksen & Yeh, 1985; LaBerge & Brown, 1989; McMains & Somers, 2005; Pylyshyn & Storm, 1988; Yantis, 1992). I predict that the inhibitory gain that determines the strength of inhibition across shrouds (Figure 10.2b) is under volitional control by the basal ganglia. Weaker inhibition allows more than one shroud to exist at a time. One possible target of such volitional control is the inhibitory interneurons in cortical Layer 4. Volitional control of the balance between cortical excitation and inhibition is predicted to be a general brain mechanism that expresses itself behaviorally in strikingly different ways.

For example, in the visual cortex, top-down expectations provide attentional modulation of bottom-up inputs. They do so via a top-down, *modulatory* on-center, off-surround network that has its effect on Layer 4 cells (see Grossberg, 1999a, 2003, for supportive experimental data). The modulatory on-center can sensitize target cells to respond more vigorously and synchronously to attended visual feature combinations. If increasing volitional gain inhibits the inhibitory interneurons, it can convert the modulatory on-center into one that can drive suprathreshold activation of its target cells via a top-down expectation. This volitional mechanism has been predicted to enable top-down expectations to generate suprathreshold conscious percepts of visual imagery and fantasy (Grossberg, 2000b). When phasic volitional control over visual imagery and fantasy is replaced by tonic hyperactivity, hallucinations can occur, as in schizophrenia.

The same sort of volitional control is predicted in ventrolateral prefrontal cortex to control when a sequence of items is stored in a cognitive working memory (Grossberg & Pearson, 2008). These predictions suggest how homologous mechanisms within laminar neocortical circuits can carry out different functions: allocation of spatial attention in the parietal cortex, visual imagery and fantasy in the visual cortex, and working memory storage in the prefrontal cortex.

Scene Understanding: Gist, Texture, and Multiple-Scale Shrouds

Attentional shrouds can be allocated on multiple spatial scales to enable scene understanding to occur. This clarifies how humans may rapidly recognize a scene by shifting spatial attention from global gist to more local properties of textures and objects. The ARTSCENE neural model (Grossberg & Huang, 2009) proposes how to learn and predict scene identity incrementally by learning a scene's gist as a large-scale texture category and how to improve scenic prediction by sequentially scrutinizing finer textures of a scene that are selected by attentional shrouds (Figure 10.3). Scene identity is predicted via a learned mapping from multiple-scale gist and texture category activations. Tested on the real scene images from Oliva and Torralba (2001), this gist-plus-texture system can distinguish natural scene categories up to 92% correct, outperforms alternative models in the literature that use biologically implausible computations, and outperforms systems that use either gist or texture information alone. It was sufficient to combine texture information from the three largest annotated regions in an image to achieve good scene recognition. These texture measures correlate highly with scene identity, and the correlation strength is proportional to the texture size. On average, in the scenic database that was used to benchmark the model, three principal textures together constitute 92.7% of the total area of a landscape image in the data set and appear much more salient than small objects and textures.

The ARTSCENE model is consistent with several studies in global-to-local visual processing (e.g., Navon, 1977; Schyns & Oliva, 1994) and with the fact that human viewers can detect a named object in a scene within approximately 150 ms, that is, less than the average fixation time (~300 ms; Potter, 1975). The ARTSCENE computation of texture builds on circuits that combine multiple stages of oriented filtering, rectification, and lateral inhibition that were introduced in Grossberg and Mingolla (1985b) and then adapted by other authors (e.g., Chubb, Sperling, & Solomon, 1989; Solomon, Sperling, & Chubb, 1993; Sutter, Beck, & Graham, 1989).

Motion-Defined Objects, Formotion Interactions, and Eye Movement Control

Both the ARTSCAN and ARTSCENE models involve What cortical processing stream mechanisms of object category learning and recognition, and how they interact with Where cortical processing stream mechanisms of spatial attention and action. Both models consider the processing of object forms, which may be stationary or may move and thereby change their visible views with respect to an observer. However, neither model analyzes the related problems of motion-defined objects, how form and motion information interact to generate object percepts, and how the eye movements that enable tracking of moving objects to occur are controlled. Neural models of these processes have been developed with various colleagues over the years, and integrating of these remains a goal of current research.

Models of how smooth pursuit and saccadic eye movements are controlled have become ever more detailed in the characterization of their underlying brain processes and their explanatory and predictive range (e.g., Gancarz & Grossberg, 1998; Grossberg & Kuperstein, 1986, 1989; Grossberg, Roberts, Aguilar, & Bullock, 1997; Pack, Grossberg, & Mingolla, 2001; Srihasam, Bullock, & Grossberg, 2009).

The same is true about how motion-defined objects are perceived and how form and motion interact to generate object percepts and thereby to overcome

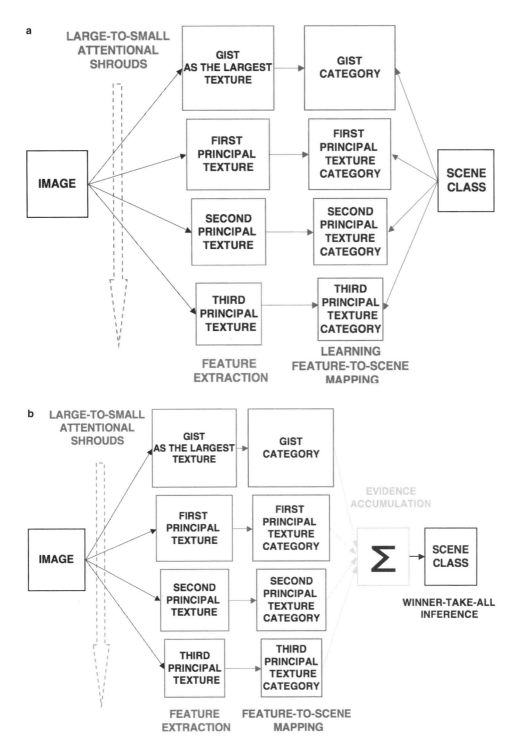

Figure 10.3. ARTSCENE model. (a) ARTSCENE training mode. (b) ARTSCENE testing mode. From "ARTSCENE: A Neural System for Natural Scene Classification," by S. Grossberg & T.-R. Huang, 2009, *Journal of Vision, 9,* p. 4. doi:10.1167/9.4.6 Copyright 2009 by Association for Research in Vision and Ophthalmology. Reprinted with permission.

the complementary deficiencies (Grossberg, 2000a) of the What and Where cortical processing streams, taken separately, in computing effective representations to define and track moving-objects-in-depth. To understand such processes, one needs to answer the following question: How do visual form and motion processes cooperate to compute object motion when each process separately is insufficient? Consider, for example, a deer moving behind a bush. Here the partially occluded fragments of motion signals available to an observer must be coherently grouped into the motion of a single object. A 3D FORMOTION model has been developed to answer this question (Baloch & Grossberg, 1997; Baloch, Grossberg, Mingolla, & Nogueira, 1999; Berzhanskaya, Grossberg, & Mingolla, 2007; Chey, Grossberg, & Mingolla, 1997, 1998; Grossberg, Mingolla, & Viswanathan, 2001; Grossberg & Rudd, 1989, 1992) and thereby to propose a solution of the global *aperture problem*. Wallach (1935) first showed that the motion of a featureless line seen behind a circular aperture is perceptually ambiguous: no matter what the real direction of motion may be, the perceived direction is perpendicular to the orientation of the line, that is, the *normal component* of motion. The aperture problem is faced by any localized neural motion sensor, such as a neuron in the early visual pathway, which responds to a local contour moving through an aperture-like receptive field. In contrast, a moving dot, line end, or corner provides unambiguous information about an object's true motion direction (Shimojo, Silverman, & Nakayama, 1989). The 3D FORMOTION model proposes how such moving visual features activate cells in the brain that compute *feature-tracking* signals which can disambiguate an object's true direction of motion.

In its current form, the 3D FORMOTION model comprises five important functional interactions involving the brain's form and motion systems that address such situations. In the first, 3D boundary representations, in which figures are separated from their backgrounds, are formed in cortical area V2, just as in Figure 10.2a. These depth-selective V2 boundaries select motion signals at the appropriate depths in middle temporal cortical area (MT) via V2-to-MT signals. In the second, motion signals in MT disambiguate locally incomplete or ambiguous boundary signals in V2 via MT-to-V1-to-V2 feedback. The third functional property concerns resolution of the aperture problem along straight moving contours by propagating the influence of unambiguous motion signals generated at contour terminators or corners. Here is where sparse feature-tracking signals, for example, from line ends, are amplified to overwhelm numerically superior ambiguous motion signals along line segment interiors. In the fourth, a spatially anisotropic motion grouping process takes place across perceptual space via feedback between MT and medial superior temporal cortical area (MST) to integrate veridical feature tracking and ambiguous motion signals to determine a global object motion percept. The fifth property can also use the MT–MST feedback loop to convey an attentional priming signal from higher brain areas back to V1 and V2. Baloch et al. (1999) have proposed how such form-motion, or *formotion,* interactions provide a neurobiological account of the type of *third-order motion* that George Sperling and his colleagues (e.g., Lu & Sperling, 1995a, 1995b) have so brilliantly articulated.

The 3D FORMOTION model has been used to simulate a wide range of perceptual data about motion perception, most of them without any other explanation at the present time. Rather than review these explanations, I would like to illustrate how a model can explain many data other than the ones that were used to discover its underlying design principles and brain mechanisms.

Temporal Dynamics of Decision Making During Motion Perception in the Visual Cortex

One such database concerns perceptual decision making, as exhibited by saccadic eye movements, during visual motion perception. Speed and accuracy of perceptual decisions are known from many types of experiments to covary with certainty in the input (Gold & Shadlen, 2007; Luce, 1986) and have been modeled by using statistical models. Recently, neurophysiologic data have been collected that correlate with the rate of evidence accumulation in parietal and frontal cortical "decision neurons." Such data challenge us to go beyond statistical models to discover how the brain accomplishes such decision making. A biophysically realistic model of interactions within and between retina/LGN and cortical areas V1, MT, MST, and lateral intraparietal (LIP), gated by basal ganglia, has been developed to quantitatively simulate dynamic properties of decision making in response to ambiguous visual motion stimuli (Grossberg & Pilly, 2008). This Motion Decision, or MODE, model clarifies how the brain circuits that were characterized in the 3D FORMOTION model to solve the aperture problem can also contribute to making probabilistic decisions in real time.

Some scientists have claimed that perception and decision-making can be described using Bayesian inference, or related general statistical ideas, that estimate the optimal interpretation of the stimulus given priors and likelihoods. However, such concepts do not disclose the neocortical mechanisms that enable perception and make decisions. The MODE model explains behavioral and neurophysiological decision-making data without an appeal to Bayesian concepts and, unlike other existing models of these data, generates perceptual representations and choice dynamics in response to the moving experimental visual stimuli. Quantitative model simulations include the time course of LIP neuronal dynamics, as well as behavioral accuracy and reaction time properties, during both correct and error trials at different levels of input ambiguity in both fixed duration (FD) and RT tasks. Model MT–MST interactions compute the global direction of random dot motion stimuli, whereas model LIP computes the stochastic perceptual decision that leads to a saccadic eye movement.

A valuable paradigm for studying decision making, which links psychophysics and neurophysiology, has been developed by Newsome, Shadlen, and colleagues (Roitman & Shadlen, 2002; Shadlen & Newsome, 2001). This research studies how brain dynamics in the LIP area relate to saccadic behavior of monkeys (percentage accuracy, RT) that are based on discriminating the motion direction of random dot motion stimuli at various degrees of coherence.

In these experiments, two kinds of tasks were used: FD and RT tasks. Macaques were trained to discriminate net motion direction and report it via a saccade. Random dot motion displays, covering a 5° diameter aperture centered at the fixation point on a computer monitor, were used to control motion coherence—namely, the fraction of dots moving nonrandomly in a particular direction from one frame to the next in each of the three interleaved sequences. Varying the motion coherence provided a quantitative way to manipulate the ambiguity of directional information that a monkey could use to make a saccadic eye movement to a peripheral choice target in the judged motion direction, and thus the task difficulty. More coherence resulted in better accuracy and faster responses.

In the FD task (Roitman & Shadlen, 2002; Shadlen & Newsome, 2001), monkeys viewed the moving dots for a fixed duration of 1 s and then made a saccade to the target in the judged direction after a variable delay. In the RT task (Roitman & Shadlen, 2002), monkeys had theoretically unlimited viewing time and were trained to report their decision as soon as the motion direction was determined. The RT task allowed measurement of how long it took the monkey to make a decision, which was defined as the time from the onset of the motion until when the monkey initiated a saccade. The two monkeys in the Roitman & Shadlen (2002, p. 9476) experiment were shaped during RT task training to initiate the choice saccade within "approximately 1 s" after the dots turn on. In each RT task trial, the monkeys had to wait for a minimum of about 1 s (one monkey: 800 ms; the other: 1,200 ms) after motion onset to receive a reward, however rapidly they responded. Human subjects in a similar RT task usually respond around 1 s from motion onset for the weakest coherence without any speed instruction (Palmer, Huk, & Shadlen, 2005, p. 385).

Neurophysiological recordings were done in LIP while the monkeys performed these tasks. The recorded neurons had receptive fields that encompassed just one target and did not include the circular aperture in which the moving dots were displayed. Additionally, they were among those that showed sustained activity during the delay period in a memory-guided saccade task. It was found that the speed and accuracy of perceptual decisions covaried strongly with the rate of evidence accumulation in LIP cells.

Figure 10.4 summarizes the MODE model processing stages. All the stages through MSTv are part of the 3D FORMOTION model. The new processes include saccadic target selection in cortical area LIP and gating of LIP cell responses by the basal ganglia. As noted earlier, the 3D FORMOTION model proposes a solution of the aperture problem. The LIP processing stage embodies a solution of the *noise-saturation problem* (Grossberg, 1973, 1980), which is faced by all neurons because their activations fluctuate within a small interval of possible values: How does a network of cells, or cell populations, remain sensitive to the spatially distributed pattern of their inputs as they vary greatly in size through time? Cells that interact in shunting recurrent on-center, off-surround networks are capable of solving this problem. A special case of such networks shows how the most highly activated cell, or cell population, is selected to make a decision.

In the Roitman and Shadlen (2002) and Shadlen and Newsome (2001) experiments, a fraction of the dots move randomly through time and another fraction move in a fixed direction. Local directional processes can be fooled when there are multiple dots in each frame, some dots move incoherently, or independent random dot motion sequences are interleaved through time. The directional transient cells (Figure 10.4) generate local directional signals between any two dots that occur with an appropriate spatiotemporal displacement.

Each processing stage in Figure 10.4 has been used to explain neurophysiological and anatomical data in the articles that introduced the 3D FORMOTION model. Here one comparison worth noting is between the elaborated Reichardt (1961) detectors that van Santen and Sperling (1985) put to good use in explaining various motion data, and the directional transient cells used in the 3D FORMOTION model. In the 3D FORMOTION model, directional transient cells build on the motion-veto directional circuit that was proposed by Barlow and Levick (1965). Grossberg, Mingolla, and Viswanathan (2001) elaborated that model to propose how directional selectivity could be ensured in response to targets moving with variable speeds. This was accomplished by a circuit in which nondirectional transient cells send signals to inhibitory directional interneurons and directional transient cells, and the inhibitory interneurons interact with each other and with the directional transient cells. This predicted interaction is consistent with recent retinal data concerning how bipolar cells interact with inhibitory starburst amacrine cells and direction-selective ganglion cells, and how starburst cells interact with each other and with ganglion cells (Fried, Münch, & Werblin, 2002). The possible role of starburst cell inhibitory interneurons in ensuring directional selectivity at a wide range of target speeds has not yet been tested.

The directional short-range filter (Figure 10.4) integrates directional evidence from any active directional transient cells that occur within its directionally selective receptive field. Typically some directions will be amplified more than others by the short-range filter. However, lower motion coherence, higher dot density, and more interleaving of stimulus frames in the definition of the random dot stimuli increase the probability that incorrect directional signals will be generated in the short-range filter and thereby reduce the impact of correct local groupings in determining a clear motion directional percept. Apart from being few in number, these correct directional signals also have a short life span because a new set of signal dots are chosen every frame. Therefore, the motion stream must somehow enable a relatively sparse set of short-lived and correct feature tracking signals to gradually discount the more numerous incorrect local directional groupings. This problem is in many ways similar to the aperture problem, even though individual moving dots do not cause an aperture problem.

Spatial and opponent directional competition selectively strengthen feature-tracking signals, weaken ambiguous motion signals, and create speed-sensitive receptive fields (Figure 10.4). These cells are predicted to be a Where cortical stream analog of the simple cells for form perception that are well known to occur in the What cortical stream. A directional long-range filter (Figure 10.4) then gives rise to true directional cells by pooling output signals with the same, or nearly the same, directional preference over multiple orientations, opposite contrast polarities, both eyes, and a larger spatial scale. The cells that receive inputs from the directional long-range filter are also predicted to be depth-selective. They are predicted to occur in cortical area MT and to be analogous to complex cells in the form pathway. The properties of sensitivity to speed, as well as pooling across multiple orientations, opposite contrast polarities, both eyes, and a range of depths, are not needed in our current simulations of direction discrimination.

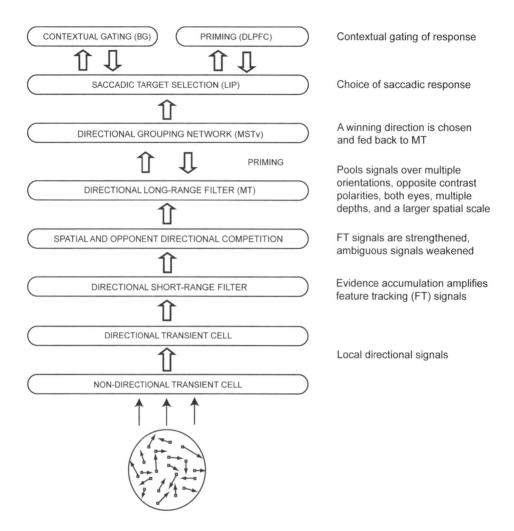

Figure 10.4.   Retina/LGN–V1–MT–MST–LIP–BG model processing stages. The first two model stages (change-sensitive receptors and directional transient cells) in Retina/ LGN compute local directional signals in response to image luminance increments or decrements. These signals feed into the directional short-range filter in V1, which accumulates evidence for motion in a given direction and thereby amplifies the feature tracking (FT) signals. Spatial and opponent directional competitions selectively strengthen FT signals, weaken ambiguous motion signals, and create speed-sensitive receptive fields. A long-range filter gives rise to true directional cells by pooling output signals with the same directional preference that survive the competitive stages. Within each direction, these signals are pooled over multiple orientations, opposite contrast polarities, both eyes, multiple depths, and a larger spatial scale. Pooling across multiple depths, both eyes, and opposite contrast polarities is not needed in the current simulations. These directional cells activate a directional grouping network, proposed to occur within cortical area MST, within which directions compete to determine a local winner. Enhanced feature tracking signals typically win this competition over ambiguous motion signals. Model MST cells that encode the winning direction feed back to model MT cells via a top-down spatial filter, where they indirectly boost directionally consistent cell activities by suppressing inconsistent activities over the spatial region to which they project. This

Figure 10.5 schematizes the LIP shunting recurrent on-center, off-surround network, also called a *recurrent competitive field,* that converts a spatially distributed, representation of motion into a directional saccadic decision, or command. Variants of this model, since its origin in Grossberg (1968) and Sperling and Sondhi (1968), as well as its mathematical analysis in Grossberg (1973), have been used by later authors to simulate the dynamics of perceptual or motor decisions in both deterministic models (e.g., Brown, Bullock, & Grossberg, 2004; Chey et al., 1997; Francis & Grossberg, 1996a, 1996b; Francis, Grossberg, & Mingolla, 1994) and stochastic models (Boardman, Grossberg, Myers, & Cohen, 1999; Cisek, 2006; Grossberg, Boardman, & Cohen, 1997; Usher & McClelland, 2001). Even a deterministic recurrent competitive field typically describes the temporal evolution of population mean activities and cell firing frequencies. It is only when properties that depend on the variance of cell firing become rate-limiting that explicit noise terms add explanatory power. Figures 10.6 through 10.8 illustrate the model's ability to simulate these data about decision making in response to motion stimuli, using the motion stimuli themselves as model inputs.

Concluding Remarks: Toward Solving the Mind–Body Problem

The several model examples that have been reviewed here are a small sample of those now being developed (see http://cns.bu.edu/~steve) for quantitatively explaining and predicting how brain mechanisms give rise to mental functions. These models embody new design principles that have been discovered by trying to explain psychological data as the result of an individual adapting autonomously to a changing world moment-by-moment in real time. The models have provided an ever-improving horizontal and a vertical understanding of behavioral and brain organization and dynamics: *horizontal* by showing how

---

(Continued.) feedback accomplishes directional and depthful motion capture within that region, whereas ambiguous or incoherent motion directions are suppressed. This shift in the spatial locus of unambiguous feature tracking signals continues to propagate across space as the MT-to-MST feedback process cycles through time. It is the action of this feedback loop that is predicted to solve the aperture problem and to generate a representation of global object direction and speed (Grossberg et al., 2001). This feedback loop between MT and MST is what regulates the temporal dynamics of decision making in the neurophysiological and behavioral data. The feedback loop needs more time to capture incoherent motion signals when there are more of them and cannot achieve as high a level of asymptotic response magnitude when more of them compete with the emerging winning direction. The motion information from MST is passed onto LIP, which converts it into an eye movement command, whereby the monkey reports its decision via a saccade. BG = basal ganglia; LIP = lateral intraparietal cortex; LGN = lateral geniculate nucleus; MST = medial superior temporal cortical area; MT = middle temporal cortical area; PFC = prefrontal cortex; SC = superior colliculus; V1 = primary visual area; V4 = visual area 4. From "Temporal Dynamics of Decision-Making During Motion Perception in the Visual Cortex," by S. Grossberg & P. Pilly, 2008, *Vision Research, 48,* p. 1347. Copyright 2008 by Elsevier. Reprinted with permission.

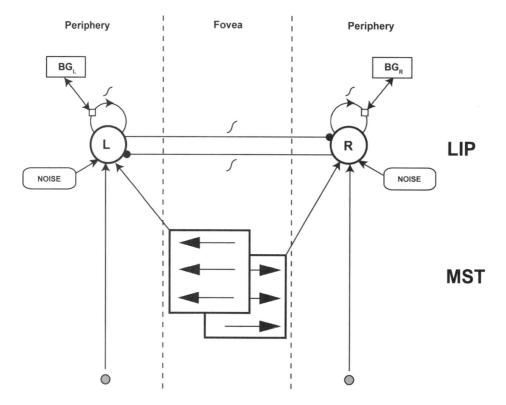

Figure 10.5. Lateral intraparietal cortex (LIP) decision circuit. The activities of cells in the recurrent competitive field predict the direction of the randomly moving dots. Each cell receives two bottom-up inputs: one from the form stream due to the presence of the peripheral choice target (indicated by a small circle) in the response field, and the other from the foveal medial superior temporal cortical area (MST) pool of the motion stream tuned to its preferred direction. The latter sensory input comes from outside the response field. This nonclassical neural connection is thought to result from training on the stereotypical task. Also, each cell self-excites itself and is inhibited by other competing cells in the field via different sigmoidal signal functions, which are indicated on the respective connections. The gain of the recurrent self-excitation is regulated by the basal ganglia. Internal noise processes to each cell help to simulate the probabilistic nature of perceptual decisions. BG = basal ganglia. From "Temporal Dynamics of Decision-Making During Motion Perception in the Visual Cortex," by S. Grossberg & P. Pilly, 2008, *Vision Research, 48,* p. 1351. Copyright 2008 by Elsevier. Reprinted with permission.

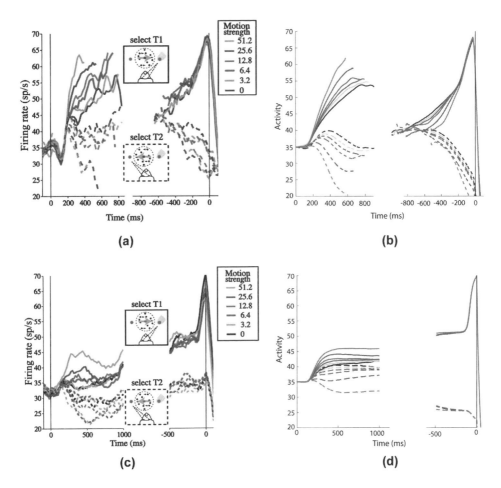

Figure 10.6. Temporal dynamics of lateral intraparietal cortex (LIP) neuronal responses during the fixed duration (FD) and reaction time (RT) tasks. (a) Average responses of a population of 54 LIP neurons among correct trials during the RT task (Roitman & Shadlen, 2002). The left part of the plot is time-aligned to the motion onset, includes activity only up to the median RT, and excludes any activity within 100 ms backward from saccade initiation (which roughly corresponds to presaccadic enhancement in firing). The right part of the plot is time-aligned to the saccade initiation and excludes any activity within 200 ms forward from motion onset (which corresponds to initial transient pause in firing). (b) Model simulations replicate LIP cell recordings during the RT task. In both data and simulations for the RT task, the average responses were smoothed with a 60-ms running mean. (c) Average responses of a population of 38 LIP neurons among correct trials during the 2002 FD task (Roitman & Shadlen, 2002) during both the motion viewing period (1 s) and a part (0.5 s) of the delay period before the saccade is made. (d) Model simulations mimic LIP cell recordings during the 2002 FD task.

(continued on next page)

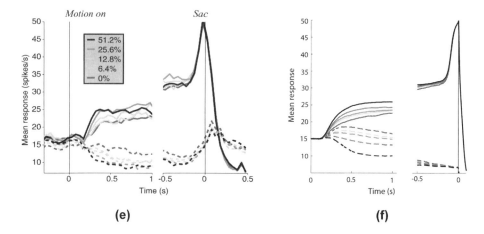

(e)   **(f)**

Figure 10.6. *(Continued).* (e) Average responses of a population of 104 LIP neurons among correct trials during the 2001 FD task (Shadlen & Newsome, 2001), during both the motion viewing period (1 s) and a part (0.5 s) of the delay period before the saccade is made. (f) Model simulations emulate LIP cell recordings during the 2001 FD task. In panels a through f, solid and dashed curves correspond to trials in which the monkey correctly chose the right target (T_{in}) and the left target (T_{out}), respectively. Cell dynamics (rate of rise or decline in both tasks and response magnitude in FD task) reflect the incoming sensory ambiguity and the perceptual decision (solid: T_{in} choices, dashed: T_{out} choices). Note that for 0% coherence, even though there is no correct choice per se, the average LIP response rose or declined depending on whether the monkey chose T_{in} or T_{out}, respectively. From "Temporal Dynamics of Decision-Making During Motion Perception in the Visual Cortex," by S. Grossberg & P. Pilly, 2008, *Vision Research, 48,* p. 1352. Copyright 2008 by Elsevier. Reprinted with permission.

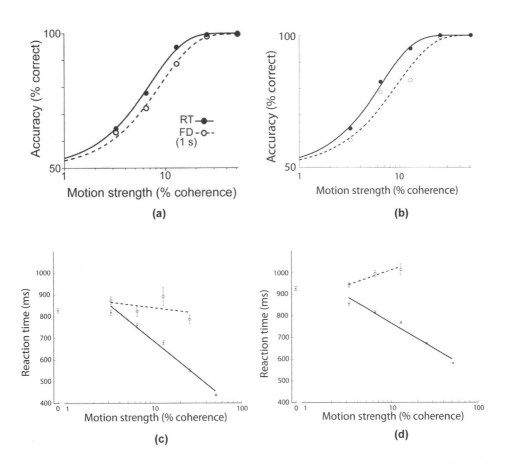

Figure 10.7. Psychometric and chronometric data during the fixed duration (FD) and reaction time (RT) tasks (Roitman & Shadlen, 2002). (a) Accuracy data (% correct) as a function of motion coherence (% certainty) is fit using a cumulative Weibull distribution function for both FD and RT tasks (Figure 6B in Mazurek et al., 2003). The ability to discriminate motion direction depends on the stimulus strength. Accuracy in the RT task is slightly better than that in the FD task for lower coherence levels. (b) Model simulations emulate these data. Solid curve corresponds to the RT task, and dashed curve to the 1-s FD task. Number of trials is 500. (c) Reaction time data (milliseconds) as a function of motion coherence (% certainty) is linear fit using a weighted, least squares estimate (as per the convention in Figure 3B of Roitman & Shadlen, 2002). The plot is prepared from the data for T_{out} (left target) choices in Table 2 of Roitman and Shadlen (2002). Data for T_{in} (right target) choices gives a similar plot. Less ambiguity implies a faster decision. Solid line corresponds to correct trials and dashed line to error trials. Error bars shown are standard errors of mean (SEM). SEMs decrease with coherence on correct trials but increase with coherence on error trials. Moreover, error trials have relatively higher SEMs. (d) Model simulations emulate the RT data on both correct and error trials. The behavior of SEMs with respect to coherence and correctness of trials is captured in the simulations. Number of trials is 500. In panels a through d, the abscissa is in the $\log_{10}$ scale. From "Temporal Dynamics of Decision-Making During Motion Perception in the Visual Cortex," by S. Grossberg & P. Pilly, 2008, *Vision Research, 48,* p. 1353. Copyright 2008 by Elsevier. Reprinted with permission.

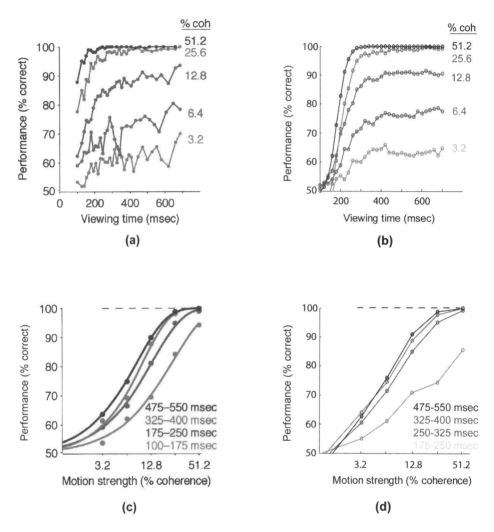

Figure 10.8. Influence of viewing duration on performance at various coherences in the fixed duration (FD) task paradigm. (a) Data from Gold and Shadlen (2003) show that the more time the dots are observed, the better the performance. This effect saturates at every coherence level. (b) Model simulations (2001 FD task) reproduce this influence of viewing time. (c) The psychometric function as a function of duration ranges. More viewing time tends to shift the psychometric function to the left, thus reducing the discrimination threshold. (d) The simulated psychometric functions capture these data trends. coh = coherence. From "Temporal Dynamics of Decision-Making During Motion Perception in the Visual Cortex," by S. Grossberg & P. Pilly, 2008, *Vision Research, 48,* p. 1354. Copyright 2008 by Elsevier. Reprinted with permission.

multiple brain regions cooperate to overcome the complementary deficiencies of individual regions acting alone (Grossberg, 2000a); *vertical* by explaining how multiple levels of organization, including behavior, neuroanatomy, neurophysiology, biophysics, and biochemistry, work together to control adaptive behaviors (e.g., Fiala, Grossberg, & Bullock, 1996; Grossberg & Versace, 2008). Such models illustrate how the classical mind–body problem is finally getting solved during our time.

References

Abbott, L. F., Sen, K., Varela, J. A., & Nelson, S. B. (1997). Synaptic depression and cortical gain control. *Science, 275,* 221–224. doi:10.1126/science.275.5297.221

Backus, B. T., Fleet, D. J., Parker, A. J., & Heeger, D. J. (2001). Human cortical activity correlates with stereoscopic depth perception. *Journal of Neurophysiology, 86,* 2054–2068.

Baloch, A. A., & Grossberg, S. (1997). A neural model of high-level motion processing: Line motion and formotion dynamics. *Vision Research, 37,* 3037–3059. doi:10.1016/S0042-6989(97)00103-X

Baloch, A. A., Grossberg, S., Mingolla, E., & Nogueira, C. A. M. (1999). A neural model of first-order and second-order motion perception and magnocellular dynamics. *Journal of the Optical Society of America A: Optics, Image Science, and Vision, 16,* 953–978. doi:10.1364/JOSAA.16.000953

Barlow, H. B., & Levick, W. R. (1965). The mechanism of directionally selective units in the rabbit's retina. *The Journal of Physiology, 178,* 477–504.

Berzhanskaya, J., Grossberg, S., & Mingolla, E. (2007). Laminar cortical dynamics of visual form and motion interactions during coherent object motion perception. *Spatial Vision, 20,* 337–395. doi:10.1163/156856807780919000

Boardman, I., Grossberg, S., Myers, C., & Cohen, M. (1999). Neural dynamics of perceptual order and context effects for variable-rate speech syllables. *Perception & Psychophysics, 61,* 1477–1500. doi:10.3758/BF03213112

Brown, J. M., & Denney, H. I. (2007). Shifting attention into and out of objects: Evaluating the processes underlying the object advantage. *Perception & Psychophysics, 69,* 606–618. doi:10.3758/BF03193918

Brown, J. W., Bullock, D., & Grossberg, S. (2004). How laminar frontal cortex and basal ganglia circuits interact to control planned and reactive saccades. *Neural Networks, 17,* 471–510. doi:10.1016/j.neunet.2003.08.006

Cao, Y., & Grossberg, S. (2005). A laminar cortical model of stereopsis and 3D surface perception: Closure and da Vinci stereopsis. *Spatial Vision, 18,* 515–578. doi:10.1163/156856805774406756

Caplovitz, G. P., & Tse, P. U. (2007). V3A processes contour curvature as a trackable feature for the perception of rotational motion. *Cerebral Cortex, 17,* 1179–1189. doi:10.1093/cercor/bhl029

Carpenter, G. A., & Grossberg, S. (1993). Normal and amnesic learning, recognition and memory by a neural model of cortico-hippocampal interactions. *Trends in Neurosciences, 16,* 131–137. doi:10.1016/0166-2236(93)90118-6

Carrasco, M., Penpeci-Talgar, C., & Eckstein, M. (2000). Spatial covert attention increases contrast sensitivity across the CSF: Support for signal enhancement. *Vision Research, 40,* 1203–1215. doi:10.1016/S0042-6989(00)00024-9

Cavada, C., & Goldman-Rakic, P. S. (1989). Posterior parietal cortex in rhesus monkey: II. Evidence for segregated corticocortical networks linking sensory and limbic areas with the frontal lobe. *The Journal of Comparative Neurology, 287,* 422–445. doi:10.1002/cne.902870403

Cavada, C., & Goldman-Rakic, P. S. (1991). Topographic segregation of corticostriatal projections from posterior parietal subdivisions in the macaque monkey. *Neuroscience, 42,* 683–696. doi:10.1016/0306-4522(91)90037-O

Chey, J., Grossberg, S., & Mingolla, E. (1997). Neural dynamics of motion grouping: From aperture ambiguity to object speed and direction. *Journal of the Optical Society of America A: Optics, Image Science, & Vision, 14,* 2570–2594. doi:10.1364/JOSAA.14.002570

Chey, J., Grossberg, S., & Mingolla, E. (1998). Neural dynamics of motion processing and speed discrimination. *Vision Research, 38,* 2769–2786. doi:10.1016/S0042-6989(97)00372-6

Chiu, Y.-C., & Yantis, S. (2009). A domain-independent source of cognitive control for task sets: Shifting spatial attention and switching categorization rules. *The Journal of Neuroscience, 29,* 3930–3938. doi:10.1523/JNEUROSCI.5737-08.2009

Chubb, C., Sperling, G., & Solomon, J. A. (1989). Texture interactions determine perceived contrast. *Proceedings of the National Academy of Sciences of the United States of America, 86,* 9631–9635. doi:10.1073/pnas.86.23.9631

Cisek, P. (2006). Integrated neural processes for defining potential actions and deciding between them: A computational model. *The Journal of Neuroscience, 26,* 9761–9770. doi:10.1523/JNEUROSCI.5605-05.2006

Daniel, P. M., & Whitteridge, D. (1961). The representation of the visual field on the cerebral cortex in monkeys. *The Journal of Physiology, 159,* 203–221.

Distler, C., Boussaoud, D., Desimone, R., & Ungerleider, L. G. (1993). Cortical connections of inferior temporal area TEO in macaque monkeys. *The Journal of Comparative Neurology, 334,* 125–150. doi:10.1002/cne.903340111

Dosher, B. A., Sperling, G., & Wurst, S. A. (1986). Tradeoffs between stereopsis and proximity luminance covariance as determinants of perceived 3D structure. *Vision Research, 26,* 973–990. doi:10.1016/0042-6989(86)90154-9

Downing, C. J. (1988). Expectancy and visual-spatial attention: effects on perceptual quality. *Journal of Experimental Psychology: Human Perception and Performance, 14,* 188–202. doi:10.1037/0096-1523.14.2.188

Drasdo, N. (1977, April 7). The neural representation of visual space [Letter]. *Nature, 266,* 554–556. doi:10.1038/266554a0

Duncan, J. (1984). Selective attention and the organization of visual information. *Journal of Experimental Psychology: General, 113,* 501–517. doi:10.1037/0096-3445.113.4.501

Egly, R., Driver, J., & Rafal, R. D. (1994). Shifting visual attention between objects and locations: Evidence from normal and parietal lesion subjects. *Journal of Experimental Psychology: General, 123,* 161–177. doi:10.1037/0096-3445.123.2.161

Eriksen, C. W., & Yeh, Y. Y. (1985). Allocation of attention in the visual field. *Journal of Experimental Psychology: Human Perception and Performance, 11,* 583–597. doi:10.1037/0096-1523.11.5.583

Fazl, A., Grossberg, S., & Mingolla, E. (2009). View-invariant object category learning, recognition, and search: How spatial and object attention are coordinated using surface-based attentional shrouds. *Cognitive Psychology, 58,* 1–48. doi:10.1016/j.cogpsych.2008.05.001

Fiala, J. C., Grossberg, S., & Bullock, D. (1996). Metabotropic glutamate receptor activation in cerebellar Purkinje cells as substrate for adaptive timing of the classically conditioned eye blink response. *The Journal of Neuroscience, 16,* 3760–3774.

Francis, G., & Grossberg, S. (1996a). Cortical dynamics of boundary segmentation and reset: Persistence, afterimages, and residual traces. *Perception, 25,* 543–567. doi:10.1068/p250543

Francis, G., & Grossberg, S. (1996b). Cortical dynamics of form and motion integration: Persistence, apparent motion and illusory contours. *Vision Research, 36,* 149–173. doi:10.1016/0042-6989(95)00052-2

Francis, G., Grossberg, S., & Mingolla, E. (1994). Cortical dynamics of feature binding and reset: Control of visual persistence. *Vision Research, 34,* 1089–1104. doi:10.1016/0042-6989(94)90012-4

Fried, S. I., Münch, T. A., & Werblin, F. S. (2002, November 28). Mechanisms and circuitry underlying directional selectivity in the retina [Letter]. *Nature, 420,* 411–414. doi:10.1038/nature01179

Galletti, C., & Battaglini, P. P. (1989). Gaze-dependent visual neurons in area V3A of monkey prestriate cortex. *The Journal of Neuroscience, 9,* 1112–1125.

Gancarz, G., & Grossberg, G. (1998). A neural model of the saccade generator in the reticular formation. *Neural Networks, 11,* 1159–1174. doi:10.1016/S0893-6080(98)00096-3

Gold, J. I., & Shadlen, M. N. (2007). The neural basis of decision making. *Annual Review of Neuroscience, 30,* 535–574. doi:10.1146/annurev.neuro.29.051605.113038

Grossberg, S. (1968). Some physiological and biochemical consequences of psychological postulates. *Proceedings of the National Academy of Sciences of the United States of America, 60,* 758–765. doi:10.1073/pnas.60.3.758

Grossberg, S. (1973). Contour enhancement, short-term memory, and constancies in reverberating neural networks. *Studies in Applied Mathematics, 52,* 213–257.

Grossberg, S. (1978a). Behavioral contrast in short term memory: Serial binary memory models or parallel continuous memory models? *Journal of Mathematical Psychology, 17,* 199–219. doi:10.1016/0022-2496(78)90016-0

Grossberg, S. (1978b). A theory of human memory: Self-organization and performance of sensory-motor codes, maps, and plans. In R. Rosen & F. Snell (Eds.), *Progress in theoretical biology* (Vol. 5, pp. 233–374). New York, NY: Academic Press.

Grossberg, S. (1980). How does a brain build a cognitive code? *Psychological Review, 87,* 1–51. doi:10.1037/0033-295X.87.1.1

Grossberg, S. (1994). 3-D vision and figure-ground separation by visual cortex. *Perception & Psychophysics, 55,* 48–120. doi:10.3758/BF03206880

Grossberg, S. (1997). Cortical dynamics of three-dimensional figure-ground perception of two-dimensional pictures. *Psychological Review, 104,* 618–658. doi:10.1037/0033-295X.104.3.618

Grossberg, S. (1999a). How does the cerebral cortex work? Learning, attention, and grouping by the laminar circuits of visual cortex. *Spatial Vision, 12,* 163–185. doi:10.1163/156856899X00102

Grossberg, S. (1999b). The link between brain learning, attention, and consciousness. *Consciousness and Cognition: An International Journal, 8,* 1–44. doi:10.1006/ccog.1998.0372

Grossberg, S. (2000a). The complementary brain: Unifying brain dynamics and modularity. *Trends in Cognitive Sciences, 4,* 233–246. doi:10.1016/S1364-6613(00)01464-9

Grossberg, S. (2000b). How hallucinations may arise from brain mechanisms of learning, attention, and volition. Invited article for the *Journal of the International Neuropsychological Society, 6,* 579-588.

Grossberg, S. (2003). How does the cerebral cortex work? Development, learning, attention, and 3D vision by laminar circuits of visual cortex. *Behavioral and Cognitive Neuroscience Reviews, 2,* 47–76. doi:10.1177/1534582303002001003

Grossberg, S., Boardman, I., & Cohen, C. (1997). Neural dynamics of variable-rate speech categorization. *Journal of Experimental Psychology: Human Perception and Performance, 23,* 481–503. doi:10.1037/0096-1523.23.2.481

Grossberg, S., & Huang, T.-R. (2009). ARTSCENE: A neural system for natural scene classification. *Journal of Vision, 9,* 1–19. doi:10.1167/9.4.6

Grossberg, S., & Kuperstein, M. (1986). *Neural dynamics of adaptive sensory-motor control: Ballistic eye movements.* Amsterdam, North Holland: Pergamon Press.

Grossberg, S., & Kuperstein, M. (1986/1989). *Neural dynamics of adaptive sensory-motor control: Ballistic eye movements* (2nd ed.). Amsterdam, North Holland: Pergamon Press.

Grossberg, S., & Mingolla, E. (1985a). Neural dynamics of form perception: Boundary completion, illusory figures, and neon color spreading. *Psychological Review, 92,* 173–211. doi:10.1037/0033-295X.92.2.173

Grossberg, S., & Mingolla, E. (1985b). Neural dynamics of perceptual grouping: Textures, boundaries, and emergent segmentations. *Perception & Psychophysics, 38,* 141–171. doi:10.3758/BF03198851

Grossberg, S., Mingolla, E., & Viswanathan, L. (2001). Neural dynamics of motion integration and segmentation within and across apertures. *Vision Research, 41,* 2521–2553. doi:10.1016/S0042-6989(01)00131-6

Grossberg, S., & Pearson, L. (2008). Laminar cortical dynamics of cognitive and motor working memory, sequence learning and performance: Toward a unified theory of how the cerebral cortex works. *Psychological Review, 115,* 677–732. doi:10.1037/a0012618

Grossberg, S., & Pilly, P. (2008). Temporal dynamics of decision-making during motion perception in the visual cortex. *Vision Research, 48,* 1345–1373. doi:10.1016/j.visres.2008.02.019

Grossberg, S., Roberts, K., Aguilar, M., & Bullock, D. (1997). A neural model of multimodal adaptive saccadic eye movement control by superior colliculus. *The Journal of Neuroscience, 17,* 9706–9725.

Grossberg, S., & Rudd, M. (1989). A neural architecture for visual motion perception: Group and element apparent motion. *Neural Networks, 2,* 421–450. doi:10.1016/0893-6080(89)90042-7

Grossberg, S., & Rudd, M. E. (1992). Cortical dynamics of visual motion perception: Short-range and long-range apparent motion. *Psychological Review, 99,* 78–121. doi:10.1037/0033-295X.99.1.78

Grossberg, S., & Stone, G. O. (1986). Neural dynamics of attention switching and temporal order information in short-term memory. *Memory & Cognition, 14,* 451–468. doi:10.3758/BF03202517

Grossberg, S., & Versace, M. (2008). Spikes, synchrony, and attentive learning by laminar thalamo-cortical circuits. *Brain Research, 1218,* 278–312. doi:10.1016/j.brainres.2008.04.024

Grossberg, S., & Yazdanbakhsh, A. (2005). Laminar cortical dynamics of 3D surface perception: Stratification, transparency, and neon color spreading. *Vision Research, 45,* 1725–1743. doi:10.1016/j.visres.2005.01.006

Kelly, F., & Grossberg, S. (2000). Neural dynamics of 3-D surface perception: Figure-ground separation and lightness perception. *Perception & Psychophysics, 62,* 1596–1618. doi:10.3758/BF03212158

Koch, C., & Ullman, S. (1985). Shifts in selective visual attention: Toward the underlying neural circuitry. *Human Neurobiology, 4,* 219–227.

LaBerge, D., & Brown, V. (1989). Theory of attentional operations in shape identification. *Psychological Review, 96,* 101–124. doi:10.1037/0033-295X.96.1.101

Lu, Z.-L., & Sperling, G. (1995a). Attention-generated apparent motion. *Nature, 377,* 237–239.

Lu, Z.-L., & Sperling, G. (1995b). The functional architecture of human visual motion perception. *Vision Research, 35,* 2697–2722. doi:10.1016/0042-6989(95)00025-U

Luce, R. D. (1986). *Response times: Their role in inferring elementary mental organization.* New York, NY: Oxford University.

McMains, S. A., & Somers, D. C. (2005). Processing efficiency of divided spatial attention mechanisms in human visual cortex. *The Journal of Neuroscience, 25,* 9444–9448. doi:10.1523/JNEUROSCI.2647-05.2005

Nakamura, K., & Colby, C. L. (2000). Visual, saccade-related, and cognitive activation of single neurons in monkey extrastriate area V3A. *Journal of Neurophysiology, 84,* 677–692.

Nakamura, K., & Colby, C. L. (2002). Updating of the visual representation in monkey striate and extrastriate cortex during saccades. *Proceedings of the National Academy of Sciences of the United States of America, 99,* 4026–4031. doi:10.1073/pnas.052379899

Nakamura, H., Kuroda, T., Wakita, M., Kusunoki, M., Kato, A., Mikami, A., . . . Itoh, K. (2001). From three-dimensional space vision to prehensile hand movements: The lateral intraparietal area links the area V3A and the anterior intraparietal area in macaques. *The Journal of Neuroscience, 21,* 8174–8187.

Navon, D. (1977). Forest before trees: The precedence of global features in visual perception. *Cognitive Psychology, 9,* 353–383. doi:10.1016/0010-0285(77)90012-3

Oliva, A., & Torralba, A. (2001). Modeling the shape of the scene: A holistic representation of the spatial envelope. *International Journal of Computer Vision, 42,* 145–175. doi:10.1023/A:1011139631724

Pack, C., Grossberg, S., & Mingolla, E. (2001). A neural model of smooth pursuit control and motion perception by cortical area MST. *Journal of Cognitive Neuroscience, 13,* 102–120. doi:10.1162/089892901564207

Palmer, J., Huk, A., & Shadlen, M. N. (2005). The effect of stimulus strength on the speed and accuracy of a perceptual decision. *Journal of Vision, 5,* 376–404. doi:10.1167/5.5.1

Posner, M. I. (1980). Orienting of attention. *The Quarterly Journal of Experimental Psychology, 32,* 3–25. doi:10.1080/00335558008248231

Potter, M. C. (1975, March 14). Meaning in visual search. *Science, 187,* 965–966. doi:10.1126/science.1145183

Pylyshyn, Z. W., & Storm, R. W. (1988). Tracking multiple independent targets: Evidence for a parallel tracking mechanism. *Spatial Vision, 3,* 179–197. doi:10.1163/156856888X00122

Raizada, R. D., & Grossberg, S. (2003). Towards a theory of the laminar architecture of cerebral cortex: Computational clues from the visual system. *Cerebral Cortex, 13,* 100–113. doi:10.1093/cercor/13.1.100

Reeves, A., & Sperling, G. (1986). Attention gating in short-term visual memory. *Psychological Review, 93,* 180–206. doi:10.1037/0033-295X.93.2.180

Reichardt, W. (1961). Autocorrection, a principle for the evaluation of sensory information by the central nervous system. In W. A. Rosenblith (Ed.), *Sensory communication* (pp. 303–317). New York, NY: Wiley.

Reynolds, J. H., & Desimone, R. (2003). Interacting roles of attention and visual salience in V4. *Neuron, 37,* 853–863. doi:10.1016/S0896-6273(03)00097-7

Roitman, J. D., & Shadlen, M. N. (2002). Response of neurons in the lateral intraparietal area during a combined visual discrimination reaction time task. *The Journal of Neuroscience, 22,* 9475–9489.

Schwartz, E. L. (1977). Spatial mapping in the primate sensory projection: Analytic structure and relevance to perception. *Biological Cybernetics, 25,* 181–194. doi:10.1007/BF01885636

Schyns, P. G., & Oliva, A. (1994). From blobs to boundary edges: Evidence for time-and spatial-scale-dependent scene recognition. *Psychological Science, 5,* 195–200. doi:10.1111/j.1467-9280.1994.tb00500.x

Shadlen, M. N., & Newsome, W. T. (2001). Neural basis of a perceptual decision in the parietal cortex (area LIP) of the rhesus monkey. *Journal of Neurophysiology, 86,* 1916–1936.

Shih, S.-I., & Sperling, G. (2002). Measuring and modeling the trajectory of visual spatial attention. *Psychological Review, 109,* 260–305. doi:10.1037/0033-295X.109.2.260

Shimojo, S., Silverman, G. H., & Nakayama, K. (1989). Occlusion and the solution to the aperture problem for motion. *Vision Research, 29,* 619–626. doi:10.1016/0042-6989(89)90047-3

Solomon, J. A., Sperling, G., & Chubb, C. (1993). The lateral inhibition of perceived contrast is indifferent to on-center/off-center segregation, but specific to orientation. *Vision Research, 33,* 2671–2683. doi:10.1016/0042-6989(93)90227-N

Sperling, G., & Sondhi, M. M. (1968). Model for visual luminance discrimination and flicker detection. *Journal of the Optical Society of America, 58,* 1133–1145. doi:10.1364/JOSA.58.001133

Srihasam, K., Bullock, D., & Grossberg, S. (2009). Target selection by frontal cortex during coordinated saccadic and smooth pursuit eye movements. *Journal of Cognitive Neuroscience, 21,* 1611–1627. doi:10.1162/jocn.2009.21139

Sutter, A., Beck, J., & Graham, N. (1989). Contrast and spatial variables in texture segregation: Testing a simple spatial-frequency channel model. *Perception & Psychophysics, 46,* 312–332. doi:10.3758/BF03204985

Theeuwes, J., Mathot, S., & Kingstone, A. (2010). Object-based eye movements: The eyes prefer to stay within the same object. *Attention, Perception, & Psychophysics, 72,* 597–601. doi:10.3758/APP.72.3.597

Tyler, C. W., & Kontsevich, L. L. (1995). Mechanisms of stereoscopic processing: Stereoattention and surface perception in depth reconstruction. *Perception, 24,* 127–153. doi:10.1068/p240127

Usher, M., & McClelland, J. L. (2001). On the time course of perceptual choice: The leaky competing accumulator model. *Psychological Review, 108,* 550–592. doi:10.1037/0033-295X.108.3.550

van Santen, J. P. H., & Sperling, G. (1985). Elaborated Reichard detectors. *Journal of the Optical Society of America A: Optics and Image Science, 2,* 300–321. doi:10.1364/JOSAA.2.000300

Wallach, H. (1935). On the visually perceived direction of motion. *Psychologische Forschung, 20,* 325–380. doi:10.1007/BF02409790

Webster, M. J., Bachevalier, J., & Ungerleider, L. G. (1994). Connections of inferior temporal areas TEO and TE with parietal and frontal cortex in macaque monkeys. *Cerebral Cortex, 4,* 470–483. doi:10.1093/cercor/4.5.470

Weichselgartner, E., & Sperling, G. (1987). Dynamics of automatic and controlled visual attention. *Science, 238,* 778–780. doi:10.1126/science.3672124

Yantis, S. (1992). Multielement visual tracking: Attention and perceptual organization. *Cognitive Psychology, 24,* 295–340. doi:10.1016/0010-0285(92)90010-Y

Yarbus, A. L. (1961). Eye movements during the examination of complicated objects. *Biofizika, 6,* 52–56.

11

The Auditory Attention Band

Adam Reeves

When led to expect a near-threshold auditory tone of a particular "signal" frequency by cuing the signal on every trial or presenting it often, listeners preferentially detect tones in an "attention band" centered on that frequency. This is shown by a decrease in the detection of other, uncued, less common, and therefore unexpected, tones ("probes") that are progressively farther in frequency from the signal (Greenberg & Larkin, 1968). The shape of the attention band derived from these detection probabilities usually matches that of the *critical band,* the band in which neighboring frequencies interact. The critical band is fundamental in modeling auditory frequency perception; for example, threshold is elevated by noise inside the critical band centered on the signal frequency, whereas noise outside it has no effect, and tones inside the same critical band summate in loudness, whereas those in different bands do not (Scharf, 1970). That the attention band matches the critical band suggests that listeners can monitor a single critical band (Scharf, Quigley, Aoki, Peachey, & Reeves, 1987) or even two nonadjacent ones (Schlauch & Hafter, 1991), a conclusion that would be of considerable theoretical import. However, although Wright and Dai (1994) found the usual match using 295-ms tones, the attention band was much wider than the critical band for 5-ms tones. This anomaly may be explained if the frequency of the threshold-level 5-ms tone (2,500 Hz) was poorly encoded by the listeners, making it impossible to attend to a specific signal frequency, but our results with 20- and 40-ms tones make this unlikely (Experiment 1). An explanation preferred here is that the listener directs attention broadly toward the expected frequency at the start of the trial (*endogenous* control), but only when stimulated can the auditory system focus precisely onto the signal (*exogenous* control), focusing taking more than 5 ms. Focusing is probably complete within 52 ms (Reeves & Scharf, 2010); when complete, the precision of attention is limited only by the critical band. Without endogenous control, a probe tone distant in frequency would also force focusing and so would be as well detected as a signal; without exogenous control, the attention band would be broad at all durations.

DOI: 10.1037/14135-012

Human Information Processing: Vision, Memory, and Attention, C. Chubb, B. A. Dosher, Z.-L. Lu, and R. M. Shiffrin (Editors)

Like the critical band, the attention band is probably formed in the cochlea, being revealed with pure tones but not with difference tones (Scharf et al., 1987). Indeed, sectioning the olivocochlear bundle (OCB), as a by-product of vestibular nerve ablation in Meniere's patients, prevents feedback to the cochlea and almost eliminates the attention band, even though thresholds and critical bands are unaffected (Scharf, 1998). Because detection thresholds for signals in white noise are equal before and after ablation, OCB feedback must suppress probes rather than enhance signals. Thus, when tones are brief, suppression does not have time to occur, and probes may still be heard, but when tones are long, suppression has time to attenuate distant critical bands, and precise focusing is revealed. This idea can be captured by a model in which the listener is cued (endogenously) to attend to a broad range of frequencies encompassing several critical bands that surround the signal. Detection occurs if any of these critical bands is stimulated, implying that the wide detection contour found with brief tones—the wide attention band—can be modeled by probability summation across bands. However, as focusing proceeds, irrelevant filters are excluded (exogenously), so that the bands detecting distant probes are no longer processed, and the attention band narrows.

To anticipate the experimental results, the attention bands for 20- and 40-ms tones were indeed broad but also showed an unexpected asymmetry in which lower frequency probes close to the signal were favored over higher frequency probes—and in some cases even over the signal itself. This result, which has never been seen with long-duration tones, seemed incredible; why would a rarely presented lower frequency probe tone be heard better than the signal to which attention is devoted, when the experiment was carefully designed to minimize off-frequency listening? However, it turned out that the probability summation model accounts for the attention-band asymmetry even when attention is disposed symmetrically on either side of the signal, illustrating a principle of Sperling (1984) that data from compound tasks such as the one used here do not reveal attention effects in a model-free manner.

Method

Listeners were undergraduate students with normal hearing from Northeastern University, ages 18 to 24 years, who served for single-experimental sessions of 50 to 70 min for course credit. They sat in a small "Eckoustic" sound-isolated booth (Eckel Industries, Ontario, Canada). Tones (signals, probes, and cues) were generated digitally at 50-K sampling rate by a Tucker-Davis (TDT) System II interfaced to an AP2 card in Pentium computer running Pascal, or a TDT System III (RP2.1) in a Dell Optiplex computer running Matlab (with custom software). Sound was sent through a headphone driver (HB6 or HB7) to the left ear via a calibrated Sony MDR-V6 headphone. System II generated broadband background noise using an analogue noise source (WG1) and band-pass filter (PF1); noise level was checked each session. System III generated noise digitally (a new sample on each trial) simulating an analogue bi-quad five-pole bandpass filter; noise levels, being stable, were checked only at the end of each experiment. Testing was monaural (left ear). Noise cutoff frequencies were 300 and

1,800 Hz. Noise sound pressure level (SPL) was 80 dB (SL 48.2 dB or 70 dB in Experiment 2). Tones were gated sinusoids; the constant amplitude part of the waveform was 20 ms, 40 ms, or 300 ms in duration, with an additional cosine-squared rising or falling ramp of 5 ms (System II) or a 7-ms rise and 5.3-ms fall (System III). Tone duration was fixed for each session. Waveforms were checked using a Tektronix TAS220 oscilloscope, and frequency content was measured with a wave-analyzer (GRC 1900) using a 50-dB-wide filter. Thresholds were measured initially using a two-interval forced choice method converging on 79% correct (Scharf, Reeves, & Suciu, 2007) and averaged over nine to 11 naive listeners in each TDT system at each duration and frequency (570, 700, 840, 925, 1,000, 1,075, 1,170, 1,370, and 1,600 Hz). Signals and probes were set to the 79% threshold level in the main experiments, the levels being adjusted en masse by 1 or 2 dB to account for individual differences in hearing.

Probe-Signal Procedure

Each trial began with a cue tone with the duration and frequency of the signal, set 6 dB above threshold. Such a *valid* cue was designed to help the listener concentrate attention on the signal frequency. The cue was followed 300 ms later (500 ms in Experiment 1) by an *observation period,* either two 400-ms intervals, one containing a tone (in two-interval forced-choice [2IFC]) or a single interval with a tone on half the trials (in Yes–No; see Figure 11.1, insert), the intervals

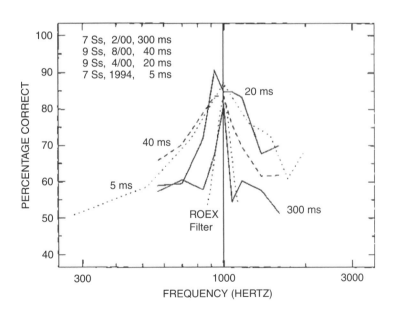

Figure 11.1. Percentage correct (2IFC) plotted against frequency in Hz. Chance is 50%. The signal (1,000 Hz) is marked by a vertical line; other data are for probes. Data at 300 ms, 40 ms, and 20 ms are ours. Data at 5 ms (Wright & Dai, 1994) are replotted and scaled down from 2,500 Hz. Dots marked ROEX (rounded exponential) model the critical band at 1,000 Hz.

being marked by visual signals. The listener pressed a button to report either the interval (in 2IFC) or the presence (Yes–No) of the tone, upon which the correct answer was fed back. In Yes–No trials, the cue was followed by noise alone on half the trials, by the signal on quarter of the trials, and by one of the eight probes on the remaining quarter, at random. In 2IFC trials, the signal occurred on half the trials and one of the eight probes on the other half, again at random. Because probes and signals were never presented on the same trial, this is a "compound" rather than a "concurrent" task (Sperling, 1984). The method (2IFC or Yes–No) was fixed in each hour-long session of 12 blocks, each block containing 64 trials. Trials were self-paced.

Experiment 1

Experiment 1 provided measurements of the attention band for 20-, 40-, and 300-ms tones in white noise, using the 2IFC method on the TDT System II. The 1,000-Hz signal occurred on half the trials and was cued on every trial. The *multiprobe method* of Dai, Scharf, and Buus (1991) was used in which each trial presents one of eight probes evenly spaced in critical bands, four above and four below the signal frequency, to minimize off-frequency listening. The attention band was expected to match the critical band for the 300-ms tones (Greenberg & Larkin, 1968), but would it match for 20- and 40-ms tones, or be broader, as with 5-ms tones? The 20- and 40-ms tones are well specified in pitch even at threshold and had the same apparent pitch as the cues, being of the same duration.

Results

Mean percentage correct for the 300-ms tones is shown in Figure 11.1 by the lower solid line for seven naive listeners. Accuracy for the 34-dB SPL, 1,000-Hz signal was 82%, as expected from the prior measurement of threshold. Accuracy for detecting the probes fell rapidly as probe frequency deviated from the 1,000-Hz signal, to reach near-chance (50%) levels. These results demonstrate once again that the attention band for long-duration tones approximates the critical band. Here, the critical band is approximated by a rounded exponential (ROEX) filter (Patterson, Nimmo-Smith, Weber, & Milroy, 1982) centered at 1,000 Hz and scaled to have the same peak (Figure 11.1, dots). The ROEX filter has central frequency f_o (1,000 Hz) and width given by the equivalent rectangular bandwidth, equivalent rectangular bandwidth (ERB) = 24.7 (1 + 0.00437f_o). The ROEX shape is given by:

$$r_f = (1 + A \times f*)\exp(-A \times f*), \text{ where } f* = |(f - f_o)/f_o| \text{ and } A = k \times f_o/\text{ERB}.$$

Filter asymmetry is controlled by k, which is 4.80 if $f > f_o$ and 3.33 if $f < f_o$. The ROEX filter describes the critical band in terms of signal level, not percent correct, but these are closely proportional over the range of accuracies shown. In vivid contrast, probe accuracy for the 20-ms and 40-ms tones (Figure 11.1, lines and dashes) declines only slowly away from the 1,000-Hz signal and, in fact, follows fairly closely the 5-ms tone data of Wright and Dai (1994), rescaled from 2,500 to 1,000 Hz (Figure 11.1, dots). The broad attention band for short-duration tones is found even with tones with frequencies that are well specific to the listener, so poor encoding of the signal frequency is unlikely to account for the results. Instead, the results provisionally support the *focusing* hypothesis, which predicted a similar shape for all these tones. However, this hypothesis does not seem compatible with an *asymmetry* seen in the 20-ms data—namely, the relatively high accuracy at 925 Hz compared with that at 1,075 Hz. It is not possible to explain away the asymmetry by appealing to the flattening (lowering) of pitch perception that occurs at short durations, because the cue and signal would be flattened to the same extent as the probes (all three had the same duration). Off-frequency listening seems unlikely, because the probes were equally spaced about the signal. What is going on?

Experiment 2

Experiment 2 was run as a check on the 2IFC procedure used in Experiment 1, which required the listener to maintain attention at the cued frequency over two intervals spanning almost 1 s. A wide attention band would appear in the data, even if attention were focused on a single critical band at each moment in time, if attention wandered during the trial. A Yes–No procedure was used in which there was just one brief interval (300 ms between cue and signal) to minimize wandering. Well-practiced listeners were run with TDT System II to check that the results of Experiment 1 were reliable across experience as well as method. Listeners were run both in the probe-signal condition and in a control condition in which all tones, probes, and signals were presented equally often and were always validly cued. Each listener ran four sessions, to obtain both control and probe-signal data at both stimulus durations, the order being randomized. Seven listeners heard 20-ms tones, and seven heard 40-ms tones.

Results

Mean percentage correct for the 20 ms tones is plotted for each of the probes and for the signal frequency in Figure 11.2; dotted lines indicate ± 1 SEM. Accuracy for the control condition in which each of the tones was fully attended was high and independent of frequency, duplicating the initial measurements of threshold. Results in probe-signal trials once again demonstrate a fairly wide attention band at both tone durations. They also showed the unexpected asymmetry, in that performance at 925 Hz was again better than that at the signal frequency. The asymmetry did not stem from poor threshold measurements, because the control data showed no spike at 925 Hz. Results at 40 ms

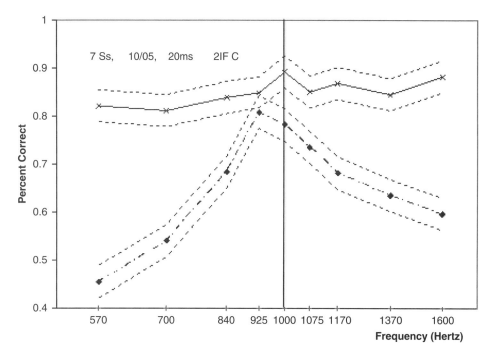

Figure 11.2. Mean data for seven practiced listeners with 20-ms tones. Control data: x's. Probe-signal: filled symbols. Yes–No method; chance is 50%.

(not shown) were similar in that control accuracy was flat and probe-signal accuracy was higher at 925 Hz than at 1,075 Hz, although not as high as at 1,000 Hz.

Experiment 3

Experiment 3 was run to check that the multiprobe method, in which the eight probes were disposed symmetrically around the signal, was not somehow responsible for the asymmetrical attention band. The multiprobe method was introduced by Dai, Scharf, and Buus (1991) to make off-frequency listening much less likely than in the original single-probe method of Greenberg and Larkin (1968), in which the listener heard only the signal and one specific probe in a trial block. However, in the multiprobe method, the listener hears each probe so infrequently, he or she may misclassify some of them as noise; the asymmetry would develop if misclassifications were more likely for high-frequency probes. Measurements were obtained for a new set of six listeners who heard the signal on 80% of trials in a trial block or a single probe on the remaining trials. The 2AFC method was used with the TDT System 2 equipment. Both probe-signal and control (probe only) trial blocks were run. Probe frequencies were 925 Hz or 1,075 Hz in different sessions. The signal was always 1,000 Hz. Tones were 40 ms. The probe-signal data (not shown) revealed the usual asymmetry, mean accuracy being 84% at 925 Hz and 73% at 1075 Hz. Control accuracy was the same (89%). These results indicate that the asymmetrical attention band is not an artifact of the multiprobe method.

Experiment 4

Experiment 4 was run to check that the asymmetrical attention band was not an artifact of some hardware or software error associated with the exact choice of stimuli. The methods of Experiment 1 were repeated for six new listeners, for 20-ms tones only, with all the frequencies downshifted by a fixed fraction so that the original signal of 1,000 Hz now became a signal at 925 Hz, and probes were now 527, 648, 777, 856, 994, 1,082, 1,267, and 1,480 Hz. The broad attention band and asymmetry occurred again.

Experiment 5

Experiment 5 was run to check on an individual difference noticed in the previous experiments; it seemed that listeners with wider attention bands showed more asymmetry. The method of Experiment 2 (the Y/N procedure, but run on TDT System 3) was repeated with 16 new listeners at each duration (20 and 40 ms).

Results

Accuracy was plotted as a function of frequency in the manner of Figures 11.1 and 11.2, but separately for each listener. Data were variable because the number of trials for each probe was small. Attention band half-widths were estimated in each plot using a smooth, single-peaked French curve to interpolate the frequencies at which accuracy fell halfway between peak accuracy and chance. Estimates were made by a trained student and by a laboratory technician with no knowledge of the hypotheses of the study; this method was more reliable than linear interpolation between adjacent values. Attention band asymmetry was estimated by subtracting percent correct (Pc) at the signal frequency (1,000 Hz) from that at the next lower probe (925 Hz). The extent of asymmetry correlated fairly well with the half-widths ($r^2 = .46$, $t_{14} = 4.69$, $p < .01$), as shown in Figure 11.3 for the 20-ms data, such that asymmetry increased with half-width.

Discussion and Model

According to "induced focusing," the attention band should be wide with brief tones when only exogenous attention (governed by the cue) has time to operate, but narrow with long-duration tones when stimulus-induced (exogenous) focusing begins to take effect, the precision of which is eventually limited only by the critical band. To model these ideas, probability summation across critical bands considered as independent filters was assumed; exogenous attention permits

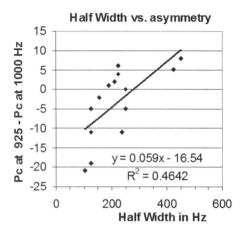

Figure 11.3. Asymmetry (percentage correct, Pc, at 925 Hz, minus that at 1,000 Hz) versus half-width for 16 listeners in Experiment 5 (two points are overwritten); tone duration is 20 ms.

several adjacent filters to contribute to detection, but focusing ultimately narrows this down to one. Critical bands were approximated by ROEX filters, which are assumed to act independently if separated by more than a specific percentage of the central frequency but whose correlated responses can be mimicked by a single filter at the mean frequency if separated by less than this amount. This simplification, which treats close filters as a single filter and distant filters as independent, made the model tractable at the cost of plausibility. The probability of detecting brief tones is then given by probability summation over the bank of filters that receive endogenous attention. For long-duration tones, only one filter remains active, explaining why the ROEX filter (the critical band) matches the attention band when the tone is long. Details follow. The probability of detection ($0 < w < 1$) by a single ROEX filter at frequency f is

$$w(f) = (1 + g \times A \times asym) \times \exp(-g \times A \times asym), \text{ if } f > H_o, \text{ and}$$

$$= (1 + g \times A/asym) \times \exp(-g \times A/asym), \text{ if } f < H_o,$$

where $g = abs(f - H_o)/H_o$ is the frequency (f) relative to the central frequency (H_o), A (the mean width) $= 4 * H_o / $ ERB, and filter asymmetry is determined by $asym$. A *frequency bank* is a set of adjacent ROEX filters to which attention is allocated at the start of a trial by endogenous attention. Let $H_c(k)$ be the center frequency of the k-th filter. Filter centers are spaced in equal steps (S) in log frequency, that is, $H_c(k + 1) = S \times H_c(k)$.

Endogenous attention is presumably centered on frequency H_o and falls off symmetrically on either side of H_o, given that the listener focuses attention primarily at H_o (i.e., no off-frequency listening.) A logistic function is used for convenience to represent the falloff. Thus, $E(k) = 1/(1 + z_k^2)$ is the endogenous weight on the k-th filter, where $z_k = [\log_{10}(H_c(k)) - \log_{10}(H_o)] / \sigma$ is the z score of log frequency and σ controls the width of attention.

Let S_0 be the chance of detecting H_o in single-band listening mode. The multiband loss obtained when the listener monitors n independent bands for a signal in one band is $S_n = S_0/\text{sqrt}(n)$ (Smith, 1982), a model that predicts the magnitude of the uncertainty effect for brief tones (Scharf, Reeves, & Suciu, 2007). The chance of filter k detecting a tone of frequency i is then the product of filter weight w, endogenous attention E, and S_n, such that $P_k(i) = S_n * E(k) * w_k(i))$. Using logs to convert products into sums, $P(i)$, the chance of detection at frequency i by any filter, is then

$$P(i) = 1 - 10 \wedge \left[\sum_k \log_{10}(1.0 - P_k(i)) \right], \text{ where } k \text{ indexes attended-to filters.}$$

Figure 11.4 illustrates the theoretical outcomes for a single ROEX filter of asymmetry (asym) 1.4 and for probability summation across 61 such filters spaced S = 1.05 units apart. Detection rates are from 0% to 100%, because guessing is not included. Probability summation clearly shifts the peak to lower frequencies, even though the filter with the greatest attention weight (and thus greatest sensitivity) remains at H_o. Filter asymmetry is such that there are more filters contributing to detection at a fixed distance below H_o than at the same fixed distance above H_o. Lacking asymmetry, the peak does not shift.

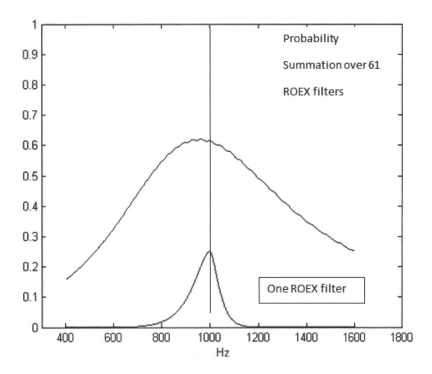

Figure 11.4. Theoretical effects of probability summation over 61 rounded exponential (ROEX) filters spaced S = 1.03 units apart. Filter asymmetry (1.4) is visible in the single ROEX filter at Ho.

Model Fitting

Parameters started at *asym* = 1.4, S_0 = 0.4 (chance of detection with just one filter), S = 1.05 (filter frequency spacing), σ = 0.6 (attention bandwidth), and *n* = 9 (number of ROEX filters); a custom iterative grid search was run, as MATLAB minimization routines (fminsearch) were often trapped in bad local minima. Grid search start values and step sizes were improved over many runs to minimize mean square error (MSE); 800 successive frequencies were calculated for each filter to obtain stability.

Data from Experiment 2 were then analyzed for half-width and asymmetry, given the relation found in Experiment 5. Listeners were then categorized as "narrow" or "broad" by a median split on the half-widths. Data and fits are plotted next for each group of six listeners (grouped by tone duration, half-width, and system). Data were corrected for guessing by rescaling (0.5–1.0) to (0.0–1.0) before fitting and are plotted in this manner. Averaging data across listeners before fitting erases some of the variation inevitable in probe data from 1-hr sessions but conflates listeners with somewhat different attention bands.

As Figures 11.5 through 11.8 illustrate (see the parameters in the figure legends), increasing the model attention bandwidth(σ) increases the number of filters contributing to the overall response profile, such that the empirical

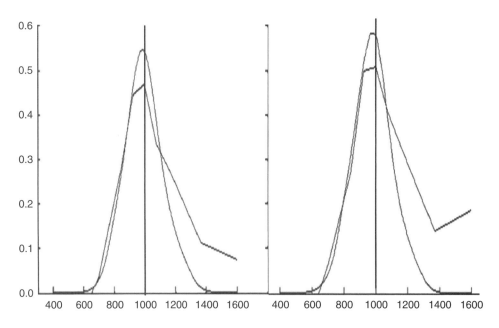

Figure 11.5.   Left panel: mean data for six "narrow" listeners; 20-ms tones, Tucker-Davis (TDT) System III. Smooth curve: model with 13 rounded exponential (ROEX) filters. Mean square error (MSE) 0.10. Parameters: asym 1.375, S_0 0.32, spacing 1.04, attention σ 0.033. Right panel: mean data for six additional "narrow" listeners; 20-ms tones, TDT System II. Smooth curve: model with 17 ROEX filters. MSE 0.06. Parameters: asym 1.20, S_0 0.235, spacing 1.033, attention σ 0.034.

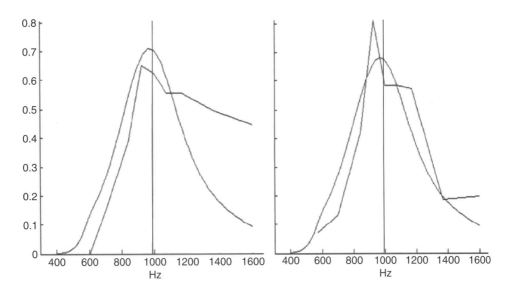

Figure 11.6. Left panel: mean data for six "broad" listeners; 20-ms tones, Tucker-Davis (TDT) System III. Smooth curve: model with 29 rounded exponential (ROEX) filters. Mean square error (MSE) = 0.18: asym 1.325, S_o 0.337, spacing 1.039, attention σ 0.068. Right panel: mean data for six additional "broad" listeners; 20-ms tones, TDT System II. Smooth curve: model with 37 ROEX filters. MSE = 0.07: asym 1.40, S_o 0.255, spacing 1.03, attention σ 0.071. That σ is larger implies more active filters.

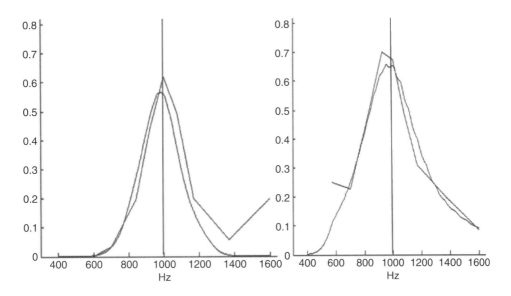

Figure 11.7. Left panel: mean data for "narrow" listeners; 40-ms tones, Tucker-Davis (TDT) System III. Smooth curve: model with 13 rounded exponential (ROEX) filters. Mean square error (MSE) = 0.09: asym 1.325, S_o 0.297, spacing 1.039, attention σ 0.031. Right panel: mean data for six additional listeners, classed as "narrow" but broader than on left; 40-ms tones, TDT System II. Rippled curve: model with 23 ROEX filters. MSE = 0.06: asym 1.40, S_o 0.375, spacing 1.053, attention σ 0.072.

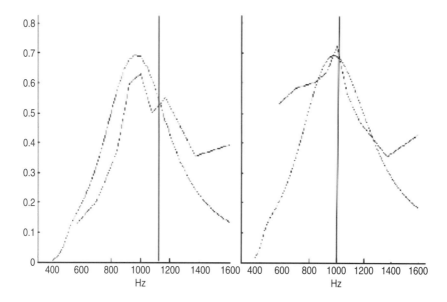

Figure 11.8. Left panel: mean data for six "broad" listeners; 40-ms tones, TDT System III. Smooth curve: model with 33 rounded exponential (ROEX) filters. Mean square error (MSE) = 0.13 asym 1.40, S_o 0.335, spacing 1.043, attention σ 0.085. Right panel: mean data for six additional "broad" listeners; 40-ms tones, TDT System II. Smooth curve: model with 53 ROEX filters. MSE = 0.16 *asym* 1.20, S_o 0.25, spacing 1.03, attention σ 0.10.

attention band widens and the asymmetry increases. (Other best-fit model parameters either varied little [S and *asym*] or acted only to scale the fitted curve to overall accuracy [S_o]). For 20-ms tones, Figure 11.5 shows that listeners classified as "narrow" showed little asymmetry, and Figure 11.6 shows that those classified as "broad" not only heard more distant probes (and were therefore "broad") but also showed asymmetry. Figures 11.7 (narrow) and 11.8 (broad) repeat this point for 40-ms tones. Model fits were generally not bad, except at 1,600 Hz, where (for no obvious reason) probe detection exceeded predictions. Comparing Figure 11.6 with Figure 11.8, it seems that the asymmetry for "broad" listeners was larger with 20-ms than with 40-ms tones, and, because the effects of certainty (vs. uncertainty) on threshold are also somewhat larger at 20 than at 40 ms (Scharf et al., 2007), the combined results suggest that focusing continues as tone duration is increased above 20 ms. However, both effects are small and need replication.

Conclusion

Attentional bandwidths have been studied before but with little evidence of the asymmetry that became the focus of this study. The experiments were repeated several times, because I was initially skeptical of the results. How could "off-frequency" listening appear when the multiprobe method made it seem impossible? How could the listener best hear a tone lower in pitch than that attended when the cues, signals, and probes all had the same duration, implying that the lowering-of-pitch consequence of reducing duration must apply equally to all the tones used? Understanding the effect of asymmetrical underlying filters explained the paradox: At a given distance below the signal frequency, more filters are active than at the same distance above the signal frequency. The specific functions used include the standard ROEX filter, the square-root expression for uncertainty, the logistic expression for the presumed symmetrical falloff of attention with log frequency on either side of the signal, and a high-threshold version of probability summation. None of these elements is without question, but the model provides an existence proof that a detection contour that appears to demonstrate off-frequency listening may do no such thing.

References

Dai, H. P., Scharf, B., & Buus, S. (1991). Effective attenuation of signals in noise under focused attention. *Journal of the Acoustical Society of America, 89,* 2837–2842. doi:10.1121/1.400721

Greenberg, G. Z., & Larkin, W. D. (1968). Frequency-response characteristics of auditory observers detecting signals of a single frequency in noise: The probe-signal method. *The Journal of the Acoustical Society of America, 44,* 1513–1523. doi:10.1121/1.1911290

Patterson, R. D., Nimmo-Smith, I., Weber, D. L., & Milroy, R. (1982). The deterioration of hearing with age: Frequency selectivity, the critical ratio, the audiogram, and speech threshold. *Journal of the Acoustical Society of America, 72,* 1788–1803. doi:10.1121/1.388652

Reeves, A., & Scharf, B. (2010). Auditory frequency focusing is very rapid. *Journal of the Acoustical Society of America, 128,* 795–803. doi:10.1121/1.3458823

Scharf, B. (1998). Auditory attention: The psychoacoustical approach. In H. Pashler (Ed.), *The psychology of attention* (pp. 75–117). London, England: Psychology Press.

Scharf, B. (1970). Critical bands. In J. V. Tobias (Ed.), *Foundations of modern auditory theory* (Vol. 1, pp. 157–202). New York, NY: Academic Press.

Scharf, B., Quigley, S., Aoki, C., Peachey, N., & Reeves, A. (1987). Focused auditory attention and frequency selectivity. *Perception & Psychophysics, 42,* 215–223. doi:10.3758/BF03203073

Scharf, B., Reeves, A., & Suciu, J. (2007). The time required to focus on a cued signal frequency. *Journal of the Acoustical Society of America, 121,* 2149–2157. doi:10.1121/1.2537461

Schlauch, R. S., & Hafter, E. R. (1991). Listening bandwidths and frequency uncertainty in pure-tone signal detection. *Journal of the Acoustical Society of America, 90,* 1332–1339. doi:10.1121/1.401925

Smith, J. E. K. (1982). Simple algorithms for M-alternative forced-choice calculations. *Perception & Psychophysics, 31,* 95–96. doi:10.3758/BF03206208

Sperling, G. (1984). A unified theory of attention and signal detection. In R. Parasuraman & D. Davies (Eds.), *Varieties of attention* (pp. 103–181). New York, NY: Academic Press.

Wright, B. A., & Dai, H. (1994). Detection of unexpected tones with short and long durations. *Journal of the Acoustical Society of America, 95,* 931–938. doi:10.1121/1.410010

Part IV

Applications

12

Perceptual Mechanisms and Learning in Anisometropic Amblyopia

Zhong-Lin Lu, Chang-Bing Huang, and Yifeng Zhou

Amblyopia, a developmental spatial vision impairment that cannot be corrected by refractive means, affects approximately 3% of the population (Ciuffreda, Levi, & Selenow, 1991). Although most researchers agree that amblyopia is a cortical impairment resulting from abnormal visual experience in early childhood, its neural basis is still not entirely clear (Barnes, Hess, Dumoulin, Achtman, & Pike, 2001; Daw, 1998; Kiorpes & McKee, 1999). Research based on animal models of amblyopia found that V1 neurons receiving primary inputs from the amblyopic eye exhibited abnormal contrast sensitivity and spatial properties (Crewther & Crewther, 1990; Kiorpes, Kiper, O'Keefe, Cavanaugh, & Movshon, 1998). However, the observed neuronal deficits in amblyopia are not sufficient to account for the behavioral deficits, suggesting that neural deficits in amblyopia are not limited to a subset of neurons in V1 (Kiorpes et al., 1998). Consistent with this view, disruption in the binocular organization of extrastriate cortical areas has been documented in primate (Movshon et al., 1987) and cat amblyopes (Schröder, Fries, Roelfsema, Singer, & Engel, 2002). Abnormal activities in extrastriate cortical areas have also been reported in human functional imaging studies (Barnes et al., 2001).

Conventional wisdom on visual development suggests that spatial vision becomes hardwired after a critical period, usually around 6 to 8 years of age (Berardi, Pizzorusso, Ratto, & Maffei, 2003); the amblyopic visual system is fully (although erroneously) developed after age 8 years and is no longer subject to therapeutic modifications. In clinical practice, only infants and young children with amblyopia are treated, and patients older than 8 years are left untreated (Greenwald & Parks, 1999). On the other hand, recent studies on perceptual learning suggest that the adult visual system retains large degrees of plasticity, and perceptual learning might be a potential treatment for adult amblyopia.

DOI: 10.1037/14135-013

Human Information Processing: Vision, Memory, and Attention, C. Chubb, B. A. Dosher, Z.-L. Lu, and R. M. Shiffrin (Editors)

In this chapter, we review some recent progress in our understanding of the mechanisms of amblyopia and evidence of perceptual learning in the amblyopic visual system. We focus primarily on anisometropic amblyopia because it is the predominant type. Other types of amblyopia, such as strabismic amblyopia, may be different (Hess & Pointer, 1985; Levi & Klein, 1982).

Mechanisms of Anisometropic Amblyopia

Traditionally, spatial vision is characterized through measures of contrast sensitivities and visual acuities (McKee, Levi, & Movshon, 2003). The external noise method (see Figure 12.1) and associated models allow us to decompose and explain contrast sensitivity and visual acuities with intrinsic limitations of the perceptual system (Lu & Dosher, 2008). By systematically manipulating the amount of external noise superimposed on the signal stimuli and measuring contrast or feature thresholds at multiple criterion performance levels (threshold vs. contrast [TvC] function), the method reveals the intrinsic limitations of the perceptual system: internal additive noise, contrast-gain control or multiplicative noise, nonlinear transducer, and statistical uncertainty (Burgess & Colborne, 1988; Eckstein, Ahumada, & Watson, 1997; Lu & Dosher, 1999; Pelli, 1985). Initially used to characterize and compare human

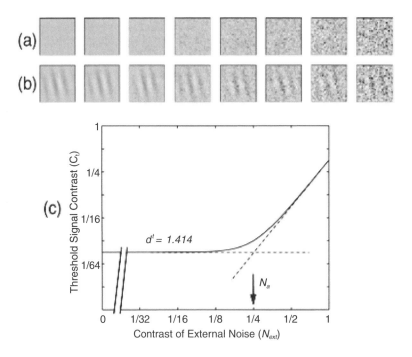

Figure 12.1. (a) From left to right, external noise images with increasing contrast. (b) A signal Gabor patch embedded in increasing levels of external noise. (c) A threshold versus external noise contrast function.

observers in various perceptual tasks (Burgess & Colborne, 1988), the external noise approach has recently been extended to identify mechanisms, that is, alterations of the intrinsic observer characteristics underlying performance changes associated with various observer states, including attention (Dosher & Lu, 2000a, 2000b; Lu & Dosher, 1998), perceptual learning (Chung, Levi, & Tjan, 2005; Dosher & Lu, 1998; Gold, Bennett, & Sekuler, 1999), and adaptation (Dao, Lu, & Dosher, 2006).

Kersten, Hess, and Plant (1988) were the first to apply the external noise method to study visual dysfunctions in clinical populations. One anisometropic and two strabismic participants with amblyopia were tested. On the basis of the linear amplifier model (LAM; Pelli, 1981), they found that two of the participants had normal or near normal sampling efficiency but increased equivalent internal noise, and one had lower sampling efficiency but near normal equivalent internal noise.

Subsequent external noise studies on amblyopia have, however, generated inconsistent results (Levi & Klein, 2003; Nordmann, Freeman, & Casanova, 1992; Pelli, Levi, & Chung, 2004; Wang, Levi, & Klein, 1998). Some authors attributed amblyopic deficits to reduced sampling efficiency; others attributed them to increased additive internal noise; and still others attributed them to increased stimulus-dependent noise. Although some of the inconsistencies might have resulted from differences in participants' characteristics, it is also possible that the same amblyopic participant may exhibit different deficits in different tasks or conditions. Studies that systematically test the same subjects over a range of tasks and conditions may help resolve some of the inconsistencies. The LAM also imposes some limitations on the theoretical interpretations of the TvC functions. This is reflected in the paradoxical decreased internal noise in amblyopia found in some of the conditions in Pelli et al. (2004). Lu and Dosher (2008) showed that the LAM must be elaborated to include both a nonlinear transducer function and multiplicative internal noise, as implemented in the perceptual template model (PTM; see Figure 12.2a), to account for all the existing data in the literature. The PTM provides an improved theoretical framework to compare amblyopic and normal visual systems in terms of the gain of the perceptual template and the magnitudes of the internal additive noise and multiplicative noise (Figure 12.2b).

Xu, Lu, Qiu, and Zhou (2006) applied the PTM framework to identify the mechanisms underlying anisometropic amblyopia. Twelve normal (22.1 ± 0.6 years) and 10 amblyopic observers (20.3 ± 0.5 years), nine anisometropic, and one strabismic-anisometropic amblyopes, participated in the study. Observers identified the orientation (either +12° or −12° from vertical) of a foveally presented Gabor embedded in white Gaussian external noise with eight standard deviations, 0, 0.02, 0.04, 0.08, 0.12, 0.16, 0.25, and 0.33. For each external noise condition, contrast thresholds at two performance criterion levels were measured with two interleaved staircases: a 3/1 staircase that converges to 79.3% correct and a 2/1 staircase that converges to 70.7% correct. All observers ran two sessions per eye with Gabors at 2.3 cycles per degree (c/deg). The order of measurements was randomly assigned. In addition, eight observers, four normal and four amblyopic, were also tested with Gabors at 1.5 c/deg and 4.6 c/deg.

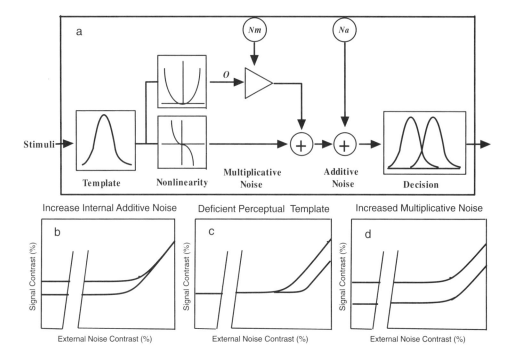

Figure 12.2. (a) Perceptual template model. (b–d) Performance signatures of the three mechanisms of amblyopia deficits. From "Treated Amblyopes Remain Deficient in Spatial Vision: A Contrast Sensitivity and External Noise Study," by C. Huang, L. Tao, Y. Zhou, and Z.-L. Lu, 2007, *Vision Research, 47,* p. 24. Copyright 2007 by Elsevier. Reprinted with permission.

For the normal and fellow eyes, only contrast thresholds in low external noise increased with increasing spatial frequency; contrast thresholds in high external noise did not change as a function of spatial frequency (see Figure 12.3). As Gabor frequency increased from 1.5 to 4.6 c/deg, the average threshold in the three lowest external noise conditions increased $85\% \pm 6\%$; the average threshold in the highest three external noise conditions did not change significantly $(-9\% \pm 3\%)$. This is consistent with Chung, Legge, and Tjan (2002), who found that the contrast sensitivity function (CSF) measured in high external noise was flat. For the amblyopic eyes, contrast thresholds in both low and high external noise conditions increased with increasing spatial frequency. As Gabor frequency increased from 1.5 to 4.6 c/deg, the average threshold in the three lowest external noise conditions increased $342\% \pm 21\%$; the average threshold in the highest three external noise conditions increased $131\% \pm 20\%$. This pattern of results is drastically different from that of the normal subjects.

For all the amblyopic subjects, the best-fitting PTM consisted of a mixture of two mechanisms: increased internal noise and increased impact of external noise (see Figure 12.4). Consistent with Pelli et al. (2004), we found a high degree of correlation between internal additive noise and visual acuity $(r = .673, p < .01)$ and a high degree of correlation between template deficiency

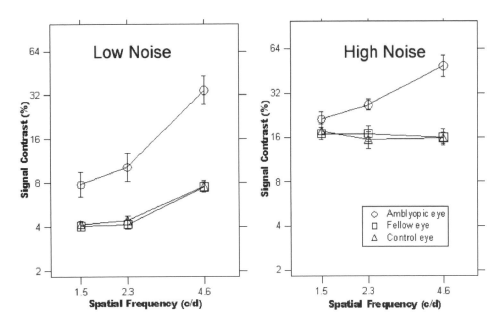

Figure 12.3. Average threshold versus spatial frequency functions in low (left panel) and high (right panel) external noise conditions for amblyopic, fellow, and normal eyes. c/d = cycles per degree. From "Identify Mechanisms of Amblyopia in Gabor Orientation Identification With External Noise," by P. Xu, Z.-L. Lu, Z. Qiu, and Y. Zhou, 2006, *Vision Research, 46,* p. 3756. Copyright 2006 by Elsevier. Reprinted with permission.

and visual acuity ($r = .838$, $p < .01$). These strong correlations were expected because visual acuity is determined by internal noise and the quality of perceptual template.

We concluded that amblyopic deficits can be attributed to two independent factors: (a) increased additive internal noise and (b) deficient perceptual templates. Whereas increased additive noise underlay performance deficits in all spatial frequencies, the degree of perceptual template deterioration increased with the spatial frequency of the Gabor stimuli. That larger template deficits were found in higher spatial frequencies is consistent with the observation that individuals with amblyopia have more profound deficits in tasks that require processing of high spatial frequencies (McKee et al., 2003).

Patients Treated for Amblyopia Remain Deficient in Spatial Vision

Outcomes of amblyopia treatments are conventionally evaluated using tests of visual acuity (Regan, 1988; Stewart, Moseley, & Fielder, 2003). In China, a treatment is completely successful if the patient achieves and maintains 1.0 minimum angle of resolution (MAR; or better) visual acuity in the amblyopic eye for more than 3 years.

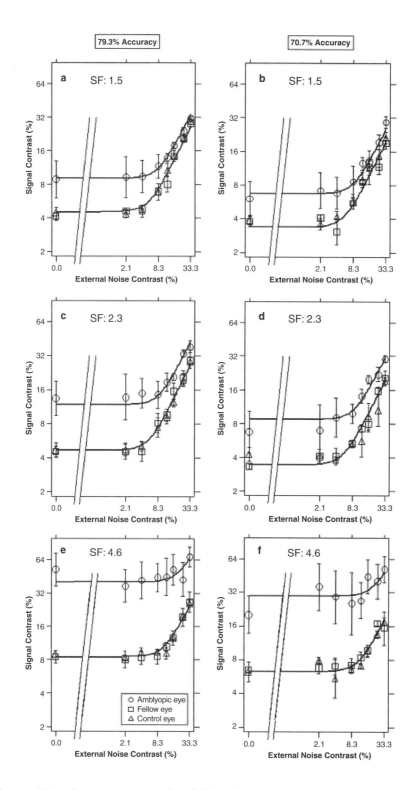

Figure 12.4. Average contrast thresholds of four amblyopic, four fellow, and four normal control eyes as functions of external noise levels for three Gabor spatial frequencies: 1.5, 2.3, and 4.6 cycles per degree. Error bars indicate ± 1 standard error. SF = spatial frequency. From "Identify Mechanisms of Amblyopia in Gabor Orientation Identification With External Noise," by P. Xu, Z.-L. Lu, Z. Qiu, and Y. Zhou, 2006, *Vision Research, 46,* p. 3755. Copyright 2006 by Elsevier. Reprinted with permission.

Although acuities provide convenient assays of the spatial resolution of the visual system, it has long been recognized that simple photopic visual acuity cannot predict performance in many other spatial vision tasks (Braddick, Campbell, & Atkinson, 1978; Pelli, Robson, & Wilkins, 1988; Watson, Barlow, & Robson, 1983). Many researchers have suggested that the CSF, which assesses spatial vision over a wide range of spatial frequencies and contrast levels, may be a better tool for detecting and diagnosing deficits in spatial vision (Jindra & Zemon, 1989; Yenice et al., 2007). On the basis of an analysis of 427 adults with amblyopia, McKee et al. (2003) concluded that measures in two orthogonal dimensions, visual acuity and contrast sensitivity, are necessary to account for the variations in amblyopic visual performance. Others suggested that patients treated for amblyopia can simultaneously exhibit normal Snellen acuities but deficits in contrast sensitivity (Cascairo, Mazow, Holladay, & Prager, 1997; Regan, 1988; Rogers, Bremer, & Leguire, 1987), based on tests using either pattern or letter charts.

Huang, Zhou, and Lu (2008) measured contrast sensitivity functions in treated amblyopes using standard psychophysical procedures with sine-wave grating stimuli in both eyes. Five treated children with amblyopia (one anisometropic, one anisometropic and strabismic, and three strabismic; 10.6 ± 1.8 years) with naturally occurring amblyopia participated in the study. The average visual acuity of the previously fellow eyes (pFEs) for these subjects was 0.936 ± 0.021 MAR. Their acuities in previously amblyopic eyes (pAEs; 0.944 ± 0.019 MAR acuity) had been maintained for at least 3 years. Contrast sensitivity functions were estimated at spatial frequencies 0.5, 1, 2, 4, 8, 12, and 16 c/deg in a two-interval forced-choice (2IFC) sine-wave grating detection task using a staircase procedure.

Figure 12.5 depicts the contrast sensitivity functions for all five subjects. A within-subject analysis of variance showed that contrast sensitivity varied significantly with both spatial frequency ($p < .001$) and eyes ($p < .05$). Interaction of the two factors was also significant ($p < .01$). In other words, contrast sensitivity was significantly higher in the pFEs than in the pAEs, and the difference depended on spatial frequency: highly significant at 12 c/deg and 16 c/deg ($p < .01$), significant at 8 c/deg ($p < .05$) and marginally significant at 2 c/deg and 4 c/deg ($.05 < p < .10$). In the pAEs, the average estimated cutoff spatial frequency was 14.8 ± 2.5 c/deg. In the pFE, the average estimated cutoff spatial frequency was 22.3 ± 2.4 c/deg.

Consistent with Xu et al. (2006), additional measurements of TvC functions identified two mechanisms of deficits in these subjects: increased internal noise at low to medium spatial frequency and increases in both internal noise and impact of external noise at high spatial frequencies.

The finding of deficient contrast sensitivity functions in the pAE of treated amblyopic patients is consistent with other reports in the literature. Although visual acuity is often thought to reflect the cutoff spatial frequency of the visual system, the acuity task in fact relies on a range of spatial frequencies. It is possible that amblyopic individuals can cope with many tasks (e.g., reading) using low and intermediate spatial frequency channels when their fellow eyes are patched. The relatively larger deficits in high spatial frequencies exhibited by observers who have completed occlusion therapy and practice in acuity tasks

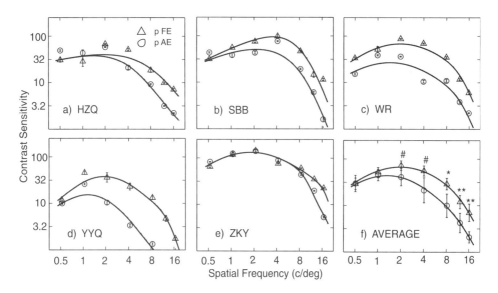

Figure 12.5. Individual subjects' (a–e) and average (f) contrast sensitivity functions. # .05 < *p* < .10. * *p* < .05. ** *p* < .01. pFE = previously fellow eyes; pAE = previously ambly-opic eyes. From "Treated Amblyopes Remain Deficient in Spatial Vision: A Contrast Sensitivity and External Noise Study," by C. Huang, L. Tao, Y. Zhou, and Z.-L. Lu, 2007, *Vision Research, 47,* p. 27. Copyright 2007 by Elsevier. Reprinted with permission.

suggest that selective training in relatively high spatial frequencies might be necessary to reduce high spatial frequency deficits in amblyopia.

Perceptual Learning Improved Spatial Vision in Adult Amblyopia

The value of perceptual learning as a potential therapy for amblyopia has been evaluated since the pioneering work of Campbell and colleagues (Campbell, Hess, Watson, & Banks, 1978). The results have been mixed (Ciuffreda, Goldner, & Connelly, 1980; Schor & Wick, 1983; Wick, Wingard, Cotter, & Scheiman, 1992). However, unlike most of the studies on perceptual learning in the normal popu-lation, these studies typically used high contrast stimuli and relatively short training periods (e.g., 7 min) that were predetermined, irrespective of the prog-ress in training and subject's ophthalmological characteristics. Later studies on perceptual learning in the normal visual system showed that it typically requires several hundreds of training trials to improve performance signifi-cantly in perceptual tasks.

Several studies (Chung, Li, & Levi, 2006; Levi & Polat, 1996; Levi, Polat, & Hu, 1997; Li & Levi, 2004; Li, Provost, & Levi, 2007; Polat, Ma-Naim, Belkin, & Sagi, 2004; Simmers & Gray, 1999; Zhou et al., 2006) found that more elabo-rate training procedures on simple spatial vision tasks can lead to significant visual acuity improvements in adults with amblyopia. For example, Levi and colleagues found that Snellen acuities in two anisometropic amblyopic subjects were significantly improved following intensive training in a Vernier acuity task (Levi & Polat, 1996; Levi et al., 1997). In addition, both Li and Levi (2004) and Li et al. (2007) showed transfer of learning of position acuity to Snellen acuity in participants with amblyopia beyond the so-called critical period (age < 8 years).

Zhou et al. (2006) trained adult and teenager amblyopic subjects in a simple visual detection task and evaluated effects of perceptual learning on visual acuity and CSF. Twenty-three naive observers with natural-occurring anisometropic amblyopia completed the study. They were randomly assigned into three treatment groups: the seven observers (18.3 ± 2.9 years) in Group I were trained in a sine-wave grating detection task near each individual's cutoff spatial frequency, defined as the spatial frequency at which the estimated contrast threshold from pretraining CSF measurements was 0.50 (the "HIGH" group). The 10 observers (20.5 ± 3.7 years) in Group II practiced the CSF task over the entire range of spatial frequencies (the ALL group). The six observers (18.7 ± 4.6 years) in Group III received no training (the NONE group). Observers were trained only in their amblyopic eyes. In pre- and posttraining assessments, CSF and visual acuity for both eyes were measured for all observers. Contrast sensitivity was calculated from sine-wave grating detection thresholds at spatial frequencies ranging from 0.5 to 16 c/deg. Visual acuity was assessed with the Chinese Tumbling E Chart (Mou, 1966) and defined as the score associated with 75% correct judgments. Observers received training in nine to 19 (mean = 12.7) sessions, each consisting of 900 trials and lasting approximately 1 hr. Training was terminated after performance reached asymptotes.

In the amblyopic eyes, training improved contrast sensitivity of the HIGH group by approximately 4.9 dB (or 76.5%; see Figure 12.6), averaged across all the spatial frequencies, and visual acuity by approximately 4.5 dB (68.4%; see Figure 12.7). In comparison, training improved the average contrast sensitivity of the ALL group by approximately 4.3 dB (64.4%) and visual acuity by approximately 3.2 dB (45.1%). No significant training effects were found in the NONE group. In the untrained fellow eyes of the HIGH group, the average contrast sensitivity improved by 0.7 dB (or 7.8%) and visual acuity by 1.0 dB (or 12.5%). Repeated training did not significantly improve CSF or visual acuity in the fellow eyes for most observers in the ALL and NONE groups.

Compared with the NONE group, both training protocols produced significant improvements in CSF and visual acuity, indicating significant performance improvements due to training rather than retesting. The HIGH group improved most in terms of CSF and visual acuity in both the amblyopic and the fellow eyes, even though the magnitudes of improvements produced by the two training protocols are not statistically different. Among the three training protocols tested, the most effective training protocol might be practice of sine-wave grating detection near the cutoff frequency.

Retention of the training effects was excellent for the eight observers tested: Improvements on visual acuity were fully retained for at least 5 months and were close to 90% 1 year posttraining. It was also fully retained for 1.5 years in the two subjects tested. The considerable degree of improvements on CSF and visual acuity as well as the excellent retention suggest that perceptual learning might be of great clinical value in treating adults with amblyopia (Polat et al., 2004).

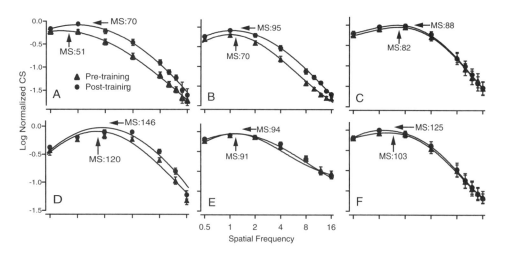

Figure 12.6. Average contrast sensitivity functions in the amblyopic eyes (A–E) and the fellow eyes (B–F) for observers in Groups I, II, and III, respectively. Error bars indicate standard error of the mean. CS = contrast sensitivity; MS = maximum sensitivity. From "Perceptual Learning Improves Contrast Sensitivity and Visual Acuity in Adults with Anisometropic Amblyopia," by Y. Zhou, C. Huang, P. Xu, L. Tao, Z. Qiu, X. Li, and Z.-L. Lu, 2006, *Vision Research, 46,* pp. 744–746. Copyright 2006 by Elsevier. Reprinted with permission.

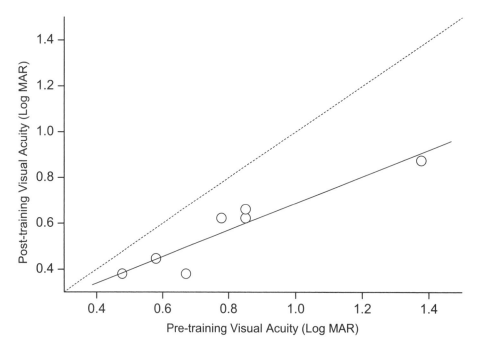

Figure 12.7. Posttraining versus pretraining visual acuity for observers in Group I. The best fitting linear regression line (R^2 = .93, p < .01) has a slope of 0.58. LogMAR = logarithm of the minimum angle of resolution. From "Perceptual Learning Improves Contrast Sensitivity and Visual Acuity in Adults with Anisometropic Amblyopia," by Y. Zhou, C. Huang, P. Xu, L. Tao, Z. Qiu, X. Li, and Z.-L. Lu, 2006, *Vision Research, 46,* p. 745. Copyright 2006 by Elsevier. Reprinted with permission.

Broad Bandwidth of Perceptual Learning
in Anisometropic Amblyopia

The hallmark of perceptual learning in the normal visual system is its specificity to the characteristics of the training stimulus (Fahle, 2002). If perceptual learning in the amblyopic visual system were also highly specific to the characteristics of the training stimuli and task, perceptual learning as a therapy for amblyopia would not be effective in improving general spatial vision. At a minimum, multiple training stimuli and tasks would have to be used to cover the range of circumstances important for daily visual functions. However, perceptual learning in the amblyopic eyes that generalizes to a wide range of untrained stimuli and task conditions would provide a basis for efficient training regimens. Although recent perceptual learning studies on amblyopia have all demonstrated some degree of transfer (e.g., Vernier acuity to visual acuity, position acuity to Snellen acuity), a systematic characterization of the degree of generalizability of perceptual learning in amblyopia is still critically important.

To evaluate and compare the generalizability of perceptual learning in amblyopic and normal vision, Huang et al. (2008) estimated the spatial bandwidth of perceptual learning in both normal and amblyopic participants. Ten teenage and adult observers (S1–S10, 18.6 ± 2.8 years) with unilateral anisometropic amblyopia and 21 teenagers and adults with normal or corrected-to-normal vision participated in this study. Fourteen (S11–S24, 22.9 ± 1.7 years) and seven (S25–S31, 22.6 ± 3.1 years) normal observers were randomly assigned into the first and second control groups. Contrast sensitivity functions and visual acuities were assessed in both eyes before and after training. During training, observers practiced a grating detection task at threshold contrast in the amblyopic eye or the nondominant eye. A staircase procedure was used to track the threshold contrast of the grating for each observer over the entire training course. A single spatial frequency was used for each observer. In the amblyopic and first control groups, observers were trained at their individual cutoff spatial frequencies (average: 7.5 ± 3.8 and 26.1 ± 4.2 c/deg; median: 9.6 and 27 c/deg), defined as the spatial frequency at which the contrast threshold was 0.50. Observers in the second control group were trained at 10 c/deg, near the median cutoff spatial frequency of the amblyopic participants.

For the amblyopic and normal observers in the first control group, training at the cutoff spatial frequency significantly improved contrast sensitivity ($p < .01$), by 10.7 dB and 5.6 dB, respectively. For the observers in the second control group, training at 10 c/deg generated a small (0.7 dB) and nonsignificant contrast sensitivity change ($p > .10$). The magnitude of improvement was not significantly correlated with age ($r = -.20, p > .10$). For the amblyopic observers, training also greatly improved visual acuities in the amblyopic eyes (average: 37.2%, $p < .01$) and fellow eyes (13.4%, $p < .01$). No significant visual acuity improvement was observed in either control group ($p > .15$).

To evaluate transfer of perceptual learning to other spatial frequencies, we compared the pre- and posttraining contrast sensitivity functions in the trained eyes. For the observers in the amblyopic (eight of 10) and first control (nine of 14) groups who showed significant contrast sensitivity improvements at the training spatial frequencies, the magnitudes of contrast sensitivity improvements at their respective training frequencies were not significantly different (9.98 vs. 8.30 dB; $p > .25$). However, the bandwidth of perceptual learning was drastically different ($p < .01$): For the amblyopic observers, the average full bandwidth was 4.04 ± 0.63 octaves; the average full bandwidth was only 1.40 ± 0.30 octaves for the normal observers (see Figure 12.8). The mode of contrast sensitivity improvement was approximately 1 octave lower than the training frequency in the amblyopic group, but at the training frequency for the normal observers, it was consistent with the last channel theory of amblyopia, that is, amblyopic individuals perform high spatial frequency tasks with lower spatial frequency channels (Levi, Waugh, & Beard, 1994).

In parafoveal vision of normal observers, Sowden, Rose, and Davies (2002) found that perceptual learning of contrast detection was specific to the trained eye with a bandwidth of 1.3 octaves. Although Sowden et al. trained their observers at 4 c/deg in parafovea and we trained our normal observers at 27 c/deg in fovea, the estimated bandwidths of perceptual learning from the two independent studies are in almost perfect agreement and consistent with the typical bandwidth of spatial frequency channels (De Valois & De Valois, 1988; Wilson, McFarlane, & Phillips, 1983).

For amblyopic observers, the estimated bandwidth of perceptual learning is much broader than the bandwidth of their spatial frequency channels, which has been estimated in sine-wave adaptation (Hess, 1980) and masking (Levi & Harwerth, 1982) paradigms, as well as in an object recognition study with filtered letters (Chung et al., 2002). All these studies found that the bandwidth of the spatial frequency channels of the amblyopic visual system is virtually identical to that of the normal observers, that is, 1 to 2 octaves. The estimated 4.04 octaves bandwidth of perceptual learning implies that the impact of perceptual

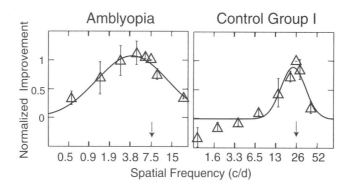

Figure 12.8. Average contrast sensitivity improvements as functions of spatial frequency for the amblyopic (a) and first control groups (b). Only subjects with significant learning effects were included in the analysis (see the texts for more details). Error bars indicate standard error of the mean. c/d = cycles per degree. From "Broad Bandwidth of Perceptual Learning in the Visual System of Adults with Anisometropic Amblyopia," by C.-B. Huang, Y. Zhou, & Z.-L. Lu, 2008, *Proceedings of the National Academy of Sciences of the United States of America, 105,* p. 4070. Copyright 2008 by the National Academy of Sciences. Reprinted with permission.

learning generalizes across spatial frequency channels in amblyopic eyes. Such a broad bandwidth of perceptual learning may underlie the improved visual acuity in the amblyopic eyes following training, a task that involves a wide range of spatial frequencies. In contrast, the approximate equivalence of learning and channel bandwidth in normal eyes suggests that perceptual learning is channel specific.

General Discussion

Physiological recordings in monkeys with experimental amblyopia (Kiorpes et al., 1998) showed that amblyopia is usually associated with a modest reduction of effective input from the amblyopic eye. Such input reduction may be one physiological basis for the increased internal noise in amblyopia. As shown by Lu and Dosher (1998), reduced stimulus input is mathematically equivalent to increased additive internal noise. Another possible physiological basis for increased internal noise in amblyopia might be increased variance of neuronal activities in the amblyopic cortex (Shadlen & Newsome, 1998; Tolhurst, Movshon, & Dean, 1983). Our results suggest that this might be a worthwhile direction for future physiological investigations on amblyopia.

The perceptual template in the PTM represents the "receptive field" of the overall observer. Using the classification image technique, a deficient perceptual template might be associated with miswiring of cortical neurons ("topographical jitter") in any or all of the many stages of visual processing (Hess & Field, 1994). It is also possible that a deficient perceptual template is due to some form of downweighting of high spatial frequency channels of the amblyopic eyes in the decision stage. On the other hand, the PTM is a model of the visual system at a rather abstract level. Although the PTM and related analysis provide some important constraints, a detailed model of the visual system is necessary to fully understand the mechanisms of amblyopia.

The relatively larger deficits in high spatial frequencies exhibited by observers who have completed occlusion therapy and practice in acuity tasks suggest that selective training in relatively high spatial frequencies might be necessary to reduce high spatial frequency deficits in amblyopia. It would be interesting to repeat the Zhou et al. (2006) study with treated amblyopic patients, using similar perceptual learning procedures to examine whether perceptual learning can provide additional improvements in high spatial frequencies. According to McKee et al. (2003), monocular contrast sensitivity might be related to the binocularity of neurons in the early visual pathway. That CSF remains deficient in patients with amblyopia treated with occlusion therapy suggests that explicit training on binocular functions may be necessary following largely monocular training and exposure therapies.

Dosher and Lu (1998) argued that specificity of perceptual learning alone is an inadequate criterion for inferring the loci of perceptual learning. Instead, a systematic task analysis is necessary for the interpretation of various specificity tests and for the design of more diagnostic tests for the level of perceptual learning. This framework has revealed that the primary mechanisms of perceptual learning are the reduction of internal noise and retuning of the perceptual template, reflecting reweighting of information from early sensory representations (Lu & Dosher, 1998, 2004; Petrov, Dosher, & Lu, 2005). We propose that the higher internal noise and defective perceptual templates in amblyopia may leave more room for improvements in perceptual learning. Specifically, if the dominant pretraining internal noise source in the amblyopic visual system is situated after the channels, then high-spatial-frequency training that retunes frequency-specific templates while simultaneously reducing postchannel internal noise will be manifest in the phenomenon of generalization across frequencies. Generalization across eyes would be observed if the internal noise source occurs after mixing of the channels in each eye. The question of generalization, and its proposed mechanism(s), requires careful investigation.

In current clinical practice, adult amblyopia is mostly left untreated. Studies have also shown that the classical "occlusion" treatment is no longer effective for older children and adults with amblyopia (Polat et al., 2004). We suggest reevaluating the conventional wisdom for treating amblyopia: that missing the critical period for treatment results in a fully (although erroneously) developed visual system that is immune to therapeutic modifications. Our studies, together with several others (Chung et al., 2006; Levi & Polat, 1996; Levi et al., 1997; Polat et al., 2004; Zhou et al., 2006), demonstrate that the adult amblyopic visual system remains remarkably plastic, and perceptual learning could lead to substantial improvements of spatial vision in adult amblyopia.

References

Barnes, G. R., Hess, R. F., Dumoulin, S. O., Achtman, R. L., & Pike, G. B. (2001). The cortical deficit in humans with strabismic amblyopia. *The Journal of Physiology, 533,* 281–297. doi:10.1111/j.1469-7793.2001.0281b.x

Berardi, N., Pizzorusso, T., Ratto, G. M., & Maffei, L. (2003). Molecular basis of plasticity in the visual cortex. *Trends in Neurosciences, 26,* 369–378. doi:10.1016/S0166-2236(03)00168-1

Braddick, O., Campbell, F. W., & Atkinson, J. (1978). Channels in vision: Basic aspects. In R. Held, H. W. Leibowitz, & H. Teuber (Eds.), *Perception* (pp. 3–38). Berlin, Germany: Springer-Verlag.

Burgess, A. E., & Colborne, B. (1988). Visual signal detection. IV. Observer inconsistency. *Journal of the Optical Society of America A: Optics and Image Science, 5,* 617–627. doi:10.1364/JOSAA.5.000617

Campbell, F. W., Hess, R. F., Watson, P. G., & Banks, R. (1978). Preliminary results of a physiologically based treatment of amblyopia. *The British Journal of Ophthalmology, 62,* 748–755. doi:10.1136/bjo.62.11.748

Cascairo, M. A., Mazow, M. L., Holladay, J. T., & Prager, T. (1997). Contrast visual acuity in treated amblyopia. *Binocular Vision & Strabismus Quarterly, 12,* 167–174.

Chung, S. T., Legge, G. E., & Tjan, B. S. (2002). Spatial-frequency characteristics of letter identification in central and peripheral vision. *Vision Research, 42,* 2137–2152. doi:10.1016/S0042-6989(02)00092-5

Chung, S. T., Levi, D. M., & Tjan, B. S. (2005). Learning letter identification in peripheral vision. *Vision Research, 45,* 1399–1412. doi:10.1016/j.visres.2004.11.021

Chung, S. T., Li, R. W., & Levi, D. M. (2006). Identification of contrast-defined letters benefits from perceptual learning in adults with amblyopia. *Vision Research, 46,* 3853–3861. doi:10.1016/j.visres.2006.06.014

Ciuffreda, K. J., Goldner, K., & Connelly, R. (1980). Lack of positive results of a physiologically based treatment of amblyopia. *The British Journal of Ophthalmology, 64,* 607–612. doi:10.1136/bjo.64.8.607

Ciuffreda, K. J., Levi, D. M., & Selenow, A. (1991). *Amblyopia: Basic and clinical aspects.* Boston, MA: Butterworth-Heinemann.

Crewther, D. P., & Crewther, S. G. (1990). Neural site of strabismic amblyopia in cats: Spatial frequency deficit in primary cortical neurons. *Experimental Brain Research, 79,* 615–622. doi:10.1007/BF00229329

Dao, D. Y., Lu, Z.-L., & Dosher, B. A. (2006). Adaptation to sine-wave gratings selectively reduces the contrast gain of the adapted stimuli. *Journal of Vision, 6,* 739–759. doi:10.1167/6.7.6

Daw, N. W. (1998). Critical periods and amblyopia. *Archives of Ophthalmology, 116,* 502–505.

De Valois, R. L., & De Valois, K. K. (1988). *Spatial vision.* New York, NY: Oxford University Press.

Dosher, B. A., & Lu, Z.-L. (1998). Perceptual learning reflects external noise filtering and internal noise reduction through channel reweighting. *Proceedings of the National Academy of Sciences of the United States of America, 95,* 13988–13993. doi:10.1073/pnas.95.23.13988

Dosher, B. A., & Lu, Z.-L. (2000a). Mechanisms of perceptual attention in precuing of location. *Vision Research, 40,* 1269–1292. doi:10.1016/S0042-6989(00)00019-5

Dosher, B. A., & Lu, Z.-L. (2000b). Noise exclusion in spatial attention. *Psychological Science, 11,* 139–146. doi:10.1111/1467-9280.00229

Eckstein, M. P., Ahumada, A. J., Jr., & Watson, A. B. (1997). Visual signal detection in structured backgrounds. II. Effects of contrast gain control, background variations, and white noise. *Journal of the Optical Society of America A: Optics, Image Science, and Vision, 14,* 2406–2419. doi:10.1364/JOSAA.14.002406

Fahle, M. (2002). *Perceptual learning.* Cambridge, MA: The MIT Press.

Gold, J., Bennett, P. J., & Sekuler, A. B. (1999). Signal but not noise changes with perceptual learning. *Nature, 402,* 176–178. doi:10.1038/46027

Greenwald, M. J., & Parks, M. M. (1999). *Clinical Ophthalmology: Vol. 1.* Hagerstown, MD: Harper & Row.

Hess, R. F. (1980). A preliminary investigation of neural function and dysfunction in amblyopia—I. Size-selective channels. *Vision Research, 20,* 749–754. doi:10.1016/0042-6989(80)90003-6

Hess, R. F., & Field, D. J. (1994). Is the spatial deficit in strabismic amblyopia due to loss of cells or an uncalibrated disarray of cells? *Vision Research, 34,* 3397–3406. doi:10.1016/0042-6989(94)90073-6

Hess, R. F., & Pointer, J. S. (1985). Differences in the neural basis of human amblyopia: The distribution of the anomaly across the visual field. *Vision Research, 25,* 1577–1594. doi:10.1016/0042-6989(85)90128-2

Huang, C., Tao, L., Zhou, Y., & Lu, Z.-L. (2007). Treated amblyopes remain deficient in spatial vision: A contrast sensitivity and external noise study. *Vision Research, 47,* 22–34.

Huang, C. B., Zhou, Y., & Lu, Z.-L. (2008). Broad bandwidth of perceptual learning in the visual system of adults with anisometropic amblyopia. *Proceedings of the National Academy of Sciences of the United States of America, 105,* 4068–4073. doi:10.1073/pnas.0800824105

Jindra, L. F., & Zemon, V. (1989). Contrast sensitivity testing: A more complete assessment of vision. *Journal of Cataract and Refractive Surgery, 15,* 141–148.

Kersten, D., Hess, R. F., & Plant, G. T. (1988). Assessing contrast sensitivity behind cloudy media. *Clinical Vision Sciences, 2,* 143–158.

Kiorpes, L., Kiper, D. C., O'Keefe, L. P., Cavanaugh, J. R., & Movshon, J. A. (1998). Neuronal correlates of amblyopia in the visual cortex of macaque monkeys with experimental strabismus and anisometropia. *The Journal of Neuroscience, 18,* 6411–6424.

Kiorpes, L., & McKee, S. P. (1999). Neural mechanisms underlying amblyopia. *Current Opinion in Neurobiology, 9,* 480–486. doi:10.1016/S0959-4388(99)80072-5

Levi, D. M., & Harwerth, R. S. (1982). Psychophysical mechanisms in humans with amblyopia. *American Journal of Optometry and Physiological Optics, 59,* 936–951. doi:10.1097/00006324-198212000-00002

Levi, D. M., & Klein, S. (1982, July 15). Hyperacuity and amblyopia. *Nature, 298,* 268–270. doi:10.1038/298268a0

Levi, D. M., & Klein, S. A. (2003). Noise provides some new signals about the spatial vision of amblyopes. *The Journal of Neuroscience, 23,* 2522–2526.

Levi, D. M., & Polat, U. (1996). Neural plasticity in adults with amblyopia. *Proceedings of the National Academy of Sciences of the United States of America, 93,* 6830–6834. doi:10.1073/pnas.93.13.6830

Levi, D. M., Polat, U., & Hu, Y. S. (1997). Improvement in Vernier acuity in adults with amblyopia. Practice makes better. *Investigative Ophthalmology & Visual Science, 38,* 1493–1510.

Levi, D. M., Waugh, S. J., & Beard, B. L. (1994). Spatial scale shifts in amblyopia. *Vision Research, 34,* 3315–3333. doi:10.1016/0042-6989(94)90067-1

Li, R. W., & Levi, D. M. (2004). Characterizing the mechanisms of improvement for position discrimination in adult amblyopia. *Journal of Vision, 4,* 476–487. doi:10.1167/4.6.7

Li, R. W., Provost, A., & Levi, D. M. (2007). Extended perceptual learning results in substantial recovery of positional acuity and visual acuity in juvenile amblyopia. *Investigative Ophthalmology & Visual Science, 48,* 5046–5051. doi:10.1167/iovs.07-0324

Lu, Z.-L., & Dosher, B. A. (1998). External noise distinguishes attention mechanisms. *Vision Research, 38,* 1183–1198. doi:10.1016/S0042-6989(97)00273-3

Lu, Z.-L., & Dosher, B. A. (1999). Characterizing human perceptual inefficiencies with equivalent internal noise. *Journal of the Optical Society of America A: Optics, Image Science, and Vision, 16,* 764–778. doi:10.1364/JOSAA.16.000764

Lu, Z.-L., & Dosher, B. A. (2004). Spatial attention excludes external noise without changing the spatial frequency tuning of the perceptual template. *Journal of Vision, 4,* 955–966. doi:10.1167/4.10.10

Lu, Z.-L., & Dosher, B. A. (2008). Characterizing observer states using external noise and observer models: Assessing internal representations with external noise. *Psychological Review, 115,* 44–82. doi:10.1037/0033-295X.115.1.44

McKee, S. P., Levi, D. M., & Movshon, J. A. (2003). The pattern of visual deficits in amblyopia. *Journal of Vision, 3,* 380–405. doi:10.1167/3.5.5

Mou, T. (1966). Logarithmic visual acuity chart and five-score recording. *Chinese Journal of Ophthalmology, 13,* 96–106.

Movshon, J. A., Eggers, H. M., Gizzi, M. S., Hendrickson, A. E., Kiorpes, L., & Boothe, R. G. (1987). Effects of early unilateral blur on the macaque's visual system. III. Physiological observations. *The Journal of Neuroscience, 7,* 1340–1351.

Nordmann, J. P., Freeman, R. D., & Casanova, C. (1992). Contrast sensitivity in amblyopia: Masking effects of noise. *Investigative Ophthalmology & Visual Science, 33,* 2975–2985.

Pelli, D. G. (1981). *Effects of visual noise.* (Unpublished doctoral dissertation). Cambridge University, Cambridge, England.

Pelli, D. G. (1985). Uncertainty explains many aspects of visual contrast detection and discrimination. *Journal of the Optical Society of America A: Optics and Image Science, 2,* 1508–1532. doi:10.1364/JOSAA.2.001508

Pelli, D. G., Levi, D. M., & Chung, S. T. (2004). Using visual noise to characterize amblyopic letter identification. *Journal of Vision, 4,* 904–920. doi:10.1167/4.10.6

Pelli, D. G., Robson, J. G., & Wilkins, A. J. (1988). The design of a new letter chart for measuring contrast sensitivity. *Clinical Vision Sciences, 2,* 187–199.

Petrov, A. A., Dosher, B. A., & Lu, Z.-L. (2005). The dynamics of perceptual learning: An incremental reweighting model. *Psychological Review, 112,* 715–743. doi:10.1037/0033-295X.112.4.715

Polat, U., Ma-Naim, T., Belkin, M., & Sagi, D. (2004). Improving vision in adult amblyopia by perceptual learning. *Proceedings of the National Academy of Sciences of the United States of America, 101,* 6692–6697. doi:10.1073/pnas.0401200101

Regan, D. (1988). Low-contrast visual acuity test for pediatric use. *Canadian Journal of Ophthalmology, 23,* 224–227.

Rogers, G. L., Bremer, D. L., & Leguire, L. E. (1987). The contrast sensitivity function and childhood amblyopia. *American Journal of Ophthalmology, 104,* 64–68.

Schor, C., & Wick, B. (1983). Rotating grating treatment of amblyopia with and without eccentric fixation. *Journal of the American Optometric Association, 54,* 545–549.

Schröder, J. H., Fries, P., Roelfsema, P. R., Singer, W., & Engel, A. K. (2002). Ocular dominance in extrastriate cortex of strabismic amblyopic cats. *Vision Research, 42,* 29–39. doi:10.1016/S0042-6989(01)00263-2

Shadlen, M. N., & Newsome, W. T. (1998). The variable discharge of cortical neurons: Implications for connectivity, computation, and information coding. *The Journal of Neuroscience, 18,* 3870–3896.

Simmers, A. J., & Gray, L. S. (1999). Improvement of visual function in an adult amblyope. *Optometry and Vision Science, 76,* 82–87. doi:10.1097/00006324-199902000-00014

Sowden, P. T., Rose, D., & Davies, I. R. (2002). Perceptual learning of luminance contrast detection: Specific for spatial frequency and retinal location but not orientation. *Vision Research, 42,* 1249–1258. doi:10.1016/S0042-6989(02)00019-6

Stewart, C. E., Moseley, M. J., & Fielder, A. R. (2003). Defining and measuring treatment outcome in unilateral amblyopia. *The British Journal of Ophthalmology, 87,* 1229–1231. doi:10.1136/bjo.87.10.1229

Tolhurst, D. J., Movshon, J. A., & Dean, A. F. (1983). The statistical reliability of signals in single neurons in cat and monkey visual cortex. *Vision Research, 23,* 775–785. doi:10.1016/0042-6989(83)90200-6

Wang, H., Levi, D. M., & Klein, S. A. (1998). Spatial uncertainty and sampling efficiency in amblyopic position acuity. *Vision Research, 38,* 1239–1251. doi:10.1016/S0042-6989(97)00278-2

Watson, A. B., Barlow, H. B., & Robson, J. G. (1983, March 31). What does the eye see best? *Nature, 302,* 419–422. doi:10.1038/302419a0

Wick, B., Wingard, M., Cotter, S., & Scheiman, M. (1992). Anisometropic amblyopia: Is the patient ever too old to treat? *Optometry and Vision Science, 69,* 866–878. doi:10.1097/00006324-199211000-00006

Wilson, H. R., McFarlane, D. K., & Phillips, G. C. (1983). Spatial frequency tuning of orientation selective units estimated by oblique masking. *Vision Research, 23,* 873–882. doi:10.1016/0042-6989(83)90055-X

Xu, P., Lu, Z.-L., Qiu, Z., & Zhou, Y. (2006). Identify mechanisms of amblyopia in Gabor orientation identification with external noise. *Vision Research, 46,* 3748–3760. doi:10.1016/j.visres.2006.06.013

Yenice, O., Onal, S., Incili, B., Temel, A., Afsar, N., & Tanrida Gcaron, T. (2007). Assessment of spatial-contrast function and short-wavelength sensitivity deficits in patients with migraine. *Eye, 21,* 218–223. doi:10.1038/sj.eye.6702251

Zhou, Y., Huang, C. B., Xu, P. J., Tao, L. M., Qiu, Z. P., Li, X. R., & Lu, Z.-L. (2006). Perceptual learning improves contrast sensitivity and visual acuity in adults with anisometropic amblyopia. *Vision Research, 46,* 739–750. doi:10.1016/j.visres.2005.07.031

13

Multimodal Perception and Simulation

Peter Werkhoven and Jan van Erp

This chapter discusses mechanisms of multimodal perception in the context of multimodal simulators and virtual worlds. We review some notable findings from psychophysical experiments with a focus on what we call *touch-inclusive multimodal perception*—that is, the sensory integration of the tactile system with other sensory systems such as vision and hearing.

The Relevance of Understanding Multimodal Perception

Humans have evolved to interact with their natural environment through multiple and highly sophisticated sensory systems, each consisting of dedicated receptors, neural pathways, and specialized parts of the brain in which processing takes place. Human sensory systems for vision, hearing (audition), touch (somatic sensation), taste (gustation), and smell (olfaction) enable us to sense physical properties from different sensory modalities such as light, sound, pressure, the flavor of substances, and volatile chemicals. Another sensory system, the vestibular system, lets us sense the gravitational force and our body accelerations.

Not trivially, our brains merge the information derived from the various sensory systems into a coherent and unambiguous multisensory percept of the world. They constantly process voluminous and parallel streams of sensory information and try to relate those sensory signals that originate from the same event, regardless of their modality. To understand the mechanisms underlying multimodal perception, we need to understand not only how information from each individual sensory modality is processed but also how information from one sensory system is integrated with and modulated by other sensory systems.

A thorough understanding of the mechanisms of multimodal perception has become of particular interest to the community of developers of rapidly evolving multimodal simulators and virtual worlds.

DOI: 10.1037/14135-014

Human Information Processing: Vision, Memory, and Attention, C. Chubb, B. A. Dosher, Z.-L. Lu, and R. M. Shiffrin (Editors)

Multimodal Simulation

Today we see interactive multimodal simulators that combine three-dimensional (3D) sound and vision, tactile feedback, and high-tech motion platforms. Among the most advanced simulators in the world is the multipurpose and multimodal simulator Desdemona, developed by the research institute TNO (Toegepast Natuurwetenschappelijk Onderzoek) Human Factors Institute in the Netherlands in collaboration with the Austrian company AMST Systemtechnik (see Figure 13.1). It has been designed to realistically simulate complex movements ranging from F16 dog fights to off-road vehicle driving and even roller coasters. It has a cabin that can contain an F16 cockpit, mounted on a fully gimbaled system that is able to rotate around any conceivable axis. The system as a whole allows 2 m of vertical movement, combined with 8 m along a horizontal sledge. The sledge itself is able to spin as well. Centrifugation enables Desdemona to generate constant G-forces up to a maximum of 3 G. Desdemona is also used for experiments on multimodal interfaces that support the pilot in keeping spatial orientation and situation awareness.

Research focuses on how to provide people with consistent multisensory cues for spatial orientation (proprioceptive, vestibular, visual, auditory) with the ambition of arriving at accurate sensory integration models (using Bayesian frameworks) that can account for the user variability observed in psychophysical experiments. The complexity of such models may be illustrated by the findings of Mesland, Bles, Werkhoven, and Wertheim (1998), who investigated the

Figure 13.1.   The multipurpose and multisensory motion simulator Desdemona, developed by TNO and AMST.

percept of passive horizontally oscillating self-motion simulated using a combination of a linear horizontal accelerator ("sled") and head-mounted displays. Remarkably, the self-motion percept for such simulation gained in quality not when the visual and proprioceptive stimuli were correctly in phase but when the visual stimulus had a small lead.

Parallel to the development of professional simulators, we see the emergence of 3D multimodal virtual game environments for social interaction, concept development, decision making, and learning. Such game environments allow people to interact with virtual worlds similar to the way they act in the real world and allow them to experience the consequences of their actions. Interaction and consistent multimodal representations (Ernst & Bulthoff, 2004) are crucial for this process of learning by doing. Consistency issues are even more complicated in the case of augmented worlds in which virtual and real worlds are combined. For example, using see-through displays in combination with auditory and tactile displays, we can perceive virtual objects embedded in our real environment. Virtual objects must behave correctly in this real world with respect to visual perspective, occlusion, shading, sound, and touch. However, technical limitations (spatiotemporal resolutions and dynamic ranges) and principle limitations (e.g., constraints of color spaces) still yield many inconsistencies.

Altogether, it is of crucial importance to have sufficient knowledge about human tolerances for inconsistencies between modalities and about modality interference effects. Furthermore, knowledge about multisensory illusions and metameric classes of sensory stimuli may lead to alternative and more feasible ways of creating a similar percept.

Sensory Substitution and Synesthetic Media

So far, we have reflected on how to convey visual properties of simulated environments to the visual sense, auditory properties to the auditory sense, and tactile properties to the touch senses in multimodal simulation. There is, however, a growing interest in exploiting our senses in less conventional ways—that is, to transduce information from one modality such that it can be sensed by other sensory systems.

Sensory transduction may serve to substitute a failing sensory system. Perhaps the most successful application of sensory substitution is Braille. Information usually acquired with our visual sensory system (reading) is transduced such that it can be acquired through the tactile sensory system (fingertips). Bach-y-Rita and Kercel (2003) suggested that reading itself can be considered the first sensory substitution system because it transduces auditory information (spoken words) such that it can be read by the visual system. With sufficient signal processing power and miniaturization of feedback devices, it has also become possible to create real-time sensory transducers. One example is the "seeing with sound" system, "vOICe," with which blind people can sense a visual scene (e.g., a street to cross). This sensory substitution system transduces images from a head-mounted camera into sound patterns that carry directional and distance information. An earlier example is the Tactile Vision Substitution System, developed by Bach-y-Rita, Collins, Saunders, White, and Scadden (1969), which transduces visual patterns from a head-mounted camera to vibrotactile patterns on the torso, enabling blind people to "see with their skin." Sensory substitution can also be applied within a sensory system, such as the finger-to-forehead of a person who has lost peripheral sensation (Bach-y-Rita, 1995).

Second, sensory transduction can be applied not as a substitution but as an augmentation of our senses or to enhance a single communication channel, such as speech or writing, into information that sends stimuli to several human senses. Waterworth (1997) termed such applications *synesthetic media*. For example, Smoliar, Waterworth, and Kellock (1995) developed a system to transduce the auditory properties such as dynamics, tempo, articulation, and synchronization of piano play to suitable visual representations to facilitate the communication between the student and the piano teacher. In another domain, TNO developed a tactile suit that transduces directional and gravitational information to vibrotactile patterns on the torso. This suit (see Figure 13.2)

Figure 13.2. The vibrotactile vest (TNO).

has been successfully tested for supporting pilots in landing their helicopter in Afghanistan during "brownouts," when clouds of dust and sand make landings based on visual information nearly impossible (van Erp, 2007). Similarly, the tactile vest has proven to support the spatial orientation of astronauts effectively under microgravity conditions in the International Space Station (van Erp & van Veen, 2006). However, it can also be used to complement the visual system, for example, in gaming applications.

Benefits of Multimodal Human–Computer Interaction

Waterworth (1997) stated that human–computer interaction (HCI) design should be seen as the art and science of sensory ergonomics for developing appropriate artifacts for sensory enhancement and communication. He assumed computers to serve as sensory transducers rather than cognitive artifacts. Today's technology makes it possible to design advanced sensory transducing multimodal human–computer interfaces, which may have various potential benefits, if designed carefully.

First, multimodal interfaces yield more robust performance. They present information in consistent complementary or redundant forms (or both). For example, the visual shape and the sound of a bird are complementary information, allowing disambiguation and enhancing the human detection and recognition performance of objects. Visual and tactile information about the size of the bird can be redundant, increasing the robustness of perceptual performance in case some sensory systems fail. Multimodal HCI can greatly improve the performance stability and robustness of recognition-based systems through disambiguation (Oviatt & Cohen, 2000).

Second, multimodal interfaces can reduce mental load. Current HCIs are strongly unimodal (usually visual), mainly consuming resources of a single sensory system and possibly causing mental overload. It has been shown, for example, that the tactile sensory systems can take over tasks of the visual system by adequately transducing the visual information to tactile patterns (van Erp, 2007).

Third, multimodal HCI has the potential to greatly expand the accessibility of virtual worlds to a larger diversity of users by adequately selecting the most appropriate combinations of modalities with respect to age, skill, style, impairments, and language (Oviatt & Cohen, 2000). For example, vision allows for a prolonged (foveal) attention to complex visual scenes and can attract attention peripherally, whereas hearing is transient but is omni-directional and has a longer short-term memory storage (Wickens, 1992). In contrast to vision and hearing, touch is capable of simultaneously sensing and acting when exploring the environment.

Fourth, multimodal presentation can promote new forms of HCI that were not previously available. For example, interfaces may adapt information presentation to the most appropriate sensory system given the preferences, needs, tasks, and context of the user, including aspects such as privacy, environmental noise and lighting, weather conditions, and protecting cloth. Adaptation of multimodal information presentation can be system controlled (the system finds out itself based on user profiles and user behavior monitoring) versus user controlled (explicit user-articulated preferences).

However, one also has to be aware of the trade-offs in multimodal HCI (Sarter, 2006). One of them is the trade-off between the benefits of adaptive multimodal HCI on the one hand and the increased cost of interface management and monitoring user demands on the other. Another is that the expected increase of robustness and decrease of mental load through the use of multimodal interfaces may lead to a higher risk that our brain can no longer converge modalities into a coherent percept and that sensory systems start to interfere, if such interfaces are not designed carefully.

Obviously, the successful design of multimodal HCI and virtual worlds relies heavily on a thorough knowledge of the underlying mechanisms of multimodal perception.

What Is Known About Touch-Inclusive Multimodal Perception

Research into the characteristics of unimodal perception has a long history; is spread across multiple disciplines, including the neurosciences, psychology, philosophy, physics, and computer sciences; and has been written down and reviewed in a huge body of literature. The first author's early contributions to the literature of human perception were also focused on unimodal visual motion perception, for example, motion detection mechanisms underlying the local extraction of linear motion patterns (Werkhoven & Koenderink, 1990) and also on rotary motion perception (Werkhoven & Koenderink, 1991), second-order motion perception (Werkhoven, Chubb, & Sperling, 1993; Werkhoven, Sperling, & Chubb, 1994), and structure from motion perception (De Vries & Werkhoven, 1995; Werkhoven & van Veen, 1995). The fact that these topics are just tiny building blocks of a single sensory system makes one realize that the world of multimodal perception will continue to challenge us with research questions for many decades to come.

Interestingly, although human perception generally has a multimodal nature, researchers only recently started to study the underlying mechanisms of multisensory perception and integration (Rock & Victor, 1964; Welch & Warren, 1980). Stein and Meredith (1993) and later Calvert, Spence, and Stein (2004) wrote excellent overviews based on the strongly fragmented literature on multisensory processing and have highlighted the most notable advances in this field. It must be noted, however, that the literature on unimodal as well as multimodal perception is strongly centered on the visual and auditory sensory systems. The synthesis of these sensory systems with the tactile sensory system has received minimal attention from the research community, given the great relevance and potential of touch in interactive virtual worlds.

In this chapter, we discuss what we call *touch-inclusive multimodal perception*: To what extent do tactile and other sensory modalities differ in their spatiotemporal characteristics? To what extent can touch-inclusive multimodal presentations enhance detection and recognition? To what extent do incongruent tactile and other sensory modalities interfere with each other?

To What Extent Do Tactile and Other Sensory Modalities Differ in Their Spatiotemporal Characteristics?

Given the increasing complexity of visual interfaces, system designers are increasingly looking toward the auditory and tactile sensory systems to provide alternative or supplementary means of information transfer (Spence & Driver, 1997; van Erp, 2001). Effective multimodal interfaces require that stimulation from several sensory channels be coordinated and made congruent informationally as well as temporally (Kolers & Brewster, 1985). Given the context of touch-inclusive multimodal interfaces and that time is an important and common dimension of all sensory modalities, we here focus on the temporal characteristics of the tactile and the visual system and aim at identifying cross-modal sensitivities and biases. For example, are time intervals when estimated by the tactile system the same as when estimated by the visual system?

Cross-Modal Biases

The relationships among the auditory, visual, and tactile channels regarding temporal duration has not been studied extensively. Only the perceived durations of visual and auditory time intervals have been compared. For temporal intervals on the order of 1 s, visual intervals had to be set longer than auditory intervals to be judged as equal in duration (Goldstone, Boardman, & Lhamon, 1959).

Modality differences have also been reported for other time-related measures and tasks, for example, in duration discrimination (Lhamon & Goldstone, 1974), temporal order judgment (Kanabus, Szelag, Rojek, & Poppel, 2002), stimulus sequence identification (Garner & Gottwald, 1968), perception of temporal rhythms (Gault & Goodfellow, 1938), and a temporal-tracking and continuation-tapping task (Kolers & Brewster, 1985). We know of only two studies that have addressed auditory–tactile interval duration comparisons. Both Ehrensing and Lhamon (1966) and Hawkes, Deardorff, and Ray (1977) found perceived tactile durations to equal auditory ones.

On the basis of the biased auditory visual relation and the unbiased auditory tactile relation, one might expect a bias in tactile visual comparisons as well: Visual intervals will probably have to be longer than tactile intervals to be judged as equal in duration. However, because manual interactions with the environment are often controlled using visual feedback, it may be expected that the perception of time intervals for the eye and for the fingertips has evolved to be consistent. Evidence for this comes from the development of visual–haptic interactions in children (Birch & Lefford, 1963, 1967).

van Erp and Werkhoven (2004) investigated the expected cross-modal bias for tactually and visually defined empty time intervals. In a forced-choice discrimination task, participants judged whether the second of two intervals was shorter or longer than the first interval. Two pulses defined the intervals. The pulse was either a vibrotactile burst presented to the fingertip or a foveally presented flash of a white square. The comparisons were made for unimodal (visual–visual or tactile–tactile) and cross-modal intervals (visual–tactile and tactile–visual) in the range of 100 to 800 ms. The standardized bias was defined as the time interval of one modality (say, visual) that was subjectively equal to the standard interval of another (say, tactile), normalized with respect to that standard interval and, thus, expressed in percentages. The results showed significant cross-modal biases between the tactile and sensory systems. Tactile empty intervals had to be set 8.5% shorter on average to be perceived as long as visual intervals. The cross-modal bias was largest for small intervals (15% for the 100-ms intervals).

Cross-Modal Sensitivity

Unimodal threshold studies have shown that the temporal resolution of the skin lies between those of hearing and vision (Kirman, 1973). This relation goes for numerous time-related measures and tasks, including discrimination of duration (Goodfellow, 1934), synchronization of finger taps (Kolers & Brewster, 1985), and adjusting empty intervals to equal pulse duration (Craig, 1973).

To be able to compare visual and tactile information in a cross-modal setting, there must be a common representation of the information from both senses. Several mechanisms for cross-modal visual–haptic comparisons have been suggested, based on two fundamentally different models (Summers & Lederman, 1990). The first is based on modality-specific representations that are used for unimodal comparisons (Lederman, Klatzky, Chataway, & Summers, 1990). These modality-specific representations must be translated into a common representation for cross-modal comparisons. This implies that cross-modal comparisons require an extra translation compared with unimodal comparisons. On the basis of the assumption that this extra translation increases the variability in the judgments, this model predicts a lower sensitivity for cross-modal comparisons than for unimodal comparisons. The second model (Ernst & Banks, 2002) states that information from the different modalities is directly processed and translated into a common (amodal) representation. This representation is used for both unimodal and cross-modal comparisons. In the latter model, unimodal and cross-modal comparisons are based on the same representation and are, therefore, hypothesized to have the same sensitivity.

van Erp and Werkhoven (2004) investigated the human sensitivity to discriminate empty intervals as a function of interval length and compared cross-modal sensitivity with unimodal sensitivity. Variances were derived from the same unimodal and cross-modal interval comparison experiments mentioned earlier. The Weber fractions (the threshold divided by the standard interval) were 20% and were constant over the standard intervals. This indicates that the Weber law holds for the range of interval lengths tested (100–800 ms).

Furthermore, the Weber fractions are consistent over unimodal and cross-modal comparisons, which suggests that there are no additional costs involved in the cross-modal comparison.

To What Extent Can Touch-Inclusive Multimodal Presentations Enhance Stimulus Detection and Recognition?

Generally, humans perceive real-world scenes through multiple sensory systems, and, most often, the information from the different sensory modalities involved is congruent, in either a complementary or a redundant way. Important questions are how scene information is processed within each modality, how information is integrated across modalities, and if and how this increases detection and recognition performance of objects or events.

Benefits of Multimodal Perception

Studies on multisensory integration have demonstrated that human perception can significantly increase in quality when the same environmental property is perceived in more than one sensory modality. For example, multimodal redundant stimuli have been shown to improve reaction time (Hershenson, 1962), stimulus identification (Doyle & Snowden, 2001), contrast detection (Lippert, Logothetis, & Kayser, 2007), perceptual organization (Vroomen & de Gelder, 2000), temporal boundaries (Vroomen & de Gelder, 2004), spatial localization (Alais & Burr, 2004), height estimation (Ernst & Banks, 2002), the reliability of depth cues (Landy, Maloney, Johnston, & Young, 1995), and size and stiffness estimates (Wu, Basdogan, & Srinivasan, 1999). Extensive reviews on neural, perceptual, and behavioral aspects of sensory integration can be found by Stein and Meredith (1993) and Calvert et al. (2004). So for congruent stimuli (derived from the same source), multisensory interaction indeed seems to improve the quality of perception. In fact, multisensory integration allows the brain to arrive at a statistically optimized integrated perceptual estimate under conditions in which the stimuli from the individual modalities involved are congruent, although each may be noisy, incomplete, and perhaps slightly different.

Interactions Between Sensory Systems

For incongruent stimuli, multisensory integration would obviously be ineffective. However, the brain cannot always determine correctly if individual signals are congruent or not. In some cases, our brain values a holistic percept so highly that incongruent stimuli lead to illusionary percept. For example, Shams, Kamitani, and Shimojo (2000, 2002) discovered that we perceive an illusory second flash when a single flash of light is accompanied by multiple auditory beeps, leading to a decrease in numerosity judgment performance. Andersen, Tiippana, and Sams (2005) extended this work by showing that the number of perceived flashes can be both increased (called *fission*) and decreased (called *fusion*) by presenting a larger or smaller number of irrelevant beeps in combination with the flashes.

Besides these audiovisual illusions, comparable effects have been reported for almost all other combinations of modalities (Bresciani, Dammeier, & Ernst, 2006; Courtney, Motes, & Hubbard, 2007; Ernst & Bulthoff, 2004; Hötting & Röder, 2004; Violentyev, Shimojo, & Shams, 2005).

Findings for incongruent stimuli have shed some light on the sensory integration process. The illusory flash effect has been explained by Bayesian models (Andersen et al., 2005; Bresciani et al., 2006; Ernst & Bulthoff, 2004; Shams, Ma, & Beierholm, 2005). These models propose that the more reliable estimate (with the smallest standard deviation) has a larger influence on the final percept. Auditory estimates are generally more reliable than visual estimates in temporal tasks, giving them dominance over visual perception in the illusory flash experiment (Andersen et al., 2005). Similarly, the tactile modality is more reliable than the visual modality and can induce visual flash illusions (Violentyev et al., 2005). In turn, the tactile modality can be modulated by auditory stimuli (Bresciani et al., 2005). Interestingly, this suggests an order of dominance (influence) for numerosity estimates equal to the order of performance found by Lechelt (1975) for unimodal temporal numerosity judgment: Hearing is best followed by touch and vision. That is, the more reliable modality in the illusory flash paradigm corresponds with the more accurate modality in his temporal numerosity judgment task.

Multimodal Numerosity Estimation

Given the growing body of models and experimental data on numerosity judgment tasks with incongruent stimuli, it may come as a surprise that multisensory numerosity judgments of congruent stimuli have hardly been studied. Only recently, Gallace, Tan, and Spence (2007) tested a spatial numerosity judgment task in which multimodal pulses were presented simultaneously at multiple locations as opposed to sequentially at a single location, as in temporal numerosity judgment. Participants had to count and sum the pulses presented in the tactile and visual modality. They found that bimodal numerosity judgments were significantly less accurate than unimodal judgments and suggested that numerosity judgments rely on a unitary amodal system. It would be interesting to know if this extends to temporal numerosity judgment.

Philippi, van Erp, and Werkhoven (2008) investigated a temporal numerosity judgment task and tested whether multimodal presentations can reduce the numerosity underestimation biases observed in unimodal conditions. Participants were presented with two to 10 pulses at different interstimulus intervals (ISIs) under unimodal conditions (visual, auditory, and tactile senses) as well as multimodal combinations. The results showed that for short ISIs (between 20 and 80 ms), multimodal presentation significantly reduced the underestimation of numerosity compared with unimodal presentation and, thus, enhanced performance. Interestingly, however, we found no differences in the variance of numerosity estimation between unimodal and multimodal presentations, suggesting that the integration process did lead to performance enhancement, but not through the variance reduction predicted by current (Bayesian) integration models.

The Cost of Multimodal Integration

We have seen convincing examples of perceptual task improvement under multimodal presentation conditions, generally for low-level perceptual tasks. For such tasks, the benefits of multimodal presentation seem to outweigh the cost of integration in terms of processing multiple resources. For higher level perceptual tasks such as object recognition, multisensory integration may come at a higher cost, for example, when information from different modalities is derived from the same scene but with different scene orientations for different modalities. Newell, Woods, Mernagh, and Bülthoff (2005) investigated the visual, haptic, and cross-modal recognition of scenes of familiar objects. Participants first learned a scene of objects in one sensory modality and were then asked to detect positional switches between objects in the same or a different modality. Newell and colleagues found a cost in scene recognition performance when there was a change in sensory modality and scene orientation between learning and test and suggested that differences between visual and haptic representations of space may affect the recognition of scenes of objects across these modalities.

To What Extent Do Incongruent Tactile and Other Sensory Modalities Interfere With Each Other, and What Is the Role of Attention in Sensory Integration?

Sensory Integration Models

Various studies on human perception of incongruent sensory inputs have determined how one sensory system was biased by task-irrelevant stimulation of other sensory systems. Some studies have shown an asymmetry of bias effects— that is, the more "appropriate" system for a particular task seemed to dominate less appropriate sensory systems. Guest and Spence (2003), for example, investigated the visuotactile assessment of roughened textile samples, in the presence of a congruent or an incongruent textile distracter, and concluded that vision influenced touch more than touch-influenced vision. The results further suggested that modality appropriateness was a function of the discriminative ability of the modality as well as ecological validity. Obviously, the order of dominance observed for temporal tasks does not seem to extend directly to spatial tasks such as texture assessment.

Early qualitative perceptual integration models assume that the more "appropriate" sensory system (i.e., most sensitive for the specific stimulus) dominates the less appropriate system, in the most extreme form, the "winner takes all" model (Welch & Warren, 1980). Other studies (Ernst & Bulthoff, 2004) have found mutual influences that can best be explained by the assumption that sensory signals are integrated with weights proportional with relative signal-to-noise ratio (the reliability of the sensory channel). On the basis of this reliability assumption, various quantitative probabilistic "ideal observer" models have been developed to explicitly model multimodal perception.

The maximum likelihood integration (MLI) approach by Andersen et al. (2005) assumes complete integration of the sensory channels and, consequently, that the sum of their weights equals 1. They found that early MLI (integration before stimulus categorization) explained the perceptual integration of rapid beeps and flashes better than late MLI (integration after categorization). Shams et al. (2005) developed a Bayesian integration scheme that could account for situations of partial integration in sound-induced flash illusions as well as complete integration.

Bresciani et al. (2006) studied experimental conditions in which visual and tactile signals were only partially integrated. They interpreted partial integration as a coupling between sensory channels and quantified the integration process using a Bayesian integration scheme with a coupling prior (e.g., prior knowledge about the probability that two sensory channel inputs originate from the same source). The free model parameter "Coupling Strength" distinguishes the model of Bresciani et al. from those of Andersen et al. (2005) and Shams et al. (2005).

The Complicating Role of Attention

Previous evidence on multimodal integration is based on experimental paradigms in which the participants' task was to ignore the "irrelevant" channel. This was done to show that multimodal integration occurs even if you want to ignore it. However, in such conditions, the strength of the integration and the ability to ignore a channel are confounded. Therefore, we explicitly distinguish two effects: (bottom-up) sensory system integration effects occurring in situations where both modalities are attended, and (top-down) sensory system suppression effects by selectively attending to the task relevant modality and ignoring the irrelevant.

Isolating Sensory System Integration

To disentangle bottom-up integration and top-down attention effects, Werkhoven, van Erp, and Philippi (2009) carried out multimodal perception experiments in which participants were exposed to incongruent sequences of visual flashes and tactile taps in two conditions. In one condition (the cue condition), they were instructed before stimulus presentation to report the number of events in a particular modality and to ignore the other (i.e., the traditional paradigms, in which sensory system integration and suppression effects are combined). In a second condition (the no-cue condition), they were instructed on which modality to report only after stimulus presentation and therefore could not ignore a channel (i.e., isolating the effect of sensory system integration). By comparing the results, Werkhoven et al. (2009) could quantify to what extent sensory integration and selective attention influence whole or partial perceptual integration.

The effects measured were fission effects and fusion effects: The task-irrelevant modality can increase (fission) or decrease (fusion) the number of perceived events in the task-relevant modality. Results showed that no-cue conditions yielded overall stronger fission and fusion effects than cue conditions, indicating that previous studies were based on the combined effects of sensory integration and selective attention. Furthermore, in no-cue conditions, the influence of vision on touch is stronger than the influence of touch on vision. However, in cue conditions, irrelevant flashes are more easily ignored than irrelevant taps. Together, these results suggest that the bottom-up influence of vision on touch is stronger but that vision is also more easily suppressed by top-down selective attention.

Consequences and Chances for Multimodal Simulation

So what has been learned so far? Because the experiments mentioned here can at most be considered to be tiny pieces of a giant puzzle of perceptual organization and because generalization of their results cannot be scientifically justified, we will just briefly speculate on some possible consequences for multimodal simulation.

Our sensory systems are all optimized for specific aspects of the outside world, often leading to different spatial and temporal characteristics. The cross-modal biases for time interval estimation between the tactile and the visual system, for example, are substantial. There is no right or wrong about an internal representation of a sensory system; there are only differences. To make time intervals congruent in simulated environments, we may have to adjust them a little bit relative to each other.

Furthermore, we have seen that multimodal estimation can improve many perceptual tasks, such as numerosity estimation. Improving numerosity estimation was not trivial back in the 1940s. At that time, Taubman (1950) reported that observers had difficulty adequately discriminating the short tones as part of characters in the international Morse code. This problem arose not only for the perception of auditory pulses, it also existed if the code consisted of flashes of light (i.e., blinker code). We may not need to optimize Morse code any longer, but the use of tactile displays (van Erp et al., 2006) to transduce information through simple spatial and temporal patterns on the skin may certainly benefit from this knowledge. The tactile vest has a wide range of current and potential applications, varying from guidance for people who are blind or have severe visual impairment, to spatial orientation in vehicles, to feedback during revalidation, to sports feedback, to teleoperations, to entirely new forms of multimodal touch-inclusive gaming.

Last but not least, we saw that incongruent stimuli can lead to illusory percepts (e.g., illusory flashes or taps) due to automatic sensory integration process. More specifically, the bottom-up interaction between sensory channels can be asymmetric, and perceptual attention can have a strong top-down influence. Such illusory percepts, when sufficiently understood, can be of interest to the community of multimodal simulator designers. The simulation of some perceptual aspects can be constrained by technical limitations or can come at high cost, similar to force feedback effects. In such cases, it may be interesting to find alternative stimulus combinations that create the same (illusory) percept. It may even allow for illusory percepts that cannot occur in the real world, such as the "rubber-hand illusion" (Ehrsson, Spence, & Passingham, 2004).

References

Alais, D., & Burr, D. (2004). The ventriloquist effect results from near-optimal cross-modal integration. *Current Biology, 14,* 257–262.

Andersen, T. S., Tiippana, K., & Sams, M. (2005). Maximum likelihood integration of rapid flashes and beeps. *Neuroscience Letters, 380,* 155–160. doi:10.1016/j.neulet.2005.01.030

Bach-y-Rita, P. (1995). *Nonsynaptic diffusion neurotransmission and late brain reorganization.* New York, NY: Demos-Vermande.

Bach-y-Rita, P., Collins, C. C., Saunders, F. A., White, B., & Scadden, L. (1969, March 8). Vision substitution by tactile image projection. *Nature, 221,* 963–964. doi:10.1038/221963a0

Bach-y-Rita, P., & Kercel, S. W. (2003). Sensory substitution and the human-machine interface. *Trends in Cognitive Sciences, 7,* 541–546. doi:10.1016/j.tics.2003.10.013

Birch, H. G., & Lefford, A. (1963). Intersensory development in children. *Monographs of the Society for Research in Child Development, 28*(5). doi:10.2307/1165681

Birch, H. G., & Lefford, A. (1967). Visual differentiation, intersensory integration, and voluntary motor control. *Monographs of the Society for Research in Child Development, 32*(2). doi:10.2307/1165792

Bresciani, J. P., Dammeier, F., & Ernst, M. O. (2006). Vision and touch are automatically integrated for the perception of sequences of events. *Journal of Vision, 6,* 554–564. doi:10.1167/6.5.2

Bresciani, J. P., Ernst, M. O., Drewing, K., Bouyer, G., Maury, V., & Kheddar, A. (2005). Feeling what you hear: Auditory signals can modulate tactile taps perception. *Experimental Brain Research, 162,* 172–180. doi:10.1007/s00221-004-2128-2

Calvert, C., Spence, C., & Stein, B. E. (2004). *The handbook of multisensory processes.* Cambridge, MA: MIT Press.

Courtney, J. R., Motes, M. A., & Hubbard, T. L. (2007). Multi- and unisensory visual flash illusions. *Perception, 36,* 516–524. doi:10.1068/p5464

Craig, J. (1973). A constant error in the perception of brief temporal intervals. *Perception & Psychophysics, 13,* 99–104. doi:10.3758/BF03207241

De Vries, S. C., & Werkhoven, P. (1995). Cross-modal slant and curvature matching of stereo- and motion-specified surfaces. *Perception & Psychophysics, 57,* 1175–1186. doi:10.3758/BF03208373

Doyle, M. C., & Snowden, R. J. (2001). Identification of visual stimuli is improved by accompanying auditory stimuli: The role of eye movements and sound location. *Perception, 30,* 795–810. doi:10.1068/p3126

Ehrensing, R. H., & Lhamon, W. T. (1966). Comparison of tactile and auditory time judgments. *Perceptual and Motor Skills, 23,* 929–930. doi:10.2466/pms.1966.23.3.929

Ehrsson, H. H., Spence, C., & Passingham, R. E. (2004, August 6). That's my hand! Activity in premotor cortex reflects feeling of ownership of a limb. *Science, 305,* 875–877. doi:10.1126/science.1097011

Ernst, M. O., & Banks, M. S. (2002, January 24). Humans integrate visual and haptic information in a statistically optimal fashion. *Nature, 415,* 429–433. doi:10.1038/415429a

Ernst, M. O., & Bulthoff, H. H. (2004). Merging the senses into a robust percept. *Trends in Cognitive Sciences, 8,* 162–169. doi:10.1016/j.tics.2004.02.002

Gallace, A., Tan, H. Z., & Spence, C. (2007). Multisensory numerosity judgments for visual and tactile stimuli. *Perception & Psychophysics, 69,* 487–501. doi:10.3758/BF03193906

Garner, W. R., & Gottwald, R. L. (1968). The perception and learning of temporal patterns. *The Quarterly Journal of Experimental Psychology, 20,* 97–109. doi:10.1080/14640746808400137

Gault, R. H., & Goodfellow, L. D. (1938). An empirical comparison of audition, vision, and touch in the discrimination of temporal patterns and ability to reproduce them. *Journal of General Psychology, 18,* 41–47. doi:10.1080/00221309.1938.9709888

Goldstone, S., Boardman, W. K., & Lhamon, W. T. (1959). Intersensory comparisons of temporal judgments. *Journal of Experimental Psychology, 57,* 243–248. doi:10.1037/h0040745

Goodfellow, L. D. (1934). An empirical comparison of audition, vision, and touch in the discrimination of short intervals of time. *The American Journal of Psychology, 46,* 243–258. doi:10.2307/1416558

Guest, S., & Spence, C. (2003). Tactile dominance in speeded discrimination of textures. *Experimental Brain Research, 150,* 201–207.

Hawkes, G. R., Deardorff, P. A., & Ray, W. S. (1977). Response delay effects with cross-modality duration judgments. *Journal of Auditory Research, 17,* 55–57.

Hershenson, M. (1962). Reaction time as a measure of intersensory facilitation. *Journal of Experimental Psychology, 63,* 289–293. doi:10.1037/h0039516

Hötting, K., & Röder, B. (2004). Hearing cheats touch, but less in congenitally blind than in sighted individuals. *Psychological Science, 15,* 60–64. doi:10.1111/j.0963-7214.2004.01501010.x

Kanabus, M., Szelag, E., Rojek, E., & Poppel, E. (2002). Temporal order judgement for auditory and visual stimuli. *Acta Neurobiologiae Experimentalis, 62,* 263–270.

Kirman, J. H. (1973). Tactile communication of speech: A review and analysis. *Psychological Bulletin, 80,* 54–74. doi:10.1037/h0034630

Kolers, P. A., & Brewster, J. M. (1985). Rhythms and responses. *Journal of Experimental Psychology: Human Perception and Performance, 11,* 150–167. doi:10.1037/0096-1523.11.2.150

Landy, M. S., Maloney, L. T., Johnston, E. B., & Young, M. (1995). Measurement and modeling of depth cue combination: In defense of weak fusion. *Vision Research, 35,* 389–412. doi:10.1016/0042-6989(94)00176-M

Lechelt, E. C. (1975). Temporal numerosity discrimination: Intermodal comparisons revisited. *British Journal of Psychology, 66,* 101–108. doi:10.1111/j.2044-8295.1975.tb01444.x

Lederman, S. J., Klatzky, R. L., Chataway, C., & Summers, C. G. (1990). Visual mediation and the haptic recognition of two-dimensional pictures of common objects. *Perception & Psychophysics, 47,* 54–64. doi:10.3758/BF03208164

Lhamon, W. T., & Goldstone, S. (1974). Studies of auditory-visual differences in human time judgment: 2. More transmitted information with sounds than lights. *Perceptual and Motor Skills, 39,* 295–307. doi:10.2466/pms.1974.39.1.295

Lippert, M., Logothetis, N. K., & Kayser, C. (2007). Improvement of visual contrast detection by a simultaneous sound. *Brain Research, 1173,* 102–109. doi:10.1016/j.brainres.2007.07.050

Mesland, B. S., Bles, W., Werkhoven, P., & Wertheim, A. H. (1998). How flexible is the self-motion system? Introducing phase and amplitude differences between visual and proprioceptive passive linear horizontal self-motion stimuli. In B. S. Mesland (Ed.), *About horizontal self-motion perception* (pp. 99–142). Utrecht, The Netherlands: University of Utrecht.

Newell, F. N., Woods, A. T., Mernagh, M., & Bülthoff, H. H. (2005). Visual, haptic and cross-modal recognition of scenes. *Experimental Brain Research, 161,* 233–242. doi:10.1007/s00221-004-2067-y

Oviatt, S. L., & Cohen, P. R. (2000). Multimodal systems that process what comes naturally. *Communications of the ACM, 43,* 45–53. doi:10.1145/330534.330538

Philippi, T. G., van Erp, J. B. F., & Werkhoven, P. J. (2008). Multisensory temporal numerosity judgment. *Brain Research, 1242,* 116–125. doi:10.1016/j.brainres.2008.05.056

Rock, I., & Victor, J. (1964, February 7). Vision and touch: An experimentally created conflict between the two senses. *Science, 143,* 594–596. doi:10.1126/science.143.3606.594

Sarter, N. B. (2006). Multimodal information presentation: Design guidance and research challenges. *International Journal of Industrial Ergonomics, 36,* 439–445. doi:10.1016/j.ergon.2006.01.007

Shams, L., Kamitani, Y., & Shimojo, S. (2000, December 14). What you see is what you hear. *Nature, 408,* 788. doi:10.1038/35048669

Shams, L., Kamitani, Y., & Shimojo, S. (2002). Visual illusion induced by sound. *Brain Research. Cognitive Brain Research, 14,* 147–152. doi:10.1016/S0926-6410(02)00069-1

Shams, L., Ma, W. J., & Beierholm, U. (2005). Sound-induced flash illusion as an optimal percept. *Neuroreport, 16*(17), 1923–1927. doi:10.1097/01.wnr.0000187634.68504.bb

Smoliar, S. W., Waterworth, J. A., & Kellock, P. R. (1995). PianoFORTE: A system for piano education beyond notation literacy. *Proceedings of the Third ACM International Conference on Multimedia,* 457–465.

Spence, C., & Driver, J. (1997). Cross-modal links in attention between audition, vision, and touch: Implications for interface design. *International Journal of Cognitive Ergonomics, 1,* 351–373.

Stein, B. E., & Meredith, M. A. (1993). *The merging of the senses.* Cambridge, MA: MIT Press.

Summers, D. C., & Lederman, S. J. (1990). Perceptual asymmetries in the somatosensory system: A dichhaptic experiment and critical review of the literature from 1929 to 1986. *Cortex, 26,* 201–226.

Taubman, R. E. (1950). Studies in judged number: I. The judgment of auditory number. *The Journal of General Psychology, 43,* 195–219. doi:10.1080/00221309.1950.9710620

van Erp, J. B. F. (2001). Tactile navigation display. In S. Brewster & R. Murray-Smith (Eds.), *Haptic human-computer interaction* (pp. 165–173). Berlin, Germany: Springer-Verlag. doi:10.1007/3-540-44589-7_18 van Erp, J. B. F. (2007). *Tactile displays for navigation and orientation: Perception and behaviour.* Leiden, The Netherlands: Mostert & Van Onderen.

van Erp, J. B. F., & van Veen, H. A. H. C. (2006). Touch down: The effect of artificial touch cues on orientation in microgravity. *Neuroscience Letters, 404,* 78–82. doi:10.1016/j.neulet.2006.05.060

van Erp, J. B. F., & Werkhoven, P. J. (2004). Perception of vibro-tactile asynchronies. *Perception, 33,* 103–111.

Violentyev, A., Shimojo, S., & Shams, L. (2005). Touch-induced visual illusion. *Neuroreport, 16,* 1107–1110. doi:10.1097/00001756-200507130-00015

Vroomen, J., & de Gelder, B. (2000). Sound enhances visual perception: Cross-modal effects of auditory organization on vision. *Journal of Experimental Psychology: Human Perception and Performance, 26,* 1583–1590. doi:10.1037/0096-1523.26.5.1583

Vroomen, J., & de Gelder, B. (2004). Temporal ventriloquism: Sound modulates the flash-lag effect. *Journal of Experimental Psychology: Human Perception and Performance, 30,* 513–518. doi:10.1037/0096-1523.30.3.513

Waterworth, J. A. (1997). Creativity and sensation: The case for synaesthetic media. *Leonardo, 30,* 327–330. doi:10.2307/1576481

Welch, R. B., & Warren, D. H. (1980). Immediate perceptual response to intersensory discrepancy. *Psychological Bulletin, 88,* 638–667. doi:10.1037/0033-2909.88.3.638

Werkhoven, P., & Koenderink, J. J. (1990). Extraction of motion parallax structure in the visual system I. *Biological Cybernetics, 63,* 185–191. doi:10.1007/BF00195857

Werkhoven, P., & Koenderink, J. J. (1991). Visual processing of rotary motion. *Perception & Psychophysics, 49,* 73–82. doi:10.3758/BF03211618

Werkhoven, P., Chubb, C., & Sperling, G. (1993). The dimensionality of texture-defined motion: A single channel theory. *Vision Research, 33,* 463–485. doi:10.1016/0042-6989(93)90253-S

Werkhoven, P., Sperling, G., & Chubb, C. (1994). Motion perception between dissimilar gratings: Spatiotemporal properties. *Vision Research, 34,* 2741–2759. doi:10.1016/0042-6989(94)90230-5

Werkhoven, P., van Erp, J. B. F., & Philippi, T. (2009). Counting visual and tactile events: The effect of attention on multisensory integration. *Attention, Perception, & Psychophysics, 71,* 1854–1861. doi:10.3758/APP.71.8.1854

Werkhoven, P., & van Veen, H. A. H. C. (1995). Extraction of relief from visual motion. *Perception & Psychophysics, 57,* 645–656. doi:10.3758/BF03213270

Wickens, C. D. (1992). *Engineering psychology and human performance* (2nd ed.). New York, NY: HarperCollins.

Wu, W.-C., Basdogan, C., & Srinivasan, M. A. (1999). Visual, haptic, and bimodal perception of size and stiffness. In virtual environments. *ASME Dynamic Systems and Control Division, 67,* 19–26.

14

Projections of a Learning Space

Jean-Claude Falmagne

Learning spaces, which are special cases of knowledge spaces (cf. Doignon & Falmagne, 1999), are mathematical structures designed to model the cognitive organization of a scholarly topic, such as Beginning Algebra or Chemistry 101. The definition of *learning space* is recalled in our Definition 1. Essentially, a learning space is a family of sets, called *knowledge states,* satisfying a couple of conditions. The elements of the sets are "items" of knowledge, such as facts or problems to be solved. A knowledge state is a set gathering some of these items. Each of the knowledge states in a learning space is intended as a possible representation of some individual's competence in the topic. Embedded in a suitable stochastic framework, the concept of a learning space provides a mechanism for the assessment of knowledge in the sense that efficient questioning of a subject on a well-chosen subset of items suffices to gauge his or her knowledge state. As such, it offers an attractive alternative to standardized testing, the theoretical basis of which is fundamentally different and based on the measurement of aptitudes (see, e.g., Nunnally & Bernstein, 1994). Many aspects of these structures have been investigated and the results reported in various publications; for a sample of these, see Doignon and Falmagne (1985); Falmagne and Doignon (1988a); Albert and Lukas (1999); and Falmagne, Cosyn, Doignon, and Thiéry (2006). The monograph by Falmagne and Doignon (2011) contains most of the results.[1]

In practice—in an educational context, for example—a learning space can be large, sometimes numbering millions of states or more. The concept of a *projection* at the core of this chapter provides a way of parsing such a large structure into meaningful components. Moreover, when the learning space concerns a scholarly

This paper is dedicated to George Sperling, whose curious, incisive mind rarely fails to produce the unexpected creative idea. George and I have been colleagues for the longest time in both of our careers. The benefit has been mine.

An earlier version of this chapter appeared in the preprint archive, arXiv. Falmagne, J.-C. (2008). Projections of a learning space. Retrieved from arXiv database: http://arxiv.org/pdf/0803.0575.pdf

[1]An extensive database on knowledge spaces, with hundreds of titles, is maintained by Cord Hockemeyer at the University of Graz: http://wundt.uni-graz.at/kst.php (see also Hockemeyer, 2001).

DOI: 10.1037/14135-015
Human Information Processing: Vision, Memory, and Attention, C. Chubb, B. A. Dosher, Z.-L. Lu, and R. M. Shiffrin (Editors)

curriculum such as high school algebra, a projection may provide a convenient instrument for the programming of a placement test. For the complete algebra curriculum comprising several hundred types of problems, a placement test of a few dozen problems can be manufactured easily via a well-chosen projection.

The key idea is that if $\mathcal{K}$ is a learning space on a domain Q, then any subset Q' of Q defines a learning space $\mathcal{K}_{|Q'}$ on Q' that is consistent with $\mathcal{K}$. We call $\mathcal{K}_{|Q'}$ a *projection* of $\mathcal{K}$ on Q', a terminology consistent with that used by Cavagnaro (2008) and Eppstein, Falmagne, and Ovchinnikov (2008) for media. Moreover, this construction defines a partition of $\mathcal{K}$ such that each equivalence class is a subfamily of $\mathcal{K}$ satisfying some of the key properties of a learning space. In fact, Q' can be chosen so that each of these equivalence classes is essentially (via a trivial transformation) either a learning space consistent with $\mathcal{K}$ or the singleton $\{\emptyset\}$.

These results, titled *projection theorems* (13 and 16), are formulated in this chapter. They could be derived from corresponding results for the projections of media (Cavagnaro, 2008; Eppstein et al., 2008; Falmagne and Ovchinnikov, 2002). Direct proofs are given here. This chapter extends previous results from Doignon and Falmagne (1999, Theorem 1.16 and Definition 1.17) and Cosyn (2002).

Basic Concepts

1 Definition

We denote by $K \triangle L = (K \setminus L) \cup (L \setminus K)$ the symmetric difference between two sets K, L, and by $d(K, L) = |K \triangle L|$ the symmetric difference distance between these sets. (All the sets considered in this chapter are finite.) The symbols $+$ and $\subset$ stand for the disjoint union and the proper inclusion of sets, respectively. A *(knowledge) structure* is a pair $(Q, \mathcal{K})$ where Q is a nonempty set and $\mathcal{K}$ is a family of subsets of Q containing $\emptyset$ and $Q = \cup\mathcal{K}$. The latter is called the *domain* of $(Q, \mathcal{K})$. The elements of Q are called *items* and the sets in $\mathcal{K}$ are *(knowledge) states*. Because $Q = \cup\mathcal{K}$, the set Q is implicitly defined by $\mathcal{K}$, and we can without ambiguity call $\mathcal{K}$ a knowledge structure. A *knowledge space* is a knowledge structure closed under union, or $\cup$-*closed*. A family of sets $\mathcal{F}$ is *well graded* if for any two sets K and L in $\mathcal{F}$ with $d(K, L) = n$ there exists a sequence $K_0 = K$, $K_1, \ldots, K_n = L$ such that $\mathrm{d}(K_i, K_{i+1}) = 1$ for $0 \leq i \leq n - 1$. We call such a sequence $K_0 = K, K_1, \ldots, K_n = L$ a *tight path* from K to L.

A knowledge structure $(Q, \mathcal{K})$ is a *learning space* (cf. Cosyn & Uzun, 2008) if it satisfies the following two conditions:

L1. Learning smoothness. For any two $K, L \in \mathcal{K}$, with $K \subset L$ and $|L \setminus K| = n$, there is a chain $K_0 = K \subset K_1 \subset \cdots \subset K_n = L$ such that, for $0 \leq i \leq n - 1$, we have $K_{i+1} = K_i + \{q_i\} \in \mathcal{K}$ for some $q_i \in Q \setminus K$.

L2. Learning consistency. If $K \subset L$ are two sets in $\mathcal{K}$ such that $K + \{q\} \in \mathcal{K}$ for some $q \in Q \setminus K$, then $L \cup \{q\} \in \mathcal{K}$.

A learning space is also known in the combinatorics literature as an *antimatroid,* a structure introduced independently by Edelman and Jamison (1985) with slightly different, but equivalent, axioms (cf. also Welsh, 1995; Björner, Las Vergnas, Sturmfels, White, & Ziegler, 1999). Another term for this is *well-graded knowledge space* (Falmagne & Doignon, 1988b); see our Theorem 10.

A family $\mathcal{F}$ of subsets of a set Q is a *partial knowledge structure* if it contains the set $Q = \cup \mathcal{F}$. We do not assume that $|\mathcal{F}| \geq 2$. We also call the sets in $\mathcal{F}$ *states*. A partial knowledge structure $\mathcal{F}$ is a *partial learning space* if it satisfies Axioms L1 and L2. Note that $\{\emptyset\}$ is vacuously well-graded and vacuously $\cup$-closed, with $\cup\{\emptyset\} = \emptyset$. Thus, it is a partial knowledge structure and a partial learning space (cf. Theorem 11).

The following preparatory result allows the shortening of some proofs.

2 Lemma

A $\cup$-closed family of sets $\mathcal{F}$ is well graded if, for any two sets $K \subset L$, there is a tight path from K to L.

Proof: Suppose that the condition holds. For any two distinct sets K and L, there exists a tight path $K_0 = K \subset K_1 \subset \cdots \subset K_n = K \cup L$ and another tight path $L_0 = L \subset L_1 \subset \cdots \subset L_m = K \cup L$. These two tight paths can be concatenated. Reversing the order of the sets in the latter tight path and redefining $K_{n+1} = L_{m-1}, K_{n+2} = L_{m-2}, \ldots, K_{n+m} = L_0 = L$ we get the tight path $K_0 = K, K_1, \ldots, K_{n+m} = L_0 = L$, with $|K \Delta L| = n + m$. □

Projections

As mentioned in our introduction, some knowledge structures may be so large that a splitting is required, for convenient storage in a computer's memory for example. Also, in some situations, only a representative part of a large knowledge structure may be needed. The concept of a projection is of critical importance in this respect. We introduce a tool for its construction.

3 Definition

Let $(Q, \mathcal{K})$ be a partial knowledge structure with $|Q| \geq 2$, and let Q' be any proper non empty subset of Q. Define a relation $\sim_{Q'}$ on $\mathcal{K}$ by

$$K \sim_{Q'} L \Longleftrightarrow K \cap Q' = L \cap Q' \quad (14.1)$$

$$\Longleftrightarrow K \Delta L \subseteq Q \backslash Q'. \quad (14.2)$$

Thus, $\sim_{Q'}$ is an equivalence relation on $\mathcal{K}$. When the context specifies the subset Q', we sometimes use the shorthand $\sim$ for $\sim_{Q'}$ in the sequel. The equivalence between the right-hand sides of Equation 14.1 and 14.2 is easily verified. We denote by $[K]$ the equivalence class of $\sim$ containing K, and by $\mathcal{K}_\sim = \{[K]\ |\ K \in \mathcal{K}\}$ the partition of $\mathcal{K}$ induced by $\sim$. We may say for short that such a partition is induced by the set Q'. In the sequel, we always assume that $|Q| \geq 2$, so that $|Q'| \geq 1$.

4 Definition

Let $(Q, \mathcal{K})$ be a partial knowledge structure and take any nonempty proper subset Q' of Q. The family

$$\mathcal{K}_{|Q'} = \{W \subseteq Q \mid W = K \cap Q' \text{ for some } K \in \mathcal{K}\} \qquad (14.3)$$

is called the *projection* of $\mathcal{K}$ on Q'. We have thus $\mathcal{K}_{|Q'} \subseteq 2^{Q'}$. As shown by Example 5, the sets in $\mathcal{K}_{|Q'}$ may not be states of $\mathcal{K}$. For any state K in $\mathcal{K}$ and with $[K]$ as in Definition 3, we define the family

$$\mathcal{K}_{[K]} = \{M \mid M = L \setminus \cap [K] \text{ for some } L \sim K\}. \qquad (14.4)$$

(If $\emptyset \in \mathcal{K}$, we have thus $\mathcal{K}_{[\emptyset]} = [\emptyset]$.) The family $\mathcal{K}_{[K]}$ is called a Q'-*child*, or simply a *child* of $\mathcal{K}$ (*induced by* Q'). As shown by the example below, a child of $\mathcal{K}$ may take the form of the singleton $\{\emptyset\}$, and we may have $\mathcal{K}_{[K]} = \mathcal{K}_{[L]}$ even when $K \not\sim L$. The set $\{\emptyset\}$ is called the *trivial* child.

5 Example

Equation 14.5 defines a learning space $\mathcal{F}$ on the domain $Q = \{a, b, c, d, e, f\}$:

$$\mathcal{F} = \{\emptyset, \{b\}, \{c\}, \{a,b\}, \{a,c\}, \{b,c\}, \{b,d\}, \{a,b,c\}, \{a,b,d\}, \{b,c,d\}, \{b,c,e\},$$
$$\{b,d,f\}, \{a,b,c,d\}, \{a,b,c,e\}, \{b,c,d,e\}, \{b,c,d,f\}, \{b,c,e,f\}, \{a,b,d,f\},$$
$$\{a,b,c,d,e\}, \{a,b,c,d,f\}, \{a,b,c,e,f\}, \{b,c,d,e,f\}, \{a,b,c,d,e,f\}, Q\}. \qquad (14.5)$$

The inclusion graph of this learning space is pictured by the gray parts of Figure 14.1. The sets marked in black in the eight ovals of the figure represent the states of the projection $\mathcal{F}_{|\{a,d,f\}}$ of $\mathcal{F}$ on the set $\{a, d, f\}$. It is clear that $\mathcal{F}_{|\{a,d,f\}}$ is a learning space.[2]

Each of the ovals in Figure 14.1 also surrounds the inclusion subgraph corresponding to an equivalence class of the partition $\mathcal{F}_\sim$. This is consistent with Lemma 7 (ii) according to which there is a 1–1 correspondence between $\mathcal{F}_\sim$ and $\mathcal{F}_{|\{a,d,f\}}$. In this example, the "learning space" property is hereditary in the sense that not only is $\mathcal{F}_{|\{a,d,f\}}$ a learning space, but also any child of $\mathcal{F}$ is a learning space or a partial learning space. Indeed, we have

$$\mathcal{F}_{[\{b,c,e\}]} = \{\emptyset, \{b\}, \{c\}, \{b, c\}, \{b, c, e\}\},$$

$$\mathcal{F}_{[\{a,b,c,e\}]} = \{\{b\}, \{c\}, \{b, c\}, \{b, c, e\}\},$$

$$\mathcal{F}_{[\{a,b,c,d,e\}]} = \mathcal{F}_{[\{b,c,d,e,f\}]} = \mathcal{F}_{[\{a,b,c,d,e\}]} = \{\emptyset, \{c\}, \{c, e\}\},$$

---

[2]This property holds in general. Notice that we have here the special case in which $\mathcal{F}_{|\{a,d,f\}}$ is the power set of $\{a, d, f\}$. However, it is not generally true that for any learning space $(Q, \mathcal{K})$ and $Q' \subset Q$, we have $\mathcal{K}_{|Q'} = 2^{Q'}$.

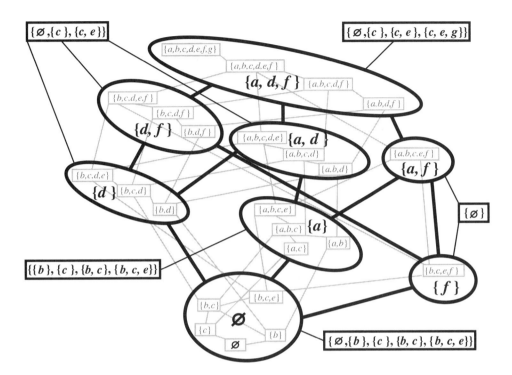

Figure 14.1. In gray, the inclusion graph of the learning space $\mathcal{F}$ of Equation 14.5. Each oval surrounds an equivalence class $[K]$ (in gray) and a particular state (in black) of the projection $\mathcal{F}_{\|a,d,f\|}$ of Q on $Q' = \{a, d, f\}$, signaling a 1–1 mapping $\mathcal{F}_{\sim} \to \mathcal{F}_{\|a,d,f\|}$ (cf. Lemma 7 (ii)). Via the defining Equation 14.4, the eight equivalence classes produce five children of $\mathcal{F}$, which are represented in the black rectangles of the figure. One of these children is the singleton set $\{\emptyset\}$ (thus, a trivial child), and the others are learning spaces or partial learning spaces (cf. Projection Theorems 13 and 16). From *Learning Spaces: Interdisciplinary Applied Mathematics* (p. 33), by J.-C. Falmagne & J.-P. Doignon, 2011, Heidelberg, Germany: Springer-Verlag. Copyright 2011 by Springer-Verlag. Reprinted with permission.

$$\mathcal{F}_{[\{a,b,c,d,e,f,g\}]} = \{\emptyset, \{c\}, \{c, e\}, \{c, e, g\}\}$$

$$\mathcal{F}_{[\{b,c,e,f\}]} = \mathcal{F}_{[\{a,b,c,e,f\}]} = \{\emptyset\}.$$

These four children are represented in the five black rectangles in Figure 14.1.

Theorem 13 shows that the well-gradedness property is always inherited by the children of a learning space. In the particular case of this example, just adding the set $\emptyset$ to the child not containing it already, that is, to the child $\mathcal{F}_{[\{b,c,e\}]} = \mathcal{F}_{[\{a,b,c,e\}]}$, would result in having all the families produced being learning spaces or trivial. This is not generally true. The situation is clarified by Theorem 16.

6 Remark

The concept of projection for learning spaces is closely related to the concept bearing the same name for media introduced by Cavagnaro (2008). The Projection

Theorems 13 and 16, the main results of this chapter, could be derived via similar results concerning the projections of media (cf. Theorem 2.11.6 in Eppstein et al., 2008). This would be a detour, however. The route followed here is direct.

In the next two lemmas, we derive a few consequences of Definition 4.

7 Lemma

The following two statements are true for any partial knowledge structure $(Q, \mathcal{K})$.

(i) The projection $\mathcal{K}_{|Q'}$, with $Q' \subset Q$, is a partial knowledge structure. If $(Q, \mathcal{K})$ is a knowledge structure, then so is $\mathcal{K}_{|Q'}$.
(ii) The function $h \colon [K] \to K \cap Q'$ is a well-defined bijection of $\mathcal{K}_\sim$ onto $\mathcal{K}_{|Q'}$.

Proof: (i) Both statements follow from the facts that $\emptyset \cap Q' = \emptyset$ and $Q \cap Q' = Q'$.

(ii) That h is a well-defined function is due to (1). It is clear that $h(\mathcal{K}_\sim) = \mathcal{K}_{|Q'}$ by the definitions of h and $\mathcal{K}_{|Q'}$. Suppose that, for some $[K], [L] \in \mathcal{K}_\sim$, we have $h([K]) = K \cap Q' = h([L]) = L \cap Q' = X$. Whether or not $X = \emptyset$, this entails $K \sim L$ and so $[K] = [L]$.   □

8 Lemma

Let $\mathcal{K}$ be any ∪-closed family, with $Q = \bigcup\mathcal{K}$ not necessarily in $\mathcal{K}$, and take any $Q' \subset Q$. The following three statements are then true:

(i) $K \sim Q' \cup[K]$ for any $K \in \mathcal{K}$.
(ii) $\mathcal{K}_{|Q'}$ is a ∪-closed family. If $\mathcal{K}$ is a knowledge space, so is $\mathcal{K}_{|Q'}$.
(iii) The children of $\mathcal{K}$ are also ∪-closed.

In (ii) and (iii), the converse implications are not true.[3]

Proof: (i) As $\bigcup[\mathcal{K}]$ is the union of states of $\mathcal{K}$, we get $\bigcup[\mathcal{K}] \in \mathcal{K}$. We must have $K \cap Q' = (\bigcup[K]) \cap Q'$ because $K \cap Q' = L \cap Q'$ for all $L \in [K]$; so $K \sim \bigcup[K]$.

(ii) Any subfamily $\mathcal{H}' \subseteq \mathcal{K}_{|Q'}$ is associated to the family

$$\mathcal{H} = \{H \in \mathcal{K} \mid H' = H \cap Q' \text{ for some } H' \in \mathcal{H}'\}.$$

Because $\mathcal{K}$ is ∪-closed, we have $\bigcup\mathcal{H} \in \mathcal{K}$, yielding $Q' \cap (\bigcup\mathcal{H}) = \bigcup\mathcal{H}' \in \mathcal{K}_{|Q'}$. If $\mathcal{K}$ is a knowledge space, then $\bigcup\mathcal{K} \in \mathcal{K}$, which implies $Q' \cap (\bigcup\mathcal{K}) = \bigcup\mathcal{K}_{|Q'} \in \mathcal{K}_{|Q'}$. Thus, $\mathcal{K}_{|Q'}$ is a knowledge space.

(iii) Take $K \in \mathcal{K}$ arbitrarily. We must show that $\mathcal{K}_{[K]}$ is ∪-closed. If $\mathcal{K}_{[K]} = \{\emptyset\}$, this is vacuously true. Otherwise, for any $\mathcal{H} \subseteq \mathcal{K}_{[K]}$ we define the associated family

---

[3]For knowledge spaces, Lemma 8 (ii) was obtained by Doignon and Falmagne (1999, Theorem 1.16 on p. 25) where the concept of a projection was referred to as a *substructure*. Their proof applies here. We include it for completeness.

$$\mathcal{H}^\dagger = \{H^\dagger \in \mathcal{K} \mid H^\dagger \sim K, H^\dagger \setminus \cap [K] \in \mathcal{H}\}.$$

Thus, $\mathcal{H}^\dagger \subseteq [K]$, which gives $L \cap Q' = K \cap Q'$ for any $L \in \mathcal{H}^\dagger$. Because $\mathcal{K}$ is $\cup$-closed, we have $\cup \mathcal{H}^\dagger \in \mathcal{K}$. We thus get $(\cup \mathcal{H}^\dagger) \cap Q' = K \cap Q'$ and $\cup \mathcal{H}^\dagger \sim K$.

The $\cup$-closure of $\mathcal{K}_{[K]}$ follows from the string of equalities

$$\cup \mathcal{H} = \cup_{H^\dagger \in \mathcal{H}^\dagger} (H^\dagger \setminus \cap [K]) = \cup_{H^\dagger \in \mathcal{H}^\dagger} \left(H^\dagger \cap \overline{(\cap [K])}\right) = (\cup_{H^\dagger \in \mathcal{H}^\dagger} H^\dagger) \setminus \cap [K],$$

which gives $\cup \mathcal{H} \in \mathcal{K}_{[K]}$ because $K \sim \cup \mathcal{H}^\dagger \in \mathcal{K}$. Example 9 shows that the reverse implications in (ii) and (iii) do not hold. $\quad\square$

9 Example

Consider the projection of the knowledge structure

$$\mathcal{G} = \{\emptyset, \{a\}, \{b\}, \{c\}, \{a,b\}, \{a,c\}, \{a,b,c\}\},$$

on the subset $\{c\}$. We have thus the two equivalence classes $[\{a, b\}]$ and $[\{a, b, c\}]$, with the projection $\mathcal{G}_{|\{c\}} = \{\emptyset, \{c\}\}$. The two $\{c\}$ children are $\mathcal{G}_{[\emptyset]} = \{\emptyset, \{a\}, \{b\}, \{a, b\}\}$ and $\mathcal{G}_{[\{c\}]} = \{\emptyset, \{a\}, \{a, b\}\}$. Both $\mathcal{G}_{[\emptyset]}$ and $\mathcal{G}_{[\{c\}]}$ are well graded and $\cup$-closed, and so is $\mathcal{G}_{|\{c\}}$, but $\mathcal{G}$ is not because $\{b, c\}$ is not a state.

We omit the proof of the next result, which is due to Cosyn and Uzun (2008; see also Falmagne & Doignon, 2010, Theorem 2.2.4).

10 Theorem

A knowledge structure $(Q, \mathcal{K})$ is a learning space if and only if it is a well-graded knowledge space.

As indicated by the next result, the equivalence ceases to hold in the case of partial spaces.

11 Theorem

Any well-graded $\cup$-closed family is a partial learning space. The converse implication is false.

Proof: Let $\mathcal{K}$ be a well-graded $\cup$-closed family. Axiom L1 is a special case of the well-gradedness condition. If $K \subset L$ for two sets K and L in $\mathcal{K}$ and $K + \{q\}$ is in $\mathcal{K}$, then the set $(K + \{q\}) \cup L = L \cup \{q\}$ is in $\mathcal{K}$ by $\cup$-closure, and so Axiom L2 holds. The example that follows disproves the converse. $\quad\square$

12 Example

The family of sets

$$\mathcal{L} = \{\{a,b,c\}, \{c,d,e\}, \{a,b,c,f\}, \{c,d,e,g\}, \{a,b,c,f,d\}, \{c,d,e,g,b\},$$
$$\{a,b,c,f,d,e\}, \{c,d,e,g,b,a\}, \{a,b,c,d,e,f,g\}\}$$

is a partial learning space because it is the union of the two chains

$$\{a,b,c\} \subset \{a,b,c,f\} \subset \{a,b,c,f,d\} \subset \{a,b,c,f,d,e\} \subset \{a,b,c,d,e,f,g\},$$

$$\{c,d,e\} \subset \{c,d,e,g\} \subset \{c,d,e,g,b\} \subset \{c,d,e,g,b,a\} \subset \{a,b,c,d,e,f,g\}$$

with the only common set $\cup \mathcal{L}$. However, $\mathcal{L}$ is neither $\cup$-closed nor well graded.
We state the first of our two projection theorems.

13 Projection Theorem

Let $\mathcal{K}$ be a learning space (respectively a well-graded $\cup$-closed family) on a domain Q with $|Q| = |\cup\mathcal{K}| \geq 2$. The following two properties hold for any proper nonempty subset Q' of Q:

(i)   The projection $\mathcal{K}_{|Q'}$ of $\mathcal{K}$ on Q' is a learning space (respectively a well-graded $\cup$-closed family).
(ii) In either case, the children of K are well-graded and $\cup$-closed families.

Note that we may have $\mathcal{K}_{[K]} = \{\emptyset\}$ in (ii) (cf. Example 5).

Proof: (i) If $\mathcal{K}$ is a learning space, then $\mathcal{K}_{|Q'}$ is a knowledge structure by Lemma 7 (i). Because $\mathcal{K}$ is $\cup$-closed by Theorem 10, so is $\mathcal{K}_{[K]}$ by Lemma 8 (ii). It remains to show that $\mathcal{K}_{[K]}$ is well graded. (By Theorem 10 again, this will imply that $\mathcal{K}_{|Q'}$ is a learning space.) We use Lemma 2 for this purpose. Take any two states $K' \subset L'$ in $\mathcal{K}_{|Q'}$ with $d(K', L') = n$ for some positive integer n. By Lemma 7 (ii), we have thus $K' = K \cap Q'$ and $L' = L \cap Q'$ for some $K, L \in \mathcal{K}$. Because $\mathcal{K}$ is well graded by Theorem 10, there exists a tight path $K_0 = K, K_1, \ldots, K_m = L$ from K to L, with either $K_j = K_{j-1} + \{p_j\}$ or $K_{j-1} = K_j + \{p_j\}$ for some $p_j \in Q$ with $1 \leq j \leq m$. Let $j \in \{1, \ldots, m\}$ be the first index such that $p_j \in Q'$.

We have then necessarily $p_j \in Q' \cap L = L'$ and $K_j = K_{j-1} + \{p_j\}$. This yields

$$K' = K_0 \cap Q' = K_1 \cap Q' = \cdots = K_{j-1} \cap Q',$$

and for $1 \leq j \leq n$,

$$K_j \cap Q' = (K_{j-1} \cap Q') + \{p\},$$

with $p \in L' \setminus K'$. Defining $K_0' = K'$ and $K_1' = K_j \cap Q'$, we have $\text{d}(K_1', L') = n - 1$, with K_1' a state of $\mathcal{K}_{|Q'}$. By induction, we conclude that $\mathcal{K}_{|Q'}$ is a well-graded $\cup$-closed knowledge structure. Because $\mathcal{K}_{|Q'}$ is $\cup$-closed, it must be a learning space by Theorem 10.

Suppose now that $\mathcal{K}$ is a well-graded $\cup$-closed family (rather than learning space). In such a case, there is no need to invoke Theorem 10, and the foregoing argument can be used to prove that $\mathcal{K}_{|Q'}$ is a well-graded $\cup$-closed family.

(ii) Take any child $\mathcal{K}_{[K]}$ of $\mathcal{K}$. By Lemma 8(iii), $\mathcal{K}_{[K]}$ is a $\cup$-closed family. We use Lemma 2 to prove that $\mathcal{K}_{[K]}$ is also well graded. Take any two states $M \subset L$ in $\mathcal{K}_{[K]}$. We have thus $L = L' \setminus (\cap[K])$ and $M = M' \setminus (\cap[K])$ for some L' and M' in $[K]$, with

$$\cap[K] \subseteq L' \subset M'. \qquad (14.6)$$

Because K is well-graded, there is a tight path

$$L_0' = L' \subset L_1' \subset \ldots \subset L_n' = M' \qquad (14.7)$$

with all its states in $[K]$. Indeed, $L' \subset L_j' \subset M'$ and $L' \cap Q' = M' \cap Q'$ imply $L' \cap Q' = L_j' \cap Q' = M' \cap Q'$ for any index $1 \leq j \leq n - 1$. We now define the sequence $L_j = L_j' \setminus \cap [K]$, $0 \leq j \leq n$. It is clear that Equations 14.6 and 14.7 imply

$$L_0 = L \subset L_1 \subset \cdots \subset L_n = M,$$

and it is easily verified that $L_0 = L, L_1, \ldots, L_n = M$ is a tight path from L to M. Applying Lemma 2, we conclude that $\mathcal{K}_{[K]}$ is well graded.

14 Remark

In Example 5, we had a situation in which the nontrivial children of a learning space were either themselves learning spaces or would become so by the addition of the set $\emptyset$. This can happen if and only if the subset Q' of the domain defining the projection satisfies the condition spelled out in the next definition.

15 Definition

Suppose that $(Q, \mathcal{K})$ is a partial knowledge structure, with $|Q| \geq 2$. A subset $Q' \subset Q$ is *yielding* if for any state L of $\mathcal{K}$ that is minimal for inclusion in some equivalence class $[K]$, we have $|L \setminus \cap [K]| \leq 1$. We recall that $[K]$ is the equivalence class containing K in the partition of $\mathcal{K}$ induced by Q' (cf. Definition 3). For any nontrivial child $\mathcal{K}_{[K]}$ of $\mathcal{K}$, we call $\mathcal{K}_{[K]}^+ = \mathcal{K}_{[K]} \cup \{\emptyset\}$ a *plus* child of $\mathcal{K}$.

16 Projection Theorem

Suppose that $(Q, \mathcal{K})$ is a learning space with $|Q| \geq 2$, and let Q' be a proper nonempty subset of Q. The two following conditions are then equivalent.

  (i) The set Q' is yielding.
  (ii) All the plus children of $\mathcal{K}$ are learning spaces.[4]

  (It is easily shown that any learning space always has at least one nontrivial child.)

  Proof: (i) $\Rightarrow$ (ii). By Lemma 8 (iii), we know that any nontrivial child $\mathcal{K}_{[K]}$ is $\cup$-closed. This implies that the associated plus child $\mathcal{K}_{[K]}^+$ is a knowledge space. We use Lemma 2 to prove that $\mathcal{K}_{[K]}^+$ is also well graded. Suppose that

---

[4]Note that we may have $\emptyset \in \mathcal{K}_{[K]}$ in which case $\mathcal{K}_{[K]}^+ = \mathcal{K}_{[K]}$ (cf. Example 5).

L and M are states of $\mathcal{K}^+_{[K]}$, with $\emptyset \subseteq L \subset M$ and that $d(L, M) = n$ for some positive integer n. We have two cases.

Case 1. Suppose that $L \neq \emptyset$. Then both L and M are in $\mathcal{K}_{[K]}$. Because $\mathcal{K}_{[K]}$ is well graded by Theorem 13(ii), there exists a tight path $L = L_0 \subset L_1 \subset \cdots \subset L_n = M$. Because $\emptyset \subset L_0$, this tight path lies entirely in the plus child $\mathcal{K}^+_{[K]}$.

Case 2. Suppose now that $L = \emptyset$. In view of what we just proved, we only have to show that for any nonempty $M \in \mathcal{K}^+$, there is a singleton set $\{q\} \in \mathcal{K}^+$ with $q \in M$. By definition of $\mathcal{K}^+_{[K]}$, we have $M = M' \setminus \cap [K]$ for some $M' \in [K]$. Take a minimal state N in $[K]$ such that $N \subseteq M'$ and so $N \setminus \cap [K] \subseteq M$. Because Q' is yielding, we get $|N \setminus \cap [K]| \leq 1$. If $|N \setminus \cap [K]| = 1$, then $N \setminus \cap [K] = \{q\} \subseteq M$ for some $q \in Q$ with $\{q\} \in \mathcal{K}^+_{[K]}$. Suppose that $|N \setminus \cap [K]| = 0$. Thus, $N \setminus \cap [K] = \emptyset$ and N must be the only minimal set in $[K]$, which implies that $\cap [K] = N$. By the well-gradedness of $\mathcal{K}$, there exists some $q \in M'$ such that $M' \supseteq N + \{q\} \in \mathcal{K}$. We have in fact $N + \{q\} \in [K]$ because $q \in M \setminus N$ implies $N \cap Q' = (N + \{q\}) \cap Q'$. We thus get

$$(N + \{q\}) \setminus \cap [K] = (N + \{q\}) \setminus N = \{q\} \subseteq M \text{ with } \{q\} \in \mathcal{K}^+_{[K]}.$$

We have proved that, in both cases, the tight path from L to M exists. The plus child $\mathcal{K}^+_{[K]}$ is thus well graded. Applying Theorem 10, we conclude that $\mathcal{K}^+_{[K]}$ is a learning space.

(ii) $\Rightarrow$ (i). Let L be a minimal element in the equivalence class $[K]$, where $K \in \mathcal{K}$. Then $\cap [K] \subseteq L$. If equality holds, we have $|L \setminus \cap [K]| = 0$. If $\cap [K] \subset L$, then $\emptyset$ and $L \setminus \cap [K]$ are distinct elements in the plus child $\mathcal{K}^+_{[K]}$. By the well-gradedness of $\mathcal{K}^+_{[K]}$, there is a tight path from $\emptyset$ to $L \setminus \cap [K]$ in $\mathcal{K}^+_{[K]}$. Because L is minimal in $[K]$ and distinct from $\cap [K]$, we see that $L \setminus \cap [K]$ must be a singleton. Hence $|L \setminus \cap [K]| = 1$. □

Summary

Various computer routines based on Markovian stochastic processes are available to perform assessments in learning spaces (see Chapters 13 and 14 in Falmagne & Doignon, 2010). However, implementing an assessment with such routines in a large learning space $(Q, \mathcal{K})$, with several million states or more, may be impractical in view of memory limitations of the computer. This chapter provides some basic results enabling a two-step procedure that can be applied in such a case. In Step 1, a representative subset Q' of items from the domain Q is selected, and an assessment is performed on the projection learning space $\mathcal{K}_{|Q'}$ induced by Q' (cf. Projection Theorem 13(i)). The outcome of this assessment is some knowledge state $K \cap Q'$ of $\mathcal{K}_{|Q'}$, which corresponds (in a 1-1 manner) to the equivalence class $[K]$ of the partition of $\mathcal{K}$ induced by Q' (cf. Lemma 7 (ii)). In Step 2, the child $\mathcal{K}_{[K]}$ is formed by removing all the common items in the states of $[K]$. The assessment can then be pursued on $\mathcal{K}_{[K]}$ of $\mathcal{K}$, which is a partial learning space (cf. Projection Theorem 13(ii)). The outcome of Step 2 is a set $L \setminus \cap [K]$, where L is a state in the learning space $\mathcal{K}$. This two-step procedure can be expanded into a n-step recursive algorithm if necessary.

References

Albert, D., & Lukas, J. (Eds.). (1999). *Knowledge spaces: Theories, empirical research, applications.* Mahwah, NJ: Erlbaum.

Björner, A., Las Vergnas, M., Sturmfels, B., White, N., & Ziegler, G. M. (1999). *Oriented matroids* (2nd ed.). New York, NY: Cambridge University Press.

Cavagnaro, D. R. (2008). Projection of a medium. *Journal of Mathematical Psychology, 52,* 55–63. doi:10.1016/j.jmp.2007.08.002

Cosyn, E. (2002). Coarsening a knowledge structure. *Journal of Mathematical Psychology, 46,* 123–139. doi:10.1006/jmps.2001.1376

Cosyn, E., & Uzun, H. B. (2008). Note on two sufficient axioms for a well-graded knowledge space. *Journal of Mathematical Psychology, 53,* 40–42. doi:10.1016/j.jmp.2008.09.005

Doignon, J.-P., & Falmagne, J.-C (1985). Spaces for the assessment of knowledge. *International Journal of Man-Machine Studies, 23,* 175–196. doi:10.1016/S0020-7373(85)80031-6

Doignon, J.-P., & Falmagne, J.-C. (1999). *Knowledge spaces.* Berlin and Heidelberg, Germany: Springer-Verlag.

Edelman, P. H., & Jamison, R. (1985). The theory of convex geometries. *Geometriae Dedicata, 19,* 247–271. doi:10.1007/BF00149365

Eppstein, D., Falmagne, J.-C., & Ovchinnikov, S. (2008). *Media theory.* Berlin and Heidelberg, Germany: Springer-Verlag.

Falmagne, J.-C., Cosyn, E., Doignon, J.-P., & Thiéry, N. (2006). The assessment of knowledge, in theory and in practice. In B. Ganter & L. Kwuida (Eds.), *Proceedings of the 4th International Conference on Formal Concept Analysis, Lecture Notes in Artificial Intelligence* (pp. 61–79). Berlin and Heidelberg, Germany: Springer-Verlag.

Falmagne, J.-C., & Doignon, J.-P. (1988a). A class of stochastic procedures for the assessment of knowledge. *British Journal of Mathematical and Statistical Psychology, 41,* 1–23.

Falmagne, J.-C., & Doignon, J.-P. (1988b). A Markovian procedure for assessing the state of a system. *Journal of Mathematical Psychology, 32,* 232–258.

Falmagne, J.-C., & Doignon, J.-P. (2011). *Learning spaces: Interdisciplinary applied mathematics.* Heidelberg, Germany: Springer-Verlag.

Falmagne, J.-C., & Ovchinnikov, S. (2002). Media theory. *Discrete Applied Mathematics, 121,* 83–101.

Hockemeyer, C. (2001). Tools and utilities for knowledge spaces. Unpublished technical report, Institut für Psychologie, Karl-Franzens-Universität Graz, Austria.

Nunnally, J., & Bernstein, I. (1994). *Psychometric theory.* New York, NY: McGraw-Hill.

Welsh, D. J. A. (1995). Matroids: Fundamental concepts. In R. L. Graham, M. Grötschel, & L. Lovász (Eds.), *Handbook of combinatorics* (Vol. 1, pp. 481–526). Cambridge, MA: The MIT Press.

Index

External noise method, 210–213
Extrastriate cortical areas, amblyopia and, 209
Extrinsic rigid object transformations, 173
Eye movement(s)
    and attention, 159–160
    feature carryover across, 117
    saccadic. *See* Saccadic planning
    smooth pursuit. *See* Smooth pursuit eye
        movements
    visual priming across, 117–121. *See* Visual
        priming

FACADE model, 171
Falmagne, J.-C., 243, 244, 247, 248
Fazl, A., 167, 169
FD tasks. *See* Fixed duration tasks
Feature contrast, 29–30. *See also* Visual
        contrast
    and contrast contrast, 33–34
    and crowding, 31–32
    and Gibsonian normalization, 29–30
    incompatibility of feature acuity and, 29–37
    and lateral inhibition between neural
        populations, 32–33
    and lateral inhibition within neural
        population, 30, 31
    and separation of target and surround,
        34–35
    and squishing, 32, 35–37
Feature-tracking signals, 176, 180
Filehne illusion, 48, 49
"Filling in," 33
Filtering, 154–155
First-order motion stimuli, 44, 45
Fission, 235, 238
Fixations, 117
Fixed duration (FD) tasks, 177, 183, 185–186
Fixed memory traces, criterion setting vs., in
        sensory memory, 96–101
Fixed memory trace theory (FMTT), 93, 111
    and discrimination learning, 101–102
    prediction of, 96–97
    test of, 99, 101
fMRI studies, 155, 160
Focusing hypothesis, 197
Formotion, 176
Four-alternative forced-choice (4-AFC) tasks,
        86–89
Fovea, 32, 39, 42, 43
Francis, W., 118
Frequency banks, 200
Functional imaging studies, of extrastriate
        cortical area activity, 209
Functional linkage, 106
Functional magnetic resonance (fMRI) studies,
        155, 160
Fusion, 235, 238

Gabor frequency, in external noise approach,
        212–214
Gabor patches (Gabor objects), 15, 19, 20, 31, 157
Gallace, A., 236
Game environments, 3D multimodal, 229
Gegenfurtner, K. R., 44–46, 48–50
Gestalt psychology, 46
Gibson, J. J., 29, 31
Gibsonian normalization, 29–30
Gilbert, C. D., 29, 31
Gist-plus-texture system, 174
Global aperture problem, 176
Global-to-local visual processing, 174
Gold, J. I., 186
Goldberg, M. E., 42
Golz, J., 69, 70
Goodale, M. A., 8, 76
Gorea, A., 76, 85
Graham, N., 13–15, 18–20, 24
Gray-to-green equisalience function, 77–78,
        83, 84
Greenberg, G. Z., 198
Greenlee, M. W., 111, 112
Grossberg, S., 169, 174–175, 179, 181, 182,
        184–186
Guest, S., 237

Hariharan, S., 32
Hawken, M. J., 44–46
Hawkes, G. R., 233
HCI (human-computer interaction),
        231–232
Heinen, S., 46
Hess, R. F., 211
Higher order motion, and smooth pursuit eye
        movements, 44–45
Hooge, I. T. C., 135
Horizontality, 7, 14, 15, 30, 107, 181, 182,
        187, 229
Huang, C. B., 215, 219
Huang, E. P., 75
Huang, T.-R, 175
Huber, D. E., 115, 116, 121, 124, 128
Human-computer interaction (HCI),
        231–232

"Ideal observer" models, 237
Ideal point, 159
Ilg, U. J., 44
Illusory flash experiment, 236
Illusory motion, and smooth pursuit eye
        movements, 45
Induced focusing, 199
Inference, visual, 115
Information, retention of, 93
International Space Station, 231
Interstimulus interval (ISI), 117, 236

About the Editors

Charles Chubb, PhD, is a professor in the Department of Cognitive Sciences at the University of California at Irvine. He also holds the position of adjunct senior scientist at the Marine Biological Laboratory in Woods Hole, Massachusetts. His research focuses on the computational basis of visual and auditory perception. His specific research interests include visual motion perception, texture perception, lightness and brightness perception, visual control of motor responses, camouflage, and also auditory perception of tonal variations. In addition, at the Marine Biological Laboratory in Woods Hole, he performs psychophysical experiments to analyze the visual processing performed by cuttlefish as they camouflage themselves in response to the visual properties of their surroundings.

Dr. Chubb received his bachelor's degree in philosophy from Princeton University in 1973. He then taught seventh and eighth grade English for 6 years at the Friends Academy in Locust Valley, New York, returning to graduate school in 1980 at New York University, from which he received his PhD in psychology in 1985. After a postdoctoral fellowship with George Sperling at New York University, in 1989 Dr. Chubb joined the psychology department at Rutgers, the State University of New Jersey, in New Brunswick, where he was a faculty member until moving to the cognitive sciences department at the University of California at Irvine in 1996. He is an associate editor for *Attention, Perception & Psychophysics* and a topical editor for the *Journal of the Optical Society of America A.*

Barbara A. Dosher, PhD, is a Distinguished Professor of Cognitive Sciences at the University of California, Irvine (UCI). She studies how humans perceive, remember, and retrieve information using a combination of behavioral testing and mathematical modeling. Her early research studied the speed and accuracy of retrieval from short-term memory and forgetting of both conscious and subconscious memories. Her recent work seeks to understand how attention and learning affect the accuracy of human perception and to develop quantitative models of state-dependent perceptual processes and visual memory. The National Science Foundation, the Air Force Office of Scientific Research, the National Institute of Mental Health, and the National Eye Institute have funded her research.

Dr. Dosher received her bachelor's degree in psychology from the University of California, San Diego, in 1973 and her PhD in experimental psychology from the University of Oregon in 1977. She was a professor of psychology at Columbia University from 1977 to 1992, when she joined the faculty of UCI in the Department of Cognitive Sciences. She is a member of the National Academy of Sciences, a fellow of the American Psychological Society and the Society for Experimental Psychologists, and is a past president of the Society for Mathematical Psychology. She is an elected member of the executive board of the Vision Sciences Society, was an associate editor for *Psychological Review* and has served on the editorial boards of journals in cognitive psychology and vision science. She has served as dean of the UCI School of Social Sciences since 2002.

Zhong-Lin Lu, PhD, obtained a BS in theoretical physics from the University of Science and Technology of China in 1989 and a PhD under Samuel J. Williamson in physics at New York University (1989–1992). This was followed by a 4-year postdoctorate in cognitive science with George Sperling at the University of California, Irvine. He joined the University of Southern California as an assistant professor in 1996 and was appointed professor of psychology and biomedical engineering in 2004 and William M. Keck Chair in Cognitive Neuroscience in 2006. In 2011, he joined the Ohio State University as Distinguished Professor of Social and Behavioral Science, professor of psychology, and director of the Center for Cognitive and Behavioral Brain Imaging. Dr. Lu is a fellow of the Society of Experimental Psychologists and the Association for Psychological Science.

The goal of Dr. Lu's research is to construct computational brain models for perception and cognition—models sufficiently computational such that they can be represented in a computer program or mathematical theory. Psychophysical experimentation, physiological investigation, clinical testing, and computational modeling are all essential ingredients and tools in his research. He has been actively engaged in the (a) computational and psychophysical study of visual and auditory perception, attention, and perceptual learning; (b) functional brain imaging study of sensory and attentional processes, second language learning, and human decision making; and (c) study of visual deficits in dyslexia, amblyopia, and Alzheimer's disease. Since 1991, he has published two edited books, three special issues, 180 articles, and more than 200 abstracts.

Richard M. Shiffrin, PhD, is Distinguished Professor and Luther Dana Waterman Professor at Indiana University, as well as professor of psychological and brain sciences, cognitive science, and statistics. He is also a member of the National Academy of Sciences, the American Academy of Arts and Sciences, and the American Philosophical Society. He is the recipient of the Rumelhart Prize, William James Fellow Award, American Psychological Association Distinguished Scientific Contribution Award, and the Society of Experimental Psychologists Warren Medal. He has published widely on human memory and information processing in journals such as *Psychological Review* and *Psychonomic Bulletin and Review* and in the book series *The Psychology of Learning and Motivation*.